Witchcraft and Magic in Europe
The Eighteenth and Nineteenth Centuries

WITCHCRAFT AND MAGIC IN EUROPE

Series Editors
Bengt Ankarloo
Stuart Clark

The roots of European witchcraft and magic lie in Hebrew and other ancient Near Eastern cultures and in the Celtic, Nordic, and Germanic traditions of the continent. For two millennia, European folklore and ritual have been imbued with the belief in the supernatural, yielding a rich trove of histories and images.

Witchcraft and Magic in Europe combines traditional approaches of political, legal, and social historians with a critical synthesis of cultural anthropology, historical psychology, and gender studies. The series provides a modern, scholarly survey of the supernatural beliefs of Europeans from ancient times to the present day. Each volume of this ambitious series contains the work of distinguished scholars chosen for their expertise in a particular era or region.

Witchcraft and Magic in Europe

The Eighteenth and Nineteenth Centuries

Edited by
BENGT ANKARLOO
and STUART CLARK

PENN

University of Pennsylvania Press
Philadelphia

First published 1999 by
The Athlone Press
1 Park Drive, London NW11 7SG

First published 1999 in the United States of America by
University of Pennsylvania Press
Philadelphia, Pennsylvania 19104−4011

British Library Cataloguing in Publication Data
*A catalogue record for this book is available
from the British Library*

Library of Congress Cataloging-in-Publication Data
Witchcraft and magic in Europe : the eighteenth and nineteenth
centuries / edited by Bengt Ankarloo and Stuart Clark.
    p.   cm.
Includes bibliographical references and index.
ISBN 0−8122−3518−5 (hardcover : alk. paper). — ISBN 0−8122−1706−3
(pbk. : alk. paper)
    1. Magic — Europe — History — 18th century. 2. Magic — Europe −
− History — 19th century. I. Ankarloo, Bengt, 1935−   . II. Clark,
Stuart.
BF1584.E9W58   1999
133.4′3′09409033 — dc21   99−26083
                                                              CIP

Typeset by Ensystems, Saffron Walden, Essex
Printed and bound in Great Britain

Contents

Introduction

Bengt Ankarloo and Stuart Clark

It is only natural that modern studies of European witchcraft should have concentrated on the period between the fifteenth and the eighteenth centuries. It was then that witchcraft was made into a serious criminal activity throughout the continent and prosecutions of witches accordingly reached their height; then, too, that witchcraft assumed major importance as a topic for debate in countless treatises, pamphlets and sermons. Magic likewise enjoyed its greatest intellectual prominence in the years between the Renaissance and the Enlightenment, even if in its popular forms it has had a more perennial significance. Almost automatically, therefore, historians have associated European witchcraft and intellectual magic mostly with the early modern centuries and sought to explain them as products of the societies and cultures of that era. They have not looked for them in the ages that followed, assuming that they belonged to a particular set of circumstances and values and that they lost their hold, and then disappeared, when these ceased to exist. Indeed, from this perspective, the history of witchcraft and magic from the later seventeenth century onwards can only be seen as one of inevitable decline; there are no other interesting questions to be asked about it. An older tradition of academic rationalism also contributed to this view. Witchcraft and magic were once thought to have been quickly and completely swept away by the intellectual changes that brought modern science and secularism to Europe. Singled out was the paradigmatic break-through in the natural sciences, in particular physics and astronomy, and perhaps also the radical criticism adopted in the philosophy of Descartes. Supposedly, these changes exposed the ignorance and prejudice that had sustained the witch trials and the beliefs on which they were based and brought them both to an end. All that needed to be done was to describe how this process came about.

Of course, not all of this can simply be discarded. Historians have become more sensitive to the social and intellectual contexts of the witch-trials, not less, and this has only reinforced the view that these were phenomena peculiar to the early modern period and, in consequence, foreign to later ones. The various European states did indeed decriminalize witchcraft during the eighteenth century and ceased to try witches even before that. European intellectuals and professionals of this period also turned their backs on witchcraft belief and on the occult sciences, disdaining them as manifestations of backwardness and superstition. In these ways, the story of witchcraft and magic from about 1650 to 1900 is clearly one of decline and retreat, a development that demands historical analysis like any other. Even so, this is not the whole story and, in certain respects, it is a misleading one. Exactly how and why decriminalization occurred remains to be considered, as does the relative importance in this process of legal, social, and intellectual influences. The relationship between modern European intellectual and professional life and the world of the occult and the supernatural cannot be reduced to one of straight-forward rejection in the name of 'enlightenment' and 'progress'. It was much more ambiguous and complementary, with Victorian supernatural-ism in Britain as a prominent example. We should therefore beware of taking eighteenth- and nineteenth-century claims about the victory of science over magic and superstition at face value. Above all, the popula-tions of Europe did not simply give up believing in witchcraft and magic, and acting on their beliefs, just because the laws against witches were removed from the statute books. To assume that they did commits us to the kind of elitism that makes ordinary people the faithful replicas of those who tried to 'improve' them. To ignore the evidence that they did not is also to miss an important ingredient in modern European life and popular culture.

This penultimate volume in the History of Witchcraft and Magic in Europe attempts to strike a balance, therefore. It takes up the preoccu-pations that have quite legitimately governed the historiography of the early modern witch trials by asking afresh the traditional questions both about how and why these trials came to an end and the way in which the Enlightenment saw a crusade against the belief system that had sustained them. But it also poses the entirely new questions that emerge when these preoccupations are set aside and not allowed to influence how the history of witchcraft and magic *after* the trials is considered. Thus, in the first contribution, Brian Levack reconsiders the chronology and causation of, first, the slackening of witchcraft prosecutions throughout Europe and, then, their final cessation. It was an uneven process in every respect – neither uniform nor linear, but varying in terms of timing, duration, and region – and Levack attributes this for the first time to the structural and procedural differences in the judicial systems involved. A striking illus-tration of this is his discovery that just as inquisitorial regimes had been quicker to accept the new demonological interpretations of witchcraft of the later medieval period, so they were also the first to abandon them once the ideological climate changed. Conversely, countries with accusa-torial systems, such as England and the Scandinavian kingdoms, were slower to introduce the modern witchcraft concept and also slower to put a final end to all prosecutions. Political elites commanded a more direct control over the inquisitorial procedure and were able to reform it as soon as they became more cautious about the guilt of the accused. By their very nature accusatorial systems were built on the active participation of wide segments of the population, and here, as a consequence, judicial practice in the courts was conservative and not so responsive to doctrinal change.

Levack's main argument, indeed, is that it is legal history, not intellectual history, that holds the key to our understanding of what happened. This is because the crucial shifts in scientific, philosophical and theological tastes that we associate with the eighteenth century came too late to affect materially a decline in witchcraft prosecutions that was already under way – in some cases, from the mid- to later-seventeenth century onwards. In this reading, the emerging reluctance of the European judicial systems to convict suspected witches, or even bring them to court, preceeded, not followed, intellectual change. Based on recent research of the type represented in Sönke Lorenz and Dieter Bauer's 1995 essay collection *Das Ende der Hexenverfolgung*, this new account of the decriminalization of witchcraft turns the old rationalist paradigm on its head while remaining within a historiography focusing on witchcraft's decline.

Marijke Gijswijt-Hofstra, by contrast, invites us to reconsider witchcraft as a continuous element in European culture throughout the eighteenth and nineteenth centuries. The evidence for doing so is certainly not yet complete. Research on witchcraft *after* decriminalization is still in its infancy and in whole areas of Europe – Scotland and Switzerland, for example – little is known about it. But she is able to draw on the pioneering work of such scholars as Owen Davies (on England) and Jürgen Scheffler (on Lippe), on her own research as a member of the Dutch study group for 'Witchcraft and Sorcery in the Netherlands' (active between 1982 and 1994), and on the findings of other members of that group, notably Willem de Blécourt (on Drenthe) and Hans de Waardt (on the province of Holland). This is an important grounding for her essay, since the Dutch study group was the first to acknowledge that the history of witchcraft could not be confined within its traditional, early modern limits. And, indeed, they have been proved right. Long after there was any scope for bringing accusations to the courts – indeed, when to do so might have brought a prosecution for slander – ordinary Europeans went on thinking and acting in terms of *maleficium*. In a culture of misfortune that has persisted throughout modern times they continued to diagnose bewitchment, identify witches, take counter-measures, consult unwitching specialists, and recognise in their own lives and in the lives of others the relevance of magic to matters of love, riches, and good health. Of course, this intense commitment of neighbours in cases of suspected witchcraft long after the official cessation of judicial prosecutions gives support retrospectively to the generalization that popular resentment against mal-evolent behaviour was a crucial ingredient in the witch hunts of the earlier centuries. In this respect, as Marijke Gijswijt-Hofstra argues, no clear break seems to have separated that period from the period that followed. But what is most significant about the new perspective is that it reveals a continuing pattern of witchcraft beliefs and actions that is richly varied in terms of gender, social position, and types of magical operations. Witch-craft and magic, it turns out, have been highly viable ingredients in community life in Europe well into modern times.

With Roy Porter we return to issues of a more traditional kind to do with ideological transformation but, again, there are fresh twists to them. Certainly, the later seventeenth and eighteenth centuries witnessed an intellectual rejection in the name of reason and progress of the beliefs and values of witch-hunting Europe. What was perceived as the modernising of science and theology made them seem irrelevant and dangerous, the product of ignorance, 'enthusiasm', and fear, not of real knowledge or confidence. In this climate of elite opinion, magic became (in Voltaire's words) 'an impossible thing' and witchcraft a crime of deception – precisely the sort of crime that was more troublesome to increasingly commercialised societies. In the new knowledge systems of the period the sorts of things previously ascribed to witches and devils became impossible in nature, improbable and superstitious (like many 'miracles') in religion, and better explained in terms of medical and other pathologies. Doctrinal 'cleansing' in particular, says Porter, brought the latitudinarian, optimistic, even utilitarian theology of the early eighteenth century into direct conflict with the demonology of the Reformation and Counter-Reformation. The whole mental world associated with the witch trials was thus discredited and attempts were made to suppress it; more devastating still, it was fictionalized and ridiculed. It became *à la mode* in the eighteenth century to tell witchcraft stories only to laugh at them. The pace and timing of disenchantment was different in the various fields of intellectual life – and different again, as we have seen, from that in jurisprudence and legal practice. But it was proposed on a widespread scale.

On the other hand, we should not be misled by the language used by the Enlightenment crusaders against witchcraft and magic. The battles of the 'witchcraft wars' were remarkably long drawn-out, lasting in the case of England throughout the period of the Restoration and down to the repeal of the witchcraft statute in 1736. To believe too much in witchcraft might have become credulous superstition; but to believe too little in it could still carry the risks of atheism. Porter shows how the European elites continued to mix what were proclaimed to be incompatible beliefs. The occult and the supernatural also had a posthumous life in the art and literature of this period. Suppressed, they returned, migrating into the world of the Gothic and into Romanticism where the supernatural could be made sublime and its terrors enjoyed without risk. From now on, explains Porter, they became the territory of writers and artists. More than anything else, however, it is the presence in eighteenth- and nineteenth-century European high culture of new forms of occult science – labelled 'pseudo' sciences by the dominant Newtonianism – that complicates any simple history of the decline of magic. Alchemy and astrology continued to appeal, alongside new studies (or new versions of old studies) like animal magnetism, physiognomy and phrenology. It seems that repudiation of the older sciences and forms of supernaturalism often led to their replacement by look-alikes.

The volume that follows, then, is concerned with both the receding of witchcraft and magic and yet their persistence too, sometimes in new and striking forms. Most obviously, it was those directly involved in the machinery of judicial prosecution who withdrew their support. It is true that witchcraft continued to have relevance in two legal contexts throughout the eighteenth and nineteenth centuries – in the redefinition of crimes hitherto ascribed to it and in the handling of cases of the slandering or maltreatment of individuals as 'witches' (the latter brought to an end in England, it has been suggested, partly by the creation of a police force). It is also the case that, at first, jurists and magistrates did not necessarily give up believing in witchcraft in principle. Instead, they concentrated on procedural reforms that meant greater control by the central legal authorities over the local administration of justice (where the worst excesses against witches had occurred), the regulation or abolition of torture, the establishing of new standards of evidence, and the provision of legal representation for suspects. Nevertheless, it cannot be supposed that witchcraft was anything but eclipsed as a criminal act, with philosophical corroboration for this step following on behind. Similarly, there was a clear ideological withdrawal from the belief in witchcraft and from some forms of traditional magic by large numbers of European intellectuals and professionals. What became the dominant scientific and religious paradigms were largely inimical to early modern demonology and in fields like ethics, political thought and history writing it became difficult, if not impossible, to find a place for demons at all. Even among those who continued to think in terms of witchcraft the longest, Marijke Gijswijt-Hofstra notes a diminution in its role and scope. Cases became less frequent and there was a narrowing in their social complexion – they became restricted to the countryside, to the lower socio-economic classes, and to non-professionals. There was a reduction in the range of misfortunes attributed to *maleficium* and less anxiety to attribute them to a particular person. There is some indication, finally, that men withdrew from witchcraft matters, leaving them more and more to the women in their communities. All these trends are apparent by the close of the nineteenth century.

At the same time, this volume testifies to the continuing significance of witchcraft and magic in European culture at every level. In this respect, it seeks to make good the neglect of an historical topic that has scarcely been acknowledged, let alone fully researched. To those who carried on believing that witches could cause real misfortune all the typical ingredients of the traditional culture of witchcraft were available as a kind of communal resource. And just as this particular logic continued to make sense of aspects of their lives, so historians too can go on using the evidence of witchcraft in eighteenth- and nineteenth-century communities as an indication, even a measure, of their social and cultural dynamics. But the same sort of principle applies to the study of those who very much *rejected* the idea that witches could cause misfortune. For even as it was being refused, witchcraft played a role – perhaps even a crucial one – in the changing ideology of the time. As it ceased to be a crime, or even a physical possibility, witchcraft carried on being a topic of debate, and, in particular, a point of reference for cultural and social disparagement. Witchcraft was the 'other' of eighteenth-century rationalism, a much-despised example of all that was deemed to be wrong with traditional religion and unenlightened societies. Its denunciation was also a political and social matter, and not just a question of philosophy. It was a way of establishing the values of order and politeness and the cultural boundaries appropriate to societies increasingly subject to commercial interests. As Roy Porter stresses, it was an aspect of ideological changes that were driven by conflict. Later still, in the somewhat calmer waters of the nineteenth century, witchcraft and magic became more and more the subjects of academic investigation – by theorists of cultural change and secularization, by folklorists and anthropologists, and by psychopathologists. The scholarly explanations for them that then emerged have had a profound effect on the historiography of witchcraft and magic ever since. All this is equal testimony to their continued power to resonate in the minds of Europeans long after the last witch was executed.

PART 1

The Decline and End of Witchcraft Prosecutions

Brian P. Levack

Introduction

During the seventeenth and eighteenth centuries, prosecutions and executions for the crime of witchcraft declined in number and eventually came to an end. The decline occurred in all European countries where witch-hunts had taken place, from Scotland to Transylvania and from Portugal to Finland. The same process took place in those colonial possessions of Spain, Portugal, England and France where ecclesiastical or temporal authorities had brought witches to trial. The decline was marked by an increasing reluctance to prosecute witches, the acquittal of many who were tried, the reversal of convictions on appeal, and eventually the repeal of the laws that had authorized the prosecutions. By 1782 the last officially sanctioned witchcraft execution had taken place, and in many jurisdictions witchcraft, at least as it had been defined in the sixteenth and seventeenth centuries, had ceased to be a crime. Individuals continued to name their neighbours as witches, and in some cases they took violent action against them, but they did so illegally and at the risk of being prosecuted themselves.

The purpose of this essay is to explain how and why the great European witch-hunt declined in intensity and eventually came to an end. It will cover the entire period of that decline, from the time when the prosecutions first began to taper off until the conclusion of the last trial. It does not deal with temporary lulls in the process of witch-hunting. Periodic reductions in the number of trials and executions occurred in almost every European jurisdiction during the sixteenth and seventeenth centuries, and they merit close historical investigation, but they do not concern us here. This essay deals only with the later stages of the process, when witch-hunting finally lost its grip on local communities and when a decline in the number of trials led to their complete termination. In some cases that final decline was related, as either cause or effect, to formal declarations that witchcraft was no longer a crime.

In studying the decline of witch-hunting, we need to distinguish between the number of prosecutions and the number of executions. Marked reductions in both of these totals occurred in the late seventeenth and eighteenth centuries but they did not always coincide. In many jurisdictions, most notably in England and Denmark, the last executions long preceded the last trials. We must also distinguish between the end of large witch-panics or chain-reaction hunts and the end of all prosecutions, including occasional, isolated trials. In many German territories, for example, the great panics, which had always involved charges of collective Devil-worship, had all but disappeared by 1670, but individual trials, and even a few small panics, continued for nearly another one hundred years.

The reduction and eventual end of witch-hunting occurred at different times in the various kingdoms and regions of Europe. In some countries, such as the Dutch Republic, the decline in prosecutions became evident before the end of the sixteenth century, while in others, like Poland, it did not begin until the middle of the eighteenth century. The length of time that the entire process took also varied greatly from place to place. In Scotland, for example, the initial reduction in the number of prosecutions was followed by more than 50 years of trials, whereas in Franche-Comté and colonial Massachusetts witch-hunts came to a complete end only a few years after the courts started to discourage prosecutions. Even the legislation declaring that witchcraft was no longer a crime was passed at different stages of the process. In some kingdoms, such as Hungary and Prussia, the formal decriminalization of witchcraft preceded and was largely responsible for the end of witch-hunting, whereas in Great Britain and Denmark it did not occur until long after the trials had stopped.

Historians of witchcraft have traditionally given much more thought to the question why the trials began than why they came to an end. Until the middle of the twentieth century those who bothered to address the latter question at all attributed the decline in one way or another to the emergence of modern rationalism, the rise of science, or an even vaguer dispelling of ignorance and 'superstition'(Lecky, 1910: 1–138). This interpretation arose during the Enlightenment, and it became the backbone of late nineteenth- and early twentieth-century liberal and Whig historiography. Historians writing in this tradition focused mainly on the content of published witchcraft treatises and the theological and philosophical controversies to which those treatises contributed. They assumed that the decline of witchcraft prosecutions had been caused by a decline in the witch-beliefs of the educated classes and therefore made little distinction between the two developments. The end of the trials thus became synonymous with the enlightened rejection of the demonological ideas that had provided the intellectual foundations of the witch-hunt.

In the last thirty years historians of witchcraft have begun to take different approaches to this problem of the decline of witchcraft. While by no means ignoring the published treatises, whose influence remains a subject of scholarly debate, they have begun to focus on the decisions of the judges, inquisitors, jurists and magistrates who staffed the courts where witches were tried. Historians have, for example, studied the ways in which Spanish Inquisitors, the members of the parlement of Paris, jurists on the law faculties at German universities, and the judges who presided at the English county assizes succeeded in reducing the number of executions for witchcraft within their jurisdictions (Mandrou, 1968; Soman, 1978; Henningsen, 1980; Lorenz, 1995; Sharpe, 1996: 213–34). These studies have shown, moreover, that the judges who brought the trials to an end displayed a much deeper belief in the reality of witchcraft than the 'enlightened' authors of contemporary witchcraft treatises. Further questions regarding the validity of the 'enlightenment model' of the decline of witchcraft have come from social, economic and cultural historians who have suggested that changes in the system of poor relief, the altered mood of local communities in the wake of large witch-hunts, the reform of the profession of popular healers, and the success of the state in christianizing and disciplining the rural population may have played a role in reducing the number of witchcraft accusations and prosecutions (Thomas, 1971: ch. 18; Midelfort, 1972: ch. 6; Várkonyi, 1991–2).

Research on the decline and end of witch-hunting has resulted in the formulation of very few general theories that apply to all of Europe (Soman, 1989). Almost all of the modern scholarship on the subject has had a local, regional or national focus, and interpretations emerging from the study of one locale do not always apply to others (Monter, 1976: 37–41; Soman, 1978; Klaits, 1982; Johansen, 1991–2; Lorenz and Bauer, 1995b). The vast chronological gulf that separates the decline of witch-hunting in the Netherlands and France from the parallel phenomenon in Hungary and Poland makes it even more difficult to establish working models or unifying themes (Muchembled, 1991–2). What is more, the developments that account for the initial decline of witchcraft prosecutions in many jurisdictions do not always explain why the trials came to a complete end or why witchcraft officially ceased to be a crime.

This essay will take three different approaches to the problem of the decline of witch-hunting throughout Europe. First, it will identify and illustrate by way of example the general reasons why prosecutions declined in number throughout Europe. It will attempt to be comprehensive in this regard, covering legal, intellectual, religious and social explanations, but it will emphasize changes in judicial procedure and the growth of judicial caution in the trial of witches. Second, it will trace the decline of witch-hunting in five national case studies as a way of illustrating the intersection of some of the general causes discussed in the first part of the essay. These case studies will also establish similarities and differences between the patterns of decline in countries which followed different judicial procedures. The third part of the essay will explore the actual decriminalization of witchcraft in the various countries of Europe and two broad shifts in the administration of criminal justice that accompanied the entire process of decline: the trial of individuals for specific crimes once included within the general category of witchcraft and the prosecution of those who took malicious, violent or otherwise illegal action against persons whom they suspected as witches.

CHAPTER 1

General Reasons for the Decline in Prosecutions

JUDICIAL SCEPTICISM AND PROCEDURAL CAUTION

The starting point for any investigation of the decline of witch-hunting must be the development of a growing awareness by those persons who controlled the judicial machinery that many witches were being convicted and executed for crimes they had not committed. This realization, which usually arose in response to the excesses of witch-hunting in certain localities, led judges and other persons involved in the hunts to criticize the ways in which the trials were being conducted. These critiques led in turn to the formulation and implementation of stricter procedural rules for the conduct of witchcraft trials, including greater restraint in the administration of torture and the application of more demanding standards of evidence. As a result of these changes in the judicial process, the trials of witches resulted in a larger number of acquittals, the mass panics in which scores of witches perished no longer recurred, and the courts became increasingly reluctant to initiate prosecutions in the first place.

I have used the phrase judicial scepticism to describe the attitude of those judges, inquisitors, magistrates, and writers who responded to the trials in this way. In the context of witchcraft the word scepticism usually denotes the attitudes of those who doubt or deny the existence of witches or the possibility of their crime. Judicial sceptics did not necessarily adopt such a stance. The essence of their intellectual position was a genuine doubt whether those persons who were being prosecuted were actually guilty as charged, and this concern led in turn to a more general uncertainty whether the crime could ever be proved at law. Some judicial sceptics may have also harboured a more fundamental, philosophical doubt whether witchcraft even existed. But judicial scepticism could, and in many cases did, coexist with a firm belief in the reality and possibility of the crime.

Let us look at five examples of the emergence of this type of scepticism and the role it played in the decline of witch-hunting. In all five cases the process began as a reaction to witch-panics that claimed large numbers of victims. The first was a chain-reaction hunt in the cathedral city of Würzburg which lasted from 1627 to 1629 and took the lives of 160 persons. Like many similar hunts in other German localities, especially in the episcopal principalities, this hunt involved the extensive use of torture. That procedure was used not only to secure confessions and convictions of those who had been accused by their neighbours but also to obtain the names of the witches' alleged accomplices. This tactic allowed for a rapid expansion of the number of victims, but it also led to the naming of witches who did not conform to the traditional stereotype of the witch, which was that of an adult female from the lower levels of society. In the early trials at Würzburg the overwhelming majority of the victims fit this description. At the height of the panic, however, the web of accusations had embraced people 'high and low, of every rank and sex', including clerics, electoral councillors and doctors, city officials, court assessors and law students (Burr, 1903: 29). It also included large numbers of children who at one point supplied more than half the victims (Midelfort, 1979: 282–3). This breakdown of the witch stereotype inclined many members of the community to question seriously whether the officials who were conducting the trials had succeeded in identifying the real witches. It also led to the frightening realization by members of the city's elite that they themselves might just as easily be named as witches. As a result of this crisis of confidence in the mechanisms by which witches were identified and prosecuted, the Würzburg trials came grinding to a halt, and witch-hunting in that bishopric entered a long period of decline. The last trial would not take place until 1749, but never again did the city experience the ravages of witch-hunting as it had in 1627–29.

The excesses of witch-hunting at Würzburg also inspired a devastating critique of the legal procedures used in the witchcraft trials. In 1631 Friedrich Spee, a Jesuit priest who held a professorship of moral theology at the University of Paderborn, published an anonymous treatise, entitled *Cautio Criminalis*, which exposed the insurmountable judicial pressures to which the accused were subject during their interrogations and the unreliability of their confessions as evidence of the crime (Spee, 1631). This book, the work of the quintessential judicial sceptic, emerged from Spee's actual experience as a confessor during the trials at Würzburg as well as from his first-hand experience with another chain-reaction hunt at Paderborn in 1631. The *Cautio* did not at first have a profound impact on the conduct of witchcraft trials, but later translations into German (1647 and 1649), Dutch (1657), French (1660) and Polish (1697 and 1710) enabled it to exercise a moderating influence throughout Europe, even in Protestant lands. It gained its greatest fame from the publicity given it by Christian Thomasius, the Protestant jurist at the University of Halle who relied heavily on it in writing his own treatises on torture and witchcraft in the early eighteenth century. Thus the *Cautio* contributed in this indirect way to the final end of the trials almost 100 years after its author had died (van Oorschot, 1995; Behringer, 1987: 366–99).

The second example of the way in which judicial scepticism developed in response to the excesses of witch-hunting comes from Sweden, where a major chain-reaction hunt took place between 1668 and 1676. Prior to this panic witch-hunting in Sweden had been relatively restrained, mainly as a result of the caution and scepticism exhibited by the clergy and the members of the royal Court of Appeal in Stockholm. In the late 1660s, however, confessions by hundreds of children that witches were taking them to the sabbath at a mythical place called Blåkulla triggered a massive hunt which began in the northern province of Dalarna and then spread to the provinces of Hälsingland, Ångermanland, Gästrikland, Norland, Uppland and ultimately Stockholm. In response to extraordinary pressure from local communities, King Charles XI appointed a series of royal commissions, consisting of local judges, clergymen and farmers as well as appellate judges and law professors, to try these cases. The lawyers on the commission objected to the acceptance of testimony from children and alleged accomplices, and they entertained serious doubts about the authenticity of the children's statements. But those sceptics constituted a minority, and the commissions secured a large number of convictions. The Court of Appeal provided less support for the panic, but it did confirm a number of sentences sent to it from local courts. The panic did not come to an end until the trials moved south to Stockholm. There the Court of Appeal began to interrogate witnesses directly rather than rely on the criminal dossier submitted by the lower courts. Shortly thereafter some of the children who had lodged the accusations began to confess before the royal commission that their stories were fabricated and that the accused were innocent. The trials came to an abrupt end and the government prosecuted some of the main witnesses, including a thirteen year-old boy (Ankarloo, 1990: 294–300).

The great Swedish trials of the 1660s and 1670s did not bring a complete end to witch-hunting in Sweden, but they certainly marked the beginning of its precipitate decline. It appears that Swedish lawyers, and probably also many members of local communities, experienced a crisis of confidence not unlike that which had occurred in places like Würzburg. After 1676 there were only isolated trials in different parts of the country, and the Court of Appeal, taking more care in the evaluation of evidence than it had in the hunt of 1668–76, confirmed only a few sentences. When another panic occurred in the western province of Värmland in the 1720s, complete with child witnesses, stories of flying to Blåkulla, and the illegal use of torture, the court of Appeal reversed all the sentences and, as it had in 1676, prosecuted those who had brought the charges of witchcraft in the first place. The experience of 1668–76 had introduced a level of caution and judicial scepticism that prevented intense witch-hunting from ever occurring again.

A third large hunt that led directly to the expression of judicial scepticism and the decline of witchcraft prosecutions was the operation conducted by the Spanish Inquisition in the Basque country between 1609 and 1611. This hunt, the largest and most famous in Spanish history, had many of the characteristics of the large chain-reaction hunts, although it did not involve the extensive use of torture. The episode began with the apparently uncoerced confessions of some villagers in Zugarramurdi in the kingdom of Navarre that they were attending sabbaths where they worshipped the Devil with large numbers of their neighbors. A panel of inquisitors investigated these confessions, tried those who had confessed or had been accused, executed six of the witches and another five in effigy, and solicited new confessions by promulgating an edict of Faith by which those admitting their crime would be reconciled with the Church. In the course of the hunt inquisitors received the confessions of some 1,300 children, who admitted that they had been taken to the sabbath. In the midst of this investigation, one of the inquisitors, Alonso Salazar de Frías, became sceptical regarding the reality of the witches' confessions, especially those of the children. He conducted a painstaking interrogation of all those who had confessed, ultimately reaching the conclusion that the entire thing was a 'chimera' and that the confessions were the result of fantasy which had arisen from youthful imagination, parental or clerical suggestion, or local rumour (Henningsen, 1980).

Salazar did not deny the possibility of witchcraft, but his recognition that in this case hundreds of persons had made false confessions and that a smaller number had been wrongly convicted and executed led him to propose a strict set of procedural rules for the Inquisition to follow in all future investigations and trials of the crime. These rules, which included the mandatory review of all sentences by the highest tribunal of the Inquisition in Madrid, had a powerful impact on the prosecution of witches in Spain for the remainder of the seventeenth century (Henningsen, 1980: 358–86). Prosecutions for various forms of magic continued, some of which were classified as witchcraft, but the records of the Inquisition after 1614 reveal few trials for attending the witches' sabbath, and capital punishment for witchcraft became a rarity. The new guidelines did not put an end to prosecutions in the local secular courts, especially in the kingdom of Aragon (Gari Lacruz, 1980; Monter, 1990b: 274–5), but there is no question that the steps Salazar and the Inquisitors at Madrid took in response to the excesses of the Basque witch-hunt of 1609–11 marked a turning point in the history of Spanish witchcraft, signaling the beginning of a long decline (Henningsen, 1980: 387–9).

The last two witch-hunts illustrating the development of legal scepticism involved the accusation of witches by persons who were allegedly possessed by demons. These accusations, much more than the naming of accomplices under torture, were the main mechanisms by which these hunts spread. The first occurred in the Roman Catholic bishopric of Paderborn in the late 1650s. It began when two young nuns from the small village of Brakel displayed the symptoms of demonic possession. The symptoms spread rapidly among the female teenage population in the village and ultimately infected about 200 persons in Paderborn itself. The entire episode received great encouragement from Bernhard Loeper, a Jesuit professor of theology at the University of Paderborn who performed a number of exorcisms mainly to prove that the Roman Catholic church was the one true church founded by Christ. As in many cases of possession, the demoniacs accused others of harming them by witchcraft, and these accusations led to the execution of approximately twenty witches and the murder of another ten, (Decker, 1995).

During this hunt the bishop of the diocese, Dietrich Adolf von der Recke, engaged in a correspondence with the Vatican regarding the treatment of possession and exorcism. The main spokesman for the Vatican, Ferdinand von Fürstenberg, was highly sceptical of the authenticity of the possessions, and he also made a series of recommendations regarding the proper procedure for prosecuting witches. These recommendations, which reflect the traditional caution of the Roman Inquisition regarding both possession and witchcraft, helped to bring the hunt to an end in 1658. When Dietrich Adolf died in 1661 Fürstenberg was appointed to succeed him. With the knowledge of what had happened a few years before, Fürstenberg insisted upon due process in all witchcraft cases originating within his jurisdiction, and he confirmed only one execution during his entire episcopate. By the time he died in 1683 Paderborn had witnessed its last witchcraft trial, although prosecutions in the neighbouring duchy of Westphalia, which had its own judicial apparatus, continued with a vengeance until the end of the century (Decker, 1981–2).

The witchcraft episode at Paderborn in the 1650s can be compared in a number of respects with the much more famous one that occurred at Salem, Massachusetts, in 1692. This hunt began when a group of teenage girls, manifesting the signs of demonic possession, accused three women of afflicting them by means of witchcraft. The hunt spread rapidly, aided greatly by the girls' identification of other individuals whom they claimed were the source of their afflictions. Further accusations came from other people in nearby towns like Andover who, in the midst of the tremendous fear generated by the trials, accused their neighbours of maleficent and diabolical activities. The number of individuals named as witches rose to almost 200, of whom 30 were convicted and 19 were executed. In the midst of the trials, however, the leading men in the colony, especially the clergy, began to doubt whether those who had been accused and executed were in fact guilty as charged. One of the most prominent ministers, Increase Mather, delivered a sermon in which he claimed it would be better for ten suspected witches to be set free than one innocent one condemned. In response to these concerns the colonial government forbade further imprisonments, released those still in gaol, and dissolved the court that had conducted the prosecutions (Boyer and Nissenbaum, 1974: 9–21; Hoffer, 1996).

There were two main sources of the judicial scepticism that emerged during the Salem trials. The first was a breakdown of the stereotype of the witch, similar to that which had occurred at Würzburg and in other German territories. The original set of accusations at Salem had been directed at old, relatively poor or marginalized women within the community, but as the accusations spread, men and women of much higher social standing, including some wealthy Bostonian merchants and Lady Phipps, the wife of the governor of Massachusetts, were implicated (Boyer and Nissenbaum, 1974: 32; Midelfort, 1979: 285–8). The second source was a growing recognition that the special court of oyer et terminer which had been established to try the witches had failed to adhere to prevailing standards of judicial proof. Contemporary critiques of the trials by Increase Mather, Thomas Brattle, Samuel Willard, Robert Calef and John Hale all focused on the insufficiency of the evidence that was used (Willard, 1692; Mather, 1693; Calef, 1700; Hale, 1702; Burr, 1914: 69–90). In particular they denied the reliability of spectral evidence, the testimony of afflicted persons that they could see the spectres of the witches who were allegedly harming them. The jurors who had returned the guilty verdicts in the trials echoed this line of argument in 1693 when they issued a public recantation, claiming that they had been deluded by the powers of darkness and had condemned persons to death on the basis of insufficient evidence (Drake, 1866). This criticism of the trials and the recantation of the jurors not only brought the Salem witch-hunt to a sudden halt, but it also signaled the end of witch-hunting throughout New England. After 1692 only one witch, Mary Disborough of Hartford, was convicted, and she was reprieved on the grounds that the evidence against her was insufficient (Taylor, 1908). The last trial in New England, which resulted in an acquittal, took place in Massachusetts in 1697.

The judicial scepticism that emerged in the wake of these large witch-hunts was in large part responsible for the significant changes that occurred in the conduct and supervision of witchcraft trials in virtually every European jurisdiction in the late seventeenth and early eighteenth centuries. These changes were sometimes prescribed in formal documents, such as the procedural guidelines that Spanish and Italian inquisitors received from their superiors or the edicts that royal governments published concerning the trial of witches. At other times judges and inquisitors made the changes themselves, on their own initiative, during the trials. Four changes in particular had a bearing on the number of witchcraft trials and convictions and executions: 1) the tighter control, supervision and regulation of local witchcraft trials by central or superior courts; 2) the restriction and in some cases the prohibition of torture in witchcraft cases; 3) the adherence of trial judges to more demanding standards of proof; and 4) the admission of more lawyers to represent witches at their trials.

The regulation of local justice

The most clear-cut and decisive change that took place in the conduct of witchcraft prosecutions, one that was linked to the other three, was the greater regulation of local justice by either central or superior judicial authorities. In order to appreciate the importance of such control, we must recognize that the most severe witch-hunts in early modern Europe were conducted by local officials who operated with a certain amount of independence from central state control. This is not to say that central governments did not from time to time participate in or even initiate witch-hunts. In a few instances even the rulers of kingdoms and principalities helped to fuel witch-hunts. King James VI of Scotland played an active role in starting the great witch-hunt that took place in his kingdom in 1591, while Christian IV of Denmark apparently had a hand in the hunt at Køge in 1612 (Larner, 1984: 3–33; Johansen, 1990: 345–6). In seventeenth-century Hungary two Transylvanian princes, Gábor Bathlen and Mihály Apafy, brought charges of witchcraft against their aristocratic enemies, leading to a set of high profile trials (Klaniczay, 1991–2: 75). Even in the early eighteenth century, when witch-hunting was declining in most parts of Europe, the senate of the kingdom of Piedmont initiated a series of witchcraft trials in which the primary victim of the crime was none other than the first-born son of King Vittorio Amedeo II (Loriga, 1994).

It is also true that throughout the entire period of the witch-hunts central state authorities granted local judges and magistrates the legal authority they needed in order to hold witch trials. But there is an enormous body of evidence showing that the areas in which witch-hunting was most intense over a long period of time were those jurisdictions in which central state power was relatively weak (Soman, 1989; Levack, 1996). Indeed, this is one of the main reasons why so many witch-panics took place in the relatively small duchies, principalities, and bishoprics within the Holy Roman Empire. There is also evidence that in those states that did have relatively strong central judicial establishments, the most serious witch-hunts occurred in communities which found ways to ignore or circumvent active state supervision of witch trials.

There were two main reasons why central authorities tended to exercise much more restraint than local judges in handling witchcraft cases. The first has to do with the level of involvement in witch-hunting. Judges from central courts, whether they were hearing cases on appeal or serving as itinerant justices, tended to be less likely than village or municipal judges to share the fears regarding witchcraft that gripped all members of the local communities. It is true that occasionally a zealous witch-hunter or inquisitor coming from outside the community would actually instill fears of witchcraft that had not previously arisen, but the more common sources of witch-hunting were the fears and animosities that prevailed within the local community. The second reason is that central judicial authorities had more legal training than local judges and usually were more deeply committed to the maintenance of what we would today call due process. They were therefore less likely than local authorities to tolerate the gross judicial abuses, such as the improper administration of torture, that frequently characterized local witch-hunts. In his discussion of the proper administration of torture, the Saxon jurist Benedikt Carpzov, observed that in small jurisdictions, county districts, and even in the larger towns, where legally ignorant plebeians and mechanics served as judges, innocent men and women were often tortured and forced to confess. Carpzov, who was no friend to witches, concluded that without judicial supervision the guilty would be set free and the innocent punished (Carpzov, 1670).

The differences in judicial outlook between central and local authorities often resulted in deliberate efforts by judges from the central legal establishment to enforce stricter rules of criminal procedure, to demand that all prosecutions be warranted by central authority, to insist that death sentences in witchcraft cases be reviewed on appeal, and to punish those local officials who violated established procedural norms. These efforts were often sustained over a long period of time, and they did not always meet with success. Occasionally the central authorities tolerated violations of their own high procedural standards. Ultimately, however, the state authorities that made such efforts succeeded in bringing about a permanent reduction in the number of prosecutions and executions.

The classic example of the way in which central authorities contained the witch-hunting zeal of local officials comes from the large portion of northern France that was subject to the jurisdiction of the parlement of Paris, one of the nine royal courts that exercised an appellate jurisdiction in the country. In 1587–8 a large witch-panic broke out in the Champagne-Ardennes region, which fell within the jurisdiction of the Parisian tribunal. In this local panic, which claimed hundreds of lives, all semblance of due process appears to have vanished. In an effort to discover the identity of witches, village judges were using the popular method of swimming those who had been named, a vestige of the medieval ordeal by cold water which was now illegal. Local officials were also torturing suspects without restraint and executing them in summary fashion. In response to this crisis the parlement proposed a policy of obligatory judicial review of all witchcraft convictions, an unprecedented imposition of central judicial authority on the French localities. The implementation of this policy, which involved the punishment of local officials for violating procedural norms, was a most delicate process. Nevertheless, the policy of automatic appeals was formally adopted in 1604 and published as an edict in 1624. From the adoption of that policy one can trace the decline of witch-hunting within the parlement's jurisdiction, even if some of the later sentences were upheld on appeal (Soman, 1986, 1978).

A similar pattern to that which obtained in France can be found in Spain, where witchcraft was considered a crime of mixed jurisdiction and could be prosecuted either by the Spanish Inquisition, an ecclesiastical institution that was under the authority of the king, or the secular courts. The Inquisition was a highly centralized, national institution, consisting of nineteen (ultimately 21) regional tribunals which reported to, and were supervised by, a central court, *la Suprema*, in Madrid. One of the functions of this central tribunal, which was headed by the Inquisitor General, was to enforce procedural rules in the trial of the crimes brought before it. The first set of guidelines, which were issued in 1526 in the wake of a witch-hunt in Navarre, were intended to govern the activities of inquisitors who tried witches in the regional tribunals. These guidelines restricted the practice of confiscating a witch's property, required consultation with the Suprema before convicting a witch a second time, and forbade the arrest or conviction of a witch solely on the basis of another witch's confession. These rules, coupled with a tradition of leniency that those rules encouraged, were in large part responsible for keeping executions for witchcraft in Spain at extremely low levels during the sixteenth century. Indeed, on a number of occasions the Inquisition succeeded in acquiring jurisdiction over cases of witchcraft that had originated in the secular courts and reversed the sentences of death that had been pronounced on the victims (Monter, 1990b: 268–9).

The Spanish Inquisition's impressive record of tight regulation and judicial leniency in witchcraft cases did not remain unblemished. A major lapse occurred in the great Basque witch-hunt of 1609–11. As we have seen, however, the inquisitor Alonso Salazar de Frias succeeded in returning the Inquisition to its traditional posture of judicial restraint. The new instructions that Salazar drafted and which the Inquisition issued in 1614 stand as a testament to the efforts of central authorities to regulate the conduct of officials in lower courts in order to contain the spread of witch panics. In addition to restating many of the guidelines of 1526, and issuing new instructions regarding the taking and recording of confessions and denunciations, the Inquisition also dissociated itself from the tactics followed by local authorities who had, 'without any legal authority, exposed the subjects to such abuses in order to make them confess and witness against others'. Moreover, as in France, the Inquisition took steps to punish the parties that had been responsible for these miscarriages of justice, turning them over to the High Court of Navarre and promising that in the future the Inquisition itself would proceed against them with the greatest severity (Henningsen, 1980: 375).

The conflict between the Suprema and local authorities continued after the publication of the new instructions. In a number of cases, most notably in northern Vizcaya, the Inquisition found it necessary to intervene in local witch-hunts conducted by secular authorities, reversing sentences and preventing executions. In a few other localities, most notably in Catalonia and Aragon, it chose to intervene belatedly if at all, and consequently hundreds of witches were executed (Monter, 1990b: 275). But in the long run la Suprema, which was the most highly centralized judicial institution in Spain, succeeded in enforcing a policy of judicial caution that not only kept executions for witchcraft at a minimum after 1614 but also brought about their ultimate termination.

The Spanish pattern was in many respects mirrored in Italy, where a centralized Roman Inquisition, which had been established in 1542, maintained control over witchcraft prosecutions long after ecclesiastical tribunals in northern European lands had deferred to secular courts in prosecuting witches. The record of the Roman Inquisition regarding witchcraft is even more impressive than that of its Spanish counterpart. Not only did it develop a strong tradition of leniency in sentencing witches, but it also insisted upon adherence to strict procedural rules in the conduct of witchcraft trials (Tedeschi, 1990). As in Spain, the enforcement of these rules was entrusted to the highest tribunal in the Inquisitorial organization, the Congregation of the Holy Office in Rome. Thus once again, as in France and Spain, a centralized institution assumed the role of regulating justice on a lower level.

The quintessential statement of the judicial caution that characterized the Roman Inquisition was the *Instructio pro formandis processibus in causis strigum sortilegiorum et maleficiorum*. Drafted in the early 1620s during the pontificate of Gregory XV, it circulated widely in manuscript until 1655, when Cesare Carena, fiscal of the Roman Inquisition, annotated and published it as an appendix to his *Tractatus de officio sanctissimae Inquisitione*.[1] Reflecting the influence of the Spanish Inquisition's new instructions of 1614, the *Instructio* dealt with all aspects of criminal procedure, establishing strict rules for examining accused witches, calling for restraint in the administration of torture and recommending particular care in the evaluation of witches' confessions. The most revealing part of this document, however, is the preface, which explains why the instructions had been drafted in the first place. The authors referred to the grave errors that were committed daily by ordinaries, vicars and inquisitors in witchcraft trials, including the use of defective forms of process, the administration of excessive torture, conviction on the most slender evidence, and the turning over of suspects to the secular courts. As Carena observed in his commentary, the atrocity of the crime had led inferior judges to disregard all the rules (Lea, 1939: 952–3). The *Instructio* was intended to remedy this problem.

The instructions drafted by the Roman Inquisition in the 1620s may have had an even more pronounced effect on witch-hunting than the rules adopted by the Spanish Inquisition in 1614. We know for example that in 1649 Cardinal Barberini of the Holy Office used the guidelines contained in the manuscript version of the document to prevent the execution of one of the *benandanti* or sleepwalkers who had confessed to infanticide before the Venetian Inquisition (Ginzburg, 1983: 125–9). After the publication of the *Instructio* in 1657 convictions for witchcraft throughout Italy declined dramatically, even in the secular courts, over which the Inquisition established its jurisdictional supremacy (Martin, 1989: 203–4). Nor did the influence of the Roman Holy Office and its procedures end there. The *Instructio* appeared in many different editions in the late seventeenth and eighteenth centuries, and it was also appended to various editions and translations of Friedrich Spee's *Cautio Criminalis*. In 1669 Cardinal Czartoriski of Poland used the instructions in order to restrain witch-hunting in his native country. The *Instructio* also served as the basis of the advice that Ferdinand von Fürstenberg sent to the bishop of Paderborn in 1657 and which Fürstenberg himself enforced as bishop after 1661, the year in which the *Instructio* was translated into German (Decker, 1995: 112). Just as the publication of demonological works had helped to disseminate the learned concept of witchcraft and thus encourage prosecutions, so the printing of cautious or sceptical works like the *Instructio* helped to make the legal community throughout Europe aware of the dangers of the unrestrained prosecution of the crime.

Even in countries which did not have strong central governments, higher judicial authorities who supervised the conduct of local courts demonstrated an ability to moderate the excesses of witch-hunting. This was particularly true in certain parts of Germany. Most German territories lay within the Holy Roman Empire, a political structure not known for the strength of its central judicial institutions. Indeed, one of the main reasons why the overwhelming majority of European witchcraft prosecutions and executions occurred in German territories, especially those that were relatively small, was the inability of imperial judicial authorities to control the operation of criminal justice in the numerous duchies, principalities and other political units within the Empire. In particular the Empire was never able to develop a regular and effective process by which cases could be referred or appealed to the *Reichskammergericht* or imperial supreme court which sat at Speyer, although that tribunal did succeed in reversing a number of sentences during the period of witch-hunting (Merzbacher, 1970: 63–4; Wolf, 1995: 785). There were, however, two other types of 'superior' judicial institutions in Germany that could, and at times did, exercise a restraining influence on witch-hunting, contributing eventually to its decline. The first were the central courts of the various duchies and principalities, especially those in the largest states, where witch-hunting tended to be more moderate than in the mid-sized territories and bishoprics. Judicial councils in places like Stuttgart, Munich, and Berlin all tended to have this negative effect on witch-hunting, especially in the late seventeenth and eighteenth centuries.

The second set of superior judicial institutions in Germany were not courts at all but the law faculties of the German universities. The imperial code promulgated by Charles V in 1532, the *Constitutio criminalis Carolina* required that when local courts confronted difficult cases, they would consult with the jurists in the law faculty of the nearest university. These consultations, which dealt with the successive stages of arrest, torture and judgment in the criminal process, served as one of the few mechanisms that could prevent local German courts from violating due process and conducting large witch-hunts.

During most of the period of witch-hunting, consultation with the law faculties in cases of witchcraft did little to restrain witch-hunting. Indeed, the consultations often had the opposite effect, as jurists, being familiar with demonological theory and committed to the rigorous prosecution of the crime, probably did more to facilitate than to restrain the prosecution of the accused and to spread learned witch-beliefs throughout Germany (Schormann, 1977: 9–44, 158; Lorenz, 1982). In the late seventeenth century, however, the consultations began to have the opposite effect, as jurists started to advise the use of extreme caution in the prosecution of the crime and to secure acquittals rather than convictions.[2] This change was particularly evident at the University of Tübingen, which began to recommend against torturing witches and in favour of acquitting them in a majority of cases in the 1660s (Schormann, 1977: 20–1). A similar but less dramatic change occurred at the University of Helmstedt in the 1660s, and that change contributed to the striking decline in the percentage of executions for witchcraft in the principality of Braunschweig-Wolfenbüttel, which consulted with the Helmstedt jurists on a regular basis. Between 1648 and 1670 the number of acquittals in witchcraft cases in that principality exceeded the number of capital sentences for the first time (Schormann, 1977: 24, 57).

One of the earliest examples of this insistence on judicial caution by members of the university law faculties comes from an opinion of Ernst Cothmann, professor of law at Rostock in the 1620s, the decade in which the Roman *Instructio* was written. The opinion, which recommended and secured the acquittal of an accused witch, is largely taken up with a critique of the various *indicia*, or pieces of circumstantial evidence, upon which the local judge had based his decision to torture the accused. It also reveals the insufficiency of the proofs that the judge had used to convict her. Just like the *Instructio*, this opinion took local officials to task for proceeding recklessly in the prosecution of witchcraft and thus for sending innocent people to the stake (Hauber, 1738: 2. 27–55). A similar decision, drafted by Paul von Fuchs, a jurist at the University of Duisburg, in 1662 concluded that the burgomaster of the town of Rietberg in Westphalia in 1662, who had been accused of witchcraft, should be acquitted and released (Hauber, 1738: 1. 614–35). That decision apparently put a permanent end to witch-hunting in Rietberg. A third decision, drafted by the law faculty at the University of Halle regarding the procedures used in the trial of Barbara Labarentin in 1694, had an even wider impact, since it led one of the members of that faculty, Christian Thomasius, to develop his ideas regarding witch trials.[3] In 1699 Thomasius recommended that students in his faculty be taught that witchcraft prosecutions should have their own distinctive form of *inquisitionsprozess*, in which special caution was to be observed (Wolf, 1995: 865). Two years later he published his treatise *De Crimine Magiae*, in which he claimed that all witchcraft prosecutions should be abandoned (Thomasius, 1701). Thomasius's scepticism, therefore, just like that of Spee and Salazar, had its origins in his efforts to contain the excesses of local justice.

The restriction and prohibition of torture

When superior judicial authorities took steps to remedy the procedural abuses that occurred in local jurisdictions they were almost always concerned, at least in part, with the improper administration of torture. This should not surprise us. Not only was torture frequently used in the prosecution of witches, especially in those areas of Europe influenced by Roman law,[4] but as a judicial practice it was particularly open to abuse. When torture was revived in the ecclesiastical and secular courts in the thirteenth century, with the clear purpose of obtaining confessions to concealed crimes, jurists recognized that the procedure might easily lead innocent persons to make false confessions in order to stop the pain. In order to prevent this from happening and thus to make the evidence obtained from confessions more reliable, jurists formulated a set of rules requiring that a certain amount of evidence of guilt be produced before torture could be administered. This evidence was usually weighted as a percentage of a full proof, which in the Roman-canonical tradition consisted of either the testimony of two-eye-witnesses or a confession. One eye-witness or circumstantial evidence that was the equivalent of this half-proof was usually required for torture to proceed. In order to prevent prosecution on trumped up-charges there also had to be evidence that a crime had actually been committed – the famous *corpus delicti*. Other rules governed the duration and intensity of the torture, and all confessions obtained under torture had to be repeated outside the torture chamber. Yet another set of rules was intended to restrict or deny the prosecution of a criminal's alleged accomplices on the basis of confessions obtained under torture.

These rules did not serve as a rationale for the system of torture, but they did attempt to limit its arbitrary potential and made judges more confident that it would serve its intended purpose. The problem arose when those rules were either relaxed or completely ignored in the interests of obtaining convictions from persons who were assumed to be guilty but for whose guilt there was little tangible evidence. Relaxation of this sort was very common in trials for witchcraft, since it was widely regarded as a *crimen exceptum*, an excepted crime, in which the usual standards of proof did not apply. And while relaxation became the rule in courts administered by trained judges, the complete ignorance or suspension of the rules occurred frequently in trials conducted by untrained laymen or clerics in small communities.

In the seventeenth and early eighteenth centuries the administration of torture in all criminal cases, and particularly in witchcraft cases, came under attack, resulting ultimately in the prohibition of torture in all European jurisdictions. The earliest critiques appeared in the first half of the seventeenth century. In addition to Spee, two Jesuits from Ingolstadt, Adam Tanner and Paul Laymann, wrote large works on moral theology that included sections on the use of torture in witchcraft trials (Tanner, 1626–7: 3. 981–22; Laymann, 1629; Kneubühler, 1977: 142–59; Behringer, 1987: 256–8). Both of these books, like Spee's, reflected first-hand experience with the trials themselves. From the Protestant side came works by Johann Meyfarth, a Lutheran professor from Erfurt whose work betrayed a heavy reliance on Spee, and Johannes Grevius, a Dutch Arminian theologian who condemned the use of torture by Christians for any purpose whatsoever (Grevius, 1624; Meyfarth, 1635).

This body of critical work on torture continued to grow in the late seventeenth century. The appearance of new works at that late date attests to the continued use of the procedure, even after its employment in witchcraft prosecutions had become less frequent. Three of these later works achieved fairly widespread circulation. In 1682 the Burgundian judge Augustin Nicolas wrote a closely reasoned assault on the practice, *Si la Torture est un moyen seur à verifier les crimes secrets: dissertation morale et juridique*. The second work, a dissertation by Meint Johan Sassen, of the University of Halle, was published in 1697 and went into several printings, while the third, which also came from the law faculty at Halle, was a dissertation by Christian Thomasius, the jurist who is known mainly for his earlier work, *De Crimine Magiae* (1701). Thomasius's dissertation on torture, which was published in 1705, also provided the basis for his more comprehensive treatise on criminal procedure in witchcraft cases that appeared in print in 1712 (Thomasius, 1705, 1712, 1986). Thomasius drew heavily on the earlier works of Spee, Tanner, and Meyfarth, but he also gave his treatise a distinctly Protestant flavour. A Pietist known for his anti-clericalism, Thomasius argued in the manner of Grevius that torture was an unchristian means of extorting the truth, that it was never mentioned in Scripture, and that the 'tyrannical' papacy had used it to strike down their enemies under the pretext of heresy and witchcraft (Thomasius, 1705).

The main criticism of torture in all these works was not so much that the procedure was inhumane, although Grevius, Nicolas and Thomasius all made that point,[5] but that the evidence obtained by means of its administration was unreliable, since innocent persons would make false admissions in order to stop the pain. This criticism of torture was therefore just one manifestation of a more general change in attitudes towards legal evidence and proof that will be discussed below. The criticism possessed more than mere academic significance. In those jurisdictions where torture was routinely administered in witchcraft cases, it contributed directly to a reduction in the number of convictions and executions and ultimately to a decline in the number of trials as well.

Before looking at the specific elements of this critique, it is important to make three qualifications. First, the arguments against torture, as they were articulated in the seventeenth century, were not new. Many of the criticisms of the procedure had been advanced in the late Middle Ages in the context of heresy trials, while the judicial reformers and witchcraft sceptics of the sixteenth and early seventeenth centuries, especially the Dutch priest Cornelius Loos (1546–95), had applied them to trials for witchcraft.[6] What made seventeenth-century judges and jurists more receptive than their predecessors to the arguments for restraint and caution was a more general change in attitude towards the evaluation of judicial evidence, coupled with the recognition that justice had obviously miscarried in the large chain-reaction hunts of the seventeenth century.

Second, even when the critics began to command an audience, the witch-hunters always managed to restate the traditional defence of the practice. Shortly after the publication of Adam Tanner and Friedrich Spee's passionate attacks on the system of torture, the Saxon judge and jurist Benedikt Carpzov published his famous *Practica Rerum Criminalium* (1635). In this manual on the criminal law, known later as 'the Lutheran *Malleus*,' Carpzov presented a systematic defence of the procedure and claimed that in cases of witchcraft proof was so difficult to obtain that the judge need not be restricted by the rules (Carpzov, 1670: 145–207). For every Hermann Löher, the German judicial official who condemned the torture of innocent witches at Rheinbach in the 1630s and whose opposition to the trials forced him to flee to Amsterdam, there was a Nikolaus von Beckman, the German-born jurist and convert to Catholicism who conducted a number of brutal witch trials near Graz and Steiermark in the 1680s and who complained that the Devil appeared as a squirrel during torture in order to help the guilty survive (Löher, 1676; Robbins, 1959: 308–9; Wolf, 1995: 932). In other words, the arguments of the judicial sceptics, just like those of the philosophical sceptics, were always contested.

Third, the actual abolition of torture in most European jurisdictions came after the effective end of witchcraft prosecutions and sometimes even after formal decriminalization. Only in two countries, Scotland and Hungary, did abolition take place before the last witchcraft trial. Most of the prohibitions of torture formed part of a broader reform of criminal procedure that many continental European states undertook in the last quarter of the eighteenth century and first quarter of the nineteenth. The first country in continental Europe to abolish torture was Prussia in 1754, forty years after King Frederick William I had issued an edict against witch-hunting. The last European territory to follow suit was the Swiss canton of Glarus, which took the step in 1851, long after the last legal execution for witchcraft in that territory (and in all of Europe) in 1782.[7] Moreover, the abolition of torture in Europe was in large part inspired by humanitarian concerns that had not been prominent in earlier critiques. The decline of witch-prosecutions therefore had much more to do with the *regulation* and *limitation* of torture than with its formal elimination.

The seventeenth- and early eighteenth-century critics of torture, writing in the context of witchcraft trials, made four specific points. The first was that torture should not be allowed on the basis of mere ill fame (*infamia*) or insufficient circumstantial evidence (*indicia*). The rationale for torturing witches on the basis of such limited or unsubstantiated evidence was the claim that witchcraft was a *crimen exceptum*, an exceptional crime in which the normal rules of evidence do not apply. Beginning in the 1620s, which was a particularly intense period of witch-hunting in Germany, a number of jurists, most notably Ernst Cothmann, presented the unorthodox but not entirely novel argument that witchcraft was not a *crimen exceptum*.[8] If that were the case, trials for witchcraft would have to conform to the more exacting legal requirements spelled out in the *Carolina*. Cothmann also argued that the less demanding evidentiary requirements in hidden crimes should apply only to the initiation of legal proceedings, not to the administration of torture, an argument that was later fully developed by Cesare Carena in the 1650s (Hauber, 1738; Lea, 1939, 2: 601–4). Soon after the appearance of Cothmann's decision, Paul Laymann argued that in cases of witchcraft and heresy the *indicia* must be *stronger* rather than weaker than in other criminal cases, so much so that judges for all intents and purposes had to be persuaded of the guilt of the accused before resorting to torture, the confession being needed simply to establish the technical requirements of full proof (Laymann, 1629).

A second criticism, closely related to the first, was directed against the arbitrary or excessive use of torture, a practice which once again had been justified on the basis of the exceptional nature of the crime. Extreme cruelty was by far the most widespread abuse of the system, and the criticism of such excesses, on both moral and legal grounds, became the most powerful and enduring argument against the entire procedure. It was central to Hermann Löher's *Hochnötige Klage*, which claimed that victims would confess to almost anything when torture was repeated, as well as to the critiques presented by Spee and Tanner. It is important to note that the same criticism of torture was often voiced by those who accepted the practice under certain circumstances, such as the Spanish and Italian inquisitors who drafted the instructions of 1614 and 1623 respectively. The Roman *Instructio*, for example, prohibited the administration of torture by jerking the ropes in the administration of *strappado*, by attaching weights to the feet, and for periods of more than one hour. Repetition was to be forbidden except in the most serious cases, in which the court was required to consult with the Congregation before proceeding. As this last rule suggests, the criticism of excessive torture was also closely bound up with the regulation of local justice, since the most flagrant abuses of the practice had occurred within relatively small or minor jurisdictions.

The third criticism of torture, which may have done more to reduce the number of prosecutions than any other single factor, was directed at the common practice of torturing those who were named by confessing witches as their accomplices. In ordinary crimes such denunciations could not be admitted as evidence, but once again the definition of witchcraft as a *crimen exceptum* allowed the judge to ignore the standard cautionary rules. The use of torture in this way had become routine in areas where belief in the sabbath was strong, and in some German bishoprics, such as Trier, Bamberg and Würzburg, it had resulted in hundreds of executions. The practice raised two legal questions. The first was whether witches whose torture had led to their conviction could be tortured a second time to extract the names of accomplices. The second was whether those persons whom the convicted witch named as accomplices could themselves be tortured without any other supporting evidence. On both legal questions learned opinion was divided,[9] although it is important to note that the most widely read demonologist of the seventeenth century, the Jesuit Martin Del Rio, had defended the practice in unequivocal terms, and had even claimed that the judge's suggestion of names during the adminis-tration of torture was legal. The torture of those persons had been deemed necessary in order to confirm the testimony of the witches (Lea, 1939: 649). The first scholar to engage Del Rio on this issue was Adam Tanner. Tanner did not deny the propriety of seeking evidence from accomplices of those who had confessed to exceptional crimes. But he objected that mere denunciation, even by more than one confessing witch, did not justify either torture or condemnation of those who had been of good reputation prior to their denunciation. The danger was that under torture innocent persons would confess to crimes they did not commit, the same danger that Spee identified in his *Cautio Criminalis*.

The final criticism of torture was a rebuttal of the claim that God would intervene in the process in order to protect the innocent. This same argument had served as a defence of the medieval ordeals before their abolition in 1215. Tanner, Grevius, and even the French jurists who drafted the *Grande ordonnance criminelle* of 1670, which identified torture as an archaic practice similar to the old ordeals, had shown the weakness of this defence (Peters, 1985: 85). Tanner was particularly eloquent in destroying this argument, claiming that if God had permitted martyrdoms, wars and massacres, there was no assurance that he would not permit the execution of innocent persons named as witches by allowing them to incriminate themselves under torture (Tanner, 1626–7).

The arguments of Tanner and Grevius against providential intervention in the torture chamber went hand in hand with criticisms of the swimming of witches, a popular and technically illegal practice which stood as a remnant of the practice of the water ordeal and which had been formally abolished as a method of judicial proof in 1215. Most lawyers, including the German jurist Johann Goedelmann and even Jean Bodin, condemned it, denying that it had any probative value. Goedelmann considered it a superstition invented by the Devil and claimed that judges who used it should be prosecuted (Goedelmann, 1592: 1: cap. 5: 21–30). In England the physician John Cotta characterized this 'vulgar trial of witchcraft' as a barbarous exercise of 'uncivil force and lawless violence.'[10] Nevertheless it did not lack learned or powerful advocates, including King James VI of Scotland, who claimed it could serve as an indication of the divine will (James VI, 1597: 81; Unsworth, 1989: 96–8). Swimming never became an accepted part of the legal process against witches in England or Scotland, but in some European localities it served as one of the *indicia* that justified the use of torture. In France village judges occasionally authorized its use, although they did so without the permission of the superior courts (Soman, 1986: 11–12; 1989: 6). In Hungary, where the old ordeals persisted well into the eighteenth century, municipal courts used the swimming test and compurgation on a regular basis (Kristóf, 1991–2: 99–100). In parts of Westphalia the swimming test apparently served as a final proof of guilt as late as the seventeenth century (Lea, 1939: 892–3). German jurists, however, uniformly condemned the procedure, and by the eighteenth century it had became the exclusive property of the popular community (Brähm, 1709: 47). In many parts of Europe the swimming of witches continued long after decriminalization (Gijswijt-Hofstra in this volume).

As legal writers and judges began to adopt a more cautious approach to the administration of torture, a more fundamental change in legal procedure began to reduce the premium on obtaining confessions under torture. This was the emergence of the possibility of non-capital punishments in all felony convictions, including witchcraft. Such sentences had always been possible in England, where the witchcraft statutes of 1563 and 1604 had provided for non-capital punishment for certain categories of offences, but these options were more difficult to exercise on the Continent, where judicial discretion was greatly limited and where the only officially recognized punishment for a crime like witchcraft was death. Recognition that the only alternative to capital punishment was acquittal provided judges with a powerful incentive to use torture to extort the requisite confession for conviction. The introduction of transportation, imprisonment and corporal punishment (classified as *poena extraordinaria*) as penalties for major crimes in continental jurisdictions changed all this, while the precedent of punishing a person for the 'suspicion' of a capital crime (*Verdachtstrafe*) without full proof gave judges a legal justification for the new sentences (Langbein, 1976; Damaska, 1978). These sentences were meted out in large numbers in Italy, Spain, and Portugal, where both torture and executions for the crimes of magic and witchcraft almost disappeared in the late seventeenth and eighteenth centuries. The new punishments in witchcraft cases also became common in France after the edict of 1682 and in the Austrian Empire after the promulgation of the *Constitutio Theresiana* in 1768. Both of those laws, just like the Prussian edict of 1714, also made it virtually impossible for judges to administer torture in witchcraft cases.

New Standards of Evidence

As suggested above, the questions raised regarding the administration of torture in witchcraft cases formed part of a more general set of concerns about the admission and evaluation of judicial evidence. During the seventeenth century judges and legal writers throughout Europe showed themselves increasingly reluctant to accept the evidence that was presented to them to justify the conviction and execution of witches. This caution led to the realization that the crime of witchcraft was extremely difficult, if not impossible to prove.[11] This conclusion may have contributed to, or received support from, a more fundamental belief that witchcraft itself was an impossible act, as shall be discussed below. But the legal conclusion, taken by itself, was of incalculable importance in bringing witchcraft trials to an end. It led directly to the increasing number of acquittals that occurred in virtually all jurisdictions, and it also contributed to the ultimate realization that witchcraft as a crime could no longer be effectively prosecuted.

The sceptical attitude towards evidence in witchcraft cases, just like scepticism regarding the possibility of the crime, was not completely absent in earlier periods of witch-hunting. There had always been judges who demanded that proof of witchcraft be absolutely conclusive before proceeding to sentence. Some of the temporary reductions in the prosecution of the crime in various jurisdictions, such as in Spain between 1550 and 1610, Scotland in the period 1597–1628, and Italy after 1520, can be attributed at least in part to the insistence upon rigid standards of proof. Underlying this caution was the fear that if such standards were not enforced, innocent persons would suffer torture and death. But whereas those early recommendations of caution were eventually ignored or contradicted, on the grounds that society needed to be protected, in the late seventeenth century they found more widespread and lasting acceptance. In this way an erratic pattern of witchcraft prosecution, in which courts oscillated between periods of intense prosecution and relative leniency, gave way to an enduring pattern of judicial caution and restraint.

Scepticism regarding the sufficiency of evidence in witchcraft cases took a number of different forms. It can be seen, first and foremost, in a growing reluctance among judges and legal writers to accept confessions, traditionally regarded as the queen of proofs, as sufficient proof of guilt. This scepticism was not restricted to those confessions that were adduced under torture, which, as we have seen, had their own special evidentiary problems. Judges and lawyers seemed just as unwilling to accept at face value those confessions that witches had allegedly made 'freely'. This scepticism arose mainly when the confessions had a high diabolical content, i.e., when the witches had confessed to either a pact with the Devil or attendance at the sabbath. Reginald Scot had argued that confessions of this sort were the least reliable of all evidence, while the other great sixteenth-century sceptic, Johan Wier (Johann Weyer), attributed them to the mental weakness of the women who had made them (Scot, 1930: 14; Weyer, 1991). An even more sophisticated interpretation of free confessions as the product of dreams or illusions, especially juvenile dreams, emerged during the investigation conducted by Alonso Salazar in the great Basque witch-hunt of 1609–11. By the late seventeenth century judges were willing to accept confessions to witchcraft (or any other crime) only if such confessions were in no way extorted, if they contained nothing that was impossible or improbable, and if the person confessing was not either melancholic or suicidal (Mackenzie, 1678: 86–7; Larner, 1981: 177). In 1788 the Danish jurist Laurits Nørregard, in urging the greatest possible caution in witchcraft cases, warned that the last thing an authority should do would be to believe the accused person's own confession (Henningsen, 1988: 108).

A second and even more frequent expression of judicial caution in the interpretation of evidence was based on the possibility that events attributed to supernatural agency may have had natural causes. This was particularly relevant to charges of *maleficium*, in which it was claimed that witches had inflicted harm by supernatural, i.e., diabolical, means. The sceptical response to such allegations, frequently adopted when lawyers defended witches against such charges, was that the act had natural causes, and that in order to convict a person of the crime, the possibility of natural causation had to be ruled out. Thus in Spain, in the wake of the hunts of 1526 and 1609–11, inquisitors were instructed to inquire whether the maleficent deeds that witches confessed to, such as having killed children or destroyed crops, might have had natural causes (Henningsen, 1980: 371). Inquiries of this sort became more and more common in later seventeenth-century trials. In Italy inquisitors from the Congregation of the Holy Office insisted that in cases of infanticide by witchcraft, the physicians who had treated the children should be examined to discover whether they could determine 'if the illness was or *could have been* natural' (Ginzburg, 1983: 126). The burden of proof was on the prosecution; all that was necessary to secure acquittal was evidence that natural causation was *possible*. In a number of trials in Scotland in the late 1620s, advocates for the witches went to great lengths to prove that malefices might not have been the product of supernatural intervention (Larner, 1981: 178). In securing the acquittal of a witch accused of murder by sorcery in 1662, Paul von Fuchs was content to show that the alleged supernatural cause of the disease which killed his victim could not be proved (Hauber, 1738: 617–21).

Even if the court could be satisfied that harm was done by supernatural means, on the grounds that there was no possible natural explanation of a particular act of malefice, cautious lawyers and officials could demand concrete evidence that the witch had actually been responsible for its infliction. Proof of this sort was obviously difficult to obtain, precisely because the very nature of magic was that it could act on substances at a distance, without direct physical contact. The evidence for commission, therefore, could only be circumstantial, such as the pronouncement of a curse on the victim, close physical proximity between the witch and the victim before the misfortune occurred, or even the report of a glance on the victim that could be represented as the evil eye. To sceptical seventeenth-century legal minds this evidence was not terribly persuasive, and it led some lawyers to claim that the only way to establish the guilt of the witch and demonic agency in the infliction of *maleficium* was to prove that she had made a pact with the Devil (Dalton, 1630; Fox, 1968: 64–5). Of course that undertaking had its own evidentiary problems. In the absence of a confession, courts would have to rely on the discovery of the witches' marks, the content of their speeches, or the testimony of accomplices to prove that she had made a pact (Bernard, 1630: 212–21). The difficulty of convicting persons on those grounds alone became evident in colonial Massachusetts, where judges required evidence of the pact for conviction. Because of that requirement, more than 80 per cent of all witchcraft cases brought before the Massachusetts courts before the Salem witch-hunt resulted in acquittals (Godbeer, 1992: 153–78).

The question whether afflictions were caused by diabolical or natural means arose in a particularly telling fashion in those cases of witchcraft which involved demonic possession. During the seventeenth century, which has been referred to as 'the golden age of the demoniac,' witchcraft cases of this sort became increasingly frequent, especially in England and France (Lea, 1939: 1041; Monter, 1976: 60). Demoniacs, very often women and children, identified witches as the cause of their possession, claiming that the witches had commanded demons to occupy their bodies and to afflict them with the fits, contortions and other forms of abnormal behaviour that had become associated with possession. The question naturally arose how such symptoms should be interpreted. Those who did not readily accept a demonological explanation of what had occurred had two alternatives. The first was fraud. In some of these cases the demoniacs staged their fits and then falsely accused individuals for their afflictions. The case of the English teenage girl Anne Gunter, who at the urging of her father feigned various signs of possession and then accused three women from her village of afflicting her in 1604, falls into this category. The other explanation was disease, the argument being that the maladies from which demoniacs suffered, which could be counted among the *maleficia* performed by witches, had natural causes. The most common interpretation of this sort in the seventeenth century was hysteria, or what in England was referred to as the suffocation of the mother. One of the first and most influential treatises to advance this was written by Edward Jorden, a London physician who was invited to observe both Mary Glover in 1602 and Anne Gunter in 1604 (Jorden, 1603).

The role that cases of demonic possession played in bringing about the decline of witch-hunting has not gone unnoticed by historians (Mandrou, 1968; Walker, 1981: 1, 75–84; Karlsen, 1987: 253–4; MacDonald, 1990: li–lvi). The revelation of frauds associated with possession contributed to greater caution in the handling of all witchcraft accusations, while the highly publicized exorcisms of possessed nuns in France led theologians, especially Protestants, to entertain and advance serious doubts about the extent of demonic interference in the world. But the most direct effect was that it made judges uncertain whether the behavior of possessed persons was sufficient to convict the witches whom they named as the source of their bodily afflictions. In 1697 a Scotsman, James Johnstone, shortly after the conclusion of a case of mass possession-cum-witchcraft at Paisley in his native land (Millar, 1809), observed that 'the parliaments of France and other judicatories who are persuaded of the being of witches never try them now because of the experience they have had that it's impossible to distinguish possession from nature in disorder' (HMC, 1894: 132). The French may have had other compelling reasons for not trying witches in 1697, but Johnstone's explanation at the very least reveals how the evidentiary problems associated with possession could lead to a state of judicial paralysis in witchcraft cases.

Demonic possession also highlighted two further evidentiary problems that had arisen in the context of numerous witch trials. The first arose from the possibility that when possession occurred, demons entered the body directly, without any human agency.[12] This possibility, which was fully accepted in contemporary demonological theory, could also lead to greater reluctance to try witches for causing possession. Indeed, the Roman *Instructio* directly criticized those judges who argued that all possession came from sorcery, claiming that the Devil could vex anyone's body directly with God's permission. Mere possession, therefore, did not provide *the corpus delicti*, the legal prerequisite for further investigation of a crime (Lea, 1939: 958). This line of reasoning was analogous to that of the Spanish inquisitors who argued that storms attributed to the malefi- cence of witches could very well be sent directly by God to punish people for their sins. In other words, direct supernatural agency, by either God or the Devil with God's permission, could serve as an alternative explanation of the witch's *maleficia*.

A further evidentiary problem connected with demonic possession arose in connection with spectral evidence, which was the testimony by possessed persons that they could see the specters or ghosts of the witches who were responsible for their afflictions. Evidence of this sort had been introduced into witchcraft trials at various times in the seventeenth century. In England it found a place in witchcraft trials as late as 1696 or possibly even 1712 (Kittredge, 1929: 363–4). Opinion on the value of such evidence varied, with writers like George Gifford proclaiming its insufficiency while others accepted its worth. The most effective challenge to its judicial use, however, came from those who claimed that the Devil might have used his powers of illusion to misrepresent innocent persons in spectral form, just as he might have misrepresented innocent persons at the sabbath.[13] It was precisely this line of reasoning that caused the clergy in Massachusetts to abandon the trials that they had originally supported in 1692 and to conclude that some of the victims had been falsely accused. Similar reasoning led German jurists in the late seventeenth century to refuse the admission of spectral evidence unless it was confirmed by other proof (Becker, 1700).

A final source of judicial caution in matters of evidence concerned the acceptance of the testimony of witnesses. In the trial of ordinary crimes excommunicants, children, criminals, heretics, and the defendant's relatives, servants and alleged accomplices were not allowed to testify against him. In many Continental jurisdictions, however, these same persons were permitted to testify against witches, on the grounds that witchcraft was a *crimen exceptum* that would otherwise be incapable of legal proof (Bodin, 1580: lib. 4, cap. 2; Carpzov, 1670: 130; Kramer and Sprenger, 1928: 209). In the seventeenth century children in particular played an increasingly prominent role as witnesses in witchcraft trials (Sebald, 1995: 104–5). The policy of allowing them to testify, however, began to encounter opposition as the trials started to take a heavy toll. In 1584 Reginald Scot criticized Continental judicial procedure precisely on these grounds (Scot, 1930: 11). About the same time the parlement of Paris, denying the entreaties of Jean Bodin, refused to allow testimony from children and other witnesses in witchcraft cases.[14] The exclusion of testimony from unqualified witnesses had the demonstrated ability to bring witch-hunts to a swift end. In 1614 the earl of Dunfermline, the Scottish lord chancellor, successfully derailed a prosecution to which he was opposed by excluding all 14 of the prosecution's witnesses against the accused, arguing that witchcraft was not a *crimen exceptum* and that therefore there was no reason to admit them (Wasser and Yeoman, forthcoming). Many of the acquittals in German witchcraft cases in the late seventeenth and early eighteenth centuries can also be attributed to the enforcement of a more demanding policy regarding the admission of testimony during the trial.

Legal representation

Closely connected to the careful and sceptical handling of evidence was the increasing frequency with which witches gained legal assistance as the trials declined in number. Although witches were entitled to defence counsel in all Continental and Scottish trials, few lawyers took their cases during the peak periods of the great witch-hunt.[15] Not only was legal counsel too costly for the typical lower-class witch, but lawyers were reluctant to defend witches on the grounds that they might thereby encourage the Devil's activities and incur suspicion themselves. There was in fact a considerable literature regarding the propriety of a lawyer's serving as a witch's advocate in such trials, and the warnings given to lawyers in this regard were probably effective in discouraging widespread representation (Kramer and Sprenger, 1928: 217–20). These warnings virtually disappeared in the demonological literature of the seventeenth century.

Although we cannot possibly gain any kind of accurate figures regarding the number of witches who had the benefit of counsel, there is a sufficiently large record of legal representation in the seventeenth century to suggest that the number of cases in which lawyers defended the accused was increasing. The large volume of business that was directed to the appellate courts of France by itself accounts for some of this increase, since legal representation at such trials was mandatory. Even in trials in the first instance, however, lawyers started pleading for witches in greater numbers during the seventeenth century. In Scotland lawyers began to defend witches in the court of justiciary in the 1620s, and in some cases they succeeded in securing acquittals (Larner, 1981: 178–91). Most of those acquittals came after 1670, such as that of the witch known as Maevia, whom Sir George Mackenzie successfully defended before the High Court of Justiciary (Mackenzie, 1672: 185–97). To this can be added the acquittals of Margaret Clerke in 1674 and Bessie Gibb in 1680, each of whom had an attorney, who in the latter case was her own husband (Scottish Record Office, 1674: fos. 181–2; 1680: fo. 103). By the 1660s the legal representation of German witches also seems to have become fairly common (Hauber, 1738: 1. 617–21; Wolf, 1995: 867). In Hungary counsel for accused witches appear as early as the 1650s and receive frequent reference in the records of eighteenth-century cases, when the number of trials finally began to decline (Várkonyi, 1991–2: 470).

Legal assistance of this sort benefited witches more than those accused of any other crime precisely because the evidence in witchcraft cases was so vulnerable to challenge by a person skilled in the law. Lawyers in witchcraft cases could easily raise doubts regarding the supernatural causes of alleged *maleficia*, demand evidence of the *corpus delicti*, and impeach the credibility of witnesses who would not have been allowed to testify in the trial of ordinary crimes. They could also point out the insufficiency of the evidence, especially when it was hearsay, and the irrelevancy of the evidence that was presented in the indictment or the libel. They could even go so far as to deny the existence of witchcraft and call for a ban on the trials, as one Hungarian lawyer did in 1671 (Várkonyi, 1991–2: 470). No wonder that in the previous century Martin Luther, in one of his outbursts regarding the crime of witchcraft, complained that lawyers 'want

too much evidence and deny open and flagrant proofs of witchcraft'
(Monter, 1976: 31). It was doubtless a similar frustration with the tactics
of lawyers that led members of the Spanish Inquisition to complain in
1526 that none of the jurists in Castile believed in witchcraft. Nor should
it surprise us that the one person acquitted of witchcraft in the central
Scottish courts between 1605 and 1622 had been wealthy enough to hire
no fewer than three lawyers (Wasser and Yeoman, forthcoming).

As a result of all these procedural changes and the persistent demands
for the exercise of legal caution, witchcraft prosecutions in the late
seventeenth and early eighteenth centuries looked very different from
those undertaken at the height of the great witch-hunt. Trials tended to
last longer and to become more deliberative, as sceptical judges, lawyers,
and juries engaged in a scrupulous examination of the evidence brought
before them. This tendency towards longer, more exacting trials became
most apparent in the central or higher courts, where many cases were
heard on appeal, but there is also some evidence of a similar trend at the
English assizes.[16] In all the European courts where witches were tried, the
summary processes that had been common in the late sixteenth and early
seventeenth century virtually disappeared. So did the large chain-reaction
hunts. Torture continued to be used in some jurisdictions, but its application was closely regulated and monitored by the superior courts, and many
of the witches who were subjected to torture managed to withstand it and
thus purge all the presumptions against them.

It should come as no surprise that as a result of these changes the
number of acquittals in witchcraft cases began to increase, in some cases
quite dramatically. Even more striking was the growing reluctance of
judges and officials to initiate witchcraft proceedings. One of the main
characteristics of the roman-canonical form of criminal procedure, which
was adopted in one form or another in most continental European courts
by the sixteenth century, was that the officials of the state could initiate
criminal prosecutions by themselves, by virtue of their office, on the basis
of ill fame. This procedure by inquisition, which had its origins in the
prosecution of heretics in the church courts, had greatly facilitated the
development of witch-hunting. Most prosecutions for witchcraft in the
sixteenth and early seventeenth centuries had begun in this manner, and
in many jurisdictions a legal official, known variously as the procurator
fiscal or advocate, acquired the function of bringing such charges before
the court.[17] Now, as the number of prosecutions began to drop off, this
pattern of official prosecution began to wane. In the duchy of Württemberg official prosecutions for witchcraft virtually disappeared after 1660.
All subsequent trials began when private subjects brought accusations
against their neighbours. In Prussia almost all witchcraft trials in the late
seventeenth and early eighteenth centuries originated in private suits. This

option had always been available under the system of justice that we broadly label as inquisitorial, and the *Carolina* had specifically provided for it (Goedelmann, 1592: 3: cap. 2; Langbein, 1974: 177–8; Unverhau, 1983: 59–142). What makes the seventeenth century distinctive in this regard was the frequency with which individuals began to exercise that option.

The reduction in the number of official witchcraft prosecutions, coupled with the new policy of restraint in the application of torture and the refusal to consider witchcraft an excepted crime, were largely responsible for giving witchcraft trials their new look. In Germany the courts that tried witches began to adhere much more closely to the criminal procedures set down in the *Carolina*, which had made special provisions for the protection of the defendant's rights (Trusen, 1995: 225). This return to the procedures of the *Carolina* did not constitute a rejection of the system of criminal justice that we generally label inquisitorial. In fact the *Carolina* served as the quintessential statement of inquisitorial procedure. Even when private citizens initiated legal actions, those suits were still handled within the framework of officialized justice. Written depositions were still taken by officers of the court for inclusion within a criminal dossier, while judges, as opposed to lay juries, continued to decide the guilt or innocence of the accused. The essence of the inquisitorial system was not the initiation of cases *ex officio* but the judicial investigation and determination of the crime by the judge regardless of the mode of initiation (Schmidt, 1940: 9; Langbein, 1974: 129–31). This inquisitorial system of justice, especially after its abuses and excesses had been eliminated, proved to be far more effective in bringing an end to witch-hunting than the accusatorial system, as a comparison between the end of witch-hunting in France and England will reveal.

CHANGES IN WITCH-BELIEFS

The responsibility for the end of witch-hunting lies mainly with the judges, inquisitors and magistrates who controlled the operation of the judicial machinery in the various secular and ecclesiastical courts of Europe in the late seventeenth and eighteenth centuries. These men not only implemented the procedural changes that we have just discussed but gradually became more uncertain whether the witchcraft accusations brought before their courts were either capable of legal proof or had any foundation whatsoever. As a result of this uncertainty they released an increasingly large number of witches, reversed capital sentences on appeal, and eventually stopped hearing cases altogether.

The behaviour of these judges and officials raises the fundamental question whether the judicial scepticism they manifested proceeded from or contributed to a more fundamental philosophical scepticism or disbelief regarding the power of the Devil, the existence of witches, and the theoretical possibility of their crime. Put another way, the question is whether the men who stopped the trials did so because they no longer believed in witchcraft. As we have seen, the decline of witchcraft prosecutions has traditionally been associated with a rational, scientific, and secular world view that denied the reality of witchcraft and the possibility of demonic intervention in the physical world. Prior to the late seventeenth century such 'enlightenment' was rare. Few educated men denied the existence of witches, and even fewer denied the possibility of their crime, especially its magical component. Those who adopted a sceptical position usually doubted the collective aspects of witchcraft, especially the sabbath, and the explicit pact with the devil, rather than the possibility that a person could harm man or beast by means of the devil's power. It is fairly safe to assume that if jurists in the kingdom of Castile did in fact 'hold it as a certainty that there were no witches,' as the supreme council of the Spanish Inquisition claimed in 1526, they were referring to the witches' alleged worship of the devil, not their practice of harmful magic. None of the most famous witchcraft sceptics of the sixteenth century denied the possibility of the crime they were discussing. Certainly Wier and Goedelman did not deny it, however bitterly they attacked the activities of witch-hunters. Cornelius Loos and Reginald Scot came much closer to a full denial, but neither made a categorical statement to that effect. Loos, like almost all the others, denied the reality of the sabbath, night flight, and the explicit pact with the Devil, but not magic itself (Lea, 1939: 603–4). Scot insisted in good Calvinist fashion that the age of miracles had passed and that a sovereign God would not permit human beings to exercise supernatural power, but he did not include the 'working of wonders by supernatural means' in his summary of the 'absurd and impossible crimes' attributed to witches.[18]

Samuel Harsnett, the cleric who did so much to discredit exorcism in early seventeenth century England, came close to denying the reality of witchcraft when he referred to witches as part of 'all that lymphatical chimera', but he went no further than his fellow countryman Scot (Harsnett, 1603: 299). Friedrich Spee, in his passionate plea for the lives of the witches who were forced to confessed in the 1620s in Germany, argued that witchcraft was a terrible crime. His belief in the reality of witchcraft may have actually made his book more acceptable in conservative circles (Monter, 1976: 84–5). Tanner and Meyfarth, like Spee, professed their belief in witchcraft. Of course it is always possible that these men made such cautious statements of orthodox belief in order to avoid the charges of atheism, but aside from Loos's formal recantation in order to avoid execution as a heretic, their expressions of belief bear signs of genuine intellectual discrimination rather than self-serving political convenience.

Among the lawyers, Salazar developed his stinging critique of inquisitorial practice within the context of a firm belief in magic as well as the sabbath. None of the judges who were members of the parlement of Paris during the early seventeenth century ever denied the reality of the crime they were adjudicating, and in some cases they confirmed sentences against the accused. Carena, whose insistence on judicial caution matches that of Salazar and the Parisian *parlementaires*, insisted that there was much illusion but also much reality regarding witchcraft (Lea, 1939: 953). Ernst Cothmann, in a pattern that became increasingly evident in the later seventeenth century, denied the reality of the sabbath but did not dispute that of *maleficium* (Hauber, 1738: 2. 217–55). A few years later Paul von Fuchs, defending his client against charges of witchcraft, disagreed with those unidentified sceptics who said there were no witches, since he believed that magicians did exist and that they should be put to death (Hauber, 1738: 1: 627–8). In Scotland, the famous defender of witches and inveterate critic of those who prosecuted them, Sir George Mackenzie, began his exposition on the subject with a response to Wier, 'the great Patron of Witchcraft', claiming that witches should suffer death not just for poisoning and murder but also for 'enchanting and deluding the world' and that even charmers were guilty of at least apostasy and heresy (Mackenzie, 1678: 81–4). In Denmark, where learned witch-beliefs tended to last longer than in other parts of Europe, it was not until the 1850 that a lawyer, T. Algreen-Ussing, declared the crime of witchcraft to be impossible (Henningsen, 1988: 108).

One reason for the rarity of categorical denials of witchcraft, even among the most sceptical and cautious critics of witch-hunting, was that until the late seventeenth century the philosophical systems that prevailed in academic, theological and judicial circles made the existence of witchcraft possible, even likely. Late medieval scholasticism readily accommodated the operation of demons in the world and provided a solid intellectual foundation for the great witchcraft treatises of the period from 1450 to 1650. Neo-Platonism, which served as the main challenge to scholasticism in the fifteenth and sixteenth centuries, was more predisposed to see magic in natural rather than supernatural or demonic terms, and that outlook gave rise to some of the earliest challenges to learned witch-beliefs (Thomas, 1971: 578–9). But neo-Platonism, with its belief in a magical world of various occult forces and its acceptance of the existence of demonic as well as angelic spirits within that 'natural' world, proved to be an insufficient foundation upon which to mount an assault on the entire set of learned witch-beliefs. A neo-Platonist would have found it difficult to argue that witchcraft and magic were impossible crimes.[19]

Only in the seventeenth century did a new philosophy emerge that had the potential to undermine the belief in the reality of witchcraft. The mechanical philosophy, which ranged itself equally against scholasticism and neo-Platonism, viewed the earth as a machine that followed regular, immutable laws of nature. The challenge that this new philosophy presented to the belief in witchcraft became evident in the work of mechanists René Descartes, Thomas Hobbes, and Baruch Spinoza, all of whom denied that spirits, if they existed at all (and the materialist Hobbes would not even accept that), could exercise influence on the operation of the material world. Because of the strength of this philosophical challenge to witchcraft, and the ability of this new philosophy to spread among the learned elite in a culture increasingly dominated by print, the decline of witchcraft prosecutions and executions is often attributed to its influence. Only when the members of the ruling and educated classes began to think in this new way, so it is argued, did witchcraft prosecutions enter a permanent and irreversible decline. According to Trevor-Roper, it was the new philosophy of Descartes that 'dealt the final blow to the witch-craze in western Europe' (Trevor-Roper, 1969: 110).

Categorical statements like this require serious qualification. The mechanical philosophy may very well have helped to undermine the *beliefs* that many educated persons had in the reality of witchcraft (Thomas, 1971: 577; Easlea, 1980: 5, 198), although recent scholarship has tended to minimize its role in this regard, especially in England (Bostridge, 1997: 4, 105, 242–3; Clark, 1997: ch. 19). Whether the dissemination of the new philosophy had anything to do with the decline and end of witchcraft *prosecutions* is much more problematic. The problem is largely one of chronology. We have seen that the decline in prosecutions began in some areas as early as 1600 and in most other areas by 1670, with the exception of a few countries on the eastern and northern periphery of Europe. These were the years when the new mechanical philosophy first made its appearance. The spread of this philosophy, however, was a gradual process, and it was not uncontested. A few natural philosophers embraced the new ideas in the 1650s (Easlea, 1980: 135) but it took some time for mechanism to exercise a more pervasive influence within the universities, the legal profession and the bureaucracies of the state. It is unlikely that the judges and officials who applied the early brakes to witch-hunting during the first 70 years of the seventeenth century were even exposed to, let alone influenced by, the new ideas. When the ideas did reach them, moreover, they had often undergone significant modification at the hands of natural philosophers who had tried to reconcile the harsh mechanism of Descartes and Hobbes with their belief in a providential, if not an immanent God.

The critical period in the reception of the new philosophy appears to have been the years between 1690 and 1720, the period of the early

Enlightenment. Thus the new philosophy did not appreciably affect the mental outlook of the educated classes until well after prosecutions had begun to decline in number and in some cases until after they had stopped altogether. In Geneva, for example, the first magistrate to profess an adherence to Cartesian ideas, Robert Chouet, wrote a critical commentary on Geneva's prosecution of witches in 1690, almost 40 years after the last witch had been executed in that republic (Monter, 1976: 38). Even in France, where the new philosophy may have taken root somewhat earlier than in Geneva, Cartesianism probably did not have the negative influence on the level of prosecutions that scholars have often attributed to it (Mandrou, 1968; Trevor-Roper, 1969: 110). Certainly the members of the parlement of Paris who played a decisive role in the decline of French witch-hunting, could not have been influenced by Cartesianism or any other aspect of the 'intellectual revolution' until long after they had brought executions for witchcraft to an end within their jurisdiction in the early seventeenth century.[20] If the new philosophy played any role at all in the decline of witch-hunting, it was at the *end* of the process in the late seventeenth and early eighteenth centuries, when the last trials took place and witchcraft was decriminalized, not in the earlier decades of the seventeenth century, when the initial and usually the most dramatic reduction in the number of trials occurred.

Even in this later period, the extent of the influence of the new philosophy on the process of witch-hunting remains in doubt. This can be seen first by looking at the impact of two of the most celebrated critics of witch-hunting around the turn of the eighteenth century, the Dutch Reformed minister and theologian Balthasar Bekker and the Saxon jurist Christian Thomasius. Both wrote in the 1690s and early 1700s, after the decline of prosecutions had begun in all western European countries, but before the last trials had taken place. The works of both men, moreover, commanded an international audience. Their scepticism was much more fundamental than that of any of their predecessors, especially Wier, and they are both considered to be participants in the early Enlightenment (Pott, 1995). Most important, the two men came to the same crucial conclusion that the crime of witchcraft was not only impossible to prove (the position of the judicial sceptics) but impossible to perform.

Of the two men, Bekker's views were the more radical. His attack on witch-beliefs took the form of a massive treatise, *De Betoverde Weereld*, which was published in four parts in the Netherlands in 1691 and 1693 and translated into English, German and French shortly thereafter. It would be hard to identify a more comprehensive assault upon the cumulative concept of witchcraft before the end of the great witch-hunt. In 1701 the sceptical German jurist Felix Brähm hailed the book as the chief assailant of the superstition of witchcraft (Brähm, 1709; Attfield,

1985: 4). Bekker denied the pact with the Devil, the sabbath, metamorphosis, flight, conception by a demon, demonic possession and the reality of harmful magic itself. At the basis of this denial lay a powerful critique of contemporary demonology. Whereas Wier could not bring himself to abandon the belief in a powerful, knowledgeable and deceptive Devil, Bekker denied that the Devil even possessed knowledge, much less a capacity to intervene in the operation of the material world.

The basis of Bekker's argument is two-fold: on the one hand, Bekker was clearly a Cartesian, a rationalist who endorsed the mechanical philosophy and who accepted Descartes' rigid distinction between matter and spirit. He gave an early preview of this outlook in his earlier rejection of the traditional interpretation of signs and wonders as indicators of supernatural displeasure and as portents of the future. On the other hand he was also a biblical scholar in the Erasmian tradition, who argued for a proper historically contextualized interpretation of those Scriptural passages that referred to witches and devils. It was in fact Bekker's biblical scholarship, much more than his Cartesianism, that lay at the basis of his radical conception of the Devil. To claim that Bekker 'had not repudiated belief in the Devil' is to miss the point, which is that for Bekker the devil was merely a symbol of evil and was incapable of exercising power over the physical world, even the power of illusion that figured so prominently in the work of Wier (Trevor-Roper, 1969: 102; Pott, 1995: 190–3). Once the devil was reduced to this status, the possibility that a human being could commit the crime of witchcraft vanished. Indeed, Bekker boldly suggested that when accusations of witchcraft are made, the state should prosecute the accusers, not the accused, a course of action that was becoming common at precisely this time.

The impact of Bekker's book on the prosecution of witches is a matter of some controversy.[21] It obviously had little judicial effect in the Netherlands, where witches had not been tried in decades, or in England, where the last execution had also occurred eight years before the first volume of the book appeared in print. The same could be said of France, which was executing its last witches in the 1690s. But it has been claimed that Bekker's book saved the lives of countless victims in other parts of Europe where his book was read, especially in the German lands near the Netherlands. On closer analysis, however, we realize that there were relatively few prosecutions even in those German lands by the time Bekker wrote. The one northwestern German territory where witch panics continued to take a heavy toll into the 1690s was the duchy of Westphalia. Only in 1696 did the courts in that duchy begin to acquit witches in significant numbers (Decker, 1981–2: 386). It would be difficult, however, to show that the judges in places like Olpe and Hallenberg, where the trials in the late 1690s were held, acted under the influence of Bekker's book. However important Bekker's book may be in the history of learned witch-*beliefs*, its effect on witch-*hunting* was apparently limited. It may have provided a foundation for the decision of some judges and magistrates to abandon prosecutions entirely in the eighteenth century, but even that influence cannot be established.

Christian Thomasius, the jurist who became the chancellor of the University of Halle in Brandenburg, appears to have exercised more influence on the later stages of witch-hunting than Bekker, if only because he wrote as a criminalist and because he and the jurists with whom he was associated were actually involved in the adjudication of the witchcraft cases that were still being heard in German courts. As we have seen, Thomasius was the quintessential judicial sceptic who exposed the evidentiary problems associated with the administration of torture in his dissertation on that subject and who published a full-scale critique on the trial of witches. His most famous work, *Dissertatio de crimine magiae*, which was translated into German as *Kurze Lehr-Sätze* in 1703, was also largely concerned with questions of judicial proof. It recommended that when cases of witchcraft came before the courts, judges needed to proceed with great caution, investigate the possibility of deception and demand more proof than was required under the existing criminal law.[22] Even if it could be proved that the Devil had been responsible for the injury or illness that had been inflicted (a point on which Thomasius was himself highly dubious), one could not prove that the accused was responsible for the deed by means of the pact. The entire procedure for trying witches was therefore worthless, and all prosecutions should cease.

The important question here is the content of the witch-beliefs that underlay this demand for judicial restraint. It appears on the surface that the position Thomasius took was just as radical as that of Bekker. In *De Crimine* he stated emphatically that the reason why all witchcraft trials should end was that 'witchcraft is only an imaginary crime.' In a full-scale assault on the cumulative concept of witchcraft, he denied the existence of a pact with the Devil, the sabbath and the influence of evil spirits over corporeal bodies. Thomasius, like Bekker, never denied the existence of the Devil, but his concept of demonic power was so limited that it rendered the crime of witchcraft impossible, with the confessions of witches being the product of either delusion or 'inhuman torture.' Thomasius believed that the power of the Devil was exercised only invisibly in the spiritual sphere; it thus had 'only moral influence' (Pott, 1995: 193–8; Trusen, 1995: 224).

Despite the apparent similarity of Thomasius's position to that of Bekker, there are grounds for drawing a distinction between them. Thomasius was not, like Bekker, a mechanist or a Cartesian. Indeed he admitted in *De Crimine Magiae* that he could not go as far as Bekker in separating the material from the spiritual world. Although he praised Bekker for his destruction of scholastic fantasies, he could not accept his dualism. The intellectual basis of Thomasius' view of demonic power was not Cartesianism, as it was with Bekker, but the theological tradition of German Pietism, which emphasized the sovereignty of God and attributed all misfortune directly to him.

The other difference between Bekker and Thomasius is that the latter never denied the reality of certain forms of magic. Thomasius fully admitted that sorcerers and witches could injure people by occult means and that those individuals should be put to death. In defending his book against his critics in 1702 he even made the apparent concession that sorcerers could bring on diseases with the Devil's help.[23] He would not, however, make any concessions on his main point, which was the non-existence of the pact with the Devil. For Thomasius it was the demonic pact, not the inflicting of harm, that constituted 'the crime of magic.' Thomasius justified this definition of magic on the grounds that according to Saxon and Prussian law, the pact with the devil remained the essence of witchcraft. The reason for declaring the crime of magic to be impossible was that human beings could not make an explicit pact with a physical Devil. The scholastic view that witches could also perform *maleficium* by means of an implicit demonic pact did not enter the discussion.

The philosophical position that underlay Thomasius's judicial scepticism did not go much beyond that of Wier, Scot and the other sixteenth-century critics of witch-hunting. The same can be said for the other jurists who wrote about the crime of witchcraft in the early eighteenth century, like Johann Reiche and Jacob Brunnemann, and the judges who tried the last cases. These men had rejected the reality of the sabbath and the pact with the Devil, but they had not yet embraced a philosophy or a theology that would lead them to reject the reality of natural or even demonic magic. This suggests that in Germany and other lands where witchcraft prosecutions continued into the eighteenth century, the judges who brought an end to the trials, no less than those who had been responsible for their initial reduction in number, were not as 'enlightened' as is often claimed.

RELIGIOUS CHANGES

Thomasius and Bekker were both committed Protestants who relied extensively upon Biblical citation and ecclesiastical history to destroy contemporary witch beliefs (Haustein, 1995: 249, 259). Both men also claimed that the theory of witchcraft was the invention of the papacy. For Bekker its purpose was to confiscate the property of witches and pay the salaries of inquisitors, whereas for Thomasius, an indefatigable opponent of clericalism, it had emerged in the misguided papal briefs that formed canon law. The prominence of religious themes in the works of these two critics of witch-hunting raises the further and much debated question whether changes in religious thought might have contributed in some part to the decline of witchcraft prosecutions.

This is not the place to evaluate the role of the Protestant and Catholic Reformations in the rise of witch-hunting (Levack, 1995a: 100–24). Suffice it to say that the demonization of European culture that preceded and accompanied the Reformation, the reliance upon Biblical injunctions against witchcraft (especially Exodus 22:18), the determination of religious reformers to eliminate magic in its various forms, the subjection of the rural masses to a rigorous moral discipline as part of a program of Christianization, and the determination of public. authorities to establish a godly state by taking legal action against moral deviants and blasphemers all contributed significantly to the intensification of witch prosecutions in the sixteenth and early seventeenth centuries. At the same time, however, it is possible to identify elements of Protestant and reformed Catholic culture that contributed in one way or another to the growing reluctance to prosecute witches in the late seventeenth and eighteenth centuries.

Certainly the Protestant biblicism that had been effectively pressed into the service of witch-hunting could just as easily be used by the opponents of the trials to discredit the entire process. In 1584 Reginald Scot revealed the full potential of this approach in his full-scale assault on prevailing witch-beliefs, *The Discoverie of Witchcraft*. This book, arguably the most radical witchcraft treatise to appear in the sixteenth century, was based in large part on the Bible and the works of its Protestant interpreters. In the seventeenth century other critics of witch-hunting, relying on a growing consensus among biblical scholars, took pains to emphasize that the Bible said nothing about witchcraft as that term was understood in the early modern period and to insist that the condemnation of 'witches' in the Bible should have no relevance to the prosecution of the crime. In 1650 the Alsatian jurist Andreas Sandherr argued before a court at Colmar that witch-beliefs had no biblical foundation (Klaits, 1982: 163), while three years later in England the political thinker Sir Robert Filmer, in the wake of the witchcraft trials at Maidstone, Kent, appended a long discourse on the difference between an English and a Hebrew witch to a tract advising members of juries how to deal with charges of witchcraft.[24]

In similar fashion the Protestant emphasis on the sovereignty of God, which underlay the prosecution of those magicians and witches who were believed to have challenged that sovereignty, could just as easily be invoked to deprive the Devil of much of his alleged worldly power. This line of thought finds its clearest expression in the 'providential' theological tradition that flourished at Tübingen in the sixteenth and seventeenth centuries. Contrary to the position taken in the *Malleus maleficarum*, the theologians at Tübingen attributed all misfortune to the work of a providential God, denying that any intermediate demonic forces played a role in the process. This tradition not only contributed to the moderation and ultimately the decline of witch-hunting in the duchy of Württemberg, but it also made inroads in Denmark, where pastors trained in the Tübingen tradition were largely responsible for the decline of witch-hunting that began in that kingdom as early as 1625 (Johansen, 1991–2: 413–20). One finds a similar theme in the works of some of the early German Pietists, including Christian Thomasius, whose strictly spiritual view of demonic power allowed him to bring faith and reason into harmony.

Perhaps the most important religious source of the decline of witch-hunting was the new attitude of tolerance that began to characterize some Protestant and even a few Catholic communities in the second half of the seventeenth century. There is a solid foundation for this religious tolerance in the Protestant tradition, most notably in the *Heidelberg Catechism*, even though intolerance was more characteristic of Protestant practice during the first century of the Reformation. This Protestant tolerance was manifested mainly towards members of other religious denominations, but the same sentiment could be extended to those suspected of witchcraft, since they were widely regarded as either heretics or at least as religious transgressors. It is probably no coincidence, therefore, that witch-hunting first began to decline in the Dutch Republic, a country known for its early religious tolerance.[25] When Bekker pleaded eloquently in 1691 that Protestants should not pass judgment on other Christians, he was reflecting a Dutch tradition that reached back to Erasmus in the early sixteenth century (Stronks, 1991: 154–5). It was also no coincidence that Poland, the Roman Catholic 'state without stakes,' not only tolerated religious diversity but also did not prosecute many witches in the sixteenth century, although both religious persecution and witch-hunting did develop belatedly in that kingdom in the late seventeenth century.

Not unrelated to this new spirit of tolerance was the abandonment of the determination by both Protestant and Catholic public authorities in many states to use their secular power to create an ideal Christian community. This determination to establish a godly state, which was widely evident in many small German states as well as in Scotland, Denmark and colonial Massachusetts, often involved the imposition of a strict moral discipline on the population. In response to clerical pressure, the legislatures of these states had passed laws against blasphemy, drunkenness, adultery, and sodomy as well as witchcraft, and on the basis of these laws the courts had prosecuted these sinners with a vengeance. In some cases this effort to impose God's will on the people was inspired by millenarian fervour. In the late seventeenth and eighteenth centuries, however, the various states of Europe abandoned this type of moral crusading, a process indicative of the secularization of both law and politics. The end of prosecutions in many of these states can be linked, at least in general terms, with this change in thinking regarding the functions of the state (Midelfort, 1972: 127; Larner, 1981: 57–9, 193–9; Roeck, 1988; Ankarloo, 1990: 291–2).

In establishing the religious sources for the decline of witch-hunting, it is important to maintain a sense of perspective. Opposition to the trials on religious grounds was more than balanced by the determination of zealous clerics and laymen to keep the trials going. Among the Protestant theologians and pastors who spoke or wrote about witchcraft in the late seventeenth and early eighteenth centuries there was a wide range of sentiment, just as there had been in the late sixteenth century, but more of it was enlisted in support of witch-hunting than against it. Let us not forget that Bekker directed his work against two of the most respected Calvinist theologians in the Netherlands in the seventeenth century, Johannes Coccejus and Gisbertus Voetius; that the leadership of the Reformed Church expelled him from his ministry for his faulty exegesis of the Bible regarding the power of the Devil; and that the large number of Dutch polemicists who attacked his book anchored their position in Calvinist theological orthodoxy.[26] In similar fashion Thomasius encountered strong opposition from the theologians at German universities, including Johann Weidner, of the University of Rostock, who in 1722 attacked both Thomasius and his stalwart supporter Jacob Brunnemann, and who defended the proposition that the Devil can transport witches through the air and breed with them corporeally.'[27]

Some of the strongest defenders of witch-hunting during the period of decline, including a number of judges and jurists, grounded their position on a biblical fundamentalism that flourished within the Protestant tradition. In England the learned judge Matthew Hale, who presided over the trial and conviction of three witches at Bury St Edmunds in 1662, explained that his belief in the reality of witchcraft derived from the Bible. Hale's religious views also led him to adopt a mechanical world view that allowed for the operation of a supernatural will, a modification of Descartes' philosophy espoused by the natural philosopher Jean Baptiste van Helmont (Cromartie, 1995: 206–8). A friend and admirer of Hale, the nonconformist Richard Baxter, likewise based his *Certainty of the World of Spirits* (1691) upon his Protestant views, supplemented by uncorroborated experience. The core of the Cotton Mather's treatise on witchcraft, *The Wonders of the Invisible World* (1692) consisted of propositions, corollaries and conjectures revealing an uncompromising biblicism. A biblically based demand for the continued prosecution of witches also emerged in Hungary, where in 1758 the Palatine Lajos Batthyány protested against Empress Maria Theresa's recently announced policy of leniency towards witches on the grounds that the Bible confirmed the existence of witches (Klaniczay, 1990a: 171).

The Bible remained a main source of witch-beliefs long after the trials had ended. In 1738 E. J. F. Mantzel, a professor at the University of Halle, defended the prosecution of witches on the ground that they, 'having denied God and made a pact with the Devil, should be punished with death in accordance with divine command' (Mantzel, 1738). In 1760 the Danish jurist C. D. Hedegaard claimed that 'when one believes the Scriptures or the revealed word of God', the reality of sorcery or witchcraft 'cannot generally be denied' (Henningsen, 1988: 107). The eighteenth-century English Methodist preacher John Wesley declared that 'giving up witchcraft is, in effect, giving up the Bible,' while his contemporary, the systematic English jurist William Blackstone, stated even more emphatically that 'to deny the possibility, nay, the actual existence of witchcraft and sorcery is at once to contradict the revealed word of God' (Blackstone, 1769: 4: 60; Wesley, 1906: 3: 330). In 1773 the Presbyterian clergy of the Church of Scotland, citing the Bible as their authority, made a common declaration in the reality of witchcraft, just as they had in 1736, the year in which the witchcraft statute of 1563 had been repealed.[28]

SOCIAL AND ECONOMIC CHANGES

In this survey of general reasons for the decline of witch-hunting we have focused almost exclusively on the work of those persons who controlled the judicial machinery and the writers who might have influenced them. But what about the members of the lower classes, who were primarily responsible for bringing the initial accusations of *maleficium* against their neighbours and for testifying against them in court? Without their support witch-hunting would not have been successful, at least not over a long period of time. Could these same members of the lower classes have been at least partially responsible for the decline of witch-hunting? Did the number of trials decrease because fewer members of the lower classes were attributing their misfortunes to the magical powers of their neighbours? If that were the case, the lower number of formal accusations might very well be explained by social, economic and demographic change.

There is little doubt that the dramatic changes in the fabric of European social life during the period 1550–1650 contributed to the great European witch-hunt. Over-population, an unprecedented rise in prices, a decline in real wages among the poor, chronic famine and dearth, especially during years of climatic severity, periodic outbreaks of the plague, extra-ordinarily high levels of infant mortality, migration of the poor from the countryside to the town, pestilence among men and beasts, and the social dislocations that resulted from widespread domestic and international warfare often lay at the root of those personal conflicts that found expression in witchcraft accusations.[29] The question for our purposes is whether there was a sufficient improvement in, or reversal of, these adverse economic and social conditions to bring about a reduction in the number of charges brought before the courts.

It is true that the demographic explosion of the sixteenth and seven-teenth centuries came to an end around 1660, and the inflation that had been fueled primarily by that demographic growth also showed signs of levelling off. Real wages registered some improvement, and the effects of warfare on the civilian population were greatly reduced. Whether these improvements made daily village life more secure and personal tensions in small communities less acute is certainly problematic; one could argue that significant changes in the quality of rural life did not take place in most European countries until the nineteenth century. The same might be said of the quality of medical care in those same communities; the country physician did not replace the wise woman in rural areas until long after the witch-trials were over. The most that we can say with any degree of certainty is that communal provision for the poor became more systematic and effective in most European countries after 1660, and that may very well have eliminated some of the social tension between the dependent members of the community and their more well-off neighbours (Thomas, 1971: 581; Labouvie, 1995: 73–6).

In the final analysis it remains impossible to determine to what extent the social and economic improvements and the changes in culture that did take place after 1660 helped to reduce the number of formal accusations made by members of the lower classes. It is difficult enough to identify the social and economic tensions that lay behind the specific quarrels leading to witchcraft accusations, but at least we have some tangible evidence, in the form of depositions taken from witnesses, to work with. But when communities did *not* bring charges of witchcraft against their neighbours, at least not as frequently as they had in the past, they rarely left written evidence regarding the reasons for their inaction. The most that the legal record tells us is the suggestive report from the Scottish justiciary court in 1671 that two witches were set free because 'there was no one to insist', i.e. for lack of a formal accuser (Scott-Moncrieff, 1905: 56). We can only speculate, therefore, whether the decline in formal accusations reflects a real reduction in the number and gravity of personal conflicts at the village level or the more pragmatic calculation that judicial authorities would not be receptive to complaints brought before them.

There are of course other possibilities. One is that popular witch beliefs actually changed, following the same pattern that occurred first among the more highly educated members of society. One possible source of such a transformation would have been the sermons of sceptical and tolerant ministers, such as those delivered by Danish pastors trained in the providential tradition in the middle of the seventeenth century or the more admonitory one given in the next century by Joseph Juxon, the vicar of Twyford, after a local witch-swimming (Johansen, 1991–2: 415–18; Gaskill, 1994b: 91). Sermons served as one of the few vehicles for contact and interaction between popular and learned culture during this period. But there is little evidence that popular beliefs actually changed in response to such religious instruction, either before or after decriminal-ization, and there is much to suggest that they continued in their earlier form. Indeed, the frequency with which local communities took illegal counter-action against suspected witches suggests strongly that popular witch-beliefs persisted for many generations after the trials had stopped. As one scholar has observed, witchcraft 'died hard in the public mind – if it died at all' (Carnochan, 1971: 389). In her contribution to this volume Marijke Gijswijt-Hofstra provides substantial evidence to support this observation.

Another possibility is that people stopped bringing charges against witches because the prosecutions themselves became too costly. We know from isolated examples that the confinement and trial of witches could be terribly expensive, even when the assets of the accused were used to defray the cost of incarceration and transportation. These financial burdens arising from the prosecution of witches fell on the entire community. In order to avoid further expenses a number of accused witches were actually released from gaol, and that result might easily have made villagers more reluctant to support further prosecutions (Monter, 1990b: 273; Levack, 1995a: 180–1). It is unlikely, however, that the larger patterns of decline can be attributed to such financial considerations. It is more likely that residents of villages and small towns would have abandoned witch-hunting after experiencing the fear that gripped the entire community during the panics. The realization that no one was safe from the cycle of accusations and implications, coupled with the recognition that innocent people were being executed, was just as capable of affecting the members of the lower classes as the members of the local ruling elite.

In any event we still do not have any hard evidence showing that members of the lower classes became reluctant to accuse and prosecute witches. Faced with a dearth of evidence from popular sources, we can only return to the sources we do have, which are statistics showing a reduction in the number of trials and executions, the records of those trials that ended in acquittals, and the statements of those individuals who criticized the process of witch-hunting. These sources suggest that the main reason for the decline in prosecutions was the increasing reluctance of lay and clerical judicial authorities to convict persons of witchcraft, an attitude that was only occasionally and belatedly reinforced by a growing scepticism regarding the possibility of the crime. It remains to be seen, however, how this reluctance to convict actually brought about a reduction of witchcraft prosecutions in different parts of Europe.

Patterns and Dynamics of Decline:
Five Case-Studies

The decline of witchcraft prosecutions, as suggested in the previous chapter, was neither a uniform nor a linear process. It took place at different times in various European jurisdictions, and it followed different patterns of development. It had some common causes, as we have seen, but the decline was every bit as diverse as the rise in prosecutions that had preceded it. In order to illustrate this diversity, as well as to give substance to the general causes we have identified, we shall investigate five national case-studies: France, England, Scotland, Germany and Hungary. These five countries followed very different patterns of witch-hunting and recorded different numbers of prosecutions and executions. The most fundamental distinction among them, however, is that each operated on the basis of a different judicial system. They varied in the degree of judicial power that the central government exercised over local courts, the extent to which ecclesiastical and judicial authorities were involved in witch-hunting, and the type of procedures that the courts used in criminal trials. These judicial differences, both structural and procedural, help to explain the widely varying patterns, dynamics, and timing of the decline in the five areas.

France
The kingdom of France presents us with the classic example of the way in which a country with an increasingly powerful central government could use an appellate system of justice to reduce the intensity of witch-hunting. In the early seventeenth century France was divided into nine separate legal areas, each of which came under the supreme jurisdiction of a provincial parlement. The largest of these was the parlement of Paris, which had jurisdiction over most of northern France and which because of both its territorial reach and its location in the capital can be considered a central judicial institution, even if was not part of the royal administration. The decline of witch-hunting within the jurisdiction of this Parisian tribunal can be dated to the 1590s, when the parlement began to insist on its formal right to review the death sentences passed against witches by local judges.

The background of the beginning of this attempt to enforce central judicial policy was a truly appalling set of witch-trials in the Champagne-Ardennes region in 1587 and 1588. In these trials the boundaries between official and popular justice, between judicial executions and lynchings, became hard to draw. Judges, alarmed by reports of thousands of witches in their districts, took peremptory and illegal action against the accused, swimming and torturing them and then allowing members of the local community to lynch them. In response to this witch-panic, which bears many of the characteristics of the scandalous miscarriages of justice that took place in Würzburg and other parts of Germany, the parlement banned all water ordeals and then made all witchcraft convictions subject to automatic appeal to the high court. This meant that the local courts had to pay the costs of sending the appellants themselves (and not just the written record of the proceedings in the lower court) to Paris. Associated with this new appellate policy was a further effort, already underway by 1587, of insisting on the exclusive prerogative of the parlement of Paris to torture a suspect in a case of witchcraft.

As Alfred Soman has shown, this policy was not immediately successful. There was widespread local resistance to it, on the highly questionable legal grounds that witchcraft was a *crimen exceptum* and therefore not subject to appeal. The parlement, in a number of decisions that reflected its growing power, rejected this argument and then, in a series of cases against local officials who conducted illegal or abusive prosecutions, established the principle of obligatory review. Twenty years later, after adjudicating a number of witchcraft cases, the ruling of 1604 was reenacted and printed. The appeals were governed by scrupulous adherence to due process, including the right of legal representation and the strictest rules regarding the application of torture. Not unexpectedly the appellate process resulted in an increasingly large number of acquittals.[1] As these reversals were handed down, the number of cases that were appealed began to dwindle, reflecting the reluctance of lower courts to pass death sentences that would only be reversed on appeal. As Soman has argued, the cases dried up at the source. We cannot claim that as a result of these decisions witchcraft was 'decriminalized' in France by 1625, any more than we can say that it was decriminalized in England by the same time (Soman, 1989: 1–10). But it is clear that by 1640 the number of cases reaching the parlement had been reduced to a mere trickle. The virtual collapse of witch-hunting in this jurisdiction stands as the best example of the negative effect an appellate system could have on witch-hunting. It depended for its success on the assembly of the criminal dossier, the cumulative body of depositions and rulings that was transmitted from lower to higher tribunals as the case progressed. It also depended on the determination of central state authorities, including the king, to support the demands of the parlementaires for compliance by lower courts. In both respects the parlement of Paris set the standard for the other countries of Europe which required the appeal of sentences in witchcraft cases, especially Sweden (and its province Finland), Denmark, Austria and Russia. All of these countries experienced a decline in witch-hunting much later than did northern France.

The remarkable and precipitate decline of executions and prosecutions within the jurisdiction of the parlement of Paris did not have an immediate effect on the other eight parlements. Four of them — the tribunals at Bordeaux, Rouen, Toulouse and Pau — became involved in substantial witch-hunts in the seventeenth century, and those hunts exposed the complex relationship between central and provincial power within the entire country. The early seventeenth-century witch-trials in the Basque-speaking Pays de Labourd, which claimed eighty lives and which spilled over into the neighbouring regions of the Spanish Basque country in 1609, provide an early example of the growing differences between the provincial and the central government. The parlement at Bordeaux originally took the initiative in requesting royal assistance in suppressing the witch panic in Labourd. King Henry IV responded by granting broad jurisdictional powers to two members of the Bordeaux parlement, Pierre de Lancre and Jean d'Espagnet. Their commission, however, was abruptly suspended, apparently by royal authority, when it became known that one of the judges was not following due process of law (Henningsen, 1980: 25, 130–1).

The tension between local and central control that was evident in the Pays de Labourd in 1609 was greatly magnified later in the seventeenth century in Normandy, where the provincial parlement at Rouen confirmed the death sentences of 46 witches in a major chain-reaction witch-hunt involving the naming of 525 individuals in 1669. By this time the parlement of Paris had succeeded in virtually ending the trials in northern France, and the ministers of King Louis XIV had for various reasons become more sceptical regarding the crime of witchcraft. When the parlement of Rouen, which possessed the same appellate authority over inferior jurisdictions as did the parlement of Paris, confirmed the first twelve sentences in this witch-hunt and was planning to review another 34, the families of the convicted witches petitioned the king for clemency. The king responded by remitting their sentences to banishment and restoring the property that the state had confiscated. Despite a vigorous protest from the Rouen parlement, the king's reprieve prevailed, and the parlement's confirmation of the other sentences was abandoned (Mandrou, 1968: 439–58).

The conflict between the central government of France and the parlement of Rouen in 1669–70 stands as the classic confrontation between local and provincial hostility to witchcraft and central judicial scepticism. Normandy was however not the only province where the royal government felt compelled to intervene in witchcraft cases in the early 1670s. Severe witch-hunts in the two southwestern provinces of Guyenne and Bearn prompted the government of Louis XIV, acting under the direction of his minister Jean Baptiste Colbert, to register edicts in the parlements of Bordeaux and Pau regarding the proper conduct of witchcraft prosecutions. In those two provinces the parlements were much more coöperative with the central government than Rouen had proved to be, but the government still felt obliged to provide direction in the conduct of witchcraft cases. In particular it considered establishing a common form of proceeding against witches, as a remedy for the violations of due process by the local courts.

The royal interventions at Rouen, Pau and Bordeaux in 1670–72 have been invested with even deeper significance because they preceded and apparently contributed to the decision to promulgate a royal edict decriminalizing witchcraft throughout France in July 1682. That edict, registered by Louis XIV, has gained the reputation as the first legislative denial of the reality of the crime of witchcraft in Europe. If in fact such a denial was one of its objectives, it achieved it in a most indirect way, since its title identified it as an ordinance against various 'diviners, magicians and enchanters', and it never used the word witchcraft (*sorcellerie*) as such. It ordered diviners and fortune-tellers to leave their houses on pain of corporal punishment, while prescribing summary punishment for practitioners of 'pretended' magic and superstition according to the gravity of their offences. The death penalty was reserved for those who compounded superstition with impiety and sacrilege, as well as for poisoners, even if their victims did not die. These last two provisions, as well as a number of articles governing the production and sale of poisons, were included mainly in response to a scandal, known as 'the affair of the poisons,' which had rocked the highest levels of Parisian society, including the royal court, between 1676 and 1681. The affair, which centered on the activities of a widow known as La Voisin, not only involved the discovery of poisoning, infanticide and alleged child-sacrifice but also the saying of amatory masses.

The implications of the edict of 1682 for witchcraft were two-fold. On the one hand witchcraft was implicitly reclassified as practical superstition and pretended magic, thereby implicitly dissociating it from the diabolism with which the crime had become closely identified while at the same time denying that the magic had any efficacy. It thus combined scepticism with a redefinition of the crime itself, a process that occurred throughout Europe in this period and will be discussed below. On the other hand, the edict provided for greater leniency in the prosecution of what once passed as witchcraft by reserving the death penalty to cases involving sacrilege, blasphemy, or poisoning. The provision for punishing witches according to the gravity of the offence, however, left open the possibility of harsh treatment for reputed witches, while the prohibition of sacrilege could be extended to include the diabolism that had been excluded from the definition of the crime. Sorcerers could still be charged with profaning the sacred host, renouncing God, and adoring the demon, as they were at Marseilles in 1693 (Mandrou, 1968: 505). The edict did not therefore, ban all witchcraft trials or even result in the reversal of all capital sentences on appeal. But the few trials that did take place under the terms of the edict, especially in Brie, Normandy and Alsace, employed the more precise language of the new jurisprudence. The witches, most of them shepherds, were accused of various acts of poisoning and sacrilege. The term 'witchcraft' was used only in an enumeration of the sundry '*maléfices, empoisonnements, sacrilèges et sorcelleries*' allegedly performed by the accused, and even then the word appeared in the plural form and almost as an afterthought (Mandrou, 1968: 499–537; Klaits, 1982: 161–2).

Despite its revolutionary implications Louis XIV's edict had little effect on the actual volume of witchcraft prosecutions in his kingdom. In northern France the trials had for all practical purposes ended by the time the edict appeared, and in the provinces of the west and southwest the royal interventions of 1670–2 had already turned the tide permanently against witch-hunting. Even in the province of Franche-Comté, which was incorporated into the kingdom of France in 1674, the last large witch-hunt had ended in 1660, the year in which a French translation of Friedrich Spee's *Cautio Criminalis* appeared (Spee, 1660). One might speculate that the edict of 1682 prevented a recurrence of another such episode in Franche-Comté, since intense prosecutions had followed periods of relative inactivity throughout the seventeenth century, but there is no evidence that pressure for a revival of the trials was mounting when the edict was published (Monter, 1976: 84–7). The duchy of Luxembourg had also brought witch-hunting to an end around 1660, twenty years before Louis XIV acquired this territory and imposed French law on it. The magistrates in Luxembourg may also have been influenced by the translation of the *Cautio Criminalis* when they decided to stop the trials (Dupont-Bouchat, 1978: 144–6).

The decline of French witch-hunting can be written mainly in terms of judicial caution and central supervision of the judicial process, but it did not lack an intellectual dimension. During the early seventeenth century a lively and important public debate took place regarding the reality of the Devil and witchcraft. The stimulus of this debate was a series of scandals involving the mass possession of nuns in urban convents at Aix en Provence (1609–11), Loudun (1634) and Louviers (1643–7). These episodes, which involved accusations of witchcraft against priests, created wide-spread scepticism regarding the various manifestations of diabolical power, including witchcraft, among theologians and physicians. It has been argued that the issues raised in this debate created uncertainty, confusion and ultimately a 'crisis of conscience' among the members of the parlement of Paris, leading to greater leniency in the treatment of witches and to the 'abandonment of the crime of witchcraft' in the period after 1640 (Mandrou, 1968: 195–363). The discovery that their policy of leniency dated from the late sixteenth century, however, suggests that their reluctance to sentence witches to their death had much more to do with adherence to increasingly rigorous French standards of judicial proof than with some new philosophical or theological misgivings about the extent of Satan's power (Soman, 1978: 33–8). If we are looking for signs of a genuine philosophical scepticism among the men who controlled the judicial and administrative machinery in France, we are more likely to find it among those men who drafted the edict of 1682 than the lawyers who staffed the parlement of Paris before 1660.

England

England is often cited as a major exception to the pattern of European witch-hunting, although recent comparative work on witch-hunting throughout Europe suggests the number of English trials per capita was not much lower than in many other jurisdictions outside German-speaking lands. England does rank fairly low in the percentage of trials that resulted in both convictions and executions, and very few English witches were executed during large panics, the one exception being the witch-hunt directed by Matthew Hopkins and John Stearne in 1645–7. The relatively low death toll in English witchcraft trials is usually attributed to the weakness of the belief in collective Devil-worship and the strict prohibition of torture in all English criminal trials. Belief in diabolism was not absent in English witchcraft treatises, especially in the early seventeenth century, but without the application of torture it was difficult for prosecutors to secure the confessions that gave such ideas legitimacy. Indeed, it was only during the great witch-hunt of 1645–47, when torture was administered illegally, that diabolism became a distinctive features of the confessions of English witches.

The categorical prohibition of torture in witchcraft cases, which was apparently unique in Europe, was only one of the features of English criminal justice that contributed to the low number of convictions and executions. Just as important was the absence of inquisitorial procedure, the system of officialized criminal justice that operated most effectively in France, Germany, the Netherlands, Spain and Italy. Efforts have been made to show that English criminal procedure grew closer to the continental model in the sixteenth century, even to the extent that we might refer to it as 'sub-inquisitorial' procedure (Unsworth, 1989), but in two respects it remained distinct from that which operated in France. The first was that a grand jury was needed to approve all draft indictments or bills before a case could go to trial. The government, therefore, was unable to initiate prosecutions on its own authority, without the approval of fairly prominent residents of the county where the accused resided. This also meant that it could not conduct open-ended witch-hunts, such as those that occurred in parts of Germany, where judges could bring to trial those persons whom confessing witches had named as accomplices. Second, judges could not secure the conviction of witches without the determination of the facts of the case by a trial jury composed of laymen. This requirement could and did serve as a restraint on intense witch-hunting: juries were directly responsible for the high number of acquittals in English witch trials. But English juries did not always lean in that direction, and in the late seventeenth century they often returned guilty verdicts after the judge had recommended acquittal.

One further characteristic of English criminal justice was that most trials for felony (and hence most witchcraft trials) took place at the county assizes, circuit courts over which judges from the central courts at Westminster presided. This system could work both for and against the successful prosecution of the accused. On the one hand the system ensured that the trials would take place near the communities where the witches lived, thus allowing those who knew the witch to take part in her prosecution and trial. On the other hand, a justice from one of the central courts presided at the assizes, thus facilitating his supervision of the trial. There were of course both witch-hanging and merciful judges, but on balance we can say that the assize judges, being committed to due process and not having any personal knowledge of the witch or her associates, tended to serve as a restraining influence on the process.[2]

It is uncertain whether we should begin the study of the decline of witch-hunting in England in the first decade of the seventeenth century or in the 1640s, after the last large hunt. Having reached a peak in the late sixteenth century, the number of English witchcraft prosecutions entered a long period of decline (Ewen, 1929: 101, 110). Likewise the percentage of executions, after hitting a high point in the years 1597–1607, also began to drop.[3] The problem is that Matthew Hopkins's witch-hunt of 1645–7 interrupted the process, sending the number of prosecutions and executions sky-rocketing for a brief period of time before dropping back to their low levels. If we chose to view that last major hunt as an exception, being the product of governmental and judicial chaos during the Civil War, then we should begin our analysis of the decline in English witch-hunting with the scepticism that developed among high churchmen like Samuel Harsnett and Richard Bancroft regarding a series of witchcraft-cum-possession cases in the last years of Queen Elizabeth's reign (1558–1603) and the early years of King James's (1603–25). In their efforts to discredit both Puritan and Jesuit exorcists, mainly for reasons of ecclesiastical politics, this group of clerics managed to turn the tide against witch-hunting in general. They secured the support of the medical establishment to declare that the symptoms of possession were caused by the natural malady of hysteria; they won over the new King to their side, a task that had been facilitated by James's growing scepticism before he left Scotland; and most important, they brought charges against those who had used fraudulent symptoms of possession to try individuals for witch-craft. The unprecedented prosecution of the demoniac Anne Gunter and her father Brian Gunter in the court of Star Chamber in 1606 for conspiring to indict two innocent women for witchcraft in many ways marks the turning point in the history of English witch-hunting and the beginning of its decline (MacDonald, 1990; Levack, 1995b).

The judiciary also played a critical role in this process, as assize judges used their limited powers over the course of the trials to secure acquittals. In one trial at Abingdon, Berkshire, in 1604 the judge deliberately selected sceptical jurymen and supervised the presentation of evidence in court in such a way as to virtually guarantee the acquittal of two accused witches (Levack, 1995b). At another trial in 1636, the assize judge, Sir John Finch, appointed four eminent barristers to counsel an accused witch on points of law (Cockburn, 1972: 120). During the archiepiscopate of William Laud in the 1630s, a period in which other crimes of a religious nature were prosecuted with the utmost vigour, the number of witchcraft cases fell to an unprecedented low.

The imminent end of witchcraft prosecutions at that time, however, was put on hold by the deadly witch-hunt of Matthew Hopkins and John Stearne during the disruptions of the Civil War. Concerning this hunt, which took about 200 lives, much has been written, and there is no need to rehearse it here (Notestein, 1911: 164–205; Deacon, 1976, Gaskill, 1994a; Sharpe, 1996: 128–47). Suffice it to say, that some of the exceptional features of the hunt – the prominence of diabolism in the confessions, the use of the torture of forced sleeplessness, the high rate of convictions – can be attributed in large measure to the breakdown of central governmental control over the judicial process. This was especially the case at the Chelmsford assizes in 1645, when 36 witches were tried, of whom 19 were put to death. At those trials the judges from the Westminster courts failed to put in an appearance, and the earl of Warwick, a legally untrained nobleman acting in a military capacity, took their place.

After the Restoration the number of witchcraft prosecutions and executions continued the downward trend that had developed in the first part of the century. One of the striking features of that decline was the elimination of charges of Devil-worship after 1664. Cases of possession persisted, but the charges of face-to-face pacts with the Devil and witches' assemblies (always tame by Continental standards) quickly disappeared. The cases that remained were characteristic of those that had predominated during the Elizabethan period: charges of *maleficium*, originating in the tensions of everyday life and lodged against one of two witches at a time. In fact, the criteria for a witchcraft indictment after 1660 became more demanding than they had been during the Elizabethan period. After the Restoration magistrates and lawyers became reluctant to frame indictments for witchcraft unless the acts of maleficient magic had resulted in the death of the victim (Holmes, 1993: 49).

The most striking feature of the chronology of English witch-hunting is the length of time that the entire process took. One would expect that in a country where the defendants had many advantages that were not available to witches on the Continent, prosecutions would have died a very early death. But that was not the case. The last execution of an English witch, Alice Molland, took place in Devonshire in 1684, while the last conviction, that of Jane Wenham, came as late as 1712 in Hertfordshsire. Wenham was actually condemned to death, but a sceptical assize judge, Sir John Powell, granted a reprieve. It was the same justice Powell who allegedly interrupted testimony regarding the claim that Wenham was accustomed to flying with the wry response that flying was not against English law (Notestein, 1911: 328). Powell made no effort to disguise his contempt for the superstitious witch beliefs of the population. The final trial was not held until 1717 in Leicestershire, while the formal decriminalization of witchcraft did not come about until 1736, when the British parliament repealed the English statute of 1604, together with the harsher Scottish statute of 1563.

During this long period of decline the institutions that were responsible for moderating the excesses of English witch-hunting clearly helped to reduce the number of trials and executions. Grand juries continued to indict witches, but in lower numbers than in the past, probably because of the new demand that the *maleficia* must have resulted in death. We do not know how many bills they rejected. The percentage of bills known to have been returned as *ignoramus* was fairly low, but the statistical record is hardly complete.[4] We have more evidence of the action taken by the trial juries, which brought in a series of acquittals after 1675, especially in the home circuit. In 1682 a Surrey jury returned a verdict of non-guilty in the trial of Joan Buts despite the evidence of some twenty witnesses, leading some observers to comment on 'the great difficulty in proving a witch' (Gaskill, 1994b: 98). In many of these acquittals the members of these juries were guided in their evaluation of the evidence by sceptical judges who 'gave small or no encouragement to such accusations' (Anon., 1676). The most famous of these judges was Sir John Holt, the Whig chief justice of the court of King's Bench who presided over twelve trials that ended in acquittals between 1689 and 1711.

Even though juries acquitted large numbers of witches in the late seventeenth century, they were also directly responsible for the few convictions that took place after the decline began. The irony of English witch-hunting was that the same features of the judicial system that had kept the number of convictions and executions fairly low by Continental standards also explain why sporadic trials and convictions stretched well into the eighteenth century. The contrast with France, which operated under a highly officialized judicial system in which judges made the final decisions of guilt or innocence, could not be clearer. Whatever the drawbacks of the inquisitorial system, its use in France gave judges much tighter control of the judicial process than their English counterparts ever could achieve. When French judges began to exercise caution in witch-craft cases, they were therefore able to discourage prosecutions unilaterally and to achieve their objectives much more quickly and decisively than their English counterparts. Unlike English judges, they did not have to persuade, supervise, control or otherwise deal with juries when they tried witchcraft cases. Indeed, they exercised their judicial authority over such cases in an appellate capacity. In England on the other hand, where the central judges presided over cases in the first instance, juries continued to establish the facts of the case and to reach independent verdicts, and there was no system of regular appeals in criminal causes. Judges might try to influence the jury by refusing to admit the testimony of certain witnesses and by demonstrating the weakness of the prosecution's case during their summation of the evidence, but with the law of evidence still in its infancy and with even sceptical judges still respecting traditions of jury indepen-dence, occasional convictions and even executions occurred long after they had been abandoned in other parts of western Europe. The pressure from juries to convict could be formidable. It certainly explains why Temperance Lloyd, Susanna Edwards and Mary Trembles were executed for witchcraft at Exeter in 1682, despite the scepticism of the assize judge, Lord North. North learned that he had to tread very warily in dealing with juries in witchcraft cases, fearing that if he denied the reality of the witches' powers they would accuse him of irreligion and find the witches guilty (North, 1890, Anon., 1682). Even the sceptical Justice Powell, presiding over the trial of Jane Wenham in 1712, left it to the jury 'to weigh the matter very well' (Gaskill, 1994b: 97). Having done that, the jury returned the guilty verdict, the last conviction in an English witchcraft trial. Only then did Powell intervene by granting a reprieve.

If we study English witch-beliefs, at least those that prevailed among the educated, we also find a surprising persistence of belief in the reality of the crime. Once again, we would expect that the land which produced Reginald Scot, Samuel Harsnett and Thomas Hobbes and which never fully accepted the belief in the sabbath would have taken the lead in denying the reality of witchcraft altogether. It is true that in 1677 John Webster published *The Displaying of Supposed Witchcraft*, in which he asserted that it was 'simply impossible for either the Devil or witches to change or alter the course that God hath set in nature' (Webster, 1677: 68). Webster's views, however, encountered significant opposition within English scientific circles, especially from Joseph Glanvill and Henry More, who reconciled their belief in the reality of witchcraft with the new science by using arguments drawn from natural theology (Jobe, 1981). The important question for our purposes, however, is whether Hobbesian or Websterian ideas on witchcraft attracted any identifiable support within the educated and ruling classes and might have contributed therefore to the decline of witchcraft prosecutions. Until 1690, which seems to have marked a turning point in the spread of the new philosophy throughout western Europe, very few educated men, especially members of the English legal profession, expressed open disbelief in the reality of the crime. Only in 1695, a full decade after the last witchcraft execution, do we find an English lawyer referring to the belief in witchcraft as a thing of the past, in the same way that Robert Chouet had handled the subject at Geneva in 1690 (Anon., 1695). During the period between 1660 and 1690, when judicial scepticism flourished within the English bar and bench, philosophical scepticism apparently exercised much less influence.

The case of Sir Matthew Hale provides one of the most striking examples of the persistence of belief in witchcraft within the English judiciary. Hale was a man of immense learning, not only in the law but also in religion and natural philosophy. He was arguably the most scientific English jurist since Bacon, and his systematic approach to the uncodified body of English common law had an enormous impact on Blackstone. As we have seen, Hale's belief in witchcraft was grounded in his Protestant biblicism, as well as in a mechanical philosophy that preserved an important role for the operation of the divine will. In his *Pleas of the Crown* (1678) he classified the crime, together with heresy, as a 'capital offence immediately against God' (Hale, 1972: 1–2, 6–8). Hale had only a limited involvement in witch-hunting, but it exposed the difficulty that the English system had in bringing witch-hunting to an end. One of the few opportunities an English judge had to influence the outcome of a criminal trial arose in his summing up of the evidence. In the famous trial and execution of Amy Duny and Rose Cullender at Bury St Edmunds in 1662, a trial that involved the acceptance of spectral evidence, Hale refused to make such a summation, despite the evident weakness of the case against the accused. Instead, Hale simply made a statement regarding the reality of the crime, based on Scripture and the laws of all nations, and left it to the jury to decide the facts of the case (Anon., 1682; Geis and Bunn, 1981: 8), The two witches were convicted and hanged. Hale's action could be interpreted as a conservative respect for the tradition of jury independence at a time when it was coming under attack, but it stands as a better example of the role Scripture played in securing convictions for witchcraft. It is interesting to note that the report of this trial, which was published in 1682, became one of the sources Cotton Mather cited in his treatise supporting the Salem witchcraft trials of 1692 (Mather, 1692: 92–9).

Even in the early eighteenth century, long after the last execution, many English judges refused to deny the reality of the crime. The charge that Whitelocke Bulstrode, a distinguished judge, delivered to a grand jury in 1718 provides us with a interesting illustration of this conservatism. Bulstrode gave his charge six years after the last English conviction, and one would expect therefore that he would have made some statement regarding the impossibility of the crime. Instead he told his audience that he need not trouble them with discussions of witchcraft, sorcery or enchantments, which had formerly been classified as offences against God, because 'there were no such practitioners within the kingdom'(Lamoine, 1992: 358). This was indeed a curious statement, a celebration of the eradication of witchcraft (the last trial had been held one year before) rather than a denial of its status as a crime. Bulstrode's words echo those of Martin Luther, who nearly two hundred years earlier had claimed that preaching the gospel had been responsible for a decline in the number of witches (Kors and Peters, 1972: 291). The coincidence should not surprise us, in light of what we have already seen regarding the enduring strength of religiously inspired belief in the reality of witchcraft, even after decriminalization.

Scotland

Although James VI of Scotland became James I of England in 1603, thus joining the two countries in a regal union, Scotland existed as a separate kingdom during the entire period of witch-hunting. It had its own parliament, privy council, national church and legal system. Witch-hunting in Scotland, therefore, has its own history, distinct from that of England. Indeed, witch-hunting was much more intense in Scotland than in England, claiming far more lives in a kingdom with less than one quarter of England's population. Many of those Scottish witchcraft executions occurred during the six large witch-hunts that occurred in 1591, 1597, 1628–30, 1643, 1649 and 1661–2. Scottish witch-beliefs, especially those concerning collective Devil-worship, were more extreme than in

England, and the clergy took a more active role in the prosecution of the crime. Most important for our purposes, the decline of witchcraft followed a somewhat different course from that which it took in England. The most severe prosecutions did not come to an end until 1662, and a fairly large hunt, involving twenty trials and seven executions, occurred at Paisley as late as 1697. The last legal executions recorded in the central records of the country took place in 1706, more than twenty years later than in England, and contemporary sources reported the trial and execution of two witches at Perth in 1715. The last trial, which was held in the court of a sheriff-depute at Dornoch in 1727, was also of questionable legality. Certainly the death of one of the two witches condemned on that occasion appears to have been the work of the local community, not the courts (Black, 1937–8: 56; Larner, 1981: 78).

Scotland's system of criminal justice, which combined features found in those of both France and England, supplies us with a framework for this analysis. On the one hand Scottish trial procedure resembled that of England, especially in the use of trial by jury and in the formal rule that all torture be conducted by warrant from the Privy Council. As in England there was also no system of appeals in criminal causes. On the other hand many of the features associated with inquisitorial justice, including the compilation of criminal dossiers, the presence of defence counsel at trials, and the central management of prosecutions reveal the emulation or at least the influence of continental jurisprudence. What set Scotland apart from both countries was its difficulty in controlling the excesses of local justice and the strength of religious sentiment in favour of witch-hunting.

As we have seen, France and England, like all European countries, had to deal with powerful local pressure to prosecute witches. Central authorities in France, especially the members of the parlement of Paris, dealt with this pressure by insisting upon the right of their tribunal to review all convictions by the local courts and to insist upon its exclusive right to apply torture. In England the central government also exercised control over local justice by means of the circuit court system, although it did not have the added control offered by an appellate procedure. In Scotland the central government was less successful in its efforts to control local justice. Part of the problem was that the government did not have the administrative resources to enforce its will on the localities. The Scottish government was also inconsistent in its attitude towards witchcraft, and at certain times during this period the Privy Council took steps to encourage, rather than to restrain witch-hunting. The result was an erratic pattern of witch-hunting and a delayed end to the entire process.

When intense witch-hunting began in Scotland in the 1590s, the government lent its support to the trials. The king himself, James VI, became convinced that he was the target of witches' malevolence, and therefore his government conducted a number of trials by its own authority. The council also issued standing commissions that allowed local authorities to conduct open-ended witch-hunts. In 1597 the Privy Council, aware of the procedural abuses that had resulted in the executions of countless innocent victims, recalled those commissions and decided that in the future it would review all requests to conduct witchcraft trials on a case-by-case basis. After that time trials for witchcraft either had to be conducted in the central criminal court, the court of justiciary, or by a commission of local authorities who possessed a warrant from the Privy Council (or Parliament) giving them permission to proceed. This system, especially the review of local requests, brought about a rather sharp decline in the total number of trials held during the next thirty years. Indeed, during the chancellorship of Alexander Seton, the earl of Dunfermline (1605–22), there were signs of a genuine judicial scepticism operating in the Privy Council, resulting in the apparent denial of at least some petitions from local communities.

Although the situation improved after 1597, Scottish witch-hunting did not follow the pattern of decline that was being set at this time in northern France. Not only did a steady stream of trials and executions continue, but at four critical junctures later in the seventeenth century, major hunts took place, with the great hunt of 1661–2 being the largest in the country's history (Levack, 1980). Two situations in particular explain this persistence of witch-hunting in Scotland throughout much of the seventeenth century. The first is that the Privy Council's screening of local requests for witchcraft trials was hardly rigorous. The great majority of the requests for commissions of justiciary were granted, and whenever they were, it was almost a certainty that the accused would be convicted and executed. The problem was that these local trials were conducted by untrained magistrates rather than by lawyers or judges, and this opened the possibility of procedural abuse, especially since the local authorities, who almost always knew the witches personally, were convinced of their guilt. The greatest of these procedural abuses was the application of torture. Torture could be administered officially in Scotland only by special warrant from the Privy Council or Parliament, but we have an abundance of evidence that it was applied illegally on a regular basis in these local prosecutions, usually during the original interrogations that followed the arrest of the witch. Occasionally the Privy Council took action against those who administered torture in this manner, but they were unable to root out the practice (Levack, 1996: 100–7).

The second reason for the continuation of witch-hunting was that from time to time the Privy Council actually encouraged local initiatives against witch-hunting. It never reinstated the standing commissions of 1591–7, but for various political and religious reasons it urged local communities to discover witches at the time of the large hunts. These initiatives were usually undertaken as part of a general crackdown on crime, especially crimes of a religious nature, the goal being to establish Scotland as a godly state. Thus in 1628 specially appointed commissioners were instructed to collect charges against people for more than 70 different crimes, with witchcraft close to the top of the list (Brown, 1900: 437–8). In 1649, the year in which King Charles I was executed and Scotland was involved in military conflict with England, the Council conducted nothing less than a moral crusade against a variety of moral crimes, including adultery and witchcraft. In 1661, shortly after the Restoration of King Charles II, the prosecution of witches took on a more political colour, as it became associated with a campaign waged by victorious royalists against rebellious Covenanters. In all these cases the central government catered to, if it did not take steps to stimulate, local demand for prosecution. At the same time local pressures to prosecute, often inspired or reinforced by religious fervour, intensified.

We cannot speak of a real decline in Scottish witch-hunting until after the mass panic of 1661–2, and even then there were to be many more trials and executions before prosecutions came to a complete end. But the decline had begun, and changes in judicial administration and legal procedure seem to have been largely responsible. The first of these changes was a significant decline in the number of conciliar or parliamentary commissions and a corresponding increase in the number of trials being funneled into Edinburgh.[5] This meant that the summary local justice that usually followed the granting of local commission gave way to the careful evaluation of the evidence that characterized criminal trials in the High Court of Justiciary. The pleadings that have survived from these cases reveal the skillful ways in which lawyers challenged the relevance of particular pieces of evidence to the libel, which is the proposition stating the reasons for the defendant's guilt. These debates on relevancy took place before the evidence was presented to the jury, and the judge's decision on these points of law could effectively lead to acquittals (Larner, 1981: 178ff). Sceptical judges could also control the legal process by disqualifying certain witnesses and by excluding apparently hostile persons from the list of potential jurors. In the famous East Lothian trials of 1678 the judges released a group of witches who were about to implicate 'sundry gentlewomen and others of fashion,' attributing their confessions to malice, or melancholy, or the Devil's deception' (Larner, 1981: 117).

A second legal development that contributed to the decline of Scottish witch-hunting was the successful implementation of an effective circuit court system after 1671. This system, the heir to the old medieval justice eyres and a counterpart to the English assizes, had been proposed from time to time in the sixteenth and seventeenth centuries, especially as part of the legal reforms of 1587, but the plan had never really got off the ground. Only during the Cromwellian occupation of the 1650s did the circuit courts operate as intended. After 1670, however, these courts began to function in a regular fashion, and an increasingly large number of witchcraft cases were brought before them. These local trials, presided over by judges from the central courts, yielded far more acquittals than those warranted by a commission of justiciary from the Privy Council. Between 1671 and 1709 only two witches are known to have been executed by circuit court judges (Larner, Lee and McLachlan, 1977: 58–60).

Underlying these procedural changes and the acquittals that resulted from them was an unprecedented determination on the part of officials in the central government to control the administration of local justice. That had clearly been the rationale for the Council's orders of 1662 and their restatement in 1678 after a series of trials on the basis of conciliar commissions had taken a heavy toll. In these new directives the Council forbade pricking, torture, and proceeding against witches without the express approval of the Council. Mackenzie, who served as Lord Advocate from 1677 until 1686, was particularly determined to eliminate justice by 'ignorant local men' and by inferior judges who were not competent to try witches. In 1680 he secured the acquittal of the accused witch Bessie Gibb, mainly on the grounds that the magistrates and the baillie of the burgh of Burrowstones who had proceeded against her were not competent to try her (Scottish Record Office, 1680: fo. 103).

Mackenzie was likewise critical of the use of torture in Scottish witchcraft trials, and upon his recommendation in 1680 five witches whose confessions were shown to have been the product of 'several types of torture' were set at liberty (Scottish Record Office, 1680: fo. 159). It was not torture as such to which 'Bluidy' Mackenzie, the persecutor of Covenanters, objected: he defended his own use of the practice in treason trials on the basis of reason of state and claimed that its use was authorized by the law of nations (Mackenzie, 1691a; 1691b: fo. 127). But he insisted that its use be restricted to the Privy Council and the Justice General, a policy paralleling that of the parlement of Paris proclaimed in 1624. The official prohibition of torture in Scotland – for 'ordinary crimes' by the Claim of Right at the time of the Glorious Revolution in 1689 and for all crimes by a British statute in 1709 – did not bear any direct reference to witchcraft trials.

The key to the slow, erratic decline of witch-hunting in Scotland lies, therefore, in the attitudes of the legal establishment and the gradually shifting policy of the government regarding local criminal justice. The role of philosophical or religious sentiment appears to have been less significant than in either France or England. Among the judges and lawyers one struggles to find even a hint of the argument that witchcraft was an impossible crime, a suggestion that admittedly would not have found favour in the conservative religious atmosphere of seventeenth-century Scotland. Certainly we do not find it in Mackenzie, the judicial sceptic, either in his defence of Maevia or in his summary of Scots criminal law (Mackenzie, 1672, 1678). In both books he took pains to establish the existence of witches, even if they were not as numerous as many contemporaries claimed. His defense of Maevia consists of the argument that malefices can only be proved by either confession or the testimony of two respectable eye-witnesses and that diseases cannot be said to have been inflicted by magical means just because those diseases had no known natural causes (Mackenzie, 1672: 187–8; 1678: 81–5).

What is even more striking about Mackenzie's defence is his reliance upon scripture and religious writing to support his client's cause. He made an eloquent statement of the Protestant belief in the sovereignty of God, citing scriptural passages regarding Christ's casting out of the Devil, and asking rhetorically how he could have allowed Satan 'to reign like a Soveraign, as our fabulous representations would now persuade us.' In discrediting the charge of flight he invoked the authority of the canon *Episcopi*, St. Augustine and even the Jesuit Martin Del Rio, insisting that flight, like metamorphosis, was the product of illusion (Mackenzie, 1672: 185, 194). This was all calculated to disarm his critics and to ward off charges of atheism, but it also reveals how sceptics could use religious arguments to reinforce their position.

One could hardly argue on the basis of this one example that Protestantism contributed in any direct way to the decline of witchcraft in Scotland. Quite to the contrary, Presbyterian sentiment in Scotland, especially in its extreme form, helped to perpetuate witch-beliefs and witch-hunting. Certainly the sermon that Rev. James Hutchinson preached before the specially appointed commissioners of Justiciary at Paisley in 1697 stands as a text-book example of the way in which Protestant biblicism could be marshalled in support of witch-hunting. Not only did Hutchinson trot out the traditional scriptural warrants for executing witches, but he used his knowledge of Greek, Latin and Hebrew to demonstrate, against the claims of sceptics, that the biblical passage did in fact refer to the activities of contemporary witches. It was a harsh, vindictive sermon which stated among other things that children of witches might be justly regarded as being in league with the Devil and that witchcraft was caused by 'unmortified lust and corruption.' Hutchinson's full discussion of the punishment of the reprobate and his conclusion bemoaning the great evil that there should be so many witches in an area 'where the gospel of Christ has been purely preached' also gave his sermon a distinctly Protestant cast (Larner, 1981: 163–5).

Some of the same Protestant hostility to witchcraft characterized an anonymous pamphlet, *Witch-craft Proven*, printed in the same year as Hutchinson's sermon. A work of almost unqualified belief in witchcraft, it too betrays its distinctive Protestant origins in both its biblicism and its Calvinist mythology of heaven and hell. Indeed, the Bible is virtually the only source that is cited in this work. No less Calvinist, but very different in its approach is a treatise entitled *The Tryal of Witchcraft*, probably written by John Bell, a Presbyterian minister from Glasgow, in 1705. Bell's work was more cautious than *Witch-craft Proven*, especially in his insistence that witches should not be convicted of malefices that might have natural causes. But there is nothing else that would associate him with the sceptical tradition of Mackenzie or his English counterparts. Besides his citation of the Bible to support the harsh treatment of witches, Bell relies heavily on the pamphlet literature produced by English Puritans like William Perkins and Richard Bernard in the early seventeenth century, echoing their discussion of the presumptions and proofs necessary to indict and convict witches and emphasizing the centrality of the pact with the Devil in the definition of witchcraft (Larner 1977). By that time, however, the judges of the Scottish central courts had almost completely abandoned such attempts to prove that witches were guilty and thus had brought Scottish witch-hunting to a virtual end. Within a year of the publication of Bell's treatise Scotland executed its last witch.

Germany: Württemberg

Because of the multiplicity and variety of the jurisdictional areas within the Holy Roman Empire and the weakness of central imperial control, the decline of witch-hunting followed different patterns in the various duchies and principalities that constituted the Empire. Rather than trying to isolate the few common patterns that prevailed throughout all German lands this essay will focus on just one of these individual political units, the duchy of Württemberg, where the decline of the witch-hunting can be attributed to the intersection of legal, intellectual, religious, and social developments.

The duchy of Württemberg, a fairly large territory situated in the southwestern part of Germany, was hardly an epicenter of witch-hunting, but, with no fewer than 415 trials, it nonetheless produced its fair share of victims. The duchy's criminal code of 1567 facilitated the prosecution of the crime by including prohibitions against both the pact with the Devil and the practice of maleficent magic. The number of trials had fluctuated during the period 1550–1670, but the duchy never experienced the large panics that plagued the smaller German territories in the southwest. A reduction in the number of trials occurred during the last two decades of the Thirty Years' War (as was the case in many German lands) but this was followed by a surge to near-record levels during the 1660s. These trials clearly marked the turning point in the history of witchcraft in the duchy. In the 1670s and 1680s the number of trials began to plummet, so that by the 1690s at most only one trial was held each year. These very low levels of prosecution persisted into the eighteenth century, with the last execution taking place in 1749 and the last trial in 1805 (Midelfort, 1972: 77–81; Bever, 1983: table 2.3).

The decline of witch-hunting in Württemberg can be attributed in large measure to the efforts of a sceptical and legally demanding central government to restrain the determination of local magistrates to extirpate witchcraft from their communities. The central authority in this case, however, was not the imperial *Reichskammergericht* at Speyer but the central council or *Oberrat* of the duchy, situated in Stuttgart, which attempted to regulate the justice administered by local magistrates. After the spate of prosecutions in the early 1660s, which took a heavy toll in lives, the *Oberrat* began to insist that local magistrates not accept testimony from children or from melancholic old women and that they investigate whether allegedly supernatural acts of malefice might have been caused naturally (Bever, 1983: 337–52). At the same time the government, faced with a swelling in the number of witchcraft accusations being brought before the courts, and aware that justice had been miscarried in the past, took steps to prevent the process from getting out of control. The officers of the central courts virtually stopped the practice of initiating proceedings themselves, used torture less frequently, followed the prescribed legal procedure with deliberate scrupulousness, and produced a large number of acquittals. The law faculty of the University of Tübingen deserves some of the credit for this new policy of restraint, since during the 1660s they directed the release of prisoners or the administration of non-capital sentences in a number of the cases referred to them. The jurists at Tübingen had hardly been lenient on witches during the 1610s and 1620s, but they now tended towards a more moderate approach. After 1670 their involvement in witchcraft cases slackened, as they heard very few witchcraft cases, the last in 1719.[6]

One of the most interesting features of the decline of witchcraft in Württemberg was the role that religion played in the process. The most important and influential theological tradition within the duchy was that of the providential school, according to which unfortunate events were interpreted as manifestations of divine providence rather than demonic intervention in the world. Throughout the period of the witch-hunt this tradition remained strong among the theologians at Tübingen, a university known for its Lutheran orthodoxy (Midelfort, 1972: 30–66). During the 1660s and 1670s the same theological tradition, which found expression in the works of Georg Heinrich Häberlin and Johann Adam Osiander, apparently influenced the judges to abandon the customary theological examination of any person accused of witchcraft, a clear sign of scepticism regarding the diabolical dimension of the crime. The theological currents within the university also influenced the jurist Erich Mauritius to insist that a pact with the devil was not to be punished as severely as the use of harmful magic, a recommendation that contradicted the policy followed in other Protestant jurisdictions, such as Puritan Massachusetts, at this time.[7] In the early eighteenth century the providential tradition formed the basis of Pietism, which as we have seen contributed to the decline of witch-hunting in a number of German territories and in Denmark. The most influential Pietists in Württemberg during this later period were Georg Bilfinger, who was one of Christian Wolff's disciples, and Johann Albrecht Bengel.

The combined effect of religiously inspired scepticism, the determination of jurists to exercise legal caution in the trial of witches, and the efforts of the central government to supervise the operation of local justice within the duchy of Württemberg can be seen in the defusing of a potentially lethal witch-hunt in the city of Calw in 1683–4. That hunt had originated in the longstanding suspicion of a young boy, Bartholomaeus Sieben, and his aged step-grandmother, Anna Hafnerin, for poisoning. When an eleven-year old boy confessed in 1683 that Anna had seduced him into witchcraft and had taken him to a witches' dance, where he saw many of his classmates, many children in Calw started telling wild stories about nocturnal diabolical journeys. The confession of Sieben to having poisoned his schoolmaster led ultimately to his execution and that of his grandmother on the grounds that the two had made pacts with the devil. But the hunt at Calw, which continued to grow as some 38 children made confessions, did not claim any more lives. The faculty at Tübingen displayed profound scepticism regarding the confessions from the other children, and the government at Stuttgart appointed a commission consisting of four jurists and one theologian, to investigate the affair. The commissioners effectively put an end to the panic, although not before a mob killed one of the members of the Hafnerin family and other suspects were forced to flee for their lives. The commissioners even banished three members of the Hafnerin family for their safety. They revealed the unreliability of the evidence contained in the confessions and proved that the children who made them could never have attended the dances because they were known to have been in bed at the time. Häberlin preached sermons explaining that because the Devil was deceptive, one could never tell from spectral evidence who was in fact a witch. The witch-hunt at Calw, the last panic in the duchy of Württemberg, ended very much the way that a similar episode at Salem, Massachusetts, was to end eight years later. The only difference is that in this case jurists, theologians and representatives of the central government were able to intervene in the process at an earlier stage and thus nip the entire hunt in the bud (Midelfort, 1972: 158–63).

The final development that may have influenced the decline of witch-hunting in Württemberg was an improvement in social and economic conditions in the late seventeenth century. There is little question that the dire circumstances of the pre-war years, especially over-population, depression and famine, had contributed to the intensification of pros-ecutions in the first part of the seventeenth century. After 1660 those circumstances changed. The population, having been sharply reduced by the Thirty Years' War, remained within more reasonable bounds as a result of considerable emigration to America, and even the French wars of the late seventeenth and early eighteenth centuries could not hinder economic recovery. After those wars there was a remarkable expansion in agricultural and industrial production, which brought relative prosperity to all but the lowest 10 per cent of the population. This change in economic circumstances almost certainly explains the gradual reduction in the number of witchcraft cases brought before local magistrates. After the 1650s virtually all accusations of witchcraft in Württemberg came from this source, as officials virtually stopped initiating cases. The first stage of the criminal process, in other words, became entirely accusatory, even though the state still handled such accusations in the manner that had become the hallmark of the inquisitorial system.[8] The gradual decline in popular accusations, therefore, might very well have been the product of the greater economic security that affected a large segment of the popula-tion (Bever, 1983: 373–6).

Hungary
The decline of witch-hunting in the kingdom of Hungary began much later than in any western European country. Trials and executions for witchcraft in Hungary had occurred since the middle of the sixteenth century, but they did not peak until the 1710s and 1720s, when the first large panics occurred. Prosecutions continued to take a heavy toll well into the 1750s, when they entered a sudden and precipitate decline (Klaniczay, 1990b: 222–5). The only other country in which a similar chronological pattern occurred was Poland, where the trials also peaked in the first quarter of the eighteenth century (Baranowski, 1952: 179; Tazbir, 1980: 280–1). In other eastern and northern 'peripheral' countries, such as Austria, Bohemia, the Scandinavian kingdoms, and the North American colonies, witchcraft trials reached their height between 1670 and 1700, which was later than in other European lands but significantly before the first Hungarian panics occurred. By the time the Hungarian and Polish trials peaked, the last Danish, Finnish, Swedish and Massachusetts witches

had been executed, and prosecutions in Austria and Bohemia had dropped to fairly moderate levels.

The Hungarian case merits special attention not only for its belated occurrence but for the peculiarities of the criminal procedures used in the trials. Unlike many of the countries in western Europe, Hungary did not adopt inquisitorial procedure until well into the eighteenth century. Not only did the old accusatorial system persist, complete with the principle of the liable accuser, but many courts continued to use the ordeal and purgation, the modes of judicial proof that had vanished in most European jurisdictions shortly after Fourth Lateran Council had banned them in 1215. Despite this reliance on older forms of judicial procedure, Hungarian courts did have recourse to torture in many witchcraft cases, especially during the intense trials of the early eighteenth century. The main foundation for the use of torture, apart from some vague references to it in a statute book of 1517, was the *Practica Rerum Criminalium* compiled by the Saxon jurist Benedikt Carpzov in 1635. This guide, which has demonological as well as procedural significance, was adopted as the law code for Austria and Bohemia in 1656 and was subsequently incorporated into the Hungarian code of 1696. It is probably no coincidence that its adoption was followed by the intensification of witch-hunting in Hungary. Not only did that code authorize torture, especially in witchcraft cases, but it served as an agent of procedural innovation, since Carpzov had emphasized and justified the use of inquisitorial procedure in hidden crimes. Nevertheless the code was not followed in all parts of the Hungary. The procedures that Carpzov prescribed, moreover, especially those concerning torture, encountered opposition from jurists, especially Mátyás Bodó in his study of criminal jurisprudence published in 1751 (Bodó, 1751; Klaniczay, 1990b: 226; Kristóf, 1991–2: 99–101; Várkonyi, 1991–2: 470).

It was only after the mass trials of the 1750s that Hungarian witch-hunting began to decline. The turning point, not only for Hungary but for the entire Habsburg Empire, came in 1756, when the Empress Maria Theresa ordered that all witchcraft cases be submitted to her conciliar appellate court for confirmation before sentences could be carried out. This decree bears a striking resemblance to the policy established by the parlement of Paris between 1588 and 1624, even if the Parisian policy did not proceed from a royal initiative. Maria Theresa's action appears to have been greatly inspired by the work of the court physician Gerard van Swieten. Like the Parisian edict of 1624, the imperial decree of 1756 encountered considerable opposition from the local courts, but the government nonetheless managed to secure widespread compliance within a fairly brief period of time. The number of witchcraft prosecutions and executions plummeted to minimal levels immediately after the edict, and they never experienced a revival, coming to a complete end in 1777, the year after torture was abolished.

This downward spiral in the number of trials was greatly aided by the passage of a new witchcraft law in 1766 and its codification in the *Constitutio Criminalis Theresiana* of 1768. Officially intended 'to extirpate superstition' and to achieve 'a rational criminal adjudication of magic and sorcery,' this law did not formally decriminalize witchcraft in Hungary any more than Louis XIV's edict of 1682 had in France.[9] But it did greatly reduce the possibility of a successful prosecution, and it virtually ended all executions. Individuals who made fraudulent witchcraft accusations or defamed their neighbors were to be prosecuted, while those whose confessions or accusations were the product of mental illness were to be hospitalized. Individuals who seriously tried to make pacts with the Devil, even if such pacts were impossible, would be banished. Finally, cases in which there was certain proof of harm caused by sorcery or demonic assistance would be referred directly to the empress (Byloff, 1934: 161–2; Kneubühler, 1977: 239–41).

The decline of witchcraft prosecutions in Hungary can readily be explained in terms of the central/local dynamic that operated in France, Spain, Scotland, and to some extent in Württemberg. The decrees that reduced witchcraft prosecutions to a trickle originated at the court of an enlightened despot in Vienna, and they were implemented not only in the different territories within a large multi-national empire but more particularly in the local courts, where resistance to the new rules was strongest. The decline of witchcraft in Hungary also involved much of the same judicial scepticism that accompanied the decline of witch-hunting in virtually all Western European countries. The law of 1766 has so much to say about the ignorance and superstition of the 'simple common people' that one can easily miss its central concern with judicial procedure. The new law complains about gross abuses of due process in the arrest and trial of witches, forbids the use of torture in witchcraft cases, warns against searching for the Devil's mark, and forbids the use of the water ordeal, which until recently had been employed on a regular basis in local jurisdictions. The law insists, moreover, that local magistrates refrain from even initiating cases against witches unless there was clear and certain proof that the crime had been committed – the elusive *corpus deliciti* that had always presented a major challenge to scrupulous legal minds when charges of witchcraft arose. The imperial law of 1766 appears therefore to have originated in the same evidentiary and procedural concerns that came to the fore in the Basque country in 1614, France in 1624, Italy in 1623, Würzburg in 1629, Württemberg in 1656, Paderborn in 1657 and Massachusetts in 1692.

In Hungary, however, the judicial concerns of the imperial court at

Vienna also appear to have had a foundation in a more fundamental philosophical scepticism or 'enlightenment' that had come into play only in the later stages of French, English and German witch-hunting. It makes sense that such an outlook would contribute to the decline of witch-hunting in Hungary, since the decline of witchcraft in that country began so much later than in the rest of Europe. By the middle of the eighteenth century it is no longer anachronistic to speak of the possible influence of the Enlightenment on witch-hunting. Certainly Gábor Klaniczay is correct to identify van Swieten as a figure of the Enlightenment, one whose thought was apparently influenced by Bekker and the Italian neo-Platonist Girolamo Tartarotti, who published a history of witch-beliefs from antiquity to the present in 1749 (Klaniczay, 1990a: 175–7). The proclaimed radicalism of van Swieten's ideas regarding witchcraft, however, deserves reconsideration.

Van Swieten, like many other sceptics, took three positions regarding witchcraft that were reflected in the various provisions of the edict of 1766. The first was that many accusations of witchcraft were the product of fantasy, imagination, or some form of mental illness. The second was that the pact with the Devil had no basis in reality, while the third was that many phenomena attributed to sorcery had natural causes. None of these ideas was particularly original, and they could easily be found in the works of the early sceptics, such as Wier, Scot and even Salazar. What one does not find in van Swieten's work is a recognition that all aspects of the witch's crime, especially her maleficent magic, were impossible. Van Swieten's scepticism, in other words, does not even approach the radical position of Hobbes, Bekker or Thomasius. Nor does it approach that of the Italians Scipio Maffei and Gian Rinaldo Carli, who attacked Tartarotti precisely on the grounds that he would not deny the possibility of all magic (Maffei, 1750). It should not surprise us that in 1762 Maria Theresa tried in vain to have a memorial erected to the neo-Platonist Tartarotti, not to his Italian critics (Behringer, 1987: 369–70; Klaniczay, 1990a: 177). It should also not surprise us that the witchcraft law of 1766, for all its scepticism and modernity, did not deny the possibility of sorcery, even in its diabolical form. What is more, the practice of such maleficent magic still could carry the death penalty, subject to imperial confirmation (Article 4).

The most distinctive feature of Hungarian witch-hunting was its association with a native Hungarian belief in vampires. Indeed, the law of 1766 was formulated in the context of a public debate on this belief. Van Swieten and his allies waged a campaign against the belief in vampires, which like many witch-beliefs was attributed to popular ignorance and superstition and was considered blasphemous and unchristian. As Klaniczay has shown, the extreme nature of vampire beliefs, which involved a challenge to the Christian doctrine of the resurrection of the dead, had an effect similar to that of the possession scandals in early seventeenth-century France, since they led many people to call into question their beliefs regarding the extent of demonic power in the world. This analogy can take us only so far. The concern with vampires did not create a scandal comparable to those that developed in the wake of the mass possessions and exorcisms at Loudun and Louviers. Nor can it be shown that a concern with vampires was the main source of the legislation of 1756 and 1766, both of which served as responses to the witch-hunts that had devastated Hungary and to a lesser extent Bohemia during the previous three decades. In 1755 Maria Theresa had published a resolution condemning the popular belief in vampires, but the immediate context of the edict of 1756 was the conviction of a Bohemian shepherd, Johan Polak, solely on the basis of the Devil's mark. In that decree the empress had claimed that 'witches could be found only where there was ignorance,' and that Polak was no more a witch than she herself (Byloff, 1934: 161).

One final approach to the decline of witch-hunting in Hungary focuses more on official concern with the practice of lay healing than with either legal abuses or extreme witch-beliefs. As in many European lands, a sizable proportion of those women accused of witchcraft in Hungary were engaged in some form of popular healing, which usually involved the practice of beneficent magic. The accusations of witchcraft came not only from those whose cures had failed but also from the cunning folk, healers and midwives themselves, as an expression of their professional rivalry (Klaniczay, 1990b: 253–4). Charges against these persons, moreover, tended to become more common as Calvinist ministers insisted that beneficent magic was just as diabolical as its maleficent form (Clark, 1990: 62–5; Kristóf, 1991–2: 107). It stands to reason therefore that successful efforts to train lay healers, to give their profession legitimacy, and to distinguish their art from the superstitions attached to witchcraft would help to reduce the number of accusations coming from below. Efforts along these lines were made in the seventeenth century, mainly by the Cartesian natural philosopher and encyclopedist János Apáczai Csere (1625–59), the doctor Sámuel Enyedi (1627–61) and the botanist János Nadányi (1643–1707), but it was not until the middle of the eighteenth century, after the mass trials of the 1710s and 1720s, that the Viennese government became involved in the process. Agnes Várkonyi has shown that the witchcraft legislation of the 1750s and 1760s was part of a much larger program of improving public health within the empire, an undertaking that involved not only futile attempts to increase the number of physicians within the country but also to legitimize and train the lay healers. The new witchcraft law of 1766 conforms nicely to this pattern, since it enumerates the various activities of lay healers in order to distinguish them from witches (Varkonyi, 1991–2: 448–65). We can only speculate that the rapid decline of prosecutions after the passage of this law discouraged accusations that had only recently been levelled against the healers.

CHAPTER 3

The End of Prosecutions

THE PROCESS OF DECRIMINALIZATION

Having explored the general reasons for the decline of witchcraft prosecutions and having charted the process in selected jurisdictions, we need now to discuss the means by which the prosecution of this crime finally came to a complete end and when judicial authorities ceased to consider witchcraft a crime. The word chosen to identify this development, decriminalization, can be viewed as a process taking place over a long period of time. In this sense it can virtually be identified with the decline of witchcraft prosecutions (Soman, 1989: 1–4). In this essay I will use the word more specifically to denote the *terminus ad quem* of the process, the time when witchcraft actually ceased to be a crime and when legal prosecutions came to a complete end.

Decriminalization in this latter sense took one of two forms. The first, which is formal or *de jure* decriminalization, involved the explicit repeal of the laws upon which prosecutions were based. *De jure* decriminalization, as we shall see, occurred in very few jurisdictions prior to the end of the eighteenth century, and in those where it did, the repeal of the laws was often incomplete, leaving some activities encompassed within the definition of witchcraft as prohibited. The second form, *de facto* decriminalization, was realized when judicial authorities simply stopped prosecuting and executing witches, either because they had concluded that the crime was incapable of legal proof or because they denied the reality of the crime. Although we can often discover the date of the last witchcraft trials and executions in various jurisdictions, it is more difficult to identify the time when the members of a ruling and administrative elite came to the conclusion that the crime should no longer be prosecuted, especially since there may have been disagreement among the members of those elites on that very question.

The repeal of laws against witchcraft serves as an early example of a process that has occurred much more frequently in the late twentieth century. Within the last 50 years many Western societies have repealed laws against such practices as abortion, homosexuality, adultery, divorce, suicide, blasphemy, and the use of narcotics. Many of these offences have been viewed more as sins than as crimes and thus might be classified as 'offences against Moral Justice' a phrase once used to describe the crimes of witchcraft and magic (Kittredge, 1929: 596 n. 189). They also might be described as 'offences against God,' the official category encompassing witchcraft in late seventeenth-century England. The moral dimension of these offences also explains why their repeal, just like that of laws against witchcraft, has often been preceded by extensive public debate, usually among groups sharing different religious outlooks.

Since the decline and end of witchcraft prosecutions occurred everywhere in Europe, historians often assume that *de jure* decriminalization was a universal phenomenon, with witchcraft laws falling like dominoes throughout Europe. The legislative record, however, does not support this assumption. Before the dawn of the nineteenth century witchcraft laws were repealed or significantly modified in only seven kingdoms: France in 1682, Prussia in 1714, Great Britain in 1736, the Habsburg Empire in 1766, Russia in 1770, Poland in 1776 and Sweden in 1779. Only the last two kingdoms legislated a complete ban on witchcraft trials. The Swedish National Code of 1779 certainly had that effect, since it simply omitted the clause regarding witchcraft in the old Code of 1734, thus rendering prosecutions impossible (Ankarloo, 1990: 300). The Polish statute, passed by the diet a year after a witch-hunt in the village of Doruchowo had claimed the lives of fourteen women, forbade the prosecution of witches by all tribunals, including the court of the small town of Grabowo which had conducted the trials at Doruchowo. The Polish statute also forbade the use of torture in all criminal cases (Soldan and Heppe, 1912: ii: 26; Baranowski, 1952; Tazbir, 1980: 305–6).

The earlier British statute of 1736 also bears most of the signs of a blanket prohibition of witchcraft prosecutions, since it repealed the English statute of 1604 and its Scottish counterpart of 1563. But by making it an offence to 'pretend to exercise or use any kind of witchcraft, sorcery, enchantment or conjuration or undertake to tell fortunes' on the pain of imprisonment for one year, parliament failed to completely decriminalize all those activities that once marched under the broad banner of witchcraft. Prosecutions for conjuration under the statute of 1736 were rare, but they did take place, and the judges who charged grand juries continued to remind them that it was 'very penal' to pretend to be a witch (Lamoine, 1992: 365; Gaskill, 1994b: 123–4). This provision of the new witchcraft law was not repealed until 1951 (Bostridge, 1996: 333).

The French royal edict of 1682, as we have seen, achieved even less than the British law of 1736. It is true that the edict, just like the later British statute, referred to magic as 'pretended,' possibly to offer protection against impostors. But as far as witchcraft prosecutions were concerned the law was far more qualified than the British statute. Designed in part to prevent a recurrence of the affair of the poisons, it left intact the death penalty for forms of magic that were overtly sacrilegious, and it permitted some of the prosecutions of *maleficium* that continued in France during the following decade. The same was true of the Habsburg imperial law of 1766. While eliminating prosecutions in cases arising from fraud and mental illness, it nonetheless ordered the banishment of those who made pacts with the Devil and even allowed the possibility of the death penalty in cases of *maleficium* performed with the assistance of the Devil.

Russian efforts to decriminalize witchcraft bore a faint resemblance to the Habsburg legislation of Maria Theresa. As early as 1731, during the reign of Empress Anna, the Russian Senate had passed a law classifying witchcraft as fraud, but conviction still carried the death penalty. Catherine II's legislation of 1770 reduced the penalty for this special type of fraud to non-capital punishment, but it left open the possibility that the parties involved could be prosecuted for popular superstition. Ten years later the empress encouraged the courts to try cases of alleged witchcraft as fraud, leaving those who made accusations, especially women who claimed to be possessed, to be tried in special courts of conscience for popular superstition. Those same courts of conscience dealt with the criminally insane (Zguta, 1977b: 1200-1).

The least comprehensive of these laws was the Prussian edict of 1714, issued by King Frederick William I less than two years after his accession to the throne. This mandate was designed entirely to reform the criminal procedures used in witchcraft trials, so that innocent persons would no longer be tortured, forced to confess, and executed. Its concern with legal procedure reflects the influence of Thomasius, the chancellor at the 'liberal' University of Halle, and indirectly that of Spee, upon whom Thomasius relied heavily in his work. The edict, which was to be proclaimed in the local courts, demanded that all judicial decisions either to torture or execute witches be submitted to the king for confirmation before being implemented. This provision, which echoes French policy and anticipates that of the Habsburg Empire, provides further evidence of the role played by central authorities in restricting witchcraft prosecutions. The law did not, however, ban witchcraft trials or even executions, although it did require the removal of all the stakes from the public places where witches had been burned. In 1721 a Prussian Landrecht abolished the death penalty in all witchcraft trials (Lea, 1939: 1431).

In all the other countries of Europe *de jure* decriminalization did not take place until after 1800, and in some jurisdictions it never occurred at all. In the duchy of Württemberg, the Provincial Code which had authorized the prosecution of witchcraft was not changed until well into the nineteenth century. The same was true in Saxony, where the code drafted by Benedikt Carpzov in 1635 was not rewritten, with the provisions against witchcraft now omitted, until the period of the Napoleonic wars. Likewise the Bavarian edict of 1611, renewed in 1665 and 1746, remained at least nominally in force until the criminal reforms of 1813 (Behringer, 1987: 297). This German pattern of late repeal, long after the *de facto* end of prosecutions, was also followed in Denmark, where the decline of witch-hunting had begun as early as 1625 and where the last legal execution had taken place in 1693. In that kingdom an article authorizing the execution of witches by burning, which had been incorporated into the Danish Code of 1683, was not repealed until 1866 (Henningsen, 1988: 106–7).

The formal decriminalization of witchcraft had little bearing on the broader process of decline that we have been discussing. The blanket repeals that took place in Great Britain and Sweden had no effect whatsoever on witchcraft prosecutions in those countries because the last trial had long preceded the legislation effecting the change. The same could be said of the large number of states which repealed their laws only in the nineteenth century. Even in those countries which passed witchcraft statutes before the end of the trials, the new laws had only a limited effect on the volume of prosecutions. The first of these laws, the French edict of 1682, probably prevented prosecutions only in the few outlying regions of the country where trials were still taking place. The same could be said of Frederick William I's edict of 1714, since prosecutions in Prussia had slackened considerably since the 1690s. The Polish law of 1776 affected only those isolated villages like Doruchowo where there was still pressure to prosecute. Only Maria Theresa's imperial law of 1766 seems to have led to a demonstrable curtailment in the number of trials and executions. Even then, however, witch-hunting was taking place only in certain parts of the Habsburg Empire, mainly in Hungary. In Austria itself trials had long since ended, with the last execution occurring in 1750 (Byloff, 1934: 154–6).

The more common pattern of decriminalization was the *de facto* cessation of trials, without any accompanying edict. This, as we have seen, was achieved at different times in various territories, but in almost all cases the very last trials occurred long after the decline in prosecutions had begun. The following table, which lists both the last execution and the last trial in those territories for which data are available, gives a clear indication of how long witch-hunting continued, at least in some attenuated form:

Country or region	Last execution	Last trial
Parlement of Paris	1625	1693
Alsace	1683	1683
Franche–Comté	1661	1667
Cambrésis	1679	1783

Dutch Republic[1]	1609	1659
Luxembourg	1685	1685
Switzerland	1782	1782
Geneva	1652	1681
England	1684	1717
Essex County	1645	1675
Scotland	1706	1727
Ireland	1711	1711
New England	1692	1697
Denmark	1693	1762
Sweden	1710	1779
Finland	1691?	1699
Württemberg	1749	1805
Westphalia	1728	1732
Würzburg	1749	1749
Bavaria	1756	1792
Augsburg	1728	1738
Kempten	1775	1775
Nuremberg	1660	1725
Prussia	1714	1728
Austria	1750	1775
Hungary	1756	1777
Slovenia	1720	1746
Poland	1775	1776
Spain	1781	1820
Portugal	1626	1802
Palermo	1724	1788

JUDICIAL EFFECTS OF THE DECLINE

As the prosecution of witchcraft entered its final stages, and the number of trials and executions declined, the courts made two significant changes in the conduct of criminal proceedings relating to witchcraft. The first was the prosecution of some of those persons accused of witchcraft for the non-diabolical crimes of poisoning and infanticide or for practicing certain types of magic. The second was the more frequent and determined prosecution of those individuals who had slandered, maliciously prosecuted or lynched other persons as witches. Both sets of criminal proceedings continued after the last trials for witchcraft, and both attest to the enduring strength of popular witch-beliefs. In the prosecution of witches for offences other than witchcraft the courts revealed an important shift in their understanding of the crime. By taking action against those who verbally or physically assaulted suspected witches, the courts effected a change in the relationship between accused witches and the law, serving now as their protector rather than their prosecutor.

Judicial reclassification

Witchcraft, as it was defined in the sixteenth and seventeenth centuries, was a composite crime. In its most elaborate form it combined the crime of maleficent magic with that of devil-worship, although the relative emphasis placed on these two components of the crime varied from place to place and also changed over time. More specifically, the crime of witchcraft encompassed a variety of activities that by themselves possessed criminal status at either the temporal or the ecclesiastical law. Witchcraft could denote heresy, apostasy, blasphemy, maiming, murder, poisoning, theft, the destruction of crops, the killing of livestock, arson, sodomy, fornication, adultery, infanticide and conspiracy.[2]

The crime of witchcraft also overlapped with, and was often grouped together with, the crime of magic, which included such practices as necromancy, conjuration, alchemy, astrology, magical healing, love magic, fortune-telling, and magical treasure-hunting. Most European languages used different words to distinguish witchcraft from magic (e.g., *hexerei* and *zauberei*; *sorcellerie* and *magie*), but a close relationship had always existed between them. One form of ritual magic, necromancy, had contributed directly to the development of witchcraft in the fourteenth and fifteenth centuries; in a certain sense the necromancer had been transformed into the witch (Cohn, 1975: 164–205; Peters, 1978). During the period of the witch trials witchcraft usually involved *maleficium*, the alleged practice of harmful magic, although in some jurisdictions a mere pact with the devil was sufficient to establish a person's identity as a witch. Even beneficent forms of magic were sometimes grouped together with witchcraft, especially by Protestant ministers and Catholic inquisitors who considered them equally sinful uses of demonic power. Women who practised magical healing and love magic were therefore vulnerable to charges of witchcraft, even when these practices did not allegedly result in the infliction of harm. More often than not, however, white magicians were prosecuted separately from maleficent witches, and they received less severe punishments. In many cases ecclesiastical rather than secular courts exercised jurisdiction over these cases of beneficent magic.

As the number of witchcraft trials declined, and as the percentage of acquittals rose, the courts that heard witchcraft cases tried and convicted a number of accused witches for specific crimes that had once been included in, or related to, the broader category of witchcraft. This reclassification of the charges against accused witches often involved the judicial abandonment of the general word for witchcraft (*hexerei, sorcellerie, brujeria, stregoneria, toverij, troldom, hekseri, trolldom, noituus*) and its replacement with more specific terms designating either the type of harm the witch inflicted or the type of magic she employed (Midelfort, 1972: 82–3; Klaits, 1982: 160; Bever, 1983: 360–1). As we have seen, the French royal edict of 1682, which did not use the term *sorcellerie* but referred instead to pretended magic, sacrilege and poisoning, serves as an example of this trend towards greater terminological precision. In many German territories the courts actually developed distinct criminal processes in order to try the new offences. The use of more precise terminology meant that when members of the community charged their neighbours with witchcraft, it became less likely that the courts would also charge them with making a pact with the devil and attending the sabbath. The growing reluctance of judges to use torture, the means by which such charges of diabolism had traditionally been introduced into the trials, only helped to accelerate this dissociation of *maleficium* from Devil-worship.

The clearest example of the reclassification of witchcraft as a different crime can be seen in the prosecution of some 'witches' as poisoners. The crimes of witchcraft and poisoning had always been closely linked, even though they were often prosecuted separately. Charges against witches often included the use of poisons, which could be viewed as either natural or magical. One of the most common Latin words for witchcraft, *veneficium*, denoted poisoning as well as magical harm. Throughout the sixteenth and seventeenth centuries critics of witch-hunting, beginning with Wier and Scot, had tried to distinguish the two crimes, claiming that those 'witches' who actually harmed their neighbours did so by means of poison, not supernatural power, and therefore should be prosecuted accordingly (Scot, 1930: 68–9; Weyer, 1991: 267–80, 354–8, 559–61). The French royal edict of 1682, which originated in the context of the 'affair of the poisons,' devoted eight of its eleven articles to poisoning, and distinguished it from the offences of magic, superstition and sacrilege, which themselves were being separated from the broader crime of witch-craft. In 1716 Hermann Meinders, a judge from Rabensburg, responding to the publication of Frederick William's edict, recommended that 'witches' who actually caused death by administering harmful concoctions to their victims be prosecuted as simple poisoners. Other 'witches' were either to be hospitalized for mental illness or punished less severely as magicians (Meinders, 1716: 103).

Scattered evidence suggests that during the period of decline the courts began to act upon these recommendations, trying at least some accused witches as poisoners. In Württemberg, for example, the number of witchcraft trials in the 1670s dropped from 46 to 16, while during the same decade prosecutions for poisoning increased from six to 15 (Bever, 1983: 378–9). In France, shepherds from the Pécy region, Brie, and

Normandy who were accused of killing their flocks by witchcraft between 1687 and 1691 were officially charged and executed as poisoners under the terms of the royal edict, although some of these persons were also tried for sacrilege (Mandrou, 1968: 499–512). In late eighteenth-century Palermo the trial of an old woman, Giovanna Bonanno, for selling her customers a vinegar mixture that was guaranteed to kill their enemies had a similar result. Bonanno was reputed to be a witch, but when she was charged with witchcraft in 1788, the secular judges reclassified her crime as poisoning and convicted her on those grounds. Since poisoning, unlike witchcraft, was susceptible to objective, empirical investigation, this reclassification has been viewed as reflective of the 'modernization' of the crime of witchcraft (Fiume, 1994). It also reflected its secularization.

A similar modernization may be seen in the trial of witches for infanticide. Intensive prosecutions for both of these crimes began about the same time in the sixteenth century, and in both cases the overwhelming majority of defendants were female (Larner, 1984: 60–1; Hoffer and Hull, 1984: 28–30). In some continental European jurisdictions women convicted of killing their children were burned at the stake, just as witches were. Although the two offences were usually prosecuted separately, the commission of one could arouse suspicion of the other, since the death of infants often gave rise to accusations of *maleficium* and because witches allegedly sacrificed children at the sabbath (Roper, 1994: 217). Thus in 1686 a servant woman from Augsburg who confessed to having killed her child at the behest of the Devil was tried and executed for witchcraft (Roper, 1994: 1). As witchcraft declined and gradually lost its status as a crime, such blurring of the two crimes ceased, and mothers who killed their children were tried simply for infanticide (Midelfort, 1972: 83).

More striking than these trials for poisoning and infanticide was the prosecution of accused witches for benevolent forms of magic. The clearest evidence of this change comes from Finland, where trials for white magic did not even begin until the 1660s, just about the time that prosecutions for maleficent witchcraft entered a rapid decline (Nenonen, 1992: 435–6). In other areas, where prosecutions for both crimes had been conducted separately for many years, the legal record likewise suggests a connection between the decline of one set of trials and the rise of the other. In various German territories, especially Württemberg, prosecutions for magic rose steadily after 1680, reaching a peak in the 1740s and continuing into the nineteenth century (Bever, 1983: fig. 10.4). In Scotland prosecutions in the kirk sessions for casting charms began to climb shortly after witch trials entered their period of decline, and they stretched well into the eighteenth century. In the Netherlands trials for magic continued long after those for maleficent witchcraft had stopped (Gijswijt-Hofstra, 1989: 76–7; 1991b: 103–19). Only rarely did prosecutions for magic carry the death penalty, and in many jurisdictions they were conducted in the ecclesiastical courts, but some of these trials were nonetheless the heirs (or at least the stepchildren) of the witchcraft processes that were being abandoned. In one Scottish prosecution for a form of charming known as 'scoring the brow' in 1728, the synod of Merse and Teviotdale referred to the practice as 'a sort and degree of witchcraft' (Levack, 1995a: 111).

This judicial transition from witchcraft to magic is difficult to chart in Spain, Portugal and Italy, where the Inquisition traditionally claimed jurisdiction not just over witchcraft but over all the magical arts as well. Most studies of the case-loads of these inquisitions group all these offences together, since the Inquisition, following the *Directorium Inquisitorium* of the fourteenth-century inquisitor Nicholas Eymeric, viewed them all as involving illicit commerce with demons and therefore heresy.[3] The inquisitions of southern Europe never made clear distinctions between *maleficium* and these other forms of demonic magic. Indeed, the maleficent character of the witch's magic was of little importance in these tribunals. The main concern of Iberian and Italian inquisitors was whether the defendant, by practising magic, had made either an implicit or explicit pact with the Devil (Henningsen, 1980: xxix; Martin, 1989: 255). One consequence of this failure to distinguish witchcraft from other forms of magic was that in these three countries the word 'witchcraft' (*brujeria, bruxaria, stregoneria*) was still used occasionally to describe the practice of white magic well into the late eighteenth century.

Despite this occasional semantic confusion, we can nonetheless distinguish between Spanish and Italian inquisitorial trials for witchcraft, characterized either by maleficence or collective devil worship, from those involving other, benevolent forms of magic. Witchcraft trials in the Spanish, Roman and Portuguese inquisitions ended fairly early in the seventeenth century (although somewhat later in the Spanish and Italian secular courts), but prosecutions for magic continued for decades, well into the eighteenth century. In the Venetian Inquisition, for example, where witchcraft trials ended by 1650 and the last execution took place in 1626, prosecutions for magic increased substantially during the period from 1631 to 1720, to almost double the number of cases between 1547 and 1630. Only after 1721 did they trail off, although they continued to form the largest single category of criminal offences brought before that court (Monter and Tedeschi, 1986: 135, 144). As in other parts of Europe, the decline and decriminalization of witchcraft in the Mediterranean kingdoms resulted in an increase in the prosecution of the various crimes that had once been comprehended within it or at least related to it. Rather than being simply decriminalized, witchcraft was being transformed into a number of discrete offences, real, imagined, and 'pretended.'

Counter-prosecutions

The second set of criminal proceedings that accompanied the decline of witchcraft were prosecutions of those people who verbally assaulted, maliciously prosecuted, or lynched their neighbours as witches. These counter-prosecutions, which involved a shift in the assignment of criminal responsibility from the witch to her assailant, took three different forms. The simplest was a slander suit against those who had made false allegations of witchcraft. These prosecutions, which were often initiated by the accused witches themselves, took place throughout the period of witch-hunting, both in secular and ecclesiastical courts,[4] but they tended to increase in number when judicial authorities became more sceptical regarding the reality of the crime. They became common in the Saar region shortly after prosecutions began to decline in 1635, in Alsace in the 1650s, in France in the 1680s, in Scotland in the 1680s and 1690s, and in various southwestern German lands about the same time (Mandrou, 1968: 492–9; Midelfort, 1972: 81; Larner, 1981: 116–17; Klaits, 1982: 158; Labouvie, 1995: 71–3). Danish courts heard a number of these cases in the eighteenth and nineteenth centuries (Henningsen 1988: 119–30). Maria Theresa's law of 1766, as we have seen, specifically provided for such prosecutions within the Habsburg Empire. In England one of the best documented slander cases ever to come before the common law courts occurred in 1736, the year in which the witchcraft statute was repealed.[5] Punishments for these crimes of slander varied widely, ranging from public penance and fines to banishment.

Closely related to slander suits were the trials of those whose false accusations of witchcraft had resulted in the actual trial and in some cases even the execution of innocent persons. One of the earliest examples of this type of counter-prosecution was the English trial of Anne and Brian Gunter in 1606 for conspiracy to indict two innocent women for witchcraft. That case, in which the witches were acquitted at the Abingdon assizes and the Gunters apparently convicted in the court of Star Chamber, stood at the beginning of the long, slow decline of English witch-hunting (Levack, 1995b: 1636–40). A similar case, the prosecution of the English labourer Richard Hathaway in 1702 for having Sarah Murdock tried for witchcraft on false pretenses, helped to bring it to a complete end. Hathaway had accused Morduck of bewitching him, preventing him from eating, and inflicting on him a number of diseases. In the ensuing witchcraft trial, at which the sceptical Chief Justice Holt presided, Morduck was acquitted and Hathaway was exposed as an impostor and a cheat. Nevertheless, he continued to harass Morduck after the trial, apparently with the support of his neighbors, who took up collections for him. At this point the attorney-general, Edward Northey, exhibited an information in the court of King's Bench against Hathaway, claiming that he was an impostor and that he had maliciously intended 'to bring [Morduck] into the danger of losing her life.' Hathaway was convicted at the Surrey assizes. He was also tried and convicted, together with three accomplices, of assaulting and wounding Morduck (Howell, 1816: 14. 644).

In a curious way these counter-suits for the malicious prosecution of witches, which include the punishment of several witnesses for giving false testimony in the great Swedish trials of 1668–76 (Ankarloo, 1990: 300), marked a return to the principle of the liable accuser. According to the *lex talionis* of Roman and early medieval Germanic law, those who brought charges against others under the accusatory process were themselves penalized if the charges were not proved in court. The talion had disappeared in virtually all jurisdictions when the courts had abandoned the ordeals and the other non-rational modes of proof and when the state had assumed primary responsibility for the prosecution of crime. The abolition of the talion had helped to make the great witch-hunt possible (Cohn, 1975: 161–2). Now, as witchcraft prosecutions were coming to an end, and as the courts began to view witchcraft accusations with suspicion, judges contemplated the reintroduction of this procedure in one form or another. In 1716 Hermann Meinders, complaining that most witchcraft trials were the product of personal hatred, envy and revenge, recommended to King Frederick William I that individuals no longer be allowed to use the accusation process against witches unless they would first agree to be subject to the talion.[6] In Meinders' view, the miscarriages of justice that were so common in witchcraft cases were now originating in the malice of private accusers, not the judges who heard the cases.

The most serious form of criminal proceedings against the accusers of witches was the trial of individuals who had lynched or beaten the persons whom they suspected. Since these trials were often for murder, they could result in the execution of the malefactors. The lynching of witches had long pre-dated the decline of prosecutions. At the height of the great witch-hunt lynching had served as an alternative to formal prosecution, sometimes to avoid the prohibitive costs of prosecution, at other times to serve the desire of the local populace for summary justice (Henningsen, 1980: 18, 204, 209; Soman, 1986). In Poland lynchings may have accounted for as many as half the total number of witchcraft executions.[7] Witch lynchings became more common, however, as the prosecutions began to decline in number, especially when the courts began to acquit large numbers of witches or refused to bring formal judicial action against them (Dupont-Bouchat, 1994: 245). Most of the formal criminal proceedings undertaken by the state against those who had lynched witches occurred during this later stage of witch-hunting or after the trials had ended altogether. In 1705, for example, the Scottish government brought charges of murder against the residents of the fishing village of Pittenweem in Fife for pressing to death an accused witch, Janet Cornfoot, under heavy stones after the judges in Edinburgh had released her from gaol (Anon., 1704). Judicial authorities in Denmark acted with equal decisiveness in 1722 after a group of villagers from Øster Grønning in Salling burned a woman to death for allegedly killing two children and a number of livestock by witchcraft. The courts tried and executed two of the ringleaders of this lynching for murder, outlawed one of their accomplices, and forced another five to do public penance (Henningsen, 1988: 110–19). The English government responded in similar fashion to two cases, one at Frome, Somerset in 1731 and the other at Tring, Hertfordshire in 1751, in which attacks on alleged witches had resulted in the death of the accused (Gaskill, 1994b: 88–9). The ringleader of the lynchers at Tring, a chimneysweep named Thomas Colley, was tried and executed for the murder of Ruth Osborne, a seventy-year old resident of a workhouse who had drowned when members of the local community subjected her and her husband to the swimming test (Carnochan, 1971: 388–403). Incidents like these have continued to take place from time to time from the eighteenth century to the present day, and in all these cases the state has maintained its role as the prosecutor of the witch's assailants, a role to which it had been relatively unaccustomed during the height of the great witch-hunt.

Conclusion

There is no simple answer to the question why European courts stopped prosecuting witches. The tendency to attribute the entire process to a growing belief that witches did not exist or that their crime was impossible to perform should be resisted. There is little evidence of such an intellectual transformation among the common folk, and even within learned circles disbelief of that sort did not develop among the men who controlled the judicial machinery until long after witchcraft had entered its decline. In Germany, where witchcraft trials took a greater toll than in all other parts of Europe combined, prosecutions began to decline in the 1650s and 1660s, if not earlier, before the new philosophy began to hold sway in academic and judicial circles. Some of the earlier critics of witch-hunting had questioned or even rejected the existence of the sabbath and the pact with the devil, and they had insisted that most of the persons accused of witchcraft were innocent, but they had not subscribed to a philosophy or a theology that denied the possibility of demonic intervention in the operation of the physical world. That change came slowly and belatedly, over the course of the eighteenth century, and even then it occurred only in the minds of some educated men, and not always those who controlled the judicial process.

The belated development of 'enlightenment' regarding witchcraft, coupled with a recognition of the limited nature of early seventeenth-century scepticism, turns our attention from philosophy to law, from a consideration of the devil's alleged powers to the way in which trials were conducted. The decisive turning points in the prosecution of witches in the various jurisdictions of Europe can be linked much more solidly to the demand for legal caution in handling witchcraft cases than to changes in learned witch-beliefs. This caution often arose during the trials themselves when it became clear that innocent persons had been executed for crimes they did not commit. This realization led to the limitation and ultimately to the prohibition of torture and to the establishment of new evidentiary standards, which greatly increased the chances that witches would be acquitted, especially when the accused had the benefit of counsel to demonstrate their application. By the end of the seventeenth century the entire judicial process for handling them had changed in ways that made a repetition of the holocausts of the

1620s impossible and the successful prosecution of individual witches less likely.

The judges and lawyers who presided over these later prosecutions might be described as sceptics, but the doubt that plagued them was very different from the systematic philosophical doubt with which we usually associate the term. Instead of doubting whether either the Devil existed or could exercise physical power in the world, they expressed profound uncertainty whether those individuals who had been accused of witchcraft were guilty as charged, even if they had confessed. It was this type of scepticism that underlay the demand that in witchcraft cases proof needed to be airtight. We find this demand in men as diverse as Alonso Salazar in Spain, Christian Thomasius in Prussia, Sir George Mackenzie in Scotland, and Increase Mather in Massachusetts. This demand for certain proof led to the more general recognition that witchcraft could not be proved at law, and once that point was reached, European judicial authorities began not only to direct acquittals, but to stop hearing cases altogether. Only in the latter stages of this process, in the late seventeenth and early eighteenth centuries, did some judges come to the more radical conclusion that witchcraft was not only unprovable but also impossible to perform.

The decline of witch-hunting began and ended at different times in the various kingdoms and territories of Europe, and it followed different patterns. Much of this geographical variation can be attributed to differences in judicial administration and procedure. The role that judges played in securing acquittals was much greater in France and Spain, where the inquisitorial system prevailed, than in England and Scotland, where juries continued to decide cases. In the Mediterranean lands, where both ecclesiastical and secular courts adjudicated witchcraft cases, the decline was more erratic than in countries like Denmark and Sweden, where the entire process was entrusted to secular officials. The limitation of torture had a greater impact in Germany, where the procedure had been frequently and grossly abused, than in France, where it was carefully regulated, or in England, where its use in witchcraft cases was technically illegal. Finally, in countries which had appellate procedures and required the review and confirmation of witchcraft sentences, such as in France and the Scandinavian countries, central authorities could restrict and eventually terminate witch-hunting much more directly and effectively than they could in kingdoms or empires which conceded a large measure of autonomy to local courts.

In a study that does not permit much generalization, there is one pattern of judicial change that was evident in most European states, with the notable exceptions of the Dutch Republic, where prosecutions ended very early, and some parts of Switzerland, where they ended very late. The decline and end of witch-hunting, characterized by formal restrictions on the use of torture, the reversal of convictions upon appeal, and legislation that restricted the right of local courts to try witches under any circumstances, was undertaken and enforced mainly by central judicial institutions. There is no small irony in this pattern, since it was the growth of state power, especially as it was embodied in central institutions, that had helped to make intensive witch-hunting possible. Both the introduction of inquisitorial procedure into most European jurisdictions as well as the assumption of secular control over witchcraft prosecutions reflected the growth of state power. In a number of countries, moreover, efforts to create a godly state, in which secular authorities pursued the religious and moral goals of disciplining and christianizing the population, had also helped to fuel the great witch-hunt. At the same time, however, the efforts of the state to bring all judicial institutions within the ambit of central governmental control worked against one of the main dynamics of witch-hunting, which was the determination of local authorities to purge their communities of witches. Just as the rise of witch-hunting was associated with the emergence of the modern state, its decline was also linked, sometimes in a most direct way, with the growth of state power during the age of absolutism and enlightened despotism.

The last executions for witchcraft in Europe reveal, in a negative way, the close connection between the end of witch-hunting and the exercise of central state power. There have traditionally been two contenders for this dubious distinction: the execution of Anna Göldi for bewitching her master's child in the Swiss canton of Glarus in 1782 and the execution of two women with inflamed eyes for bewitching their neighbours' cattle in the Polish city of Posnan in 1793. The trial in Glarus, which appears to have resulted in the last legal execution, appropriately occurred in a small canton in which anything even remotely resembling central state power was absent, where witchcraft had not been decriminalized, and where the prohibition of torture lay more than a half-century in the future. Witch-hunting at Glarus and in most of eastern Switzerland remained, even in the late eighteenth century, a strictly local operation (Bader, 1945: 207).

The execution at Posnan offers us a somewhat different commentary on the relationship between central and local control. Most Polish witchcraft trials in the seventeenth century were conducted by municipal authorities, usually in the villages where the charges almost always originated. In 1768 the highest court of the kingdom, the assessors' tribunal, had prohibited the small towns from conducting this type of trial. The order was not always observed, however, perhaps as much out of ignorance as a spirit of municipal independence. After the town of Glabowo executed 14 witches at Doruchowo in 1775, the Polish diet took action and forbade all witchcraft prosecutions. This exercise of central power seems to have been effective, for after that date witch-trials disappeared from the legal record.

In 1793, however, Poland was partitioned for the second time, leaving the country temporarily without any central government. A judge in the city of Posnan, situated in the province of Great Poland, which was about to pass over to Prussian control, immediately took advantage of this hiatus in government and executed the two women. The legality of the trial remains a subject of controversy; it was undertaken by a member of a properly constituted municipal government but without the sanction of higher state authorities. The royal commission that was overseeing the transfer of power from Poland to Prussia tried to prevent the execution, but it acted too late (Soldan and Heppe, 1912: ii. 332). We can be fairly certain that if either a Polish or a Prussian royal government had been fully constituted at the time, the trial would not have even taken place. Witch-hunting, even in its last gasp, remained a local affair which central governments tried to control, regulate or eliminate, but not always with complete success.

Notes

Chapter 1

1. The *Instructio* was also published by itself in 1657. On the publication and circulation of this work see Ginzburg, 1983: 200 n. 40; Tedeschi, 1991: 209. On Carena's treatise see Martin, 1989: 71–3.

2. Behringer, 1987: 344. The law faculties at Trier and Strasbourg also tended to recommend caution in witchcraft cases after 1650. These faculties exercised more influence over the criminal courts in the Saar region during the late seventeenth century, the period in which witchcraft prosecutions in that area declined (Labouvie, 1995: 70–1).

3. Lorenz, 1995: 227–8, 241. In this early decision Thomasius proved to be less lenient than his senior colleagues.

4. Torture was also used in witchcraft cases in countries like Sweden, Russia and Hungary where Roman law had little or no influence. In Sweden its use was forbidden in legal proceedings, but it was allowed in witchcraft cases, sometimes by royal decree. See Ankarloo, 1990: 290.

5. On the importance of the humanitarian argument in the debate over torture in the late eighteenth century see Peters, 1985: chap. 3.

6. Loos's book (Loos, 1592) was confiscated from the printer at Cologne. On Loos see Zenz, 1981: 146–53; Eerden, 1992; Lea, 1939: 601–4.

7. Peters, 1985: 90–1. Other dates of abolition are: Brunswick (1770), Saxony (1770), Denmark (1770), Sweden (1782), Tuscany (1786), France (1788), Lombardy (1789), the Netherlands (1798), Bavaria (1806), Spain (1808), Norway (1819), Portugal (1826), Greece (1827), Gotha (1828) Zurich (1831), Freiburg (1848), and Basel (1850).

8. Goedelmann, 1592: 3. cap. 1 had advanced this idea earlier in his attack on Bodin.

9. In 1515 Alciatus questioned the use of torture to get names of accomplices at the sabbath. See Kneubühler, 1977: 160.

10. Cotta, 1616: 111. The medical and philosophical faculties of the University of Leiden also rejected the procedure (Gijswijt-Hofstra, 1991a: 20).

11. In 1692 Hugh Hare, a justice of the peace, in his charge to the jury at the Surrey Quarter Sessions, warned that although witchcraft was a sin and a crime punishable by death, 'it is so hard a matter to have full

proof brought of it, that no jury can be too cautious and tender in a prosecution of this nature' (Kittredge, 1929: 596). For a similar charge to the grand jury in the same year from the Earl of Warrington see Gaskill, 1994b: 99.

12. For the late seventeenth-century Mexican development of the idea that the demons which possessed individuals did so as subservient instruments of God's will see Cervantes, 1991.

13. For the denial of the latter claim by demonologists see Lea, 1939: 886.

14. Soman, 1978: 36–7. The parlement never accepted the definition of witchcraft as a *crimen exceptum*.

15. In the Empire witches could not be represented by procurators, i.e., attorneys, but they were entitled to a defence by an advocate. See Carpzov, 1670: 39, 142–3; Trusen, 1995: 213. In England all criminals were denied defence counsel until the eighteenth century. They could, however, be advised on points of law relating to their indictments.

16. In the acquittal of Elizabeth Gregory and Agnes Pepwell at the Abingdon Assizes in 1604 the jury deliberated for eight hours. Public Record Office, STAC 8/4/10, fos. 9–18. At the trial of Joan Buts in Surrey in 1682 the jury deliberated three hours.

17. Merzbacher, 1970: 79. In some jurisdictions the judge brought the charges himself. See Carpzov, 1670: 6–7.

18. Scot, 1930: 7, 18–20, 89. On the question whether Scot denied the possibility of humans inflicting harm by supernatural means see Thomas, 1971: 572–3; Easlea, 1980: 42–3. Scot included these 'wonders' among the alleged crimes of witches which he denied and the witch-hunters could not prove to be true (Scot, 1930: 19)

19. On the difficulty of distinguishing between natural and demonic magic see Clark, 1984: 351–74.

20. Soman, 1978: 33, 39, 44. The last execution approved by the parlement took place in 1625.

21. On this controversy see Trevor-Roper, 1969: 173–5; Attfield, 1985; Stronks, 1991: 149–50. Much of the controversy concerns the extent of Bekker's influence in intellectual, not judicial circles.

22. On the judicial framework of the book see Trusen, 1995: 223–4

23. This admission appeared in the *Vertheidigung* which was included in the German translation of the book. See Thomasius, 1703.

24. Filmer, 1653. This tract bears comparison with Scot, 1930: Book VII.

25. de Waardt, 1995. There is of course no necessary connection between the two, and in the Netherlands there was a brief period of ecclesiastical intolerance towards Arminians. On Dutch 'tolerance' of witches see Gijswijt-Hofstra, 1991–2.

26. Stronks, 1991: 152–4. The most bitter attack on Bekker as well as Thomasius came from Peter Goldschmidt, the pastor of Sterup in the duchy of Schleswig (Goldschmidt, 1705). See Terpstra, 1965.
27. Wolf, 1995: 871. Brunnemann's treatise (1727), which was one of the first histories of witchcraft prosecutions, had been published anonymously at Stargard in 1708.
28. Baschwitz, 1963: 206; Lecky, 1910: 136. On the persistence of Scottish witch beliefs and their association with a distinctive Scottish culture after the union of 1707 see Bostridge, 1996.
29. Demos, 1982: 368ff argues that trials often did not coincide with periods of social conflict but that they could nonetheless originate as delayed responses to such conflict. On agrarian crises and witchcraft see Behringer, 1987: 98–112.

Chapter 2
1. Soman, 1978: 34–5. Between 1611 and 1624, 47 per cent of all appellants were released and only 4.7 per cent were executed.
2. Ewen, 1933: 126–30; Thomas, 1971: 459; Levack, 1996: 108–10. Unsworth, 1989: 91–2, identifies the judges who were hostile to witches. One of them, however, Brian Darcy, was not an assize judge but a justice of the peace.
3. Ewen, 1929: 100. In Essex the number of executions peaked in 1602, Macfarlane, 1970: 58.
4. Of 54 bills that have survived from the period 1660–1702, only nine were returned *ignoramus* (Ewen, 1929: 252–6).
5. Larner, Lee and McLachlan, 1977: 40–9, 147–50. In one of the last justiciary commissions, granted 'because of distance' in 1699 to try nine accused witches from Ross-shire, the Privy Council appointed a special committee to decide whether the sentences of the commission should be carried out (Chambers, 1861: 3: 216). The committee was thus serving the same function as the French parlements.
6. Bever, 1983: 369; Schormann, 1977: 19–21. On the few isolated cases in the 1710s, in which the faculty was *not* particularly lenient, see Lorenz, 1995: 239–40.
7. Bever, 1983: 369. On the centrality of the pact in the judicial process in Massachusetts see Godbeer, 1992: ch. 5.
8. See Langbein, 1974 on the place of the private accusation in the system.
9. Klaniczay, 1990b: 171 claims that it forbade 'any kind of witch-hunting'.

Chapter 3

1. Does not include executions in the region of Limburg, which did not belong to the republic at that time. Executions there continued into the 1630s (Gijswijt-Hofstra, 1989: 77–8).

2. See Dienst, 1987: 286–7 for the identification of some of these components in Steiermark witchcraft cases. Carpzov claimed that the 'most atrocious' crime of witchcraft mixed heresy, apostasy, sacrilege, blasphemy and sodomy (Kneubühler, 1977: 162). Scot, 1930: 18, identified 15 separate crimes attributed to witches and recommended separate prosecutions if witches had in fact been guilty of them.

3. Henningsen and Tedeschi, 1986. Martin, 1989, chapter 3, includes necromancy, divination conjuration, charms and magical healing in her definition of the offence of witchcraft. This same terminological imprecision makes it difficult to determine whether the late prosecutions in Spain and Portugal were in fact cases of maleficient witchcraft. For those late trials in Portugal see Corrêa de Melo, 1992: 573–8.

4. See for example the catalogue of defamation suits relating to witchcraft in seventeenth-century Massachusetts in Weisman, 1984: 208–11. For slander in the Netherlands see de Waardt, 1991b: 84–6; Gijswijt-Hofstra, 1991b: 110–11.

5. Sharpe, 1992: 20. For a revealing case towards the end of the period of witch-hunting in 1669 see Ewen, 1933: 459.

6. Meinders, 1716: 112. The *Carolina*, articles 12–14, had required that when a private accuser initiated a suit, he was required to provide surety in order to compensate the accused in the event that the complaint was found to be malicious. As an alternative to the surety, the complainant could be gaoled together with the accused.

7. Baranowski, 1952: 180; Tazbir, 1980: 281n, 299. In 1690 the residents of Gnesen took this process one step further by trying to lynch *the judges* who had acquitted a witch.

PART 2

Witchcraft after the Witch-trials

Marijke Gijswijt-Hofstra

Introduction[1]

The end of the witch-trials did not mean the end of witchcraft, and not even the end of witch-burnings. In 1895 in the Irish village of Ballyvadlea, near Clonmel, the 26-year old Bridget Cleary was beaten and burned to death by her husband in the presence of family and friends (int. al. Jenkins, 1977: 47–8). They assumed that the real Bridget had been abducted by fairies and replaced by a fairy changeling. The trial, also in 1895, was reported in the foreign press. This case (which will be discussed later in more detail) is somewhat atypical, since it did not primarily concern witchcraft, but it is by no means an isolated instance of such violence. Similar incidents occurred from the extreme west to the extreme east of Europe, from Ireland to Russia – in this respect we have less information on the extreme north and south of Europe, although it will be seen that a country such as Italy was also not exempt. In 1879 in the Novgorod district east of Moscow an old woman, allegedly a witch, was locked into her house and burned alive with hearth and home (Frank, 1987: 239–40; Worobec, 1995: 183). From the Walloon area of Belgium there are also reports of witch-burnings right up to the 1880s (Colson, 1898: 62). Even in the twentieth century such reports are not lacking. In 1960 a woman suspected of witchcraft in the Bavarian village of Mailach narrowly escaped death by fire when a neighbour set light to her house (Sebald, 1978: 222–3). In 1984 a woman in Poland was less fortunate, being burned to death in her house by villagers who suspected her of bewitching wells and spreading an epidemic (Schiffmann, 1987: 151–2).

Apart from such extremely violent cases of people taking the law into their own hands, up to the end of the nineteenth century – and also afterwards – there are numerous reports of less, or non-violent reactions to witchcraft suspicions. It is evident, therefore, that thinking and acting in terms of witchcraft continued considerably longer than the witch-trials. Nevertheless the spotlights of historical research have so far been mainly focussed on the period of the prosecutions. The spectacular elements of the 'witch-hunt' have clearly had a greater appeal to the historical imagination than what are called, perhaps in oversimplified terms, 'elementary village credulities' (Trevor-Roper, 1969: 9).

This last point certainly does not apply across the board to the witchcraft research of the past 25 years. The anthropologically inspired studies by Alan Macfarlane (1970) and Keith Thomas (1971) have set the tone for research on the functioning of witchcraft in local communities, even if their example was initially followed only to a limited extent (Gijswijt-Hofstra, 1990). Nevertheless, in so far as we have such studies at our disposal, they still mainly relate to the period of the sixteenth and seventeenth centuries – that of the witch-trials.

As far as the practice of witchcraft in daily life is concerned, the eighteenth and nineteenth centuries have received relatively little attention. Gustav Henningsen's appeal in 1975 (in Danish) that this lacuna be filled, down to the twentieth century, was probably the first of its kind, but was unknown outside this language area until an English version appeared in 1988 (Henningsen, 1975, 1988). In the meantime, however, research was starting up elsewhere into witchcraft after the witch-trials. Initially, the twentieth century enjoyed the most attention, in particular from French and German researchers such as Jeanne Favret-Saada (1977) and Inge Schöck (1978). But midway through the eighties more emphatic attention began to be given to the whole period after the witch-trials, in particular in the circle of Dutch witchcraft researchers (de Blécourt, 1986a, 1990, 1996; Gijswijt-Hofstra, 1990, 1991a). As will be seen below, substantial contributions on witchcraft in the centuries following the witch-trials have recently come from France (Traimond, 1988; Desplat, 1988), the Netherlands (de Blécourt, 1990; de Waardt, 1991a) and England (Davies, 1995), and increasing interest in this period is also apparent in Germany (Labouvie, 1992; Gestrich, 1995; Schöck, 1995).

'Witchcraft', the principal subject of this essay, is in the first instance interpreted in a broad, umbrella sense (see also chapter III, part 2 below, on Germany). Thinking and acting in terms of witchcraft is a useful and culturally accepted strategy for the people involved to employ to combat certain problems. In particular, witchcraft forms part of the whole repertoire that is available to them in the event of misfortune. This is primarily a matter of harm and the resultant reactions; that is to say, the attribution of a misfortune to bewitchment by someone else – the female or male witch – and the exercise of counter-magic or white magic to cope with or prevent such a bewitchment. The ways in which people have thought and acted in terms of witchcraft in different cultures and groups show not only similarities but also important differences. The 'witch' was expected to do her, or his, maleficent work, with or without help from the devil, by means of an evil look, a curse, a touch, or in some similar way. The identity of the person suspected of causing a bewitchment depended partly on the current image and stereotyping of witches, partly on the reputation for witchcraft which that person had built up over the years, and partly on the nature and quality of her, or his, relations with the bewitched – a neighbour or a relative with whom there might be strained relations. When anybody suspected that witchcraft was involved in a misfortune they could themselves take countermeasures or call in the help of an unwitching specialist. The examples mentioned above show that this could sometimes get seriously out of hand.

The core question in what follows is the extent to which 'enchanted' Europe lost ground after the witch-trials, and more particularly after the judicial prosecutions for harmful witchcraft had become things of the past. Clearly, the end of the trials did not by itself mark and herald the 'decline of magic'. Indeed, the marginalization of witchcraft came about much less smoothly and straightforwardly than has been assumed in the past. The question of the decline of witchcraft thus finds its counterpart in the question of its continuity. What ultimately matters is when, why, where, for whom, and in what respects thinking and acting in terms of witchcraft did or did not lose their significance. To what extent, both in the course of time and in various European regions or countries, was there a reduction in the domain and the frequency of bewitchments? Who continued to be involved in bewitchments, and who dropped out? Was witchcraft in these later centuries significantly a matter for the lower strata of society, for the rural areas, and, as indicated in Dutch research, for women? To what extent was there a depersonalization of witchcraft over time, whereby the attribution of misfortune to bewitchment was no longer accompanied by the designation of a culprit? Formulated more generally: what patterns of witchcraft can be distinguished in the course of time all over Europe, and what is the relationship between continuity and change in this history?

These and other related questions provide the guidelines for the tour through Europe that I have attempted. There can be no question of a synthesis, given the present state of research. Thus, the accent will be on drawing up the present balance of the research – a *status quaestionis* as it were – displaying its achievements, but also pointing out the hiatuses. Here, the investigation of witchcraft after the witch-trials will have to come to a provisional end about 1900, since the twentieth century is reserved for another volume of this series. Nevertheless there is no question of a distinct caesura round 1900.

The starting point, likewise, is not clear-cut: the witch-trials, especially the cases against people who were suspected of harmful witchcraft and/or a pact with the devil, ended earlier in one place and later in another. In view of the fact that this is less well documented than the end of the death sentences for this offence, the last judicial executions will be used as an indication of the usually somewhat later end of the witch-trials. For Europe as a whole this can be situated between the second half of the seventeenth and the end of the eighteenth centuries. Hence, our discussion has to begin not in the year 1700 or thereabouts, but, depending on the area in question, somewhere within this 'long eighteenth century'.

Furthermore, it should also be noted in this context that, as a rule, neither the end of the witch-trials nor the end of the witch-burnings marked an abrupt change of mentality on the part of the judiciary, let alone on the part of those directly involved in bewitchments. That from a given moment onwards no more death sentences were pronounced or no further trials were held, is to be seen, rather, as the more or less arbitrarily situated end point, often not recognized as such by contemporaries, of a process that had already started earlier and can only with hindsight be characterized as the 'decriminalization' of witchcraft (Soman, 1989). Just as the end of the death sentences or of the trials did not necessarily represent a clean break with the preceding decades, so the lack of witch-trials does not necessarily indicate that the judiciary had completely distanced itself from witchcraft and that scepticism reigned supreme.

At the beginning of the tour two other problems crop up, namely the question of what criterion to use for geographical classifications and the question of which route to follow. The choice of former political frontiers seems to cope with first of these, although there is the complication that these changed in the course of time. Moreover, the size of political units differed considerably, and, even in comparatively small countries, there could be substantial internal differences of opinion with regard to pros-ecution policy. For our purposes – we are after all concerned with the period after the witch-trials – it nevertheless seems justifiable to ignore these differences and confine ourselves to a broader approach, simply travelling from country to country.

The route is mainly determined by the chronology of the last death sentences: countries where this moment came at an early stage and for which, consequently, a longer period has to be discussed, will be dealt with first. In order not to make the route too erratic, account has also been taken of geographical proximity. The route goes (using present day names) from the Netherlands via Belgium to France and to the Mediter-ranean countries of Portugal, Spain and Italy. From there we go more abruptly to Ireland, England and Scotland, thereafter to the Scandinavian countries, followed by Eastern and Central Europe, ending up in Germany and Switzerland. It must, however, be repeated that the prosecution policy in these countries could differ considerably between jurisdictions and that the order chosen here gives only a partial and incomplete indication of the end of the witch-trials.

At the end of the tour there will be an opportunity to draw up the balance. As has been said, given the current state of research, it is too early for a synthesis. In so far as the material permits, a broad comparative indication will be given of the patterns of witchcraft which have become apparent along the way, of the changes to be seen in these patterns in the course of the eighteenth and nineteenth centuries, and of the extent to which there can be said to be a break with the preceding period. Attention will also be paid to the interpretation of these later developments, in particular of the decline of witchcraft. Finally we shall raise the yet more comprehensive subject of 'cultures of misfortune' – that is the whole repertoire on which people could draw in the event of misfortune or to prevent misfortune, and witchcraft's part in it. The disenchantment of Europe was not an isolated phenomenon and, in turn, did not leave the rest of the repertoire of misfortune untouched.

CHAPTER 1

From the Low Countries to France

THE NETHERLANDS AND THE ENCHANTED WORLD

In 1692, when Balthasar Bekker was removed from office as a minister of the Reformed church on account of the publication of the first two parts of his book *De betoverde weereld* (Stronks, 1991; Levack and Porter in this volume), he could not have imagined that three centuries later the world, in this case the Netherlands, would still to some extent be under the ban of witchcraft. Not only have bewitchments occurred in this country well into the twentieth century, even up to the present day, but historical witchcraft has also attracted considerable scholarly interest. Dutch witchcraft research, which between 1982 and 1994 was concentrated in an active interdisciplinary study group, produced some stimulating publications (Gijswijt-Hofstra, 1992). Witchcraft after the witch-burnings received a proportionately large amount of attention, at least compared with research in most other countries. Perhaps this was natural in view of the relatively early termination of the death sentences in the Dutch Republic at the beginning of the seventeenth century. What was more important, however, was the favourable situation in Dutch witchcraft research in the 1980s: a number of imaginative researchers emerged almost simultaneously and were able mutually to inspire one another.

Willem de Blécourt was the pioneer with an unpublished master's thesis on witchcraft in the Dutch province of Drenthe from the sixteenth up to and including the twentieth century (1983), followed by Willem Frijhoff with an article on witchcraft in East Gelderland from the sixteenth into the twentieth century (1984). Shortly afterwards de Blécourt advocated what he called a paradigmatic shift of attention from witch-trials towards witchcraft, which also meant that the later centuries would have to be involved in the research (1986a). He has put this into practice in numerous publications, including his doctoral thesis which is also on witchcraft in Drenthe from the sixteenth up to, and including, the twentieth century (1990). The doctoral thesis of Hans de Waardt on witchcraft in the province of Holland between 1500 and 1800 (1991a) is another example of research which traces witchcraft over a long period. The two volumes published by the study group (de Blécourt and Gijswijt-Hofstra [eds], 1986; Gijswijt-Hofstra and Frijhoff [eds], 1987) – parts of the last volume also appeared in English (1991) – contain further articles in which research into witchcraft after the witch-trials is presented. In addition, an annotated bibliography of publications on witchcraft in the Netherlands appearing between 1795 and 1985 (to about 1989) has been completed under the editorship of members of the study group (Matter et al [eds], 1990).

What has all this produced for our understanding of the later period? Above all, it has led to more systematic knowledge of the functioning of witchcraft in the northeastern Netherlands (de Blécourt), the former province of Holland (de Waardt) and, to a more modest extent, the province of Zeeland (Gijswijt-Hofstra, 1986, 1991b). The sources which have brought this to light vary from judicial, notarial and ecclesiastical archives to contemporary publications, newspaper reports and legends.

We can begin with the province of Holland, the most urbanized part of the Dutch Republic. The last witch-trial took place in 1659 in a rural area in the north of Holland. It concerned a woman who was suspected of having given her three, according to her, stillborn children to Satan. When the children's coffins were found to contain only dummies, she was imprisoned and ultimately condemned to be pilloried with three dummies in her arms, although the bailiff had demanded the death sentence. This took place some forty years after the last death sentence in this province had been carried out on a witch in 1608 in Gorinchem. During these forty years only a handful of witch-trials had been held. In some of the smaller towns or rural districts the judicial authorities had shown in other ways that they certainly took witchcraft seriously, for example when they were called upon to force a woman to unwitch a bewitched person (de Waardt, 1991a: 226–9). But in the larger towns the magistrates had already dissociated themselves from witchcraft earlier on.

Though the magistrates may have refused to hold witch-trials or to assist a bewitched person earlier in some places than others, they were nevertheless fairly regularly confronted with cases of slander or maltreatment in connection with witchcraft, and they also continued to take action against cunning men and witch-doctors. They also had to deal with lynchings. Two cases of lynching are known from the first half of the seventeenth century, namely in 1624 in Amsterdam and in 1628 in Schiedam, where the victim was thrown into the water and drowned (de Waardt, 1991a: 211–12). In the eighteenth century there was also at least one occasion in Holland (as will be described below) when someone suspected of a bewitchment was killed, though no longer by drowning.

Up to the beginning of the eighteenth century Reformed church councils took disciplinary measures against members who had accused others of causing a bewitchment or had called in the help of an unwitching specialist. People accused of witchcraft also used the services of notaries public to draw up attestations which could if necessary be useful later on to clear their own name before the courts. The involvement of all these bodies with witchcraft accusations declined steeply from the end of the seventeenth century onwards.

On the basis of various of sources, such as the archives of the Court of Holland, the criminal accounts of the provincial authorities, the register of sentences kept by aldermen's benches, the notarial and ecclesiastical archives of seven Dutch towns, and printed sources (including juridical and theological works) de Waardt established that the belief in witchcraft was still to be found around 1600 in broad strata of Dutch society, but that in practice certain categories of people no longer took part in the witchcraft discourse. This applied to university-trained doctors and lawyers, who acknowledged in theory that witchcraft was possible but, from as early as the late sixteenth century onwards, were less and less inclined to recognize witchcraft as the cause of sickness. As a rule, trained theologians from Protestant *and* Catholic circles adhered to the possibility of an explicit pact with the devil until well into the seventeenth century, but in many cases they too attached no credence to statements by members of their churches that they were bewitched or had concluded such a pact. This was with the exception of the Jesuits, who for propaganda reasons were only too keen to exorcize such people (de Waardt 1991a, 1993).

It is noticeable, in any case, that, in the sixteenth century and also in the centuries after, the devil and the pact seldom played a part in witchcraft accusations in Holland and the rest of the Dutch Republic, as these were expressed by those directly involved. Beyond the formal indictments, which were formulated during a criminal trial, there was usually no link made between the devil and bewitchments. Various examples are known from the seventeenth century of women and men who related that they had concluded a pact with the devil in exchange for certain considerations, but without there being any question of witchcraft being involved (de Waardt, 1989, 1991a; Rooijakkers, Dresen-Coenders and Geerdes [eds], 1994).

De Waardt further establishes that after 1600, apart from the above-mentioned academics, men on the whole took no further part in the witchcraft discourse. Not only was it traditionally very unusual in Holland for men to be accused of bewitching, but from the first decade of the seventeenth century they were seldom the victims of bewitchment either. Moreover, witchcraft accusations seldom came from their direction. This at least is apparent from the archives consulted by de Waardt down to the end of the seventeenth century. Whether men were no longer involved in witchcraft discourse in the domestic domain either is more difficult to establish. That men, as is shown by some incidents from around 1660, were literally kept outside the door when women wanted to entice an alleged witch into the house to bless the bewitched person, could indeed indicate, according to de Waardt, that suspicions arose predominantly among women (de Waardt, 1991a: 140–1). However, it does not seem very likely that men could completely dissociate themselves – assuming that they wanted to – from such deliberations, if only because it was usually difficult for such things to escape their notice. Even if they were not involved in the first suspicions and imputations, they would have had to come to an opinion at a later stage. That men could certainly share in the suspicions of (their) women is evident, for instance, from cases brought against them (also after the seventeenth century) for the maltreatment and even lynching of alleged witches.

As de Waardt also indicates, from around 1600 onwards a reduction can be observed in the range of targets for witchcraft. Activities which took place outside the home, in public places, were virtually no longer affected by witchcraft. Activities reserved for men, such as shipping, seem no longer to have been threatened. In the seventeenth century there were only very occasionally cases of bewitched cows or churns and sometimes of a bewitched horse. In other words, the means of livelihood were no longer threatened by witchcraft in Holland, a change which de Waardt partly ascribes to the favourable economic developments in this province. By far the majority of the bewitchments registered after 1600 concerned the health of people and, above all, of children. Those who were accused of causing them were women (de Waardt, 1991a: 283).

As unwitching experts men – and also women – certainly continued to play a role in the confirmation and steering of witchcraft suspicions. In the seventeenth century they still appear fairly regularly in the archives of Holland; after that, far less. Halfway through the seventeenth century the willingness of Catholic priests to assist the bewitched had in the meantime considerably decreased; only the Jesuits still clearly exhibited enthusiasm (de Waardt, 1991a: 245–9; 1993).

De Waardt has devoted considerably less archival research to the eighteenth century than to the preceding period. But the involvement of the various bodies with witchcraft accusations sharply decreased towards the end of the seventeenth century – judicial archives from the following century have not been systematically investigated – and in eighteenth-century writings witchcraft belief was more and more contested, while no concrete witchcraft accusations were reported. He therefore concludes that in the eighteenth century people still believed in the possibility of a bewitchment, but that preventive measures made such accusations unnecessary (de Waardt, 1991a: 285).

A more general problem presents itself here, namely the extent to which information from sources of this kind can be regarded as a reliable gauge of the course of, or the fluctuations in, witchcraft accusations in a particular period. It is after all possible that the decreasing involvement of, for example, judicial and ecclesiastical bodies says more about the attitude of these bodies themselves than about the frequency of witchcraft accusations (Holmes, 1993). A similar methodological comment must be made where shifts in the nature of the bewitchments and the involvement of women and men are concerned. On the basis of the cases found in the sources – for example, those to do with maltreatment and slander questions or against unwitching specialists – to what extent is it possible to generalize about those which did *not* come to the attention of these same bodies? These are questions which can, and really should, be asked in every enquiry, even if historians usually cannot give any answers to them because the sources are seldom adequate enough.

In any case, whether witchcraft accusations in the eighteenth century were indeed a rarity in Holland requires further examination. This applies also, for example, to the degree to which they were accompanied by violence. To what extent was the drama in Huizen in 1746 an exception? It concerned a widow, Rijntje Boom, who lived in the same house as Gerrit Slocher and his wife. Rijntje was suspected by them of having bewitched their seven weeks old child. Assisted by three men, all living in Huizen, Slocher had done literally everything possible to persuade the unwilling widow to bless his sick child and remove the bewitchment. Even a confrontation with elder tree canes, which had been fetched in the meantime, could not move her. The men had then taken it in turns to beat her back for an hour at a time. Rijntje had died as a result. The culprits were banished in absentia from Holland and Westfriesland for ever on pain of death. The background to this case is (still) obscure: had Rijntje already acquired a reputation as a witch; had the relations between her and the Slochers been tense for some time and if so, why; or did the suspicion come as a bolt from the blue (de Waardt, 1991a: 215, note 13; Gijswijt-Hofstra, 1997)?

Very little has been published on nineteenth-century witchcraft in Holland. De Waardt thinks that around 1800 belief in witchcraft had become restricted to a fairly small group of people whom he does not specify more exactly. This did not mean that in the nineteenth century, which falls outside his study, there were no more witchcraft affairs. De Waardt reports that at the beginning of the nineteenth century a saddler in Gorinchem had a flourishing practice as an unwitching specialist among the farmers in the vicinity of this town. The son who later took over his father's business also carried on the unwitching activities, as did a descendant from the following generation. This Gorinchem information indicates that in the nineteenth century men, even in the role of the bewitched, were not totally unconnected with the witchcraft discourse. The question of continuity and discontinuity with regard both to men's involvement in witchcraft – either in their capacity as unwitching specialists or as (family of) victims of a bewitchment – and to the way in which witchcraft was dealt with – preventively and/or reactively with concrete accusations – cannot be satisfactorily solved without further research.

My own research project (1986, 1991b), conducted on a more limited scale but continuing into the twentieth century, has focused on witchcraft in the much less urbanized province of Zeeland, in the south-west of the Netherlands. In 1835 and 1854 there were still two cases of maltreatment in connection with witchcraft suspicions brought before the courts. This will have been the usual tip of the usual iceberg. The dramas both took place in the village of St Annaland and they exhibit a similar pattern; in both cases the parties belonged to working-class circles; in both it was illness (of a child and a grown woman respectively) that was attributed to bewitchment; and in both a married woman – in one case in her thirties, in the other some 20 years older – was suspected of the bewitchment and was compelled by force by one or more male relatives of the sick person to remove the bewitchment. Unwitching specialists were not involved: people took the law into their own hands. Unfortunately the sources do not provide any insight regarding the quality of the relationships between the parties involved in the period preceding the bewitchment question. Thus it is not clear whether there had been tense relations earlier on. In any case, the parties were not related to one another, but lived near each other – not, however, next door – and therefore presumably had regular contact in some way.

In Zeeland, where a great deal of material from the old judicial archives has been lost, it is possible that the period without witch-trials dawned soon after 1565, the year in which two women accused of witchcraft in Veere were put to death by burning. From the subsequent period up to the mid-seventeenth century several slander cases and cases against cunning men are known, while the church council proceedings of the Reformed churches reveal, well into the second half of that century, disciplinary measures against members who had participated in counter-magic, had consulted a witch-doctor or had accused someone else of harmful witch-craft. So far the eighteenth century has not produced any witchcraft cases for Zeeland; it is certainly possible that the archives of the civil authorities and of notaries may contain witchcraft cases which have not yet been reported, but there was presumably little, if any, further ecclesiastical involvement, as in Holland and other areas of the Dutch Republic which have been examined on this point. It is difficult to establish whether church councils had less reason for disciplinary measures in this respect, or took a more detached attitude, felt less threatened by 'popish superstitions' (as they had termed counter-magic), and found it less fitting to talk about witchcraft. As has been mentioned, there were witchcraft affairs still in store for Zeeland during the nineteenth century.

Another area which has been studied for the period after the witch-trials, at least for the seventeenth century, is the county of Vollenhove in the eastern province of Overijssel (de Blécourt and Pereboom, 1991). Here too, in this predominantly rural area bordering on the Zuiderzee, criminal sentences were a thing of the past. However, the number of witchcraft cases found in judicial and ecclesiastical archives from the seventeenth century is proportionately larger than in Holland and Zeeland. Whether this can be regarded as an indication of the greater frequency of witchcraft affairs is difficult to say, partly because of lacunae in the records. In the county of Vollenhove also, church councils concerned themselves mainly with members of the congregation who had practised counter-magic or had consulted a witch-doctor. Judicial authorities took action against witch-doctors and were kept quite busy dealing with slander cases resulting from witchcraft insults.

De Blécourt's research shows that in the neighbouring province of Drenthe, where scarcely any witch-trials and no death sentences for witchcraft are known, there were also numerous slander cases in connection with being called a witch and the like, the last in 1785. Here too – up to the end of the nineteenth century – the civil authorities took action against unwitching specialists. As far as can be gathered from the source material, initially and through to about the mid-seventeenth century, both women and men were involved. After that women virtually disappeared from the picture, while male laymen replaced the Catholic priests.

On account of the lack of local sources it is only partially possible to discover the attitude of local church councils to witchcraft. According to de Blécourt it is clear from visitation reports and minutes of meetings of the classis and the synod, that the attitude of the ministers in Drenthe corresponded with that of their colleagues elsewhere in the Dutch Republic; they played a reconciliatory role in cases of witchcraft accusations. In addition, they called the attention of the civil authorities to witch-doctors, magical healers and similar types of specialists, at any rate until the beginning of the eighteenth century after which the authorities also showed little further interest in such people. As elsewhere, the Church took disciplinary measures against members who consulted such specialists. In the course of the seventeenth and eighteenth centuries this also applied to church members who had been the victims of theft and then accused a certain person with the aid of such a specialist.

What were the changes to which witchcraft in Drenthe was subject from the seventeenth to the twentieth centuries? To discover this de Blécourt has examined all the available sources dealing with witchcraft, including from the mid-nineteenth century onwards newspaper reports and later legends, and also collected other information about those involved. His analysis is based on the reconstruction of the indigenous meanings of witchcraft accusations, for the purpose of which he asks questions derived from the 'ethnography of speaking' regarding form, content, participants, effect, norms, circumstances, and genre (de Blécourt, 1990: 30–1). One of the most important aspects of this work is that it situates a witchcraft insult as a pronouncement by one person addressing another, leading to many insights into the social directions of accusations. Drenthe presents a picture which partly corresponds to that in Holland. Thus, the involvement of men in bewitchments decreased, both as accusers and also as bewitched persons. While in the seventeenth century the accusations had mainly come from them, it was predominantly women who subsequently made them, as a rule still against women. In Drenthe, however, this change happened about a century later than in Holland (de Blécourt, 1990: 242).

Moreover, in Drenthe, in contrast to what is suggested for Holland, bewitchment accusations also occurred in the eighteenth century, and would continue occurring into the twentieth century. Nevertheless, the numerical fluctuations in the Drenthe bewitchments – in so far as these are revealed by the archives – show similarities with those in Holland: in Drenthe too there were scarcely any cases between 1650 and 1750, after which the last quarter of the eighteenth century produced a fresh wave. For the nineteenth century a decrease in the number of bewitchments can be assumed, although the 1880s still show a slight peak. Just as de Waardt does for Holland, de Blécourt links the fluctuations in the witchcraft accusations to economic and demographic developments. Thus bewitchments of small children, the most prevalent type in the nineteenth century, are linked to the high degree of fertility in marriage in the peat communities of south-west Drenthe, where all bewitchments were concentrated in this period. Moreover, in these same peat areas orthodox Calvinism and Catholicism had a large following. Among the liberal Reformed farming population of the sandy areas bewitchments no longer occurred. Indeed, outside Drenthe too, orthodox Calvinism appears to have provided a fertile breeding ground for belief in witchcraft right into the twentieth century, as for instance in the previously mentioned village of St Annaland on the Zeeland island of Tholen. In this connection de Blécourt speaks of a Bible belt, or 'black belt'; and in the Netherlands people still talk about the 'black stocking church', which stretched from the islands of Zeeland in the south-west through the area between the great rivers and the lowlands of Utrecht to the borders of the former Zuiderzee and from there right into the north-east of Friesland (de Blécourt, 1989a, 1996: 349–50).

What also altered in Drenthe were the relative social positions of accuser and accused; while in the seventeenth century accusations were usually aimed lower down the social ladder, in the eighteenth century the reverse was true and witches were often women with a higher social status than the bewitched. For the nineteenth century the social trend of the accusations cannot be discovered. In Drenthe suspicion also fell mainly on a woman neighbour or someone else from the same village with whom there was regular contact.

The content of bewitchments in Drenthe between the seventeenth and the nineteenth centuries seems to have been less subject to change than in Holland; women were labelled as having caused the sickness or death of adults and children (as mentioned, the most common forms of bewitchment in the nineteenth century) or the failure of the butter making, while the few bewitchments ascribed to men concerned cattle or horses. How it came about that people attributed such misfortunes to bewitchment cannot be established in the majority of the cases. For Drenthe – and this applies for the most part to the other Dutch provinces – there are no indications that witchcraft accusations were preceded by conflicts, as in the case, for example, of Essex at the time of the witch-trials (Macfarlane, 1970). In so far as information is available, it points rather to a reasonably good relationship between accuser and accused preceding the bewitchment.

As well as bewitching, de Blécourt also distinguishes unwitching, witching and scolding. A woman from the neighbourhood would be suspected of bewitching, a man from a nearby hamlet of witching, while it was usually an outsider who gave expert advice on unwitching. Men who were taken for witches and possibly also werewolves were thought to enrich themselves with the aid of witchcraft ('to witch'). Such accusations were concentrated in periods of economic growth; obviously, some men profited from this more than others. The accusations were mainly expressed by young men who wanted to frighten off rivals in the marriage market by making the father, and thus also the family, of the desired girl suspect. Such accusations came to an end at the beginning of the eighteenth century, during the same period when men also dissociated themselves from bewitchment accusations. About this time a change can also be observed in what de Blécourt calls 'scolding'; whereas in the seventeenth century the insult 'toveres' (witch) was used both to compare a person to a witch and also as a reference to a bewitchment, in the eighteenth century the insult 'heks' (witch – this word only became established in the course of the seventeenth century) and 'heksenpak' (coven of witches) were uttered to compare the woman or family in question with a witch *without* there being any question of a bewitchment. In the eighteenth century, in so far as this can be inferred from the available sources, scolding someone as a witch, which was often accompanied by other negative characterizations, such as 'whore', had become a purely female affair. Contrary to the situation with witchcraft accusations, slanging matches of this kind, found up to the nineteenth century, gave expression to already existing conflicts.

To undo a bewitchment might require the help of an unwitching specialist. A good example from towards the end of the eighteenth century is the Catholic Derk Hilberdink of Meppel (Drenthe), an established witch-doctor and a weaver's hand (de Blécourt, 1986b, 1990: 145–52). His fame as a healer spread like wildfire when one person after another benefitted from his treatment. This was often in cases of chronic conditions for which neither the doctors nor barber-surgeons were able to produce a remedy. Hilberdink's diagnoses of bewitchment, his veiled accusations in the direction of 'evil people' and his partly ritualised remedies had the desired result. Even people who had earlier expressed their disbelief in the possibility of bewitchments, could apparently be made to change their view by clients of Hilberdink, and to join the ranks of the 'believers', albeit perhaps only temporarily, by going to see him.

It is not possible to trace how often and in what proportion people did or did not decide to consult a specialist, or how and why such a choice was usually made. But on the basis of the rather better documented cases it seems that gossip played an important role. Unwitching specialists were mostly outsiders and often lived in a different place from those who sought their help. In any case, no further unwitching specialists are to be found in the eighteenth-century archives from Drenthe. Hilberdink was an exception by the end of that century. Help in unwitching would presumably have been mainly sought outside the province. This pattern continued in the nineteenth century. From the second half of the nineteenth century onwards, witch-doctors from neighbouring Friesland were popular, in addition to those from Overijssel. What also occurred fairly regularly among this group was that the occupation passed from father to son or sometimes daughter (de Blécourt, 1988, 1990, 1991).

Their advice was no longer directed to the unmasking of witches, but to healing the harm caused by bewitchments with the aid of medicines. That a witch-doctor could also recommend unwitching rituals is evident from newspaper reports from 1862 concerning Sjoerd Brouwers. He advised two farmers to let their bewitched children drink a herbal brew and jump over their pet cat three times a day. For an 18-year old girl suffering from nausea, headaches, backache and stomachache he recommended rubbing her toes between twelve and one o'clock at night with pig's blood in which a cock's head had been boiled. After this her father had to ride her round the house three times in a wheelbarrow. The medicines were to be buried and every other day before sunrise they were to be smelt. Two weeks after this report, the newspaper announced that the girl had been delivered of a chubby baby boy (de Blécourt, 1990: 177).

Up to now no systematic research into witchcraft after the witch-trials has been carried out for other parts of the Netherlands. Apart from research on the popularity of Frisian witch-doctors (inter alia 1988, 1991), de Blécourt has done a study of cunning women in the north-eastern part of the Netherlands in the nineteenth and beginning of the twentieth centuries. This was also based on folk legends and newspaper reports (de Blécourt, 1989b). In so far as cunning women still gave advice in this period it was, apart from the odd vagrant, only available in towns such as Deventer and Zwolle. For the most part they concentrated increasingly on predicting the future, including naming future marriage partners, and by the nineteenth century had scarcely anything more to do with healing (de Blécourt, 1992). The most popular unwitching specialists in the north-eastern provinces were the predominantly male witch-doctors in the Friese Wouden. Apart from this, bewitched people from the recently opened up peat districts quite often sought help from local blessers – men who healed by means of the laying on of hands and the muttering of prayers – and from Roman Catholic priests (de Blécourt, 1989b, 1990).

Finally, from the provinces of Twente and Gelderland, which border on Germany, it can be reported that the water ordeal, which was used there as a legal means of proof up to the beginning of the seventeenth century, was used informally for some time afterwards where there was a suspicion of harmful witchcraft. Sometimes this took place at the request of the accused woman, as was the case in 1823 with the last known water ordeal in the Netherlands in the Twente village of Deldenerbroek. Hendrika Hofhuis, a 42-year old married, Reformed woman, was turned away from a neighbour's childbed and accused of having caused her sickness by bewitchment. Hendrika decided to prove her innocence by means of the water ordeal. She gave as the reason that she had heard people say that witches could walk over the water without sinking (Schlüter, 1991: 94). Watched by several hundred people she came through the ordeal with flying colours – she sank and was hauled up on a rope before it was too late. Once Hendrika's innocence was established, her relationship with the woman in childbed could be restored.

In the neighbouring Gelderland village of Eibergen, however, the water ordeal undergone by Aaltje Brouwers in 1694 proved insufficient to clear her of the suspicion of witchcraft, in spite of the fact that she sank. She decided to undergo a second test, this time in the weighing house in Oudewater in the province of Holland, where weighing took place into the first half of the eighteenth century (de Waardt, 1991a, 1994). Aaltje was not found to be too light, but the classis of the Reformed church nevertheless excluded her from the Lord's Supper. This was not because the Church suspected her of a bewitchment, but because the water ordeal and the weighing ordeal shamed the 'true Reformed religion' and served to strengthen 'superstitious popery' (Frijhoff, 1991: 178). The tension between the attitude of the Church and the witchcraft beliefs of her fellow villagers placed Aaltje in a quandary, for she was after all concerned with both the Church and her neighbours.

All in all, the Netherlands, at least as far as research has gone, presents a picture of variety. Belief in the possibility of bewitchments is reported right into the twentieth century. In urbanized areas, in the better circles, and among men witchcraft lost ground earlier than in the country, or among people on the lower rungs of the social ladder, or among women. Bewitchments became increasingly restricted to the domestic sphere, with children becoming a relatively popular target. It also seems that witchcraft found a comparatively favourable breeding ground among orthodox Calvinists. It is not inconceivable that the same applies to Roman Catholics, in view of the part which priests played as unwitching specialists at least into the nineteenth century. While in an urbanized region such as Holland a more depersonalized approach to witchcraft – invoking prevention instead of the tracing of the witch – is already apparent in the eighteenth century, a similar development in rural Drenthe can only be observed about a century later, although it seems that here it was not so much the prevention as the cure of the bewitchment that mattered most. Later reports of violent action on the part of the bewitched – such as two from Zeeland in the nineteenth century and even a last Frisian case from the mid-twentieth century – nevertheless make it clear that the depersonalization of witchcraft did not take place all over the country and certainly not to the same extent.

BELGIUM: FROM WITCH-TRIALS TO WITCH-LYNCHINGS?

There has been comparatively little research into witchcraft in Belgium after the witch-trials (Gijswijt-Hofstra, 1992), while for the Grand Duchy of Luxembourg it is virtually non-existant. The principal contributions on later Belgian witchcraft come from Marie-Sylvie Dupont-Bouchat. They comprise a study of the policy of the Roman Catholic church in the diocese of Malines with regard to witchcraft and 'superstition' in the period 1565 to 1793, reconstructed on the basis of reports of decanal visitations (Dupont-Bouchat, 1984 and 1987), and a recent essay, based on various sources, on magic and witchcraft in Belgium and France in the eighteenth and especially the nineteenth centuries (Dupont-Bouchat, 1994). Apart from this, there has been research into witchcraft and superstition in seventeenth- and eighteenth-century sermon books from the church province of Malines (Maesschalck, 1995), and individual cases of witchcraft from the eighteenth and nineteenth centuries have been rescued from obscurity in sporadic articles. The kind of systematic research, based on a diversity of sources, into eighteenth- and nineteenth-century witchcraft in specific regions or places that is available for certain areas of the Netherlands, is so far lacking for Belgium and Luxembourg. On the other hand, the use of ecclesiastical visitation reports and sermon books represents a welcome supplement and this example deserves to be followed elsewhere, including the Netherlands.

In the Southern Netherlands, which, except for the prince-bishopric of Liège, was under the rule of the Spanish Habsburgs down to 1715, the last death sentences for witchcraft, both in the Flemish and also in the Walloon region, were carried out in the 1680s. But from the 1630s onwards a considerable decrease in the number of executions at the stake can already be seen. After 1650 witch-trials, apart from a few exceptions, belonged to the past (Dupont-Bouchat, 1984: 72–3). But this did not apply to the belief in witchcraft. During the later centuries there are numerous scattered accounts of lynchings or maltreatment of supposed witches and of the actions of unwitching specialists. The problem is that in view of the state of the research, it is not possible to gain anything like a complete picture of the development, distribution and importance of witchcraft beliefs and practices among different groups of the population.

From the ecclesiastical visitation reports and sermon books, which of course primarily reflect the normative viewpoints of the Church authorities, it can be concluded that witchcraft and other forms of what the Roman Catholic church branded as superstition formed a source of concern until halfway through the eighteenth century. From the decanal visitation reports of the diocese of Malines it appears that conversion, not chastisement, was the most important issue. Indeed, this seems to be characteristic of ecclesiastical policy in general, as far as the period after the witch-trials is concerned. A similar policy was, after all, pursued by the Dutch Reformed church councils, as we have seen, and we will later find that the Mediterranean inquisitions were also primarily intent on conversion and reconciliation.

In the Malines visitation reports 87 cases of witchcraft and superstition are to be found between 1572 and 1743, only five of which were post-1700 (Dupont-Bouchat, 1987). The last report of a witch dates from 1643. After that, reports of witchcraft are almost exclusively concerned with unwitching; cunning men and women and also exorcists – always men, often priests – had to suffer for it. Moreover, male familiarity with the devil finds expression in a few cases where a satanic pact is concluded by a man. Whether women were less associated with the pact after the period of the witch-trials than before cannot be determined from this material. Nor is it clear to what extent the church intervened in favour of the accused in cases of witchcraft accusations. In any case, the involvement of priests in unwitching and exorcism, whatever their superiors thought of it, will have contributed to the reinforcement of witch-belief among their parishioners, at least up to the eighteenth century and probably later still.

From Maesschalck's analysis of sermon books and catechism explanations from predominantly Flemish Roman Catholic clergy it appears that their tendency to think in terms of witchcraft, at first strongly demonologically oriented, lost ground in the eighteenth century and 'natural' explanations of wondrous things gained in importance. The eighteenth-century authors in their midst did not go so far as to exclude the possibility of a person being affected by malevolent witchcraft. Nevertheless, they considered countermagic to be sinful; man's hope must be founded on God. Furthermore, it is interesting that these later authors were in agreement that witchcraft, in contrast to other forms of superstition, scarcely occurred in their time (Maesschalck, 1995: 118–19). To what extent their observations were in keeping with reality is naturally open to question.

Whether the Belgian cases of bewitchment known to us from the eighteenth and nineteenth centuries were exceptions or the tip of the iceberg can only be determined by further research of the kind that has been completed for the Dutch province of Drenthe. From reports in legal periodicals Dupont-Bouchat concludes that after the end of the seventeenth century, when no more witch-trials took place, the Belgian magistrates were still confronted with lynchings and maltreatment of supposed witches. She assumes that the country people, who continued to believe in witchcraft, took control of the situation out of frustration over the lack of co-operation on the part of the judges (Dupont-Bouchat, 1994: 245). This sounds plausible, although one cannot exclude the possibility that at the time of the witch-trials too cases of taking the law into one's own hands already occurred – even if it is questionable what the relative therapeutic significance of witch-trials was, compared with other, violent or non-violent countermeasures in cases of bewitchment. As we shall see in the section on France, in the jurisdiction of the *parlement* of Paris numerous lynchings took place during the very period of the witch-trials (Soman, 1985: 197–8).

Dupont-Bouchat mentions some ten, mainly Walloon, cases of lynching or maltreatment, two of which are from the end of the seventeenth century, one from the beginning of the eighteenth and the rest from the nineteenth century up to 1882. It is not clear whether in this respect she has exhausted the legal periodicals she consulted since publications by other authors show that in the nineteenth century there were more cases of a similar nature. Thus in 1898 the folklorist O. Colson mentioned ten other cases concentrated in the Walloon provinces in the years 1880 and 1890. Reports on the Flemish provinces of Belgium are somewhat scarcer in this respect. What all these cases have in common is that it was very much the rural population that was involved, that it was principally women who were set upon, and that they were not infrequently thrown into fires, resulting in a number of deaths.

One of these tragedies took place in 1815 in Flanders (Bronne, 1957; van Mello, 1984). It all started with a farmer and his wife in Onkerzele who were convinced that their daughter's illness and that of their cattle was caused by the witchcraft of a neighbour, who otherwise had a good name in the village. The farmer enticed the neighbour into his house, blocked the exits and accused her of the bewitchments. When she denied everything, he bound her hands and feet and pulled her, assisted by his wife and daughter, into the fire up to her calves. When the poor woman continued to deny the accusations, they pushed her still further into the flames. Finally, after several hours the farmer pulled her out of the fire and threw her out onto the street unconscious. Although she regained consciousness and could recount her story, she died of her injuries a week later. The farmer was condemned to death and his wife to be branded; their daughter had died in the meantime.

In the Onkerzele drama there was no intervention by an unwitching specialist, but in some of the other nineteenth-century lynchings or cases of maltreatment this did take place. Thus there are cases known from this period where a cunning woman put her client on the track of a witch, or, much less often, on that of a male witch who in the odd case turned out to be the local priest. Apart from this, a member of the clergy could be called in to conduct an exorcism, which did not as a rule imply any search for a malefactor. All in all, there is still very little known about unwitching and unwitching specialists in Belgium. From a case against a Walloon-Brabant 'grimancien' in 1762–3 it can be gathered that he not only unwitched humans and animals, with a female neighbour usually taking the blame, but also, according to the stories of his clients, traced stolen goods and hidden treasure with the help of the devil. Needless to say, these particular clients had a rude awakening (Douxchamps-Lefevre, 1987).

For the eighteenth century Dupont-Bouchat (1994: 237–40) reports a lively use of magical books by men, including priests, in rural Belgium. As indicated by the example just given, even the help of the devil was not spurned by unwitching specialists. Other men also consorted occasionally with the devil and 'witched' for their own financial gain.

Our picture of eighteenth- and nineteenth-century witchcraft in Belgium is, as has been said, far from complete. Compared with the areas dealt with in the Netherlands – the southern Catholic provinces are not included – it is noticeable that in Belgium lynchings and maltreatment of supposed witches occurred fairly regularly until well into the nineteenth century, probably substantially more so than in the Netherlands. If this was indeed the case, it could also indicate a comparatively greater and more prolonged preoccupation with bewitchments. Although principally women were accused of bewitchments, the share of men as accusers and in unwitching, whether professional or not, seems to have remained fairly large, at least until the nineteenth century. Whether men were still calling on the devil for help in the nineteenth century is not clear. It is conceivable that the pattern which is beginning to emerge for Belgium is connected to a considerable extent with the ideas about the devil (and also about the saints) disseminated by the Roman Catholic church and the services rendered by that church in unwitching. Apart from this, the lesser degree of urbanization in Belgium provided a climate in which witchcraft could continue to thrive.

FRANCE: WITCHES, PRIESTS AND THE AMBIGUITY OF UNWITCHING

While witchcraft research in the Netherlands and Belgium, but also for example in Scandinavia, and even in Great Britain, has so far been carried out purely by native speakers, the situation is different for France, the Mediterranean areas, Germany, Switzerland and Eastern Europe. There, foreign researchers, mainly American and British, have also contributed to the reconstruction of the history of witchcraft. As regards France, the harvest for the eighteenth and nineteenth centuries is bigger than else-where in the absolute sense, although there is no one study which covers these two centuries in their totality. The south, with monographs on les Landes de Gascogne (Traimond, 1988) and Béarn (Desplat, 1988) comes off best. Apart from this, attention has been paid more briefly to witchcraft in the *bocage* of the Mayenne (Denier, 1990; Liu, 1994) and in Normandy (le Tenneur, 1991), while non-regionally oriented research, for example on the views of French farmers concerning 'the supernatural' (Devlin, 1987) and on medical practices (Ramsey, 1988), contains substantial information about witchcraft.

With all its diversity as regards approach, scope and use of sources, the French research provides an interesting demonstration of the extent to which the reconstruction and representation of earlier – and also contemporary – witchcraft is determined by research traditions and the attitudes of the researchers. On the one hand, there is the watershed between the periods during and after the witch-trials; historians *of* the witch-trials, however much they differ from one another, are seldom also historians of witchcraft *after* the witch-trials. Thus it is noticeable that areas in northern and eastern France, which have received a great deal of the attention devoted to the period of the witch-trials (Monter, 1976; Muchembled, among others 1979, 1981, 1985 and 1987; Soman, 1992; Briggs, 1989 and 1996a), are among the comparatively neglected areas for the later period. On the other hand, there also tends to be a gap between research which concentrates on the repression of witchcraft and research which is primarily devoted to witchcraft as a part of daily life. This also applies to studies on witchcraft in the eighteenth and nineteenth centuries. Thus in the historian Christian Desplat's study of Béarn (1988), which spans four consecutive centuries up to the beginning of the nineteenth century, the dominant perspective is that of the upper classes who increasingly distanced themselves from witchcraft after the end of the witch-trials, thereby elevating themselves above the 'superstitious' common people. On the other hand, in the study by the ethnologist Bernard Traimond (1988) on les Landes de Gascogne in the period 1750–1926 the emphasis is on what witchcraft meant for the people directly involved and how people coped with it in practice. In addition, research can be categorized as more or less historicizing – that is to say, it is either focused on chronological development and makes allowance for historical contexts, or (and this sometimes coincides with the former) it concentrates on problems and analysis. As will be seen, these factors naturally affect the comparability of the studies, and the extent to which they supplement each other in the reconstruction of witchcraft in the past.

One thing is certain, however: that in France also, at least in the rural areas, witchcraft continued to belong to the cultural repertoire of misfortune after the end of the witch-trials (at the latest the end of the seventeenth century; Soman, 1992; Muchembled, 1994; Levack in this volume). As is shown by the research on twentieth-century witchcraft in, for instance, the *bocage* of the Mayenne (Favret-Saada, 1977), Haute-Bretagne (Camus, 1988), Anjou (Gaboriau, 1987) and Languedoc (Pinies, 1983; Bloch-Raymond and Frayssenge, 1987), this applies right down to the present day (see de Blécourt, 1999). Of course, this still does not say anything about the continuity of, or the fluctuations in witchcraft: these remain to be seen.

What is repeatedly apparent from the French research is the intertwining of witchcraft with the Roman Catholic faith, in the form in which this faith was manifest in the rural areas. Thus a helpful attitude from the village priest in cases of bewitchment could contribute to reinforcing witchcraft-belief and at the same time strengthen the ties between the parishioners and the church. This applied not only to cases of demonic possession, which, for example, in Normandy up to about 1800, if not longer, were 'fed' from this source with a certain degree of regularity (le Tenneur, 1991: 294–310), but also to other forms of bewitchment. As well as this priests did their best to stave off other disasters, such as storms or hail. Moreover, according to reports round 1900, in various parishes it was assumed that priests possessed the gift of divination (Weber, 1979: 26–7). If the priest was a powerful mediator in good fortune and adversity, then saints, of course, had the same function. In fact, the Roman Catholic church provided a whole range of rituals to cope with the ups and downs of life. Parishioners, unwitching specialists and priests could make use of them in ways that might or might not be approved of by the ecclesiastical authorities. The more the pressure that was placed on the position of the Catholic church from the time of the French Revolution onwards, the more the amount of rituals approved by it increased (Kuselman, 1983; Devlin, 1987).

Questions of gender have been given a less prominent place in French witchcraft research on the eighteenth and nineteenth centuries. The exceptions are Traimond's study (discussed below) and the recent article by Tessie P. Liu (1994) on the position of women in farming households in the *bocage* of the Mayenne in the nineteenth century. On the basis of folklore collections compiled in the late nineteenth century Liu shows how bewitchments and unwitching gave expression to conflicting interpretations of 'family interest'.

The target of a bewitchment was always the head of the economic unit – at the same time the head of the family. Regardless of whether he himself was the victim of the bewitchment, or it fell on his wife, children, cattle or harvest, it was the pater familias, as the owner of the indivisible social unit, who was affected. The attacker was to be sought among 'the neighbours'. In practice, according to Liu, he or she frequently turned out to be a member of the same family who was dissatisfied with the settlement of an inheritance. Although in principle all the children were entitled to an equal share in the inheritance, the family business was usually left to *one* male successor, and it could happen that the interests of the other children were made subservient to his. Although Liu does not say so in so many words, and is sparing with examples, her argument implies that a bewitchment was primarily an affair between male relations. This does not alter the fact that it was often the lady of the house who was the first to suggest the possibility of bewitchment, who chose the unwitching specialist, and who took further measures to ward off the attack and safeguard the family interest. In particular, the question-and-answer game between the unwitching specialist, who otherwise remains a background figure in Liu's article, and the person or persons affected by the bewitchment fulfilled an important function; all financial secrets and family conflicts were supposed to come out into the open during this discussion, so that it could become clear who the culprit was.

While Liu is not primarily concerned with witchcraft, let alone its historical development, but rather with the position of women, the article by Marie-Claude Denier (1990), which appeared four years earlier, but escaped Liu's notice, aims also at discovering the main features of witchcraft, including divination and 'magic beliefs' in the *bocage* of the Mayenne for the whole of the eighteenth and nineteenth centuries. On the basis of fifty cases of witchcraft, divination and the unauthorized practice of medicine drawn from the judicial archives, Denier concludes that witchcraft and divination scarcely underwent any change in the course of the two centuries. Indeed, he even carries this argument through to the present day by pointing out that contemporary witchcraft must have roots in past centuries (Denier, 1990: 116).

This observed continuity of witchcraft and divination seems to rest principally on the sort of misfortunes (illness, death and economic damage) which were ascribed to bewitchments and the persons who were held responsible for them or who practised divination. According to Denier, bewitching was mainly a matter for men who were on the lower rungs of the social ladder and belonged to the farming, artisanal or commercial sector in the rural areas, while divination was mainly a matter for women who lived in the country or in the town. The devil was not involved in bewitchments, but he was sometimes in divination, for example, in cases of treasure-seeking. The practice of divination could also extend to the realm of unwitching. There is, however, scarcely any information given about this.

Other matters which also receive inadequate attention in Denier's article are the circumstances under which a suspicion of bewitchment arose, the direction of the suspicion and the problems which might have given rise to it. As long as there is insufficient knowledge about the interrelations between the parties involved and the context in which the bewitchment and the unwitching took place, only very partial and thus unsatisfactory pronouncements can be made about the possible continuity of witchcraft. An additional factor here is that only four of the fifty cases mentioned by Denier date from the eighteenth century; it is not at all clear whether this points to a more active prosecution policy, an increase in bewitchments and unwitchings, or an increase in violence in matters of this kind in the nineteenth century. Moreover, no insight is provided into the distribution of cases which came before the courts in that century. All in all, this provides a somewhat shaky basis for speaking about continuity, or, as Denier puts it, about there being scarcely any change.

This does not alter the fact that Denier's article also contains interesting observations relevant to further research. While Liu concludes from late nineteenth-century folklore collections that bewitchments were ascribed to jealous relatives and unwitching was a matter for the party affected and a hired unwitching specialist, Denier sketches for the same area, but on the basis of legal documents from the nineteenth and partly eighteenth centuries, the outlines of another type of witchcraft – witchcraft as a village affair – which evidently occurred alongside or even preceded the type recorded by Liu – witchcraft as an internal family affair. For bewitchment matters that occurred within a family and were connected with an inheritance, the help of a comparative outsider was called in. In contrast to this, the whole village community was a party in the examples mentioned by Denier.

From eight eighteenth- and nineteenth-century slander cases it can be seen just how much a person's reputation as a witch resulted from the village grapevine. Thus in 1774 a day labourer, Anne Fousset, was not only branded a witch by her fellow villagers, but even thrown into a fire. She managed to escape alive. Twenty years earlier the labourer François Ménard was less fortunate. He and Jeanne Cadot, the wife of another labourer, were accused by a farmer, Mathurin Guéret, of having bewitched his sick daughter over a period of months. Ménard and Cadot already had reputations for harmful witchcraft in the village. The father of the sick child called in the help of his fellow villagers to compel Ménard and Cadot to come to his house and remove the bewitchment. The matter got out of hand when Ménard and Cadot refused; they were both beaten and then set alight, according to one witness on the insistence of the mother of the little girl. Cadot managed to save her life by taking the side of the accusers but Ménard met his death. By presenting a united front the villagers legitimised this violent action. Apparently, no unwitching specialist was involved in these cases.

Attention has already been given to the fact that in Belgium people took the law into their own hands, resorting even to lynching, after the period of the witch-trials. Dupont-Bouchat's (1994) assumption that this sort of violence replaced the witch-trials is, however, contradicted by Alfred Soman's (1985, 1988) material. At least for the jurisdiction of the *parlement* of Paris he records that the decrease in the number of witch-trials was accompanied by a decrease in the number of lynchings (Soman, 1985: 198). In other words, lynchings occurred more often in the period of the witch-trials itself than they did afterwards. But Soman's research goes no further than the seventeenth century. That people in France also took the law into their own hands in a violent manner in later ages is evident not only from the eighteenth-century cases in the Mayenne mentioned above, but also, for example, from research on les Landes de Gascogne (Traimond, 1988) and Béarn (Desplat, 1988), where this sort of reaction to bewitchments is to be found down to the 1820s. Similar occurrences are also known from other parts of France (Devlin, 1987: 113–18). As late as 1902 there was a case in the Tarn where a certain Bertrand and his son were shot dead by a man who had heard from an unwitching specialist that Bertrand had bewitched him with an illness

(Devlin, 1987: 113–14). Questions naturally arise as to how exceptional this was, what regional differences and fluctuations occurred here, and what the circumstances were which led to lynchings or other forms of violence.

As in Belgium, it appears that in France too the domestic hearth was used to force a suspect to perform unwitching. When this led to the death of the suspect, the matter certainly became one for the legal authorities and thus also for the press. But we can assume that a greater number of fire-induced unwitchings with less than fatal consequences escaped the notice of the authorities and thus remain concealed from later researchers. That burnings occurred in various parts of France is apparent from the examples given by Judith Devlin (1987: 115–18) from the years 1820 and 1830. Some of the victims paid with their deaths. For instance, an old woman, who was said to have the evil eye, died of her burns after the local people had set fire to her house at night.

For Béarn Desplat mentions cases of 'grilling' from 1748 and 1826. The outcome of the first case, mentioned only in passing, is not given. Desplat calls the 1826 case, dealt with in more detail, the last burning at the stake, despite the fact that it had no fatal consequences. The person concerned was Marie Peillon, a sixty-year old spinster, reputed to be a witch, from the municipality of Saint-Faust (Basse Pyrénées). According to her own account she was suspected of having bewitched her cousin, the widow Brocq, with an illness; according to other reports the sick person was a neighbour's niece, Sagette. Marie claimed that at the widow's house she was tied to a stake by the tailor Brocq, the brother-in-law of the widow, a certain Pondacq, his sister and Sagette, and that they had then lit a fuse which had been placed round it. Marie received burns on her legs, but managed to break loose just in time. The background to this affair remains obscure, and there are varying reports of the circumstances. As regards the subsequent course of events, it is known that the burgomaster wanted to hush it up, that the prefect then intervened and that a case was brought against Brocq, who thanks to a favourable jury verdict was nevertheless acquitted. Desplat interprets the clemency of the jury as an attempt to trivialize the facts. Whereas local worthies in the eighteenth century were still inclined to concern themselves with so-called witches ('soi-disant sorciers'), in the nineteenth century it was more a question of ignoring 'superstition', shocked as people were about its continuance (Desplat, 1988: 216).

Traimond came across no cases of burnings of supposed witches in les Landes de Gascogne before 1776, but did find other forms of violence against them. Fire entered into ten of the 26 cases of maltreatment traced for the period from 1750 to 1826. In the first half of the nineteenth century the use of fire was popular in this area. Traimond suggests that this was possibly connected with the Holy Heart cult (*le culte du Sacré-Coeur*) which was growing in popularity at that time and in which fire played an important part. But he does not exclude the possibility that the example of the Languedoc, where the earliest known witch-burning dates from 1752 (Traimond, 1988: 166–7), may have had its effect. The example from Béarn from 1748 should also be numbered among these cases (Desplat, 1988: 131).

Like Desplat, Traimond also goes more deeply into a case of burning from 1826. The parallels between the two cases are that in both a woman was suspected of having brought an illness on a woman from another household, men played an important role in the attempts to force the suspected woman to undo the bewitchment, no mention is made of the devil, and there are divergent versions of what happened. A striking difference is that in the bewitchment question dealt with by Traimond an unwitching specialist was called in at an early stage (Traimond, 1988: 17–45). However, he was not directly involved with the dénouement.

What happened here? In one of the hamlets of Mées, a village not far from Dax in the south-west of les Landes, Marie Lavielle, a young woman from a neighbouring village who was looking for work, fell ill shortly after her arrival at the tenant farmstead of Laustes. The rumour rapidly spread that witchcraft was involved and that the farmstead in question was the target. The master of the house, Jean Lacoste, decided to bring in the vet and 'magicien' Pierre Noguès, who was to be found every Saturday at the market in Dax. The healer, who was called Pierron, examined the sick Marie Lavielle in the presence of Lacoste, Pierre Lavielle, a cousin of the sick woman, and the neighbours Marie Basset and Marie Lassale. According to one witness he did this with the aid of herbs, according to another with holy water and the *Grand Albert*, the popular book on magic which repeatedly crops up in stories elsewhere in France and in Belgium. Pierron was not able to pronounce a diagnosis because the guilty party was present. He limited himself to administering medicaments and probably did not point to a culprit, let alone incite violence. In the meantime the occupants of the farmstead were quite sure of what they had to do: the unmarried, presumably somewhat older Marie Lassale, who together with her also unmarried brother and sister lived in the neighbouring farm of Batède, was the malefactor, and she had to undo the bewitchment, willingly or unwillingly. When she maintained that she did not have the bewitchment on her conscience and could not therefore comply with the request, she was beaten with a stick and dragged by her hair onto a sheaf of straw, which was then set alight. As a last resort poor Marie promised to heal the sick woman and thus managed to save her life. Pierre Lavielle and Pierre Lacoste were given prison sentences. The healer Pierre Noguès had got away in time.

There is no need here to go into this episode as exhaustively and penetratingly as Traimond has done. His conclusion is that bewitchments took place within the female circuit, and that men were only involved as outsiders in the roles of unwitching specialists or as house-mates in the event of forcing someone to undo the bewitchment. Witchcraft was one of the possibilities for expressing conflicts which arose between neighbours. A problem which, according to Traimond, occurred at this time was that a dichotomy was becoming apparent between the richer and more modern households, in which men were dominant and the women were expected to stay at home, and the poorer, more traditional households, where women had the last word and also went out to work, together with the men. The bewitchment incident of 1826 occurred between Marie Lassale, from a somewhat richer farm and with a sister who did indeed stay at home, and the poorer household of Lacoste, where things were more traditional and his mother-in-law (still) held sway. According to Traimond this development could well have given rise to a conflict which could only be formulated in terms of a bewitchment and where the richer and more modern farm was the centre of the evil (Traimond, 1988: 34–5).

Be that as it may, it is evident that bewitchments could give expression to diverse problems and that these could occur between different parties – for example, conflicts over inheritances within families, as described for the Mayenne, but also conflicts between neighbouring farmsteads that were to a great extent interdependent. In these cases unwitching specialists could, as outsiders, fulfil the role of intermediaries.

In two other case studies, based also on trial materials and newspaper reports, Traimond goes into the functioning of unwitching specialists in greater depth. In the first study he deals with three healers, two of whom were unfrocked priests, in Bordeaux in the first decade of the nineteenth century at the time of the transition from Consulate to Empire. The second study concerns the vicissitudes of a Basque barber-surgeon in Bayonne circa 1750. From both stories it is evident that bewitchments were not restricted to the countryside, but also occurred in towns. Furthermore, it becomes clear that the four specialists were distinguished from one another both as regards their fields of activity and their methods. The barber-surgeon, who in 1750 was sentenced to the galleys for life and whose *Agripa Négra* had to be burnt in public in his presence, was a man who had come down in the world and worked in prostitution circles. It was predominantly women, including the local midwife, who testified against him. He was said to have promised to trace treasure and lost goods with the aid of his magic book, and in addition he was supposed to have acted as a magical healer and exorcist. One of the three healers who were imprisoned more than half a century later was a cooper living in Bordeaux who had carried on the divination practice of his uncle after his death and given advice on bewitchments. The two rather older priests had taken the side of the Revolution in order to be able to keep their country parishes, were defrocked after the Terror, and had then taken to healing out of financial necessity. They prescribed medicines, performed exorcisms and also made use of other rituals to help remove bewitchments from the sick.

Traimond also gives later examples of healing priests; for instance, that of the popular priest-healer of Tosse (Landes) who in 1871 was accused of using magic. It is not surprising that this impression had been created: the priest was very particular about hygienic measures such as cleaning or burning mattresses and quilts. To the villagers it was obvious that these measures were intended to drive evil spirits out of the bedding and undo bewitchments. According to Traimond there was, in any case, scarcely any distinction for the country folk between the unwitching specialist and the priest. After all, they both had a healing function and used rituals which showed strong similarities. An interesting question for further research would be whether priests and also other specialists simply paid lip service to their bewitched patients or took the possibility of bewitchment seriously.

Both Traimond and Desplat discuss the question of the continuity of witchcraft. For the city of Bayonne Traimond notes a break in 1750 when the Basque barber-surgeon had to appear before the courts. For the previous period only three slander cases are known, all brought between 1707 and 1711 by women suspected of witchcraft (Traimond, 1988: 148–53). According to Traimond, a rift becomes visible in 1750 between discourse and practice in the leading circles: lip service is paid to the contention that magic cannot be effective, but in practice some of these people are still making use of it, for example to find stolen goods. For les Landes de Gascogne as a whole Traimond points to the continuation of what he calls the 'idéologie magique', as that was to be found, in particular, among the rural population. On the other hand, the ritual which was used for bewitchments had to some extent changed, as is demonstrated, for example, by an increasing use of fire. What Traimond also emphasises is that the world of witchcraft cannot be dismissed as an irrational world: experience, reason and critical analysis played an essential part in it.

When Desplat discusses the continuity of witchcraft in neighbouring Béarn, he is in principle talking about a period of some four centuries, with the 'last burning at the stake' in 1826 as the end point. Not only did a substantial part of the population continue to believe in the possibility of bewitchments, but also, during the whole of this period, it was primarily women who were held responsible for them. As is demonstrated by Desplat's research, it is more difficult to determine how the process of 'disenchantment' in the higher and also the slightly less elevated circles took place. The fact that the magistrates, after a halt had been called to the witch-trials at the end of the seventeenth century, still pursued the unwitching specialists, the 'soi-disant sorciers', and were increasingly inclined to brand witchcraft as the superstition of the common people, does not say all that much about the people who occupied responsible positions at the local level. Thus Desplat mentions numerous examples not only of priests who helped their parishioners to rid themselves of a bewitchment, but also of prominent people who believed in witchcraft just as much as their fellow villagers.

Thanks to extensive legal records and other documents from or about the years 1763 and 1777, Desplat has been able to give a fairly detailed description of two unwitching specialists (Desplat, 1988: 185–206). The first was Joandet Saubat, a vicar of humble birth at Nay, a small town with a population at that time of about 2,500. He was evidently convinced of the diabolic danger which witches represented to their fellow humans. He influenced a nine-year old orphan to such an extent that the boy pointed to a number of women as witches. Some of these women, including several members of the bourgeoisie, were persuaded to allow Saubat to exorcise them. In 1763 the affair ended in a lawsuit before the court of Pau, the capital of Béarn, where at the same time two other unwitching specialists had to appear. The authorities thus discovered the existence of a whole network of 'chasseurs de sorciers' and exorcists in this area. As later became apparent, Saubat was more or less the spiritual father of the network. As it happens, Saubat, along with one of the other defendants, had a lucky escape: well-disposed parishioners had warned him that he would be arrested and so he just managed to get away in time. After some five years he returned to Béarn.

The other principal figure, who in 1777 and like Saubat (who was in the meantime living in Pau) became involved with the law, was the 17-year old epileptic Jean Tuquet, the son of a coal merchant in the conflict-stricken village of Louvie. He had come into contact with Saubat and other unwitching specialists and had become convinced that he himself had magical powers. He made use of these by branding numerous women – who they were is not clear – as witches. He was assisted by unmarried contemporaries of both sexes. The sentence which was passed on him in 1779 in Pau was one of public penance and banishment from the kingdom for nine years. His companions got off more lightly. Saubat too only had to pay a small fine. Perhaps he owed this to episcopal intervention; although the bishop was not very happy about Saubat's activities, he never went so far as to officially condemn him.

That in this area, in particular in the 1770s, according to the observations of enlightened contemporaries, 'superstition' was rampant and numerous unwitching specialists and young people were responsible for

their share of unrest, is ascribed by Desplat to a concurrence of circumstances. There were political riots, the economic situation was also critical,
amongst other reasons because a contagious cattle disease had taken a
heavy toll, and the expulsion of the Jesuits in 1764 meant that people had
to do without their pastoral and pedagogic services.

So far we have seen a variety of unwitching specialists: a vet, a cooper,
a barber-surgeon, several priests and a vicar. All of them were men,
although women evidently also exercised this function in the Mayenne, in
particular in the towns. Nevertheless, this is only a small selection from
the even more varied choice available in France in the eighteenth and
nineteenth centuries. Thus Matthew Ramsey (1988: 264–76) also makes
mention of smiths, carpenters, poachers and shepherds. It remains to be
considered whether advice on bewitchments was given purely as a sideline.
Indeed, comparatively little attention has been paid to the social position
of unwitching specialists (Ramsey, 1988: 270–1). They by no means
formed a homogeneous group: thus the time spent on unwitching and the
amount of income derived from it varied considerably, and their position
in the local community varied from marginal to central. Some of them
operated mainly locally, while others drew their clients from miles around.

A point of discussion is the extent to which in the early modern period
bewitchments were also attributed to unwitching specialists, or, more
broadly formulated, the extent to which the man in the street made a
distinction between black and white witchcraft. On the one hand, there
are researchers who share the opinion of Keith Thomas (1971) that this
distinction was indeed made both in England and on the continent of
Europe and that unwitching specialists were not as a rule suspected of
bewitchments. On the other hand, attention has been drawn, for example
by Robert Muchembled (1985, 1979), to the fact that this distinction was
an elitist construction in northern France, without any roots in a rural
population for whom all forms of magic were fundamentally ambiguous.
A person who was feared in his or her own village as a witch could be
consulted by outsiders as an unwitching specialist. Ramsey believes that a
choice between these two interpretations will only be possible after further
research (Ramsey, 1988: 267) but both interpretations have their own
empirical embedment. It is probably best, therefore, to think in terms of a
continuum on which each region or group from a certain period could
have a place according to how close it came either to Thomas' pole
(division between black and white witchcraft) or to Muchembled's (mix-
ing of black and white witchcraft).

Perhaps this is still too clumsy a distinction and more can be gained by
systematically taking account of the perspectives of the various parties
involved in a bewitchment. To begin with, there was the person who
believed him or herself to be the victim; from his or her point of view

this was a question of harmful witchcraft and the measures to remove the bewitchment did not come into the same category, even if the witch was repaid in kind. The unwitching specialist usually shared this viewpoint. Those to whom the bewitchment was ascribed were in the ambivalent position that to cooperate in the unwitching amounted in the eyes of the other parties to an acknowledgement of guilt. Unwitching was never a neutral action; the removal of a bewitchment by the suspect represented the neutralization of the previously inflicted harm, while attempts at unwitching by the person affected or by an unwitching specialist called in for the purpose could acquire a positive force, since the source of the mischief came under fire. Moreover, the unwitching specialist could in his turn run the risk of being suspected of a bewitchment by other people. Examples of the latter are not limited to northern France, but are also known from the Mediterranean areas and from England. However, how precisely this worked out in historical practice and what it meant for the position and prestige of unwitching specialists is still very far from clear.

From the Mediterranean Countries to the British Isles, and Scandinavia

THE MEDITERRANEAN COUNTRIES: FROM THE INQUISITION WITH LOVE

Whereas witchcraft research elsewhere in Europe is principally based on sources surviving from secular authorities and there is still comparatively little use made of ecclesiastical records, in the Mediterranean countries the reverse is the case. Here research is for the most part based on the abundant archives of the Inquisition. This is not surprising in view of the dominant position of the Inquisition in these countries as far as matters of belief, and thus also witchcraft, were concerned (see Monter in volume IV of this series). What is a problem, however, is that the waning interest of the Inquisition in witchcraft (including magical healing, love magic etc.) during the eighteenth century leaves the historian of this later period with comparatively empty hands. And if research into eighteenth-century witchcraft is scanty in these countries, then for the nineteenth century, at least in translation, it is non-existent. Moreover, the Inquisition archives of the seventeenth and eighteenth centuries contain relatively little material on bewitchment questions. The attention of the Inquisitors was mainly directed to practitioners, whether or not professional, of magical healing, love magic and treasure hunting. Whether this means that bewitchments, in so far as they were independent of magical healing and love magic, played a correspondingly modest role in the day-to-day life of the population, will have to be established on the basis of other sources.

Comparatively speaking Portugal is the country where the least is known about witchcraft (Bethencourt, 1990 and 1994; in Portuguese: Paiva, 1992). Very few witch-trials were held and scarcely any smoke rose from burnings at the stake. The Portuguese Inquisition, set up in 1536 and abolished in 1821, devoted far and away the most attention to Judaizers, Jews who had converted to Christianity but who according to the Inquisition still clung too closely to their Jewish rituals. At the most, 3 per cent of all cases concerned witchcraft, and then mainly the activities of cunning men and women. In the first half of the eighteenth century, however, the tribunals of Évora and Coimbra, up to now the best researched, became more active in this respect, which still calls for an explanation (Bethencourt, 1994: 187).

Otherwise, there is very little chronological differentiation to be found; Francisco Bethencourt maintains that popular views of witchcraft in Portugal exhibited 'surprising stability' over the centuries (Bethencourt, 1990: 421). The inquisitors were evidently confronted with reports of harmful witchcraft almost up to the time of the abolition of their institution, but they did nothing about it. They were principally concerned with the more or less professional *saludadores*, healers of cattle and people in the country areas, and, much more often, with illiterate cunning women who operated chiefly in the towns and, amongst other things, provided magical assistance in love or sex problems or in improving a person's social position. It is interesting that Bethencourt does not mention any cases of healing priests (Bethencourt, 1990: 409–10). Could it be that they had nothing whatever to do with unwitching or did they adhere more strictly to the ecclesiastical regulations?

As far as Portuguese witches are concerned, we find that they were born as such, did their damage by means of a curse or the evil eye, usually struck in the country in the context of village or family conflicts, but could if necessary also remove bewitchments (presumably brought about by others) in the role of cunning women. This ambivalence led to people preferring to consult cunning women who lived somewhere else. According to Bethencourt (1990: 414), the clientèle of the cunning men and women included noblemen, priests and officers of the crown. However, he does not indicate whether this distinguished circle of clients continued down to the early nineteenth century. Nor does he discuss how 'stable' was the apparently modest role of the devil (who usually assisted in the form of an animal), or the occasionally encountered metamorphosis of witches into birds (Bethencourt, 1990: 421).

The policy of the Spanish Inquisition (1478–1834) with regard to witchcraft has so far only been systematically recorded for the Basque country in the period 1609–14 (Henningsen, 1980). After Salazar's policy of moderation in this region the Inquisition refrained from passing death sentences for witchcraft. Secular courts continued to do so for somewhat longer. In southern Spain, according to reports, no witch-trials were held at all, which Gustav Henningsen (1980: 389; 1991–92: 294) attributes to the absence of witches in this area. Unlike this essay, Henningsen reserves the concept witch(craft) for 'evil people' who flew to nocturnal meetings with the devil, changed themselves into the form of an animal and worked evil on their fellow men, doing all this with the aid of personal magical power, whether or not innate (Henningsen, 1991–92: 294). He contrasts this with sorcery, by which harm could also be done, but where only magical techniques were involved, without bringing in the devil. Jean-Pierre DeDieu confirms the gist of Henningsen's account; apparently the tribunal of Toledo only dealt with six cases of *brujería* (somewhat confusingly translated by DeDieu as 'witchcraft or sorcery'), and these in the northern part of its district. Far and away the majority of the cases concerned *hechicería* (translated by DeDieu as 'enchantment'), that is to say 'petty magic' which was used 'for revealing the future, telling fortunes, finding lost objects and attracting lovers' (DeDieu, 1987: 142–3). Nevertheless, this description pays insufficient attention to the fact that in southern Spain adversity could also be attributed to bewitchments or the casting of spells and that people here could very well feel threatened, as has been shown by María Helena Sánchez Ortega (1991 and 1992). All in all, there is good reason to recommend this intriguing question of the differences between the north and the south as a matter needing systematic research.

As far as the later period is concerned, both more generally oriented Inquisition studies and also several articles specially devoted to witchcraft provide interesting information, mainly relating to the Toledo and Valencia districts (DeDieu, 1986, 1987 and 1989; Haliczer, 1990; Sánchez Ortega, 1991 and 1992). On the basis of the resumés of the trials sent by the tribunals to the Suprema in Madrid, Jaime Contreras and Gustav Henningsen (1986) have calculated that for the whole of Spain 3,532 (7 per cent) of the 44,674 trials held by the Inquisition between 1540 and 1700 – earlier and later resumés are not available – concerned superstition and witchcraft. The Inquisition paid the most attention to heretical propositions and blasphemy (27 per cent), Moriscos (24 per cent) and, following someway behind, Judaizers (10 per cent) (Contreras and Henningsen, 1986: 114). There were, however, important regional and temporal variations. Thus, the tribunals of Aragon with 10 per cent of trials for superstition and witchcraft come out higher than the tribunals of Castile with 5 per cent, and between 1615 and 1700 these trials reached a much higher level than before – 21 per cent for the tribunals of Aragon and 12 per cent for those of Castile (Bethencourt, 1994: 186).

In so far as the tribunal of Valencia concerned itself with superstitious aberrations between 1478 and 1834, more than half the cases involved were to do with divination, over a quarter with love magic, and less than a fifth with magical healing (Haliczer, 1990: 317). As in Portugal, here too it appears from examples from the 1640s that women who practised magical healing or love magic ran the risk of being accused of harmful witchcraft. In such cases exile from the district was the heaviest punishment. Cases of divination provided by far the most work for the tribunal, in particular those concerned with hunting for enchanted treasure. At the beginning of the eighteenth century this was an exceptionally popular occupation to which also people from the upper classes devoted themselves with the cooperation of Moorish slaves, bought or engaged for the purpose. Love magic, principally practised by women, followed a similar pattern in Valencia to that in Catalonia, Andalusia and Castile, as will be explained below. This time the village priest does make an appearance in examples of magical healing; he provided sick people with amulets and prayed for their recovery. In a case brought against a certain priest in 1651 he confessed that it was the saints themselves who had given charms to the bewitched and that he was certainly not the only priest who acted in this way (Haliczer, 1990: 318).

Between 1600 and 1780 the tribunal of Toledo conducted nearly three hundred cases concerning superstition and witchcraft, of which a fifth took place in the eighteenth century after the involvement of the Inquisition was already on the decline – from the mid-seventeenth century onwards (DeDieu, 1986: 181–2; 1987: 142). Three-quarters of the cases were brought against women, the majority of whom had practised love magic or were said to have carried out bewitchments (Sánchez Ortega, 1992: 197). Sánchez Ortega gives numerous examples from the seventeenth century and a few from the eighteenth from which it is apparent that women in particular were suspected of bewitchments, whether or not they formed part of love magic. Their evil eye, their curse, the magic they practised (for example sticking pins into waxen hearts), and possibly also their invocation of the devil led to the cattle, the harvest, the neighbours, or the men desired by them becoming bewitched. People who were physically or emotionally vulnerable appear to have been particularly prone to bewitchment, especially lovers, women, and children (Sánchez Ortega, 1992: 205).

An intriguing feature of all this is what the inquisitors themselves thought about these matters. For instance, how should we interpret the sentence of exile pronounced in 1679 against a woman who was accused of having in her possession a box with suspicious contents? Would the members of the tribunal have been just as convinced as the neighbour who made the accusation was that, with the aid of the contents of the box – two pierced hearts of wax and a waxen stomach with a hole through it – a bewitchment could be performed? And what must they have thought of the men who had become impotent and, as a last resort, appeared before the court in the hope that the inquisitors would be powerful enough to neutralize the magical influence of their ex-lovers? According to Ruth Behar (1989: 184) the inquisitors of Spain and Mexico considered the magical power of women 'as illegitimate in the sense that it was a delusion and therefore not really a form of power at all.' This was indeed the official theory, but it is questionable to what extent they exhibited such scepticism in practice.

In an article which covers Catalonia, Valencia, Andalusia and Castile and in which the examples cited are again predominantly from the seventeenth century, Sánchez Ortega (1991: 58–9) shows that magical healing was practised by both men and women. On the other hand, it was principally men who were held responsible for seeking enchanted treasure, said to have been buried by both Muslims and Jews on their expulsion from the Iberian peninsula. In this connection Sánchez Ortega speaks of 'masculine magic' whereby, according to reports, use was made of knowledge derived from astrology, the cabala, the psalms and esoteric books.

Love magic was a typically feminine form of witchcraft which seems to have been very frequently practised, both by specialists in this field and also by other women. It was always a case of seducing and winning a man, where the material and social need for him was usually a more important motive than love (Sánchez Ortega, 1991: 61, 83). Love magic was used to fathom the amorous intentions of a man and to win or win back his love. Various forms of divination were applied and erotic rituals were performed – for example with menstrual blood, sperm, and pubic hair – and use was also made of chants and the invocation of demons and other rituals if it was a case of regaining someone's love. In the latter case, it could even happen that a woman resorted to the 'binding' or 'impotency spell', which made the man impotent with women other than herself. Love magic in Castile and Southern Spain was a typically urban phenomenon, as indeed in large parts of Italy (Behar, 1989: 182). As a rule the women who practised love magic were either young and unmarried, widows, had been left by their husbands, or lived in casual unions with men. They worked as maids or servants, and sometimes as prostitutes. In Southern Spain they were often *moriscas*, women of mixed Spanish and Moorish descent (Behar, 1989: 200–1).

To what extent does Spain conform to Bethencourt's characterization of Southern Europe as 'un univers saturé de magie' (Bethencourt, 1994)? The picture that we get of Spain and also of Portugal diverges quite considerably from that of the more northern countries so far discussed. The frequently mentioned love magic is particularly striking, suggesting that most women made use of it at some time, as is the masculine form of magic, searching for treasure, which also occurred frequently in Italy. It would indeed appear that these sorts of magical activities, and love magic in particular, were indeed practised more in the Mediterranean area than in regions further north. On the other hand, these very activities may have been magnified as a result of the policy of the Inquisition. Elsewhere, for example in the Dutch Republic (Roodenburg, 1990), there was also mention of love magic, which was sometimes punished by church councils, but this was by no means as extensive as in Spain. If it was indeed the case that love magic was considerably more popular in the Mediterranean regions than in more northern areas, then an explanation for this might partly be sought in the social position of women. The greater the extent to which women were dependent in material and social terms on a steady relationship with a man, and men were a comparatively scarce item, the more frequently women will have resorted to love magic. According to this argument the more independently-minded women in the prosperous Dutch Republic would have had less reason to practise love magic than women from the Mediterranean area, who had much more difficulty in keeping their heads above water without a man and who were in greater risk of social marginalization. An additional factor was that it was precisely in the Mediterranean regions that love magic was a sure means of impugning a man's honour; where virility was a sign of honour, impotence detracted from it.

The question of continuity and change in witchcraft in Spain is difficult to tackle given the present state of research. Information on the eighteenth century is scanty enough, but for the nineteenth century it is totally lacking. It is true that up to the eighteenth century the archives of the Inquisition reveal apparently similar cases, albeit fluctuating in time, of bewitchment, magical healing, love magic and treasure hunting, but information on the people involved and their interrelations and on the circumstances of bewitchment and unwitching is still extremely inadequate. The attitude taken by the local clergy with regard to bewitchments also deserves closer attention, since, up to now, attention has been focussed on the policy of the Inquisition. Moreover, we are better informed about the repression of witchcraft and related forms of 'superstition' by the Inquisition than about the effects of this repression. Thus it is quite conceivable that the Inquisition unintentionally contributed to the survival of witchcraft by giving people the impression that it continued to take these matters seriously.

The Roman Inquisition (1542–) put comparatively much more effort into combatting witchcraft and related magical activities than the Spanish and Portuguese Inquisitions. From about the mid-sixteenth to the end of the eighteenth centuries 'magical arts', including witchcraft, constituted 29 per cent of the work of the Venetian tribunal, while this figure was 33 per cent for the tribunals in the Friuli and 37 per cent for the Neapolitan tribunal (up to 1740) (Monter and Tedeschi, 1986: 144–6; Bethencourt, 1994: 187). As in Portugal and Spain significant temporal fluctuations occurred. Up to the end of the sixteenth century the tribunals of Venice and the Friuli dealt with comparatively few cases of witchcraft, but with many more of Protestantism and heresy. The Venetian court was most active concerning witchcraft in the seventeenth and early eighteenth centuries, after which there was a sharp decline. There was a similar pattern, but without the decline in the eighteenth century, in the courts of the Friuli. In Naples the fluctuations were less pronounced and by the second half of the sixteenth century witchcraft already formed an important focal point for the Inquisition's activities. In Sicily, which came under the Spanish Inquisition, there were according to Italian standards comparatively few, but by Spanish standards comparatively large numbers of trials for witchcraft and magical activities. Between 1560 and 1614 they formed 8 per cent of the total and thereafter up to 1700 25 per cent (Monter and Tedeschi, 1986: 134–5). Nevertheless, it should be pointed out that Rome did not maintain a central archive and that since a great deal of trial material has been lost comparative analyses are problematical.

Although, as has been said, the Roman Inquisition was far and away the most zealous in its combatting of witchcraft and magical practices – why this was so cannot be determined, according to Monter and Tedeschi (1986: 142) – this zeal was accompanied by the same moderate attitude towards 'witches' and 'magicians' that we have seen in the two other Inquisitions (Tedeschi, 1990: 111–15; Tedeschi, 1991: chs. 6 and 7). It is also true of Italy too that the secular trials for witchcraft deserve deeper research (Tedeschi, 1990: 185). With what sort of 'magical arts' did the Italian tribunals occupy themselves? As regards the Friulian Inquisition a more specific breakdown of the category 'illicit magic' is available (Monter and Tedeschi, 1986: 135–6). Between 1596 and 1785 777 cases were conducted, of which therapeutic magic (199 cases), maleficia-witchcraft (180), and love magic (115) emerge as the largest categories. While therapeutic magic was scarcely dealt with at all by the Inquisition after 1670, witchcraft and love magic were less unevenly distributed over time. In the trials for therapeutic magic women were slightly in the majority, as they were for love magic up to 1611, after which men accounted for an ever increasing share in the course of the seventeenth century. Here we see a striking difference from Spain where it was almost exclusively women who were called to account for love magic. Whereas women were easily in the majority in cases of maleficent witchcraft down to 1670, thereafter their preponderance narrowed considerably (29 women to 20 men). After 1670 it was predominantly men who were prosecuted for 'magical arts'. Had the Inquisition's policy with regard to women borne fruit in the meantime, or had men moved into this field more than previously?

For Italy there are three English-language monographs available which deal with witchcraft in the Friuli (Ginzburg, 1983), Venice (Martin, 1989) and Terra d'Otranto, South-Apulia (Gentilcore, 1992). Only the last of these also covers the period after 1650, continuing down to the early nineteenth century. Apart from this there are English-language articles which devote attention to witchcraft in Venice (Scully, 1995), Modena (O'Neil, 1984, 1987, 1991–2), Piedmont (Loriga, 1994) and Sicily (Henningsen, 1990, 1991–2; Fiume, 1994). The eighteenth century figures in two of these articles (Loriga, 1994; Fiume, 1994), but the nineteenth century is totally absent. It is also noticeable that the middle of Italy is still a blank spot.

Carlo Ginzburg's pioneering, but at the same time criticized (recently de Blécourt, 1993), study of the *benandanti* in the Friuli (1966, English translation 1983) shows an interesting variant on how a rural population defended itself against bewitchments. Men born with the caul and, to a lesser extent, women each offered protection against bewitchments in their own way. On certain nights the men left their bodies to go as a group to combat the witches who threatened the harvest. The women derived their knowledge of hidden affairs from their contact with the dead. Although Ginzburg emphasises the transformation that took place during the trials between the late sixteenth and early seventeenth centuries, from a story of nocturnal struggle between *benandanti* and witches into one of nocturnal meetings with the devil by *benandanti* in the role of witches, his book also contains some glimpses of everyday life. In the 1620s, for example, a male healer, known as a *benandante*, was called by a sick woman and stirred up trouble by blackening the reputation of the mother of her daughter-in-law (Ginzburg, 1983: 92–6). Another healer, also operating as a *benandante*, acted rather similarly in the 1640s, but was only prepared to help a sick boy on receipt of a cash payment, after which the sick boy's father turned as a last resort to an exorcising priest who confirmed that the boy was bewitched (Ginzburg, 1983: 114–15).

The systematic search carried out by Ruth Martin (1989) into witchcraft in the archives of the Venetian Inquisition in the period 1542 to 1650 has produced some five hundred cases. From the 1580s onwards the Inquisition began to take a more serious interest in witchcraft, that is to say *stregonaria*, the common denominator in use at that time for a variety of forms of witchcraft. *Stregonaria* comprised necromancy, conjuration, divination, the use of charms and incantations, healing and *maleficium* (Martin, 1989: 86). Although the tribunal would certainly have had to deal with accusations of bewitchment, these usually became part of a more general accusation of witchcraft which also comprised things like divination or healing. Illness and impotence, in particular, were misfortunes attributed to bewitchment. It was mainly women who were suspected and healers ran an added risk, since they had the knowledge and the opportunity to administer medicines which could either kill or cure (Martin, 1989: 195). Unfortunately, Martin scarcely touches on the relations between those suspected of witchcraft and their victims, or on the motives for bewitchments.

The devil only played a significant part in necromancy – learned ritual magic which was principally used by men in hunting for treasure – and conjuration, in the form of love magic practised either by women or by men anxious to acquire financial gain. In the case of divination – predominantly used by women to trace lost possessions, identify a thief, or be sure of the faithfulness of a husband or lover – it was not the devil, but perhaps a saint, an angel or the Trinity that was called on for help. Charms and incantations may have formed the biggest category of *stregonaria*, used in all the strata of Venetian society, again to give love a helping hand or to bring about a cure. Healers were either women of lowly birth, often widows (the majority), or immigrants who had somehow to support themselves, or priests or monks who were quite often on the lookout for easy money (Martin, 1989: 139).

About 70 per cent of the persons denounced for or accused of witchcraft offences in the period down to 1650 were women, and of the men making up the remaining 30 per cent some 40 per cent belonged to the clergy. Love magic in particular was a welcome source of income for unmarried or immigrant women. A recent article by Sally Scully (1995) significantly deepens our insight in this respect. On the basis of a case-study of two half-sisters who between 1637 and 1654 had to answer before the Venetian tribunal, she shows how witchcraft (in their case in the form of divination, love magic and/or magical healing), together with marriage and prostitution, was one of the economic strategies which could be used by women. It is interesting that during their interrogation both half-sisters exhibited due scepticism about the effectiveness of their magical activities and attributed their success to the credulity of their clients. All in all, we get a picture of a town where people from all layers of the population, young and old, men and women (but especially women), were involved in various ways and in different capacities in some form of witchcraft. Unfortunately, however, these studies of Venice do not extend beyond the mid-seventeenth century, so that the later development of witchcraft in this city remains a closed book.

As Mary O'Neil (1984, 1987, 1991–2) has demonstrated, in the late sixteenth and early seventeenth centuries the tribunal of Modena in north central Italy had to deal with a range of witchcraft activities comparable to those considered by the Venetian tribunal. She discusses amongst other things the ambivalent position of village healers, who were pre-eminently vulnerable to witchcraft accusations on the part of their (former) clients who were readily inclined to identify healing and harming with each other (O'Neil, 1991–2).

Thanks to Sabina Loriga's article (1994) on Piedmont in northwestern Italy it is also possible to catch a glimpse of the situation in the first half of the eighteenth century, this time not on the basis of Inquisition archives, but with the aid of trials held in the secular courts. The picture which she provides diverges considerably from that obtained from the Inquisition research; this time we see a royal court (attached to the House of Savoy) and a senate (the highest body of the Piedmontese government) which after the premature death of the young prince Vittorio in 1715 both became obsessed with witchcraft. In the course of a few years nine cases were heard and in ten other instances an enquiry was instigated or a suspect was arrested without this resulting in a prosecution. At least three people were condemned to death for witchcraft. Although the odd case featured sex with the devil and sabbath visits, the core of the accusations alleged that figurines modelled in the likeness of a member of the royal family had been used to bewitch victims, resulting in illness or death. Since this sort of accusation was taken very seriously in higher circles, it could be used as a means of bargaining and as a survival strategy – here we have a parallel with the Venetian cases discussed by Scully (1995) – by men or women who were dependent on the favour of the better off. Accusations were made by people who were in needy circumstances and who hoped for such things as admission to a poorhouse or the reduction of a prison sentence. This did indeed often result in the desired intervention of influential people. The accusations were as a rule directed against acquaintances or relations of the accuser, who more often than not appears to have borne a grudge against them. It is interesting that it was not the (potential) victim of a bewitchment who made the accusation, but a third party who had something to gain by it. Strained relationships and the explanatory aspects of witchcraft are much less prominent in these cases than the aspect of instrumental bargaining. Loriga rightly argues that witchcraft was not a homogeneous and undifferentiated belief, but must be seen as a 'cultural matrix where possible positions and conflicting attitudes existed simultaneously' (Loriga, 1994: 93).

Her article demonstrates yet again the extent to which the nature of the sources used can determine the results of the research. It is evident that the policy of the Inquisition concerning witchcraft cannot be accepted simply as normative for the way witchcraft functioned in everyday life, and this applies equally to the policy of the secular courts. The picture compiled on the basis of the Inquisition archives for Italy (and the Iberian Peninsula) of moderate action against witchcraft, and of relatively little attention to *maleficium* and correspondingly more to magical healing, love magic and treasure hunting, represents a distortion which can only be corrected with the help of other sources.

If we leave the north of Italy for the south, we first of all land up in the 'heel' of Italy, thanks to David Gentilcore's research based on various sorts of ecclesiastical archives into what he calls 'the system of the sacred' (Gentilcore, 1992: 2) in Terra d'Otranto, the southeastern part of the kingdom of Naples. He charts the whole range of lay and ecclesiastical cures which was available to people in the event of malady and misfortune. He shows very convincingly the extent to which ecclesiastical and lay rituals, at least up to and including the early nineteenth century (his study covers the period from 1563 to 1818), were interrelated and how they influenced one another, even though ecclesiastical policy after the Council of Trent (1563) was centred on a clear demarcation of orthodoxy and the combatting of everything which lay outside it. In practice, priests made use not only of ecclesiastically orthodox rituals but also, quite often, of unorthodox ones, while lay healers in their turn also made use of ecclesiastical means.

Those who needed help could turn to priests, wise women – almost all lay healers were women – and saints. Their special powers were, however, ambivalent; the adage *qui scit sanare, scit damnare* (he who knows how to heal, also knows how to harm) was applicable to all three. In particular, there were numerous examples of wise women who were both healers and also considered capable of bewitchments. It was these very female healers who ran the risk of being accused of performing a bewitchment. We see here the same pattern that has also been reported for northern Italy, Portugal and parts of France – Spain presumably also belongs to this group, but research has not yet confirmed this.

The most interesting aspect of Gentilcore's study is that witchcraft is not seen as a comparatively isolated phenomenon, but as part of a more comprehensive 'sacred system'. Indeed, Gentilcore reserves the term 'witchcraft' for cases where there is a satanic pact, and possibly also night flight and sabbath (Gentilcore, 1992: 238). For *maleficium* without a satanic pact he uses the term 'sorcery'. 'Witchcraft' usually went to-gether with 'sorcery', but not vice versa. Whether this distinction was valid in contemporary usage is not, however, made clear. Be that as it may, there were seldom trials for witchcraft in the form of a satanic pact in the ecclesiastical courts of the kingdom of Naples, while for the secular courts very few trial reports at all have been preserved (Gentilcore, 1992: 255, n. 1). This does not alter the fact that help from the devil or from demons was certainly not spurned, for example by men who used 'learned magic' – the necessary knowledge was obtained from books, among other sources – to trace buried treasure. In particular, bewitch-ments, magical healing and love magic came to the attention of the ecclesiastical authorities fairly regularly. It was predominantly women who were accused of bewitchments, in which case, as has been said, wise women quite often had to take the blame. Gentilcore gives examples of this right through to the first half of the eighteenth century, but does not indicate whether such cases ceased to be handled after that. What he does conclude is that the 'sacred system' exhibited a large degree of continuity, which implies that bewitchments, magical healing and other magical activities also continued.

That the catholic church was to a great extent, albeit not always in the same way as ordinary believers, involved in witchcraft (in the broad sense) and contributed to its continuity is also apparent from its attempts to take over the determination of *maleficium* and to keep the sole right to perform exorcisms. The help of a priest was indeed regularly called for when a bewitchment was suspected, and he quite often made use of means that were considered to be unorthodox. Apart from this it was especially the wise woman, the *magara*, to whom people turned, certainly if she herself was suspected of causing the bewitchment. These women were usually poor and saw in this a chance to earn something extra. In a few cases we read again of little wax figures which were supposed to cause harm, and also of charms which were placed under the threshold or in the doorway of a person's house for the same purpose. Bewitchments occurred from the highest to the lowest circles in this predominantly agrarian society, which was characterized by a high degree of illiteracy. In particular, it was strange illnesses, which developed gradually and were difficult to explain, that were attributed to bewitchment (Gentilcore, 1992: 137). An accusation, whether by a man or a woman, could be the expression of a tense relationship, but could also be used as a means of preventing loss of face or causing someone else to lose face (Gentilcore, 1992: 221–2). As well as women, men also used love magic and in this field female specialists were active, just as has been reported for northern Italy and Spain.

Finally, we cross over to Sicily, which, as has been said, also came under the authority of the Spanish Inquisition. Just as Carlo Ginzburg has reconstructed the demonization of the *benandanti* by the Inquisition in Friuli, Gustav Henningsen (1990, 1991–2) has done the same for the Sicilian *donni di fuora*, the 'women from outside'. This is on the basis of the trial summaries which were sent by the Sicilian tribunal to the *Suprema* in Madrid between 1547 and 1701. Between 1579 and 1651 the tribunal of Palermo held 65 trials of *donas*, mainly poor female (57), but also male (8) healers who specialized in healing illnesses caused by fairies. The *donas* alleged that they had sweet blood and that on certain nights they participated in spirit in gatherings with mainly female fairies. Each place had one or more 'companies' into which fairies and human *donas* were organized. The fairies formed a favourite subject of conversation among the Sicilians, and the *donas* were only too ready to relate their nocturnal adventures (Henningsen, 1990: 198).

The illnesses which were called down on humans and animals – children were spared – were the victims' own fault; if someone had insulted a fairy or a *dona*, then that inevitably resulted in some illness or other. In such cases the *dona* advised mollifying the fairies with an offering in the form of a ritual meal, and promised moreover that during a nocturnal gathering she herself would try to persuade her 'Ladies' to cure the illness. Whether these healing ladies who were in contact with the fairies were ever themselves accused of bewitchments by their clients is not reported, but this does not seem likely since the misfortunes in question were attributed to the fairies. Similar fairy cults have been found in other peripheral areas of Europe where few witch-trials took place, such as Greece, the Balkans, Ireland and Wales (Henningsen, 1991–2: 295).

In a case-study of a lawsuit in Palermo in 1788–9 Giovanna Fiume (1994) shows that bewitchments were actively sought after by women or men who wanted to get rid of their partners or kill someone else. To achieve their aim they asked Giovanna Bonanno, an old widowed beggarwoman who was known to be a *donna di fuora*, for spells and magic potions – in her case there is no further mention of the fairies. One day Bonanno had discovered that a louse poison, an odourless vinegar, was also lethal for humans. After that she had sold it to her clients as a magic potion and they in turn had used it to devastating effect; over two years there had been six deaths. It is not surprising that this resulted in a lawsuit against her and the six clients – the tribunal of the Inquisition had been abolished in 1782. However, the judges were not disposed to interpret her deeds in terms of witchcraft; for them it was simply a case of poisonings and Bonanno came off badly. She died on the gallows. Her clients almost all received long prison sentences.

In general, the lack of information makes it almost impossible to say anything about continuity and change in witchcraft in Italy. From Fiume's account it can be inferred that at the end of the eighteenth century at least, part of the population of Palermo considered bewitchment to be a possible cause of illness or other misfortune. From a report more than a century later it is evident that Italy too did not escape the phenomenon of lynching. In 1911 in the vicinity of Perugia an old woman reputed to be a witch was burnt in a limekiln by farmers (Soldan and Heppe, 1912: ii, 350). It will be clear that there are still plenty of opportunities here for further research.

THE BRITISH ISLES: FAIRIES AND WITCHES, FIRE AND WATER

Ireland, England (plus Wales) and Scotland are somewhat unequally endowed with regard to research into witchcraft after the witch-trials. Practically no research has been devoted to Scotland and Ireland does not fare much better, but England has recently been experiencing a revival in this respect.

Let us begin with Ireland, not only because this country had scarcely any witch-trials and then only among Protestant settlers from England or Scotland – the last in 1711 on the isle of Magee (Byrne, 1967: 38–47; Lapoint, 1992: 85–7) – but also because there are certain parallels with Sicily (Henningsen, 1991–2: 295). In Ireland too all sorts of misfortunes were attributed to evil people, and also to the fairies (who were otherwise considered benevolent), and there were healers who could assist the afflicted in such cases. The parallel does not, however, extend much further. There does not seem to have been any question of nocturnal group gatherings between fairies and healers, as there was in Sicily. Moreover, the Irish fairies had particular designs on children and nursing mothers, in order to maintain the level of their own fairy community, and also on cattle (Jenkins, 1977: 42–5).

As has been said, Irish witchcraft research is meagre, certainly as regards the later period. In so far as the eighteenth and nineteenth centuries come up for discussion at all, this is mainly on the basis of the stories recorded by folklorists in the nineteenth century and once or twice on the strength of lawcourt and newspaper reports, as in the case of Bridget Cleary in 1895. Apart from a summary compilation of more or less already known cases, plus some later ones (Byrne, 1967), and a similar article about a nineteenth-century wise woman (Schmitz, 1977), we have only an article by Richard P. Jenkins, published in 1977 and still well worth reading, about witches and fairies among the Irish peasantry.

The long-standing rift between the Protestant settlers and the Catholic Irish population is manifest in the realm of the witch-trials themselves, since the native Irish population, who nevertheless believed in witchcraft, had absolutely nothing to do with them. They regarded them, as Lapoint indicates, as instruments of foreign oppression (Lapoint, 1992: 90). But a distinction between the two populations must be made with regard to witchcraft belief too, as well as the somewhat related belief in fairies and the accompanying practices. In view of the fact that the available research on the later period principally concerns the native Irish population, it is worth noting here that fairy beliefs played only an extremely modest role among the settlers. The Protestant, conservative, and unionist writers of the nineteenth century were, however, pre-eminently instrumental in cultivating this belief, or, as Joep Leerssen recently remarked, in the 'fairification of Irish popular culture' (Leerssen, 1996: 164). Thus, the fairies were depicted as the descendants of the original inhabitants of Ireland and as 'representatives of a golden Otherworld for which the Irish peasantry was the privileged intermediary' (Leerssen, 1996: 165). What witches and fairies had in common was that they could both cause mischief. Jenkins concludes that both witchcraft beliefs and fairy change-ling beliefs served to symbolize deviance from behavioural norms. With witchcraft it was a question of problems between different families, with fairies of problems within one family. It was nearly always women in ambiguous positions on whom suspicion fell; the older, widowed, childless or independent woman was taken to be a witch, while the younger, married woman, who was both an outsider (marriage was patrilocal) *and* a guardian of the well-being of the family, was more likely to be diagnosed as a fairy changeling. According to Jenkins (1977: 51), the idea of fairy abduction made it possible for men to restore their authority in a socially acceptable manner without explicitly pointing to their wives as the culprits, which would have endangered the moral unity of their families.

The best known example of fairy abduction concerns the death of Bridget Cleary in 1895 in Ballyvadlea near Clonmel. She died as a result of the heavy-handed attempts made by her husband Michael Cleary — a labourer or cooper — and others to drive the fairy changeling out of her and bring back the real Bridget. The presumably childless Bridget was taken ill, a doctor was called in who diagnosed bronchial catarrh and nervous excitement, and the same day the parish priest also visited her. As well as this, a well-known herb doctor was consulted on the advice of an older neighbour. The herbalist's verdict was that Bridget was a changeling, and he prescribed a milky drink with herbs. Apart from the Cleary couple themselves, Bridget's father, an aunt and three male cousins of Bridget's (later also a female cousin) and two neighbours were also present in the house when the drink was collectively forced on the protesting Bridget. Meanwhile she was repeatedly asked if she was Bridget Boland, wife of Michael Cleary, which she confirmed. Then, on the advice of the same neighbour who had recommended the herb doctor, she was held over the turf fire and again asked if she was Bridget Boland and not a fairy — the idea being that the changeling would leave the house through the chimney. The following evening Bridget was again laid on the fire, but this time covered in lamp oil, with the result that she died from her burns. Cleary and one of the cousins buried the corpse in a nearby swamp. Nevertheless, news of the affair got out and it ended in a court case. Apart from the herb doctor and the female cousin, who were acquitted, the others were all condemned to hard labour, varying from twenty years for Cleary to six months for Bridget's father and the two other male cousins (Byrne, 1967: 56–68; Jenkins, 1977: 47–8). There are, in fact, other cases of fairy abduction with a fatal outcome reported for the decades preceding the Cleary death. In 1850, for instance, in Tipperary a six-year old girl died as a result of being subjected to not very gentle treatment at the instigation of a 'fairy woman' (report courtesy of Owen Davies).

That the borderline between fairies and witches was not sharply drawn is evident from the statement of one of the witnesses in the Cleary trial. This witness interpreted the barrage of questions which Bridget had to undergo as an attempt to ascertain whether or not she was a witch (*Folklore* 6, 1895: 378). Be that as it may, the conclusion that someone was a changeling usually meant that such a person was no longer seen as a victim, but as a non–human aggressor. The gap between changeling and witch – as human aggressor – was not, therefore, very great.

Within the category of witchcraft Jenkins distinguishes, first, the inflicting of harm by means of the evil eye, including causing the illness or death of people and cattle and the malfunction of agricultural implements. On the basis of the meagre information available, he surmises that suspicion usually fell on older women and that their victims were usually adolescent or adult and male. A second example, and the most important, was milk and churn blinking, whereby a cow was robbed of her milk or the butter-making churn was bewitched. According to Jenkins it was not purely a question here of witchcraft being *attributed* to someone, but, sometimes of witchcraft actually being practised. Here too women were the principal suspects since they were directly involved with milk and butter production. Reports of such activities have been noted throughout the nineteenth century. There were also various other forms of witchcraft, including love magic. Moreover, there is one court case form the 1890s against a woman who wanted to kill another woman with imitative magic (Jenkins, 1977: 40–1).

It was possible to take a stand against fairies and witches with the help of male or female unwitching specialists. Biddy Early, a nineteenth–century wise woman in east County Clare, was consulted from miles around (Schmitz, 1977). According to rumour, she had spent some time with the fairies and been given a magic bottle by them, the source of her special knowledge. Her activities comprised taking countermeasures in the event of bewitchments *and* in cases of harm caused by fairies.

After the appearance of the classic studies by Alan Macfarlane (1970) and Keith Thomas (1971), English witchcraft research entered a quieter period and in the 1970s and 1980s failed to produce any further monographs – though there were numerous articles. However, in the last few years there has been an impressive revival. The years 1996 and 1997 were undoubtedly high points, with monographs by James Sharpe (1996) on witchcraft in England between 1550 and 1750, Robin Briggs (1996a) on early modern European witchcraft, Stuart Clark (1997) on demonology and witchcraft in early modern Europe and Ian Bostridge (1997) on witchcraft in England between 1650 and 1750, and also the collection of essays on 25 years of witchcraft research after Keith Thomas' *Religion and the Decline of Magic* (Barry, Hester and Roberts [eds], 1996). Nevertheless, in all these books the period of the witch-trials is again the central theme, although both in the collection of essays (de Blécourt, 1996) and in Sharpe's monograph there is a plea for research into the continuation of witchcraft. Sharpe's conclusion also extends into the nineteenth century.

As well as this, the last few years have seen doctoral theses in which more and more attention has been given to the later period. Thus, in his recently published doctoral thesis of 1991, Ian Bostridge has analysed the debates over witchcraft in England in the period 1650 to 1736, including the discussions at the time of the repeal of the British witchcraft legislation in 1736 (Bostridge, 1997; see also Bostridge, 1996). In his doctoral thesis on attitudes to crime in early modern England Malcolm Gaskill (1994b) has devoted a chapter to witchcraft in the period 1680 to 1750. Finally, Owen Davies (1995) in his study of the decline in the popular belief in witchcraft and magic in England and Wales (see also Davies, 1996, 1996–7, 1997a, 1997b, 1997c) covers a considerably longer period, namely from the eighteenth through to the mid-twentieth centuries. His research therefore forms the most important foundation for what follows.

Apart from the regional study by de Blécourt into witchcraft in Drenthe (de Blécourt, 1990), Davies' research into witchcraft in England and Wales is so far the only work that covers the whole of the eighteenth and nineteenth centuries. Their approach differs in that De Blécourt has, as far as possible, investigated the background of those involved in witchcraft questions, while Davies has not ventured into questions of this kind. This is understandable in view of the much more comprehensive geographical range of his research. Davies bases himself principally on stories collected by folklorists, newspaper articles and contemporary publications on witch-craft. For the eighteenth century, moreover, there are articles available on the case of Jane Wenham in 1712 (Guskin, 1981) and the case of Thomas Colley and Ruth Osborne in 1751 (Carnochan, 1971), and an unpublished paper dealing with the Lamb Inn witchcraft case of 1762 (Barry, 1994). As for nineteenth-century witchcraft, this is discussed in, for example, a study of Lindsey, Lincolnshire (Obelkevich, 1976), and in publications dealing with cunning folk (Maple, 1960; Smith, 1977) and rural England (Bushaway, 1995).

Witch-trials in England became increasingly rare after the Civil Wars. The last death sentences were carried out on three women in 1682 in Exeter (Sharpe, 1996: 231; Guskin, 1981: 48 and Davies, 1995: 90 both quote the year 1684, while Gaskill, 1994b: 87 keeps to the year 1685). The last sentence was passed by a jury in 1712 in Hertfordshire – thanks to the intervention of a judge the condemned woman, Jane Wenham, was not executed – and the last witch-trial was held in 1717 in Leicester (Gaskill, 1994b: 87; Davies, 1995: 90). The Witchcraft Act of 1604 was not revoked until 1736. Bostridge (1996, 1997) has shown that this measure stemmed more from political and ideological considerations than from a sceptical attitude towards witchcraft. Both before and after 1736, not only can a whole range of more or less 'believing' views be observed among the educated, but also a selective use of these beliefs according to what Gaskill calls the 'context of communication' (Gaskill, 1994b: 94–5). Thus a person's public stand need not have corresponded with his private views. That in the course of the eighteenth century the educated increasingly came to dissociate themselves publicly from witchcraft does not, therefore, necessarily indicate disbelief in the existence of witchcraft on their part. Their public standpoint can be seen as an attempt to distance themselves from the common people by the condemnation of 'superstition' and ignorance, a process which, according to Gaskill (1994b: 93), had reached the stage of an almost complete 'divorce between popular and élite attitudes' by the end of the eighteenth century.

All this sheds interesting light on the 'decline of witchcraft', that is to say a loss of ground in thinking and acting in terms of witchcraft. As is also shown by Davies (1995), this process appears to have taken place in educated circles less rapidly, uniformly and consistently than has been assumed. Moreover, it seems that in the course of time witchcraft came to cover a multitude of sins. Whereas it was originally viewed in the better circles as an actual threat, it later became seen as tantamount to deception. Gaskill (1994b: 85) speaks in this connection of the reinvention of witchcraft.

But what was the situation with regard to everyday practice when harmful witchcraft no longer qualified for legal prosecution? As we have seen in the case of France, people took the law into their own hands, not only at the time of the witch-trials but afterwards as well. The scarcer the witch-trials became, the more this form of action seemed to gain in popularity. In England it was not the use of fire but of water that was the favourite method; moreover, the limelight was not shunned, quite the contrary. Numerous examples are known from the eighteenth and, to a lesser extent, the nineteenth centuries where a woman suspected of a bewitchment, or sometimes a man or a married couple, were thrown into water. It must be noted here that by no means all these swimmings got into the news, let alone resulted in legal action. The vitality of the practice must therefore not be underestimated. The water ordeal, which had been used earlier to ascertain whether or not someone was a witch, was also used in this later period as a punishment and a means of rendering the witch temporarily or permanently harmless (Davies, 1995: 110–21).

In this respect, the well-known drama of the married couple John and Ruth Osborne, which took place in 1751 in Tring in Hertfordshire, is by no means an isolated case (Carnochan, 1971; Sharpe, 1996: 1–4). A local publican and former farmer, John Butterfield, suspected Ruth of having bewitched his cows some time before – this was the reason why he had

had to stop farming – and caused him to have fits after he had refused to give her milk. He made it known in public that on 22 April two witches would be subjected to the water ordeal. Beforehand he let the drink flow freely and thereby managed to get the butcher, Thomas Colley, together with two other men, to do the dirty work for him. Amid great public interest – some five thousand people were said to have gathered – the 69-year old Ruth and her 56-year old husband John, who was also known as a witch and was unemployed, were thrown into the water on a rope. Colley went to work so heavy-handedly that Ruth met her death and he himself had to pay for it some months later on the gallows.

This is a case of a well prepared water ordeal attracting an exceptional number of onlookers, but which got out of hand. Such a happening once more underlined the reality of bewitchments. But it is doubtful whether John Butterfield took his fatal initiative primarily out of fear of the Osborne's witchcraft activities. The chance of gain was probably a more important motive and the publican saw this stunt as an opportunity to compensate for the loss he had suffered.

As Davies (1995: 135–55) has shown, it only became possible to restrain collective violence towards witches in England – apart from the water ordeal the weighing ordeal was also used and witches were scratched so that the bewitchment could be broken with their blood – when from 1856 onwards a paid and uniformed police force came into existence. Up to that point the elected, non-professional constable or his deputy had kept well out of incidents of this sort or had even supported his fellow villagers in their infamous activities. It was a different matter when the professional policeman, who often came from elsewhere, arrived on the scene. After 1880 collective actions against witches were virtually a thing of the past. This did not as yet apply to (more) individual acts of violence – a point which, it should now be evident, is certainly not applicable to England alone.

The use of physical violence against witches, whether this took place collectively or individually, was in any case based on the conviction that they could cause more or less severe misfortune and, usually, that they had indeed already done so. Whether taking the law into one's own hands with such violence was adopted mainly as a last resort, after other possibilities, such as self-medication, counter-magic, consulting healers, priests and/or (other) unwitching specialists had been tried, cannot always be discovered, but it is certainly probable. Davies points out, moreover, that after 1736 people also regularly complained to the magistrates about witches, but that naturally this no longer had any effect. Nor could those accused of witchcraft count on any support from this quarter. They were better off appealing to the local clergyman than calling on the magistrates in vain. This also applied to the victims of a bewitchment. Ministers were still supposed to have the power to cure witchcraft by praying over the bewitched. Examples from the nineteenth century demonstrate not only the then still existent demand for such services, but also the dilemma in which ministers found themselves when faced with such requests. It was obviously assumed that vicars could both unwitch and witch (Davies, 1995: II).

Although Davies, as indicated by the title of his doctoral thesis, is primarily concerned with the decline in the popular belief in witchcraft and magic, the accent in his study is more on its continuation. In any case, he convincingly demonstrates the extent to which a substantial part of the English rural population and a smaller, but not unimportant, part of the urban population continued, until well into the nineteenth century at least, to take account of the possibility of bewitchments, usually in the form of harm to the health of people or animals, or setbacks in the production of butter or cheese. Whether the malevolent work of witches was still manifested after the beginning of the nineteenth century in the possession of girls and young women is open to question. The Bristol Lamb Inn case in 1762 (Barry, 1994) and a case of possession in Halifax, Yorkshire, reported in the same year by the Methodist John Wesley, may well have been the forerunners of the end of this type of bewitchment, which had previously occurred regularly in England (Sharpe, 1996: ch. 8). Possibly the last case of all was in 1815, when the possession of a young married woman in Worcestershire was ascribed by her sister to the revenge of a rejected lover and was ultimately successfully counteracted by a Catholic priest (Summers, 1965: 234–5).

At the time of the witch-trials themselves it was believed that English witches derived their magical power from familiars, evil spirits in the shape of animals – often a cat, dog or toad – who in exchange were allowed to suck blood from them. These familiars fulfilled a similar function in England to that ascribed at the time to devils on (parts of) the continent of Europe (Briggs, 1996a: 29–30; Sharpe, 1996: 71–4). Whether familiars also played an equally important role in the subsequent period may be doubted. From folklore records it can be concluded that during the nineteenth and early twentieth centuries, in some areas at least – for example, the West Country, East Anglia, Cambridgeshire, Essex – it was assumed that witches kept familiars in the form of toads or white mice (courtesy of Owen Davies). Parting with blood also forms a constantly recurring element in these later stories. Just as the familiar was (or had been) thirsty for the blood of the witch, so her victims wanted her blood out of a conviction that she had taken it from them. In the eighteenth and nineteenth centuries scratching of witches occurred fairly regularly. Moreover, in these later tales of witchcraft repeated mention is made of witches who carried out their malevolent work through the power of the evil eye

(Sharpe, 1996: 283). In England and Wales fairies seem to have been held far less responsible for all sorts of disasters than in Ireland.

As elsewhere in Europe, cunning people in England — the majority of them men, mostly artisans or tradesmen — contributed to a considerable extent to the perpetuation of thinking and acting in terms of witchcraft, since they diagnosed the illnesses of people or animals or other forms of misfortune, such as those to do with churning, as bewitchments and provided appropriate remedies for them (Davies, 1995). They were themselves sometimes accused of having bewitched someone, not from envy or for revenge, but for financial gain (Davies, 1997a). Cunning people gave advice not only on bewitchments, but also, for example, on matters of love and stolen or lost goods. But whether these latter items formed an important part of their work, as was the case in the Mediterranean countries, cannot be determined on the basis of the available research material. In contrast to these countries (and, as will be shown, to the Saar region as well), during the eighteenth and nineteenth centuries cunning people in England and Wales were hardly ever asked to detect hidden treasure (courtesy of Owen Davies). As has been noted for the Netherlands (and will be again for Germany) it can also be said of England that in certain religious circles, in this case the Methodists, there was a noticeable inclination to interpret misfortune in terms of witchcraft (Davies, 1995 and 1997b).

Who was involved in bewitchment cases during the eighteenth and nineteenth centuries, and for what reason, is comparatively less well defined. From the examples given by Davies (1995) it does emerge that (older) women were taken for witches more frequently than men, but how great their share was proportionally is not mentioned. Nor is it clear who voiced the initial suspicion and who subsequently took action. From the examples it does not seem as though witchcraft was, or became, above all a female affair, as is for instance indicated by Sharpe for Yorkshire (Sharpe, 1991 and 1996: ch. 7). However, out of a sample of 26 cases of assault or threats against witches in nineteenth-century Somerset (the majority of cases are from the second half of the century) 25 of the accused witches were female, while about two thirds of the assaulters or accusers were female, the other third being male. Interestingly, the majority of these men were in their twenties or early thirties (courtesy of Owen Davies). Here is another task for further research. This also applies to the circumstances of the bewitchment cases, including the relations between the people involved. True, the well-known pattern of rejected demands for neighbourly help and the subsequent attribution of misfortune to witchcraft (Macfarlane, 1970; Thomas, 1971) was also to be seen in these later centuries. But as has in the meantime been shown for the period of the witch-trials themselves (see amongst others Guskin, 1981; Gregory,

1991; Gaskill, 1996), numerous other conflicts could be at the bottom of bewitchment questions. Simply the misfortune itself, whether or not in combination with the presence of a supposed 'witch', could result in such a drama. As Briggs (1996a: 265) has rightly remarked, witchcraft was 'peculiarly malleable, available to fit any kind of discord'.

Although Davies has from the empirical point of view much more to offer than has been touched on above, the moment has now come to describe his interpretation of the decline of witchcraft. Davies' conclusion for England and Wales is that the belief in the possibility of bewitchments prevailed for longer than the practice of witchcraft accusations (Davies, 1995: Conclusion). He infers from this that the decrease in witchcraft accusations resulted in the decrease in witchcraft belief, and not the other way round: 'once out of sight, the witch was very much out of mind'. Thus Davies concentrates primarily on the question of why the number of witchcraft accusations so substantially decreased from the end of the nineteenth century onwards, or, in other words, why local communities no longer generated witches.

Answers in terms of the increase in education and literacy, the greater availability of medical facilities, or offensives against popular superstition do not offer an adequate explanation. Literacy could even have been favourable to the popularity of witchcraft (more people could read magic books); the increased accessibility of medical facilities primarily represented greater choice in the medical market (the very fact that people preferred to visit the doctor rather than the unwitching specialist was a sign that witchcraft was losing ground); and attempts by the authorities to suppress superstition had only limited success. Davies does not deny that these factors had some effect. However, what he emphasises is that an 'autarkic rural culture', which produced for its own use, had to give way half way through the nineteenth century to a 'dependency culture', which was entirely reliant on external institutions for its economic survival, social organization and local government. This transition created five interrelated 'circumstances' which, according to Davies, had direct repercussions on the 'socio-economic machinery' which 'produced' witchcraft accusations.

As the first circumstance Davies cites the new instability of local communities, since it was precisely stability which was favourable to witchcraft accusations and the handing down of traditional knowledge from one generation to the other. In second place comes the decrease in self-government and the infiltration of national and local government. The introduction of a professional police force mentioned above is an example of this. A third circumstance was that cattle, except on farms, no longer belonged to the invariable elements of the household, and that factories took over the production of butter and cheese. This removed many previously popular objects of bewitchment. Fourthly, the vulnerability of farmers decreased thanks to the growing insurance market, and in 1834 a new Poor Law provided for state assistance, although this did not immediately result in fewer beggars. As the last circumstance Davies mentions urbanization, which in many respects represented a curb on witchcraft accusations.

As has been said, witchcraft after the witch-trials in Scotland is virtually virgin territory. Scottish church courts continued to deal with accusations of witchcraft well into the eighteenth century (courtesy of Owen Davies). The last judicial execution took place here in 1727 (Gaskill, 1994b: 118, n.104), after which the British legislation of 1736 also meant the definite termination of the witch-trials in Scotland. That witchcraft still occurred after this with a certain degree of regularity can be inferred from reports from almost a century and a half later. Thus a young fisherman landed up in prison in Dingwall in the 1870s, after having stabbed a sixty-year old woman, a supposed witch, with a penknife in order to collect some of her blood (Trevor Davies, 1947: 199). In issues of *Folklore Journal* from the 1880s and of *Folk-Lore* from the 1890s there is also mention of various witchcraft affairs. What we are waiting for, however, is a study such as Davies has carried out for England.

SCANDINAVIA: DIVERGENT GENDER PATTERNS

Although Gustav Henningsen in Denmark in 1975 was probably the first to call attention to the need for witchcraft research after the witch-trials, judging from the available publications in English, French and German, that was virtually where the matter rested, both in Denmark and also in Norway, Sweden, Finland and Iceland (Henningsen, 1975; English translation 1988). Apart from Henningsen's own Danish research (see also Henningsen, 1982 and 1984), Norwegian research into folk medicine in the nineteenth and twentieth centuries also provides some information on later witchcraft (Alver and Selberg, 1987; Mathisen, 1988). Sweden, Finland and Iceland fare worse, which is particularly regrettable since the research into the period of the witch-trials shows highly divergent gender patterns. Thus Iceland stands out with its very high percentage of men (more than 90 per cent) who were prosecuted in witch-trials (Hastrup, 1990a and 1990b; Ellison, 1993). This also applies to a slightly lesser extent to Finland (Heikkinen and Kervinen, 1990; Nenonen, 1993). On the other hand, in Sweden, Norway and Denmark it was mainly women who suffered this fate (Naess, 1990; Johansen, 1990 and 1991; Ankarloo, 1994).

The last executions for witchcraft took place in these nordic countries either towards the end of the seventeenth century, or, as in the case of

Sweden, at the beginning of the eighteenth. Likewise, in the Baltic regions of Estonia and northern Livonia, which were under Swedish jurisdiction at that period, the last death sentence was carried out at about the same date, namely in 1699. Shortly after this, at the beginning of the eighteenth century, these areas were to fall into Russian hands. A century later Sweden also had to cede Finland to Russia. At that time Norway and Iceland formed part of the kingdom of Denmark. Norway became part of Sweden in 1814 and gained independence nearly a century later in 1905. Iceland was to become an independent kingdom (in personal union with Denmark), after which the republic was proclaimed in 1944. From the religious point of view Scandinavia formed 'the largest bloc of solidly Lutheran lands anywhere in Europe' (Monter, 1990a: 425).

Let us look first of all at Denmark, the country which in this northern region has the most to offer on later witchcraft. At this stage of our tour of Europe it will no longer be a source of amazement that in Denmark too witchcraft affairs have been traced right down to the twentieth century and that sometimes heavy-handed action was taken against alleged witches. It is not clear whether people were already taking the law into their own hands against witches at the time of the original witch-trials. According to Henningsen (1988) the last illegal witch-burning with a fatal result took place in 1722, and 1800 saw the last murder of a witch – an 82-year old female beggar who was beaten to death by six men. Danish law courts were, as far as one can tell, still confronted with cases of maltreatment at least until the end of the nineteenth century, while slander cases were still being brought in the 1930s by people who had been branded as witches. Cunning people, whether or not through a slander case, came up against the law at least until the 1920s.

For his research into witchcraft after the witch-trials Henningsen has traced the references to witchcraft in the registers of the Danish Folklore Archives, in legal archives and, from the mid-nineteenth century, also in newspapers. The cases described by Henningsen suggest the following picture. In Denmark too bewitchments were as a rule connected with the health of people and especially of animals, and the majority of the accused were women. Whether the women concerned already had reputations as witches, as Johansen (1990 and 1991) has established for the seventeenth century, cannot be determined for the later period without further study. In the case of Dorte Jensdatter, a 50-year old, single woman in Salling, who earned her keep by spinning in other people's homes, it was clear that she had for some time been regarded as a witch. She was said to have bewitched cattle and also two children. The death of a horse in 1722 proved to be the last straw. The owner of the horse and the mother of one of the dead children mobilized the neighbours so that Dorte might be interrogated in their midst. Her evasive answers were an inducement to deal with her more drastically. Dorte was tied down in her own house and ultimately set on fire by the mother. The two chief offenders were sentenced to death for this murder, but the others got off with lighter sentences or were even acquitted. Anne Klemens, an elderly beggar who paid for this with her life in eastern Jutland in 1800, had also been reputed to be a witch for some time. However, it was not until a 22-year old itinerant cunning woman provided the initial impetus that she was attacked. The healer was beheaded, and the six men who had beaten Anne to death were banished.

Although women, and not only single women like Dorte but married women too, formed the majority of those accused of bewitchment, the role of men was by no means negligible. In one-third of some thirty witchcraft cases mentioned by Henningsen for the period between 1700 and 1934 a man was accused. Whereas to start with this was still the exception, from the mid-nineteenth century onwards it occurred more frequently. In such cases it was always a man who made the accusation, and cattle were usually the victims of the bewitchment – in 1899, for example, a cunning man was accused of such activities. In one case, from 1863, mention is made of scratching the witch: this was a matter between a smallholder and a farmer suspected of bewitchments. Whether taking blood from the witch was so much the less popular in Denmark than in England cannot, however, be established on the basis of Henningsen's survey. This also applies to the water ordeal, of which also only one example is included (a thwarted attempt in 1766). Cunning people – a man or a woman – were involved in many of the witchcraft episodes mentioned. Indeed, they were fairly regularly charged in maltreatment and libel cases. They were also brought before the courts on account of their share in tracing thieves or treasure by magical means (early nineteenth century).

The devil does not appear to have played a (significant) part in all this. Henningsen does, however, mention various eighteenth-century cases of men who sold their souls to the devil in exchange for worldly gain, while not connecting this with witchcraft. As regards the attitude of the Lutheran ministers towards witchcraft matters, we only know that they sometimes expressed their concern about what was happening in their congregations. It is not clear whether victims of bewitchments or people accused of witchcraft turned to them for help. Other matters which have received insufficient attention are the relations between the parties involved and the possible conflicts which formed the basis for witchcraft accusations.

From the Norwegian research into folk medicine in the nineteenth and twentieth centuries it can be inferred, among other things, that illness and other misfortune could be ascribed not only to witches, but also to so-called *hulder* (fairies) (Alver and Selberg, 1987: 24–5). These *hulder*, who lived in the open air, had no greater destructive powers than the Irish and Sicilian fairies. They were certainly more powerful than humans and could punish people for transgressing the rules that had to be observed in associating with them. According to oral tradition the witch, as at the time of the witch-trials, was usually a wandering beggar, tramp or outcast (Alver and Selberg, 1987: 25). As a poorer person the witch had reason to be envious. Yet well-off people also ran the risk of being accused of witchcraft: they were said to have attained their high levels of production by means of witchcraft ('witching' in the terminology of de Blécourt (1990)) and thus to have acted to the detriment of other people. According to the stories told, the witches were guilty, among other things, of stealing milk and cream from their neighbours and making their cattle sick. This often happened when the witch had been refused something for which she – the scanty examples predominantly concern women – had asked.

Witches could be rendered harmless, but there was ultimately nothing that could be done against *hulder*. As with the Irish fairies, it was assumed that the Norwegian ones could kidnap a child and leave a changeling behind instead. Pregnant women and midwives also had to watch out for them. Alver and Selberg emphasize, as Jenkins (1977) does for Ireland, that the supernatural punishment, whether it came from *hulder* or witches, implied a form of social control. However, the Norwegian material provides little insight into those concerned and their interrelations, let alone into the settlement of witchcraft questions over the centuries. Nor do we get to know much more about what Alver and Selberg call the 'wise ones', except that they were expected as the custodians of traditional knowledge to be able to discover why the problems had arisen in the first place (Alver and Selberg, 1987: 420). From another article on folk medicine it appears that some 'folk healers' of the nineteenth and also the twentieth centuries maintained contact with the *hulder* and derived their powers of healing from them (Mathisen, 1988: 172). There is, however, no mention of folk healers who were consulted in bewitchment cases.

Sweden, Iceland and Finland must of necessity be passed over, at least as far as the period after the witch-trials is concerned. And yet a short stop is not entirely superfluous, if only to draw attention to a few points. It appears from Swedish research that during the height of the witch-trials in this country in the 1670s people were also taking the law into their own hands and there were even cases of witches being lynched (Ankarloo, 1994: 209). What is nevertheless more intriguing is the deviant gender pattern occurring in Iceland and to a lesser extent also in Finland, Estonia and northern Livonia. In all these areas more witch-trials took place against men than against women. In the trials in Iceland the women even formed as small a minority as men did in countries such as England or the Dutch Republic. The question as to why this was so and whether we are dealing with comparable forms of witchcraft has scarcely been asked, let alone answered. Of the extent and manner of male and female involvement in various forms of witchcraft in the period after the witch-trials nothing at all is known, but this particular puzzle certainly deserves further study.

In some 120 witch-trials held in Iceland in the seventeenth and early eighteenth centuries on the authority of the Danish colonizers only ten of the accused were women, while only one of the 22 death sentences carried out between 1625 and 1685 involved a woman. Kirsten Hastrup (1990a, 1990b) ascribes this male overrepresentation to the native Icelandic views on magic and witchcraft, according to which the typical witch was a man. She infers this from (the use of) the words by which (benevolent *and* maleficent) witchcraft and the practitioners of harmful witchcraft were designated. Not only was the female designation for a witch much less common than the male, but it can also be deduced from the two terms for witchcraft that words were seen as the most important magical instrument of power (*galdur*) and knowledge as their ultimate source (*flölkyngi*). Hastrup adds in this connection that men had more access to knowledge in general and thus also to magical knowledge, and were therefore more often involved in magical practices, for example healing, than women. They thus ran a greater risk of becoming involved in witch-trials. Without entirely repudiating her views, R.C. Ellison (1993) does make some comments on Hastrup's interpretation. In the first place, referring to saga material in which women also operate as 'learned' witches, she doubts whether the male hegemony was indeed as great in day-to-day practice as Hastrup would have it appear. Secondly Ellison attaches less weight to the aspect of (male) erudition than to the lack of any association of witchcraft with sexual activities. The first point clearly deserves further attention, but the second is more debatable, since elsewhere in Europe it was possible to end up with a female overrepresentation even without such a sexual component.

What does not emerge sufficiently clearly, with a few exceptions, either in Hastrup or in Ellison, is the question of who made the accusations (mainly about bewitchments of people and animals) and why. At the time of the witch-trials, it looks as though men played by far the most important role, both as accusers and witnesses. It would be too much to go into more depth concerning the Icelandic community patterns at that time – predominantly self-supporting farms in which needy women were also lodged – and the consequences for the (low) number of trials and the immunity of poor women.

In Finland too the majority of those tried for witchcraft were men, with the exception of western Finland during the height of the trials in the 1660s, 1670s and 1680s (Heikkinen and Kervinen, 1990; Nenonen, 1993). Up to the 1660s only charges concerning bewitchments – of people, cattle or food – came before the courts. In the 1670s and 1680s the emphasis fell on benevolent magic, formerly a matter for the church, and, to a lesser extent, on observing the witches' sabbath. Women were convicted more often than men and mostly fined for the practice of benevolent magic, while the ratio was the other way round where charges of injuring by witchcraft were concerned (which did not usually result in a sentence) (Nenonen, 1993: 84). What the ratio was in the eighteenth century, when there was evidently still a substantial number of witch-trials (Nenonen, 1993: 83), remains to be seen.

CHAPTER 3

From Eastern and Central Europe to Germany and Switzerland

EASTERN AND CENTRAL EUROPE: WITCHES, VAMPIRES AND MORE

In so far as there has been any research (published in German, English or French) on witchcraft after the witch-trials in Eastern and Central Europe, it has mainly consisted of analyses of folktales and descriptions of rituals. Research on witchcraft accusations and other reactions to bewitchments is very thin and even so it seldom covers the eighteenth and/or nineteenth centuries (for the twentieth century see de Blécourt 1999)

Let us begin with Russia where – as in Estonia and northern Livonia under Swedish rule (Madar, 1990) – more men (68 per cent) than women (32 per cent) had to stand trial for maleficent witchcraft in the seventeenth century (Kivelson, 1991: 84–7). A substantial number of the men *and* women charged were healers. Exactly what the sex ratio was for the witch-trials held during and up to the end of the eighteenth century is not known. In view of the fact that an older overview of seventeenth- and eighteenth-century trials indicates that in about half the cases men, or men as well as women, were accused (Kovács, 1973: 78), it can be assumed that the share of women in the eighteenth century had risen considerably. This makes the transition to the nineteenth century, when it was women who were principally regarded as witches, less abrupt.

Information on the practice of witchcraft in the later period is to be found in two articles, only the more recent of which is wholly devoted to witchcraft (Frank, 1987; Worobec, 1995). For rural Russia and the Ukraine – the Ukraine passed at the end of the eighteenth century from Polish into Russian hands – Christine Worobec has traced 75 witchcraft affairs between 1861 and 1917 from ethnographic, psychiatric, juridical and newspaper reports. More than three quarters of them happened in the last three decades of the nineteenth century, a period of vast unemployment and poverty. The accused included beggars and neighbours who asked for assistance – the well-known pattern of the refusal to give alms and subsequent bewitchment – but also mainly female relatives, including wives, mothers, mothers-in-law and daughters-in-law of the accusers.

In Russia and the Ukraine taken together women represent more than 70 per cent of those accused of maleficent witchcraft between 1861 and 1917. In the Ukraine, where women had been traditionally associated with witchcraft, this percentage was 10 per cent higher, while among the Russian agrarian population two thirds of the accused consisted of women. If women were suspected of bewitchment(s), they also ran three times as great a risk as men of receiving violent treatment (Worobec, 1995: 168). In addition, women considered themselves more often to be victims of bewitchment. All in all, these are sufficient reasons for Worobec to speak of a feminization of witchcraft (Worobec, 1995: 173). She relates this to an increasing identification of women with their sexuality (with its potential dangers for the 'patriarchal world'), to their increased dependence on assistance and the thus greater visibility of older women and widows, and, as far as the victims of bewitchment are concerned, to attempts on their part to influence the power relations in the female sphere to their own advantage. The second point, the dependence on assistance, indirectly links up with Valerie A. Kivelson's explanation of the low percentage of women who stood trial for witchcraft in Russia in the seventeenth century. She suggests that the immobility imposed at that time by the state helped to strengthen the extended family as the basic economic and social unit and that women thus acquired a more stable position within the family and the community and were therefore less susceptible to accusations of witchcraft (Kivelson, 1991: 83–4).

Be that as it may, according to Worobec, the later accusations were always based on certain tensions. As at the time of the witch-trials healers of both sexes ran the risk of being accused. Those bewitchments attributed especially to men concerned the infertility of women and bad harvests. As regards the latter, men who themselves reaped a rich harvest were particularly suspect; this is a well-known pattern, designated as 'witching' by de Blécourt (1990). Furthermore, both men and women were thought capable of harming newly-weds or their guests during the wedding celebrations by a bewitchment in the form of demonic possession, by causing impotence in the bridegroom, by making the bride reluctant to engage in sexual intercourse, and by causing other illnesses which occurred during or directly after the festivities. In general, women were suspected of using witchcraft to make other people, often of the same sex, ill or even to kill them, or rob cows of their milk.

As has already been touched on at the beginning of this essay, very violent things could take place in Russia (Frank, 1987; Worobec, 1995). The woman who, in Vrachevo in 1879, was burnt alive in her house by the villagers was a 50-year old beggar and wife of a soldier. She had asked a certain couple in vain for cottage cheese. After this their daughter was taken ill. During convulsive fits she had cried out that the soldier's wife had bewitched her. When two other women also became ill, and one of them died, the neighbours decided to take action. The execution took place in the presence of almost two hundred farmers. In 1891 in the province of Moscow a 73-year old beggarwoman, alleged to be a witch, also paid with her life when she was accused by another woman, who also had convulsive fits, of having bewitched her. The old woman was so badly battered by two villagers that she died of internal injuries.

Demonic possession attributed to the maleficent work of witches occurred with a certain degree of regularity among women. In 1898–9 in a village in the province of Smolensk there was even an epidemic of possessed people involving thirteen women and two men, who suffered from convulsive fits for which a fellow villager was held responsible. It is uncertain what happened to her, but Worobec (1995: 185) reports that most possessed women had had to cope on their own after they had been widowed or because their husband was away from home for a long time as a soldier or migrant worker. For the time being this is all we have to go on as far as Russian bewitchment matters are concerned.

For the Ukraine it may be added that the practice of swimming witches was particularly common there, both in the eighteenth and far into the nineteenth centuries (Zguta, 1977a). It was usually a case of (a large part of) the female villagers being subjected to the water ordeal in order to establish which of them was responsible for a continuing drought. In addition, use was made of the so-called 'water-bearing ordeal'; women who were suspect in some way had to carry buckets of water from a river or pond to a certain cross or other religious shrine. Those who did this without spilling any water went free, but anyone who spilt water on the way was held responsible for the drought. It is striking that in such cases all the female villagers were in principle suspect, and that men went scot-free. As late as 1885 a collective swimming took place in the Ukrainian province of Kherson, and similar witch-swimmings were also used in Georgia.

Unfortunately Poland has to be passed over owing to the lack of (accessible) publications on eighteenth- and nineteenth-century witchcraft cases after the witch-trials – the last judicial executions took place in 1776 (Schiffmann, 1987: 152; Klaniczay, 1994: 221). On the basis of research on the twentieth century (Schiffmann, 1987) – see de Blécourt (1999) – there can be no doubt that in Poland misfortune, in the form of sicknesses of people and animals, was still being attributed to witchcraft. As late as 1984 a rich and attractive 40-year old widow, who had turned down offers of marriage from men from her village and had become engaged to a man from another village, was burnt alive in her house by villagers who suspected her of having bewitched their wells and spread an epidemic. Bewitchment by fairies evidently also belonged to the Polish repertoire (Schiffmann, 1987: 148). Here too the blood of the witch was used to heal the bewitched person (Schiffmann, 1987: 150).

If the journey from Poland is continued south and south-eastwards, then it appears that Hungary and Austria are the only countries where there is anything to report before finally reaching Germany and Switzerland. Neither for the Czech Republic and Slovakia nor for the territories previously belonging to the Ottoman Empire, such as present-day Rumania, Bulgaria, Greece and the former Yugoslavia is any (accessible) information available on later bewitchment matters. The Greek Orthodox southeastern area of Europe is also lacking in witchcraft research for the earlier period, although it may be safely assumed that the prosecution of witches in this part of Europe did not assume great proportions (Klaniczay, 1994: 226; Levack, 1995a: 214). Where there are essays devoted to the later period, they deal with 'folk-beliefs' derived from folk-tales concerning, for instance, (mainly female) witches, metamorphoses, flying, bewitchments, and cunning people, whether or not initiated into their art by the fairies. But none of this is related to, and checked against, actual witchcraft affairs (on the Central Balkans: Vukanović, 1989; on Croatia: Boskovic-Stulli, 1991–2). Alternatively, these articles provide overviews of present-day magical charms and healing rituals (on Yugoslavia: Conrad, 1983; on Bulgaria: Conrad, 1987). From the latter it is clear that certainly in the countryside, but also in a city such as Sofia, account must be taken, even down to the present day, of the possibility of bewitchments, that frequent use is made of magic charms, and that many villages possess a specialist, usually female, who can heal illnesses attributed to witchcraft, can offer protection against bewitchments, but can also harm people.

How inadequate such broad surveys, based on collections of folk-tales and inventories of ritual practices, turn out to be if we want to gain insight into what really took place, is evident, for example, from ethnological research in present-day villages on Rhodes (Herzfeld, 1981) and Greek-controlled Cyprus (Argyrou, 1993) (see de Blécourt, 1999). Thus, among other things, Michael Herzfeld (1981: 566) points to the discrepancy between what a respondent from the village in question recounts in general terms about the evil eye, namely that childless, elderly women are particularly prone to possess it, and what in fact takes place. He convincingly demonstrates the value and importance of a semiotic approach, in this case to evil eye accusations, and, more generally, of thorough local research. The latter point also applies to Vassos Argyrou's study of the 'strategic use of magic' in some Greek-Cypriot villages. He sees the attribution of certain things to 'magic' (read: bewitchments) as practical solutions to practical problems, as strategies whose acceptance by others depends to a considerable extent on their 'performative appropriateness' – that is, the extent to which the idiom of 'magic' fits in with existing cultural conventions – and much less on abstract notions of truth and falsity. In this way 'the thorny issue of belief' is at the same time evaded (Argyrou, 1993: 267–68).

Since the second half of the 1980s Hungarian witchcraft research has been very active in setting up a database for a computerized analysis of Hungarian witch-trials, in publishing transcriptions of these witch-trials (Klaniczay, Kristóf and Pócs [eds], 1989) and numerous publications on them and on Central European witchcraft beliefs – as these could be inferred from legal records and folk-tales – and in the organization in 1988 in Budapest of an international conference on witch beliefs and witch-hunting in Central and Eastern Europe (Klaniczay and Pócs [eds], 1991–2). As in Poland, the period without witch-trials in Hungary began comparatively late; the trials did not reach their numerical zenith until the first half of the eighteenth century. Some 90 per cent of the accused were women. The last known execution dates from 1777, nine years after witch-burning was definitely prohibited on the orders of Empress Maria Theresa, and more than 20 years after she had begun her crusade against 'superstition', prompted by a popular panic about vampires in neighbouring Moravia, and on the advice of her court physician Gerard van Swieten (Klaniczay, 1987 and 1990b; see also Levack and Porter in this volume).

Hungary, moreover, had to contend with vampires, as is apparent from various vampire cases which occurred on the periphery of the kingdom in the first half of the eighteenth century (Klaniczay, 1987). These vampires, dead people who had usually died under unusual circumstances and thereafter returned to spread death and destruction in the shape of humans or animals, were rendered harmless by digging up their not yet putrified corpses which still contained blood, piercing them with a stick, beheading them or removing the heart and burning it. Hungary was in fact, in the words of Gábor Klaniczay (1990a: 165), 'a huge cultural melting pot' in which diverse cultural traditions converged. As well as witches and vampires this country had fairies (who also often brought disaster), werewolves, and shaman–like healers.

Although the Hungarian researchers have put a lot of effort into compiling overviews of the witch-trials and reconstructing earlier 'belief-systems', we still know comparatively little about how witchcraft functioned in everyday life. Ildikó Kristóf's analysis of the witch-trials in Calvinist Debrecen comes closest in this respect (Kristóf, 1991–2). One of his most interesting findings is that wise women formed a substantial part of those who were charged with maleficent witchcraft in this town. Competition among wise women or conflicts with official barber-surgeons and midwives were at the bottom of many of the accusations of this sort. Whether the accused were wise women or not, there was usually something to be criticized about their conduct. A bad reputation, gained for example by adultery or stealing, increased a person's vulnerability to accusations of maleficent witchcraft.

Unfortunately we can say no more about the later period than that the end of formal proceedings did not mean the end of the informal accusations, that the archives of Debrecen also contain material on nineteenth-century witchcraft suspicions, and that the population of eastern Hungary could still provide plenty of information for twentieth-century folklorists in search of witch beliefs (Kristóf, 1991–2: 114).

In Austria work is also in progress on a databank for the witch-trials (Dienst, 1992). There is less emphasis on folkloristic research in Austria in comparison to that which has been carried out in Hungary. Here too there are various publications on the witch-trials, but a meagre crop for the later period. The percentages of women and men charged in the witch-trials are so divergent per region and sometimes also over time as to make Austria an interesting experimental field for gender-oriented witchcraft research (Tschaikner, 1991). Indeed, in this connection the share of female and male accusers and cunning people would itself deserve attention, quite apart from further research on the period after the witch-trials.

For this later period we shall have to make do for the time being with an older article, in which the emphasis is not on bewitchments, but on treasure hunters and exorcists in Linz and its environs towards the end of the eighteenth century (Commenda, 1960). A criminal investigation instigated in 1792 showed that a whole network, mainly of artisans, under the leadership of someone who posed as a lawyer, devised plans to line their pockets by magical means and free themselves of their financial worries. The acquisition of a certain Bible was the only obstacle still hindering the realization of these plans. How the judicial verdict turned out is not known. From the interrogations it is in any case evident that this network had at its disposal books and manuscripts in the fields of treasure hunting, conjuration, blessings, and astrology and also a book by Cornelius Agrippa. The written word represented a popular source of magical power and knowledge. Without that one could scarcely hope to achieve a successful exorcism or invoke the devil.

GERMANY AND THE DEVIL

The heart of the witch-trials was to be found in the German Länder. In some of them death sentences for witchcraft were carried out into the eighteenth century; in others this stopped earlier, in the second half of the seventeenth century. The last execution took place in Kempten (Bavaria) in 1775, while there was an execution in Würzburg in 1749 and in Württemberg in 1751 (Levack, 1995a: 250–1). Only in Switzerland is a still later judicial death sentence known, namely in 1782. Not only did witch-trials occur for a very long time in some of the German Länder, although rarely to the very end, but there is also a flourishing belief in witchcraft in Germany today (Schöck, 1978, 1987; Baumhauer, 1984; de Blécourt, 1999). An enquiry held in 1986 showed that a third of the population of the German Federal Republic believed it possible that certain people could harm their fellow human beings means of witchcraft (Schöck, 1987: 294–5).

For more than ten years now the production of German witchcraft research has shown an impressive and important increase. Three years after the concentration of Dutch witchcraft research a study group was also set up in Germany: the Interdisciplinary Study Group for Witchcraft Research (Arbeitskreis Interdisziplinäre Hexenforschung: AKIH) founded in 1985. Under the direction of Sönke Lorenz and Dieter R. Bauer this is still a flourishing concern with annual meetings, regular international conferences, and a recently initiated series of witchcraft publications (Lorenz and Bauer [eds.], 1995a, 1995b). Here too the emphasis of the research is on the period of the witch-trials. However, possibly inspired in part by Inge Schöck's research (1978) into twentieth-century witchcraft, interest is developing in the eighteenth- and nineteenth-century periods (Behringer, 1987, 1995; Labouvie, 1990, 1992, 1993, 1995; Göttsch, 1991; Sander 1991; Scheffler, 1994; Gestrich, 1995; Schöck, 1995). These articles or parts of monographs are concerned with Bavaria, Württemberg and Saarland in the south of Germany – although anachronistic this designation is used for the sake of brevity – and respectively Lippe and Schleswig-Holstein in the north-west and north. The middle and also the eastern part of Germany – the former DDR – are totally blank spots for this later period and to a great extent for the period of the witch-trials.

In the German research an analytical distinction is fairly regularly made between *Zauberei* (sorcery) and *Hexerei* (witchcraft), (see for example Schormann, 1981: 23–4; Behringer, 1987: 15–19; Labouvie, 1987: 76–7). The term *Hexerei* is reserved for diabolism, because the devil is invariably involved in it: there is a pact with the devil, sex with the devil, the witches sabbath and the accompanying flight, and usually also *maleficium* (inflicted harm). Here we can talk, as Brian Levack (following Joseph Hansen) does, about a cumulative concept of witchcraft (Levack, 1995a: 29–49). With *Zauberei* it is more a question of ritual actions in order to achieve harmful or beneficial objectives. However, this distinction only partly meshes with the original contemporary classification, although both terms, and also many others, were in circulation. How exactly the dissemination of the word *Hexerei*, which had been in use for longer in southern Germany and penetrated into the north in the first half of the seventeenth century, occurred in the early modern period and in what sense(s) this term was used, deserve further study (Kramer, 1983: 238; Lecouteux, 1985, 1995). To what extent did the cumulative, demonological *Hexerei*-concept, as developed in some theological circles and reflected in an increasing preoccupation with diabolic dangers, become adopted more generally? Was it, after all, principally a construction which was (or could be) called upon during judicial interrogations, but which did not play a significant role in the context of daily life? Recently Jonathan Barry has rightly advocated closer studies of the cultural transmission and transformation of the witch stereotype (Barry, 1996: 27).

It is customary to translate the twin German concepts *Hexerei* and *Zauberei* into English by using the terms witchcraft and sorcery. However, we must not lose sight of the fact that in contemporary usage in England itself the term witchcraft was used as an umbrella concept and without the devil being assigned a prominent place (Macfarlane, 1970: 310–12). Further differentiation could be made with the help of adjectives such as 'good' and 'bad'. In the French-speaking regions of Europe people did not even have a second term at their disposal and *sorcellerie* continued to function as an umbrella term.

This short terminological exercise shows how difficult it is in translations and international comparative research to do justice to the original meanings of certain terms. An analytical distinction between witchcraft and sorcery, however the demarcation is made, does not really help and can even damage the indigenous categories. That is why the term witchcraft is used here in an umbrella sense, with further differentiation being made with the aid of adjectives.

The question of the reception of the cumulative, demonological *Hexerei*-concept in the German Länder also arises with regard to the eighteenth and nineteenth centuries. If this concept was widely accepted during the period of the witch-trials, then there should at least be some trace of it for some time afterwards. However, as far as can be seen, this is not the case. Another point concerns the extent to which those directly involved in witchcraft affairs attributed to the devil some kind of role in them. A first indication comes from an article by Inge Schöck (1995) on the supervision by the state authorities and by the Catholic church of the moral conduct of the people of Württemberg from the mid-seventeenth to the mid-nineteenth centuries. She only mentions secular supervision as a source for future research. But as far as ecclesiastical discipline was concerned, which was entrusted to the so-called *Sittengericht* (morals tribunal), she mentions cases of divination, treasure hunting, consultation with a witch-doctor to solve a theft, and witchcraft accusations addressed to women (sickness of a cow in 1655 and 1832; illness of a child in 1797). It is also recorded that a major fire in 1731 was attributed to the work of witches.

There is an interesting case of a preceptor who in 1728 ventured to deny the existence of spirits, the devil, hell, witches and bewitchments. He had to appear before the *Sittengericht* and modify his views. He admitted that the devil and hell existed but with the proviso that devils had no bodies, but were only spirits. He also recognized the existence of witches. He did not entirely repudiate the possibility of bewitchment, but according to him this was often only imaginary (Schöck, 1995: 384). Although Schöck does not give a comprehensive survey, let alone a closer analysis of the ecclesiastical disciplinary policy, it would appear that the people of Württemberg who had to answer to the *Sittengericht* did not themselves have any demonological *Hexerei*-concept – and there was certainly no question of a cumulative demonological *Hexerei*-concept. In so far as the devil was involved, it was, as elsewhere, in more professional activities such as treasure hunting and tracing thieves.

For Schöck the central theme is not the decline of witchcraft but its continuation. In her view both the Catholic and the Protestant churches contributed to this in so far as they adhered to the existence of a personified devil. Apart from this she cites the modern occult movements of the nineteenth century, folk medicine, and the enormous poverty and the very cramped living conditions of the population, all of which produced a favourable context for the continuation of the belief in witchcraft (Schöck, 1995: 386–9).

Further information on Württemberg is provided by Andreas Gestrich (1995) in an article on the connection between the end of the witchcraft prosecutions and the rise of popular Pietism in the eighteenth century. Taking the village of Walddorf near Tübingen as an example, he investigates the effect of the end of the witch-trials on the religious views of, and social relations between, people who up to then – and also afterwards – believed in the existence and the effectiveness of witches. From the 1670s onwards Pietism, an internalized form of Protestant devoutness, had become widespread in middle-class circles in Württemberg. From the 1760s this revival movement also became popular in the rural areas, initially among Protestants, but from the beginning of the nineteenth century among the Catholic population as well. Characteristic of this popular Pietism was an overpowering concentration on life after death and deliverance from sin. The longing for spiritual rebirth and purification expressed itself in a dualism between spirit and body, and between God and the devil, which was carried to great lengths, as well as in an ascetic life style. This Pietism was also characterized by pronounced chiliasm: the second coming of Christ and the beginning of the millennium was expected in 1836, and until that moment arrived the devil continued his offensive. The real presence of the devil in the world formed a central element of popular Pietism as professed by various groups. In Walddorf alone there were three of these groups, one of which set off for Russia in 1817 to await the second coming of Christ from the East. All in all, about a quarter of the 250 families in this village had ties with one or other of the Pietist groups. On the other hand, Pietism was not a success in all Württemberg villages.

Gestrich puts forward the hypothesis that the development of this popular Pietism was closely connected with the end of the witchcraft prosecutions. Without the possibility of effectively clearing themselves of the accusation of being in contact with the devil, people turned prophylactically to driving out the witch or rather the devil in themselves by means of ascesis. In this way they hoped to join the ranks of the saints (Gestrich, 1995: 285). This is an interesting possibility, which calls for further explanation. Yet, contrary to Schöck, Gestrich suggests in his hypothesis that the Walddorfers in question adhered to demonological views of witchcraft. Where is there evidence for this? Although Gestrich reports that legal papers from the eighteenth and nineteenth centuries contain numerous cases of witchcraft accusations and charges of maleficent witchcraft, he limits himself to two examples of ecclesiastical mediation.

In 1777 the church council (*Kirchenkonvent*) of Walddorf dealt with a conflict between a married couple, the Werners, on the one hand, and the widower Wurster and his mother-in-law, on the other hand. Werner's wife had accused Wurster's mother-in-law of stealing onions from their garden. This had led to blows and Wurster had thereupon lodged a complaint with the minister. He had told the church council that his mother-in-law had been hit so hard by Werner that Werner's wife, fearing the worst, had called on him to stop and let the woman go. Thereupon his mother-in-law had asked Werner if he wanted to kill her too, just as he had her daughter when she had stolen from him. Wurster also told how his wife (the daughter of his mother-in-law) had died: she was suddenly taken ill and bereft of her senses, and after she had lain in bed for two days in this state, Werner had come to her and had put his hand under the bedclothes, whereupon she had 'let her water flow' and given up the ghost. Werner himself declared before the church council that he had only wanted to feel the sick wife's pulse. The only thing known about the further history of this case is that the sitting was adjourned on account of the illness of the minister – he died shortly afterwards – and that the case then ended up at the *Oberamt* (court of the high bailiff) (Gestrich, 1995: 272–3). What seems clear here is that we have an accusation of harmful witchcraft addressed to Werner, without the devil being mentioned even once.

The second example dates from 1822 when Johannes Gaiser appeared before the church council with his wife and declared that he could no longer live with her because she had been accused of being a witch and had not cleared her name. He also said that Jacob Lang had spread this rumour. Lang denied this and said that, in any case, he did not even know the name of the alleged witch. During the enquiry it appeared that Lang had indeed voiced his suspicion about Gaiser's wife, but that Gaiser's son had spread the rumour about his stepmother. Although Lang had to pay a small fine, it was Gaiser himself who was above all reprimanded for not having greater control over his son and for behaving discourteously to his wife. The local authorities left it at that and took no further action on the substantive aspect of the case (Gestrich, 1995: 273–4). Here too the devil does not come into the picture.

The provisional conclusion must therefore be that no empirical basis is offered for the assumed reactions of people who were taken for witches – that, failing the possibility of clearing their name before a court of law, they would have tried to exorcize the devil in themselves. This is what Gestrich suggests to explain the rise of popular Pietism. Following Mary Douglas' theory concerning the social embedment of cosmologies (Douglas, 1973), he sees both witch-belief and ascesis as symbolic manifestations of similar social experiences which find expression in corresponding dualistic views. We thus finish up again with the devil, who according to this argument would have had to have played a prominent role both in witchcraft and also in the ascesis of Pietism. Moreover, it is not clear whether the people in question, at any rate those who were suspected of witchcraft, had or came to have any ties with Pietism. After all, three quarters of the village population did not have this bond. What Gestrich does indicate is that both witchcraft accusations and also early Pietism were to be met with among people who belonged to the lowest level of the middle class (*unteren Mittelschicht*) and could scarcely keep their heads above water, but for whom it was ignominious to beg. This social experience is supposed to have found expression in a leaning towards a dualistic world view.

Although it is difficult to demonstrate a connection between the end of the witch-trials and the rise of popular Pietism, this does not alter the fact that Gestrich makes an interesting attempt to analyze particular religious views and practices, together with the whole business of witchcraft, as a function of the social experiences of those concerned. This certainly deserves further attention. Moreover, an interesting parallel becomes visible with the positive correlation noted in the Netherlands and England between orthodox Calvinism and Methodism respectively and a persistent witch-belief. There is clearly a challenge here for comparative research.

Before turning to the more northerly areas of Germany, let us make a short trip to the region bordering on Württemberg to the east, Catholic Bavaria, where a heated debate about witchcraft occurred in 1766–7 and where around 1750 a number of death sentences for witchcraft were still carried out. As Wolfgang Behringer shows (1987, 1995), the controversy known as the 'Bavarian Witch War' was between enlightened people and conservatives, in particular the Jesuits, who bombarded each other with numerous pamphlets. All levels of the population took part in the debate. Enlightened authors represented witchcraft and the devil's pact as something ridiculous; the contrary party took these matters very seriously but ultimately had to back down. Another interesting point is the role of the unwitching specialist Johann Joseph Gassner, who ascribed all sickness to bewitchment and in 1774 was taken into the household of the prince-abbot, who was said to have been responsible for the last German execution in Kempten in 1775. Otherwise, we have no information about how much support there was among the common people at the time for demonological witchcraft beliefs.

Eva Labouvie's research, which focuses on rural witchcraft beliefs and is based on civil and ecclesiastical archives, brings us to the Saar region, which bordered on present-day Luxemburg and north-eastern France and was at the time under the domination of different rulers. Here it was the village communities themselves that took the initiative in witch-hunts with the election of *Hexenausschüssen* (witch inquisitions) and, particularly between 1580 and 1635, went to work with great zeal. And yet the cumulative, demonological notion of witchcraft, as preached from the chancel, barely took root among the villagers. The pact with the devil, fornication, and renouncing the faith played an insignificant role in confessions. There was, however, a greater awareness of the need to destroy all evil-doing 'witches'. The main points of the confessions obtained under pressure of torture were to do with *maleficium* and flying to the witches' dance, a traditionally familiar concept. In so far as the devil made an appearance, it was as a human, not frightening figure (Labouvie, 1991: 105–11).

Between 1635 and 1700 only a few more witch-trials were held, which Labouvie attributes to, among other things, the devastating consequences of the second half of the Thirty Years War, the wars also waged after 1648 in this area, and the increasing scepticism among lawyers and in the high courts of law (Labouvie, 1995: 58–60). From about 1650 we see a substantial increase in slander cases in the lower courts which were brought by people who were alleged to be witches – how long and how frequently these continued to be brought is not very clear. To what extent a change in the mentality of villagers was also at the bottom of this is difficult to judge (Labouvie, 1995: 72–3). Nevertheless, Labouvie believes that from the mid-seventeenth century onwards the rural belief in witchcraft lost its rigorousness, inviolability and incentives for prosecution. This was because the conflicts which had evoked the earlier accusations were becoming things of the past and thus the 'social logic' of witch-belief was lost (Labouvie, 1991: 257–9, 265; 1995: 73–6). She establishes that the typical witchcraft accusation was directed at older, single women who were dependent on the personal support of their fellow villagers. As soon as poor relief was institutionalized in the Lutheran, Calvinist and Catholic areas, this type of conflict disappeared. Thus, according to Labouvie, the most important reason for witchcraft accusations was gone.

Although her research also covers the period after the witch-trials, the eighteenth and nineteenth centuries receive much less comprehensive and systematic treatment as far as witchcraft is concerned. Labouvie is guided by sources from ecclesiastical and secular bodies from which there is evidently more to be gleaned about their efforts to combat all forms of 'superstition' and to 'improve' the inhabitants, than about the place occupied by witchcraft in everyday life in the course of this later period. It is not for nothing that her book devoted to folk magic and rural 'superstition' bears the title *Verbotene Künste* (Forbidden Arts) (1992). In her publications there are virtually no examples of bewitchment affairs after the witch-trials. Whereas from other, neighbouring areas there are fairly regular reports about such affairs and their more or less heavy-handed resolution, Labouvie creates the impression that in the Saar area all this had become a thing of the past at an earlier stage. Whether this is a question of distortion arising from the selection and use of sources is difficult to judge, since the author is not very explicit about the method she has followed.

In any case she argues that witch-belief, including the preventive measures which were taken, suffered from loss of function from the mid-eighteenth century onwards (Labouvie, 1992: 300), that, at least in ecclesiastical visitation reports, such measures were not mentioned after that time (Labouvie, 1990: 50), that witch-belief in the nineteenth century had long since lost its importance (Labouvie, 1987: 55), and that it nevertheless continued to exist into the twentieth century (Labouvie, 1995: 76). Apart from the disappearance of the most important sources of conflict that were reflected in witchcraft accusations, she attributes this decline to new ways of interpreting and combatting sickness and other misfortunes, such as those offered by the natural sciences, medicine and technology, to the fight against 'superstition' by the churches and the secular authorities, and to the literacy programme for the population initiated at the end of the nineteenth century.

Even if bewitchment cases and also the branding of people as witches do not persist in this later period, this is partly compensated by information on related matters. For the eighteenth century in particular Labouvie notes changes in what she calls the repertoire of folk magic. Apart from the disappearance of protective measures against bewitchments, she reports a marked expansion in attempts to find treasure by magical means, a shift from harmful witchcraft practised with amulets or symbols to diverse forms of written or verbal curses and profanities (Labouvie, 1993), and a transition from forms of blessing and *Krankheitszauber* (witchcraft in cases of sickness) to *Heilzauber* (therapeutic witchcraft), which was employed independently by the population to gain prosperity and for which numerous magic manuals came into circulation (Labouvie, 1992: 300–1).

For the former county of Lippe, bordering in the west on Westphalia, Jürgen Scheffler (1994) presents a picture of witchcraft in the nineteenth and twentieth centuries which diverges considerably from that offered by Labouvie for Saarland in the eighteenth century. Lippe had also been one of the key areas of witchcraft prosecutions, in particular between 1653 and 1670 (Walz, 1993: 522), but here there was no question of a rapid decline in witch-belief and witchcraft accusations. In the nineteenth and even the beginning of the twentieth century – the eighteenth century is still a blank – witchcraft affairs were by no means a thing of the past and witch-doctors and cunning women had work in abundance, both among the country folk and also among the working class in the small towns (Scheffler, 1994: 271, 295). The belief in werewolves also died hard. Scheffler has been able to derive this from such sources as newspaper reports, minutes of provincial synods, accounts by folklorists, and legends.

Here too we see the now familiar pattern whereby sicknesses of both people and animals could be attributed to bewitchments. For confirmation of the diagnosis and to ward off the bewitchment the help of a magic specialist could be called in. Examples from the late nineteenth and early twentieth centuries demonstrate that here too, as in the Netherlands and Belgium, feather rings found in pillows provided irrefutable proof of bewitchment. Burning these in a hermetically sealed house was the prescribed remedy. If anyone knocked, the door must on no account be opened, for this would be the witch who wanted to prevent the burning. Whether this was all that happened or, as for example in Belgium and France, there was the occasional witch-burning in nineteenth-century Lippe is not reported. But at the end of the sixteenth century lynching was not an unknown phenomenon in this area (Walz, 1993: 517).

Scheffler does indicate that an unwitching ritual could regularly end in a witchcraft accusation against a concrete person – again usually a woman – though he does not specify exactly what the role of the specialist was in this (Scheffler, 1994: 274). However, none of the examples show that the professional advice implied a concrete accusation. This corresponds to the findings of de Blécourt for the north-east of the Netherlands in the same period (de Blécourt, 1989b) and of Traimond for les Landes de Gascogne in the first half of the nineteenth century (Traimond, 1988).

There are more parallels to be reported. As in the Netherlands, the profession of witch-doctor, which was mainly practised by men and often passed on within the family, could also pass to a daughter. Moreover witch-doctors and cunning women who possessed special skills appear to have attracted customers from far and wide. Although giving unwitching advice was not specifically a female affair, female specialists were greatly in the majority. Magical treasure hunting belonged, as it did everywhere, to the men's domain, while divination was a job for women. Otherwise, Scheffler reports that from half way through the nineteenth century rural witch-beliefs were under great pressure as a result of economic moderni-zation, social change and the spread of bourgeois culture (Scheffler, 1994: 294).

Although Rainer Walz's research (1993) on the county of Lippe concerns solely the period of the witch-trials and the distance from the period dealt with by Scheffler is therefore considerable, for the sake of the contrast and the different approach, it nevertheless deserves brief attention. Thus, at the time of the witch-trials unwitching, divination and healing were practised considerably more by men than by women. Witchcraft accusations and branding someone as a witch belonged much more than in later times to the customary repertoire in terms of which people attacked an opponent.

Walz offers not so much an explanation of the witchcraft prosecutions, as an insight into the functions of witchcraft belief in Lippe and an idea of the behaviour of those directly involved. His conclusion is that the two chief functions of witchcraft belief were contingency reduction through attributing misfortune to bewitchment and isolation of an adversary by means of abuse or accusation.

According to Walz ideas about production and consumption in village communities at that time were determined by the principle of the so-called zero sum game (*Summenkonstanz*): an increase in the total stock was not thought possible, therefore one person's gain was another's loss. In his opinion, this way of thinking also applied to other fields such as friendship, love, health and honour. Thus, there was always a reason for envy and distrust. The witch was one to whom goods passed which someone else had lost, whether this was a question of health or possessions. Seen in this light witch-beliefs gave expression to a concern for the maintenance of equality. An increase in witch-trials would thus point to changes in the social structure, for example a growing polarization between rich and poor (Walz, 1993: 52–5). This application of the economic metaphor of the zero sum game to matters of love, health and honour seems unwarranted. An explanation by means of nomenclature does not solve anything. Yet

Walz's analysis is also fruitful. On the basis of numerous case studies he shows how much witchcraft accusations and branding a person as a witch were part of the then village culture, which he characterizes as a retaliation-oriented 'culture of strife', full of envy, jealousy and verbal agression.

Walz's study also provides food for thought on matters such as the interpretation of both the continuation and also the marginalization or decline of witchcraft in the later period. To what extent can the continued existence of (certain forms of) witchcraft belief be attributed to the survival of the structural characteristics of village communities described by Walz? And to what extent did changes in these structural characteristics lead to changes, and possibly a decline, in witchcraft? Can the decline of witchcraft be put down wholly to such causes or, as seems more likely, were the various attempts to marginalize witchcraft and other forms of 'superstition' partly responsible?

From Lippe the journey continues northwards and we arrive in the duchies of Schleswig and Holstein, formerly Danish, which came into the possession of Prussia in 1866. The last death sentence for witchcraft in this agrarian area, which was not one of the key zones of witchcraft prosecution, was carried out in 1687, while the last witch-trial is said to have taken place in 1752 (Sander, 1991: 22). For the eighteenth century a certain amount of research is available, but for the nineteenth century there is none. The research by Kirsten Sander (1991) into 'superstition' in Schleswig-Holstein between 1580 and 1750, based mainly on bills from the lower law courts, shows that though the witch (*Hexe*) concept had indeed made its appearance in this area at the end of the seventeenth century, ideas about the devil's pact, sex with the devil and the witches' flight to the sabbath had only been adopted to a limited extent. Here too women were the main suspects in bewitchments, the health of people and animals and also milk and butter production were the targets, and both men and women were involved in magical practices, although there were more cunning women than cunning men (Sander, 1991: 81). As Silke Göttsch (1991) has shown on the basis of an incident from 1707, it could happen that witchcraft accusations were used by the owner of a country estate as a means of disciplining rebellious retainers.

At least until the middle of the eighteenth century, bewitchments, unwitching and branding someone as a witch were the order of the day, although some courts had begun to take a more lenient line (Sander, 1991: 84). After that time, these cases only came before the court very sporadically. Unfortunately, for Schleswig-Holstein too the question of continuity and change in witchcraft beliefs and practices must remain unanswered as long as researchers ignore the later period. What we do see, however, at least from the German research discussed here, is that, even during the period of the prosecutions, the cumulative, demonological

Hexerei-concept only became integrated into the ideas of the common people to a very modest extent. It was not the devil's pact, but harmful witchcraft which occupied them and against which they tried to protect themselves. Furthermore, branding people as witches and making accusations against them provided an effective means of blackening a person's character and making his (or her) life difficult.

SWITZERLAND: THE END OF THE JOURNEY

In Switzerland the witchcraft prosecutions lasted the longest: they began early and in some areas the end came very late. The last judicial death sentence was carried out in 1782 in Glarus on Anna Göldi (Monter, 1994: 58). She was accused of having bewitched her employer's daughter. About thirty years earlier in the cantons of Schwyz and Graubünden (Poschiavo) executions were still taking place. These exceptions show that in these areas members of the courts, at least, still considered witchcraft to be a serious threat. They would almost certainly not have been alone in this opinion, but even so there remains virtually nothing more to say about Switzerland from the point of view of this essay. It is true that the two monographs by David Meili (1980) on the witches living in Wasterkingen and sentenced in Zürich in 1701, and by Christian Broye (1990) on witchcraft in Geneva from the sixteenth century up to about 1750 provide valuable information, but there is no research on any later period. Nevertheless, some of the results from Broye's study are important. This is because Broye poses the question of the continuity of witchcraft. His first focus is on the period of the witch-trials themselves (1520–1681). The Genevan policy was comparatively mild and relatively few death sentences were pronounced. The last execution took place in 1652 and the last but one in 1626. Broye diagnoses a high degree of continuity in the opinions of the ordinary people of Geneva and its environs. The element of revenge was a prominent factor. Witches – three quarters of the witch-trials concerned women – did not choose their victims at random; they were always out for retaliation. The result was sicknesses of people or animals. Broye does point to a change at the beginning of the seventeenth century in the kinds of misfortunes that were attributed to witches: whereas in the sixteenth century poisoning was still regularly mentioned, there were now reports of the possession of young girls by demons instead (Broye, 1990: 26–8, 63, 71, 104).

After the end of the witch-trials 24 cases were brought against cunning men and women between 1680 and 1750. Broye regards these accused as the successors of the witches. This is an observation which has also been made for other areas, but which does not, for example, apply to the

Netherlands. Although it is of course possible that the judicial authorities only took action against unwitching specialists after the witch-trials were behind them – because they now had more time and/or started to view the activities of these specialists as a threat to public order – it could be that closer examination of the earlier legal records might show that there had already previously been cases against such specialists. Be that as it may, it is clear that Geneva, at least in the period from 1680 to 1750 cited by Broye, harboured a considerable number of cunning men (including executioners) and cunning women and that they had no lack of customers. Apart from being consulted in connection with bewitchments, they were also called in to help find lost or stolen goods. For this purpose they made use, among other things, of well-known manuals such as *Le Petit* and *Le Grand Albert* and *La Clavicule de Salomon* (Broye, 1990: 110–11). Indeed, these were books which were also very popular amongst the population. A last incident which is mentioned by Broye concerns the molestation of an older Genevan woman, married to a master tanner, who had for years had the reputation of being a witch and who also acted as a healer. She was evidently fond of children, gave them tit bits and petted them. The sickness of one of these children in 1728 – the woman had given the child nuts, after which it was taken ill – was the last straw. The parents of the child in question had reason to suppose that there was an element of revenge here. They called in the executioner, who advised them to burn the child's bonnet and after that to treat the child's clothes with a hazel rod. This would not only harm the witch responsible, but also compel her to come and account for her conduct. It is interesting that the executioner, who evidently feared for the child's life, covered himself in advance against the failure of the therapy by saying that he was not God and that he had no influence over him. When the mother of the child went to beat the clothes, this was the final confirmation needed by the people on the streets. The suspect woman was surrounded by a large crowd and could only be rescued just in time (Broye, 1990: 114–21). As this story demonstrates, half a century after the end of the witch-trials witchcraft affairs had by no means come to an end. From further research it could well turn out that this incident was not the last of its kind.

Conclusion: Cultures of Misfortune: Towards a Disenchanted Europe?

Long after the end of the witch-trials, thinking and acting in terms of witchcraft still formed part of the cultural repertoire which was available to people in cases of misfortune. For those concerned, witchcraft remained a useful, culturally accepted and therefore rational strategy for dealing with certain problems. It could explain misfortune and the responsibility for it could be attributed to someone else. At the same time, witchcraft was a means of power, an instrument which could be used to damage the position of another person and/or improve ones own. To counteract the threat of bewitchment there was the threat of accusation.

Nevertheless, although it by no means disappeared in cultural terms, witchcraft had to concede ground, both as regards content and in a social sense. How this process took place in the different European countries can only partly be reconstructed. As has become apparent, witchcraft research still exhibits numerous lacunae for the eighteenth and nineteenth centuries. Moreover, the available studies reveal a considerable diversity of approach, which impedes comparison. Let this caveat suffice here.

A variety of meanings are covered by the umbrella concept of witchcraft, and by similar terms in other languages. As mentioned earlier, for the Dutch province of Drenthe de Blécourt has identified four such meanings or types to do with bewitching, unwitching, witching and scolding. Female neighbours were suspected of bewitching, men from neighbouring hamlets of witching. For unwitching outsiders gave advice. Scolding, calling someone a witch, can be seen as a derivative of witching and especially of bewitching. De Blécourt's conclusion is that in the incidents in Drenthe there was virtually no overlapping between bewitching, witching and unwitching; these were never combined in one and the same person (de Blécourt, 1990: 237).

To what extent these different meanings, and in particular those of bewitching and witching, can also be distinguished elsewhere, is only partially clear. Accusations of enriching oneself through witchcraft (witching) have been found in the available research, but the element of causing harm (bewitching) certainly does not seem to have been absent and was even to the fore. This is because what one person appropriated was at the expense of another. This at least is the picture that emerges from research on Norway and Russia. Here too this was a question of conflicts between men.

However, there is more to be said. There are numerous examples, spread over large parts of Europe, of (predominantly) men who tried to trace buried treasure by magical means. This might or might not be with the help of the devil, and was aimed at the remuneration of other people as well as themselves. That it was possible to combine this activity with unwitching is shown by a Belgian example from the eighteenth century. Similarly numerous and widespread, though substantially overrepresented in the Mediterranean area, are the examples, predominantly of women, who practised love magic for themselves or for other women. This was usually in order to gain or regain a partner, if necessary by making it impossible for that man to make love to another woman. Magical treasure hunting and love magic might well be regarded as forms of witching, in the sense of feathering one's nest, although here too one person's gain could mean another person's loss. Certainly in the case of love magic we see forms of witching that, at least from the point of view of a man struck by impotence, were scarcely, if at all, to be distinguished from bewitching.

As indicated earlier, it is a point of discussion to what extent witchcraft, in whatever form, was experienced as fundamentally ambivalent. The combination of different sorts of witchcraft in one person is an indication of just such an ambivalent assessment. The figure of the unwitching specialist has received particular attention in this context: to what extent and by whom was this figure feared as a witch and held responsible for bewitchments? Did practitioners combine in their person both bewitching and unwitching, just as (other) witches did, who were expected to undo the bewitchments they had brought about? Accusations of bewitchment directed at unwitching specialists do not seem to be spread evenly over Europe. Not only in Drenthe, but also elsewhere in the Netherlands they have scarcely been reported at all. From the north of France, on the other hand, there are numerous indications that unwitching specialists drew their custom from outside their own village and were feared as witches by their fellow villagers or were accused of bewitchments. In the Mediterranean areas, the southeast of Europe, Hungary, Switzerland, Belgium and England there are also reports of unwitching specialists who bewitched, although the spatial distance between them and their clientele often receives inadequate attention and such reports are still not very numerous from the last three of these countries. The rest of Europe has to be passed over in this respect. Further research will have to show to what extent it was the rule or the exception in various areas for unwitching specialists of different sorts, such as cunning people and priests, and of different sex, to be also feared for bewitchments. This also applies to the question of the extent to which unwitching went hand in hand with spatial distance between the unwitching specialist and the bewitched person, and bewitching with spatial proximity, where there was the chance of overstepping certain boundaries between the witch and the bewitched (de Blécourt, 1994).

Patterns of witchcraft can also be recognized in terms of the content of bewitchments (that is to say the kinds of misfortune that were attributed to them), the participants (in their roles as bewitched, male or female witches, or unwitching specialists), the nature and quality of the relations between the bewitched and the witch, and the way in which people dealt with the misfortunes attributed to bewitchment.

Let us begin with the content of bewitchments. The range of misfortunes that were linked to bewitchment was greater during the 'zenith' of the witch-trials than afterwards. On the one hand, there were misfortunes which could in principle affect a whole community, such as extreme weather conditions or epidemics. Misfortunes of this kind were attributed to the work of witches particularly in the core areas of the witchcraft prosecutions. They were considered by the prosecutors as a serious attack on society, contrived through a demonic pact. Less extensive, but equally dramatic disasters, such as shipwrecks and fires, could just as well be interpreted as results of bewitchment. On the other hand, there were the more personal misfortunes in the form of sickness or injury, damage to possessions (including the sickness of animals), and accidents with butter making and beer brewing. Naturally, with this sort of bewitchment it was not only single persons who were affected, but also whole families. Eventually the range of misfortunes was reduced and only the more or less personal misfortunes remained. Thus, in the area of Holland shipwreck was still sometimes connected with witchcraft until virtually the end of the sixteenth century, but not afterwards. In general, the reduction of enchantment to the sphere of personal misfortune coincided with the approaching end of the witch-trials.

What kinds of personal misfortune were attributed to bewitchments in the different parts of Europe in the course of the eighteenth and nineteenth centuries, which kinds occurred most frequently, which disappeared from the scene, and which remained? From the research materials available the following picture emerges. Protracted or otherwise exceptional illnesses of children (but also of adults), and also misfortune in the domestic economic sphere, such as the sickness of animals or the failure of butter making, were attributed to bewitchment. Not surprisingly, the latter forms of misfortune disappeared from the witchcraft repertoire earlier in the towns than in the countryside. Thus, in rural England the pig, 'the cottager's friend', remained a popular target for bewitchment up to the nineteenth century (Davies, 1995: 357). In some places earlier, in others later, the realm of bewitchments became reduced to the most personal sphere – people's health. In the comparatively rich province of Holland this development had already started in the seventeenth century. Elsewhere, and particularly in the rural areas, it presumably took place much later. The more the vulnerability to misfortune in the sphere of the domestic economy decreased, the fewer were the bewitchments in this area. Thus, it has been established for the Dutch province of Drenthe and for England that with the coming of the milk factories butter making ceased to be a target for bewitchment.

As a form of bewitchment which tended above all to affect girls and as a rule younger women, possession occasionally occurred for a considerable time after the end of the witch-trials. There are various cases known in England from the second half of the eighteenth century and a possible last case in 1815, while a Russian village still experienced a real possession epidemic as late as 1898–9. In France, too, such attacks of possession did not finish directly after the witch-trials, although researchers make no mention of them for the nineteenth century (see also Porter in this volume). A similar situation occurred in the Netherlands, but there the number of cases remained comparatively small and there is no further mention of them after the seventeenth century. What happened in this respect in other countries cannot be gathered from the available research. A specifically male complaint which could be attributed to bewitchment was impotence. In the research on the Mediterranean regions in particular there is frequent mention of such bewitchments. Whether they occurred more in these countries than elsewhere needs to be investigated further. It is also difficult to say whether, in other parts of Europe as in parts of the Netherlands, men became scarcely affected by bewitchments, with children in particular, and to a lesser degree women, remaining as the vulnerable groups.

It is also interesting to note that, as the domain of bewitchments was reduced to the most personal sphere, witchcraft also became depersonalized; that is to say, the attribution of misfortune to a bewitchment was no longer, or less often, accompanied by the naming of a culprit. Examples of this have been produced for England and the Netherlands. In his study of religion in South Lindsey, Lincolnshire, James Obelkevich (1976: 285–6) reports that towards the end of the nineteenth century the failure of butter making was still blamed on witchcraft, but that no attempt was made to trace the witch responsible. 'It was witchcraft without witches', he says. In this connection Obelkevich speaks of the completion of a long-term process of depersonalization, a process which he does not, however, trace back in time. Davies maintains, on the other hand, that none of this is apparent from his research covering the whole of England, which is based on more than just stories recorded by folklorists. He concludes that 'specific individual misfortunes were hardly ever blamed on witches in general, but on known witches' (Davies, 1995: 353).

The research carried out by de Blécourt does offer some support for Obelkevich's argument. Thus, in Drenthe in the second half of the nineteenth century, specific people were no longer directly accused of bewitching the butter making and preventive measures had gained the upper hand (de Blécourt, 1990: 193). There is also a change to be observed in the same period in the methods of the Frisian witch–doctors. Their advice was no longer directed to exposing the witch (de Blécourt, 1990: 246). Indeed, it can be added here that exorcisms, in so far as they were still used as a remedy for ills attributed by the victims to bewitchment but were not aimed at tracing the witch, also represented a 'depersonalized', or rather a non-person-oriented strategy, which had been used for centuries. What significance this has in the framework of Obelkevich's argument for depersonalization is nevertheless an important question. For the present a distinction should be made between what priests and other unwitching specialists were aiming at in their rituals and the explanation which their clients attached to their actions. In tracing the process of depersonalization the views and strategies of the people bewitched must be to the fore. It will have to be shown to what extent 'depersonalized' healing rituals on the part of the specialists indeed indicate that the bewitched themselves were no longer out to expose the culprit. Here too there is a task for further research.

As far as the frequency of bewitchments is concerned, it can only be remarked in a general sense that as time passed bewitchment affairs grew less frequent. Thus, there are considerably fewer known from the twentieth century than from the nineteenth. However, there is no question of a continuous, consistent decline. From Dutch research, for instance, it emerges that in the eighteenth and nineteenth centuries marked fluctuations occurred in the number of bewitchment cases (de Blécourt, 1990: 248–52; de Waardt, 1991a: 282–91). In this connection it must be borne in mind that it is difficult to trace the extent to which the fluctuations and the ultimately decreasing frequency of such affairs, as suggested by the available sources, are a reliable gauge for the cases dealt with informally and possibly without (much) violence, which occur comparatively rarely in these same sources. After all, cases of this second kind will have constituted by far the majority, as, for instance, is reported by Davies (1995: ch. 3) for England in the eighteenth and nineteenth centuries.

Apart from the scope and the frequency of bewitchments, their social complexion also changed. This took place more by fits and starts than is suggested by research conducted as if former societies consisted only of two social strata – 'elite' and 'people' – each with its own way of thinking and acting (Harris [ed.], 1995). The end of the witch-trials did not imply that elites became 'enlightened' straightaway, and thereby rose far above the ordinary, 'superstitious' people. For some time after the witch-trials had been discontinued it appears, for instance, that parsons in rural England, Jesuits in the Dutch Republic and priests in French villages and small towns were willing to give active support to victims of bewitchment. From rural municipalities in Twente in the East of the Netherlands (te Walvaart, 1995: 44–5) and Alsace (Lea, 1939: 1529) there are comparatively late examples known from the end of the eighteenth and the end of the nineteenth century respectively of burgomasters who were involved in witchcraft, sometimes as next of kin of the bewitched. Moreover, from Dutch, German and English research it can be seen that orthodox Protestant traditions – respectively Calvinist, Pietist and Methodist – formed a comparatively favourable breeding ground for thinking and acting in terms of witchcraft (de Blécourt, 1989a; Gestrich, 1995; Davies, 1997b). For those for whom the Biblical word was law, it was but a small step from the devil to the witch. Furthermore, in addition to French research, Belgian and Mediterranean studies have shown just how closely the Roman Catholic faith, as it found expression in rural areas, was also intertwined with witchcraft.

The view often expressed in witchcraft studies, that cases of bewitchment took place principally, and after the period of the trials almost exclusively, in the countryside, appears to need adjustment. It has been established that they also occurred among the population in cities such as London, Geneva and Palermo and that there was, moreover, plenty of work for urban unwitching specialists, even if they drew their clients from the rural areas as well and could be consulted for other matters too. In London this tradition can be traced down to the early twentieth century (Davies, 1997c). It is also known from various Dutch towns that bewitchment cases survived into the nineteenth century (de Waardt, 1991a: 304, 306).

If we look at female and male involvement in witchcraft questions, then the first thing to be noticed is, as emphasized above, that highly divergent patterns emerge from different areas and over the course of time. While in many countries it was women who were primarily labelled as witches and had to stand trial, in countries such as Iceland, Finland, the Baltic States and Russia this was not the case and men were in the majority (Levack, 1995a: 133–6; Briggs, 1996a: 260–2). Broadly speaking France occupied a middle position (Briggs, 1996a: 260). Numerous explanations have been given for the overrepresentation of women among the accused, but considerably fewer for the overrepresentation, or simultaneous occurrence of men. This last point also applies to the representation of men and women among the bewitched, the accusers and the unwitching specialists.

It is not within the scope of this essay to go exhaustively into the debate that has taken place so far (for a recent discussion see: Briggs, 1996a: 259–86). Broadly speaking – and this is also relevant for the period after the witch-trials – many of the explanations for the overrepresentation of female accused suffer from the fact that, like the questions they seek to answer, they are too general. The greater the number of specific, time- and place-related questions that are asked about the 'production' of witches, and the greater the attention that is paid to the circumstances in which (and the way in which) suspicions and accusations came about, and by whom they were expressed, the greater will be the chance of satisfactory answers. In this respect, it is important to establish for each area, period and group which stereotypes of witches – male/female, young/old, rich/poor – prevailed for the various sorts of witchcraft, and to what extent the forming of suspicions and the making of accusations conformed to, or diverged from them. As is demonstrated by Herzfeld's research on present-day Rhodes (1981), we must be on the lookout for discrepancies between image and practice.

One thing which by definition should be certain for the period after the witch-trials is a decrease in male involvement in the offensive against witches, whether these were women or men. Although judicial prosecutions had come to an end, this did not necessarily mean that there was no role left for men as opponents of witchcraft. As the bewitched, as relatives or friends of the bewitched, or as unwitching specialists men do indeed still appear to have had a share in the process of insinuation, accusation and/or other actions against the witch, even if not to the same extent or in the same way in every place and time. It can only be partially established whether the development reported for the regions of Holland and Drenthe (in Holland from round 1600, in Drenthe from round 1700), that men became less and less involved with witchcraft, and that bewitchment cases increasingly took place between women and in the domestic sphere, reflected a more general pattern. As has been said, it should be borne in mind in this connection that male relatives of a bewitched person or male unwitching specialists in these regions of the Netherlands could still become involved in a bewitchment episode, certainly when the assumption and the suspicion of bewitchment in the female sphere had once taken shape and things had then deteriorated.

As far as the gender of the witch is concerned, a striking development took place in Russia where an initial male over representation had, by the nineteenth century, given way to a female. Among the bewitched too the share of women had become greater than that of men – a reason for Worobec (1995: 173) to characterize this development as a 'feminization' of witchcraft. Whether a similar 'feminization' took place in other countries with formerly predominantly male witches is not known.

In England, as in the Netherlands, women occupied virtually a monopoly position among the accused, but it must be doubted on the basis of the fairly regularly recurring reports of male witches in the eighteenth and nineteenth centuries whether this still remained true after the period of the witch-trials. Whether a 'feminization' of the bewitched and the accusers occurred in England in this later period cannot be determined on the basis of the available research. Among the unwitching specialists the male role in the later period appears to have been comparatively large. In Danish, German and French research on this same period male witches are also to be found, though not in large numbers. To what extent the creation of the witch in these countries increasingly became women's work can also be only partially examined. If male involvement in the creation and indication of witches was already decreasing, this certainly did not apply when it came to forcing them to undo their bewitchments. Ultimately both bewitchments *and* the attempts to undo them remained a family affair. Just as bewitchments affected not only the victims, but also their families, so too were unwitching activities (partly) dominated by family interests, whether or not they were primarily carried out on the initiative of, and by women.

As long as the extent of female and male involvement in witchcraft in the period after the witch-trials has not been adequately charted, it will not be possible from the interpretative point of view to get much out of comparative analyses. Generally speaking the vulnerability of (certain) women or men to accusations of bewitchment and/or 'witching' (enriching themselves) was greatest in their own domain of daily duties. For women this meant the care of members of the family and usually animals, including milking and butter making. This usually took place indoors or in the immediate vicinity of the house, and it is clear that it was all too easy for things to go wrong. The situation remained on the whole unchanged up to the nineteenth and even the twentieth century. Depending on the specific activities and the possibly diminishing risks or better risk cover, the male work domain, predominantly situated outside the home, exhibited a correspondingly diminishing vulnerability to misfortune and, therefore, fewer occasions for a man to be suspected of a possible bewitchment in this field. In so far as men or women acted as unwitching specialists they each ran the risk, depending on time and place, of being suspected of harmful witchcraft.

As regards the nature and quality of the relations between the bewitched and his or her closest relatives on the one hand and the male or female witch on the other the following observations can be made. The bewitched person attributed to the witch not only the power of bewitching but also the actual bewitchment. In his or her turn the bewitched person exercised power over the witch by possibly making an accusation or forcing him or her to undo the bewitchment or not. Once again it has been established for Drenthe that whereas accusations had usually been directed 'downwards' from the social point of view, by the eighteenth century the opposite was the case. In this region there is no evidence of previous conflicts between accuser and accused.

Scarcely nothing is known about the social direction of accusations elsewhere, certainly for the later period. As far as the quality of the relations between the parties preceding accusation is concerned, for regions outside the Netherlands and for the period of the witch-trials attention has often been drawn to their 'socially strained' nature. Whether this was a question of open conflict or of repressed tensions, there was reason for the bewitched person to attribute maleficent intentions to the witch. The later examples cited in this essay also show how diverse the background of witchcraft accusations could be. Nevertheless, it must be assumed that Briggs's broad description of witchcraft as being 'available to fit any kind of discord' (Briggs, 1996a: 265) does not always hold good for the later centuries. This is because of the already mentioned reduction in the scope of bewitchments, the depersonalization of witchcraft reported for some regions, and the decreasing participation in bewitchment affairs both as regards social composition in general and, at least in certain areas, as regards men. In this respect, it is vital to gain more insight into the actual (power) relations, not only between men and women, but also, for example, between members of different generations, between members of families and fellow villagers, and between the well-established and new-comers. What were the resulting pressure points and tensions, and to what extent and by whom were they then 'translated' into witchcraft suspicions and accusations?

Patterns of witchcraft can also be traced with regard to reactions to bewitchments. The violent reactions stand out in particular, if only because they were more likely to come to the notice of the police and the courts and to get into the newspapers. To what extent the various reactions give an indication of the perceived weight of misfortunes can be only partially established, certainly given the present state of research. Violent reactions towards the alleged witch could indicate that a misfortune was experienced as extremely serious, yet the absence of violence or even of any confrontation with the witch – if he or she had indeed been identified – does not necessarily imply that it was taken lightly. Whether taking the law violently into ones own hands represented a last resort, after self-medication, counter-magic and/or consulting healers or unwitching specialists – in so far as these were available – had all come to nothing, cannot always be discovered, although this seems likely. This does not mean, however, that direct personal violence can simply be regarded as superseding formal witch-trials. Both could occur at the same time, as Soman has shown for the jurisdiction of the *parlement* of Paris (Soman, 1985: 198).

What can hardly be ignored, partly thanks to contemporary and later reports, is that in a number of cases – presumably a small minority of the total – the use of violence was certainly not shunned in the effort to have a bewitchment removed. Into the nineteenth century, fire and beatings were repeatedly used: the witch sometimes lost her life into the bargain. Apart from those from France and Germany similar stories are known from Belgium, Ireland and Russia. Elsewhere it was not fire but water that was popular. This was the case particularly in England but also in the Ukraine and, presumably to a lesser extent, in Denmark and the Netherlands. From England there are numerous eighteenth- and nineteenth-century examples where a woman, or sometimes a man or a married couple, who were suspected of bewitchment, were thrown into water. The water ordeal, which in earlier times had been used to determine whether or not someone was a witch, was also adopted in this later period both as a punishment and as a means of rendering the witch temporarily or permanently harmless. In addition, witches were scratched in order to break their bewitchments with their own blood. In England this happened fairly regularly up to the nineteenth century. Examples of scratching the witch are also known from countries such as Denmark and the Netherlands.

From the available research material it can also be gathered that personal violence against witches did not occur everywhere or to the same extent. There are relatively few incidents of this kind known for the Netherlands, compared to Belgium, France and England. This might be traced partly to national and regional differences in the pace at which each government established a monopoly of force. As has been demonstrated for England, the introduction of a professional police force meant the final eclipse of the water ordeal (Davies, 1995: ch. 3).

From what has been said above and the preceding European survey what conclusions can be drawn about the continuity, change and decline of witchcraft in the various parts of the continent and the British Isles? Despite the necessary reservations it has to be said that no clear break in thinking and acting in terms of witchcraft is apparent between the period of and the period after the witch-trials. Well after the end of these trials, even centuries afterwards, witches were still held responsible for misfortunes. Nevertheless, this does not mean that there was complete continuity. The diminution of the domain of bewitchments, on the one hand, and narrowing of social participation in them, on the other, signify important, albeit gradually occurring, changes, first observed in the relatively prosperous and urbanized areas such as Holland. This reduction was accompanied at the same time by a decline in the frequency of bewitchments, although, as far as one can tell, this did not take place continuously or consistently. A decline in witchcraft can be said to have happened earlier in one place and later in another. However, this does not mean that Europe in about 1900 – the finishing point for this essay – was 'disenchanted'. On the contrary, there are many reports of bewitchment cases up to and including the twentieth century and from all parts of Europe. If the process of the disenchantment of Europe has still not yet been completed, this must have been very far from true in 1900.

The question as to why there was a 'decline of witchcraft' has frequently been asked but very seldom answered. In the first place, this is because all too often, and rather carelessly, another question is really intended – namely why was there an end to the witch-trials (see amongst others Levack, 1995a: 233–4; Briggs, 1996b: 49–63). This is not very helpful for our purposes. But if the question as to why there was a decline in witchcraft is really asked, it is often couched in too general terms. Further differentiation between various kinds of witchcraft and between belief and practice is called for. If we concentrate on the still very broad question of why the interpretation of misfortune in terms of witchcraft became less popular over the years, or on its counterpart, of why such interpretations retained their credibility for many people for centuries after the end of the witch-trials, then Davies' findings for England and Wales are above all relevant. These are that the belief in the possibility of bewitchments lasted longer than the practice of making witchcraft accusations (Davies, 1995: Conclusion). As mentioned earlier, he concludes from this that the decrease in witchcraft accusations resulted in the decline of witchcraft belief, and not the other way round. For him the core question is why the number of witchcraft accusations in England substantially decreased from the end of the nineteenth century onwards, or, in other words, why local communities no longer generated witches. His answer comprises the five previously mentioned 'inter-related circumstances', i.e. communal instability, decline of self-government and the intrusion of state and local government, separation from livestock and food production, personal security and state charity, and the shifting balance of population from rural to urban communities. In his view these circumstances, brought about by the transition from an autarkic rural culture to a 'dependency culture' from the mid-nineteenth century onwards, directly influenced the 'socio-economic mechanisms which produced accusations of witchcraft'.

This summing up sounds plausible, but is this all that can be said? What, for example, is the range of Davies' explanation? Is it also valid for other countries? Answering this question is a somewhat precarious undertaking in the present state of research. However, the methodology of Davies' approach does deserve some comment. A distinction between the circumstances and the mechanisms which encouraged witchcraft accusations can be enlightening, provided the mechanisms – for example the refusal of alms followed by a bewitchment – are made explicit, which Davies does too little of. I regard the circumstances as structural developments which together act on and result in the 'structure of the situation' in which people make decisions and take actions. Mechanisms, on the other hand, are the quantifiably recurring ways in which people react when placed in these situations. Next we must see how all this can be substantiated. While Davies chooses to approach the decrease in witchcraft accusations from a structural perspective, from outside as it were, the approach recommended here will be from the other direction, from within – that is to say, with those who were affected by misfortune in mind.

Although no bewitchment occurred without misfortune, not every, and also not every kind of misfortune was attributed to bewitchment. Already in the early modern period there were numerous areas of life, for example trade and administration, where bewitchments scarcely occurred (Barry, 1996: 25). The reduction in the range of misfortunes connected with bewitchments, which occurred earlier in one place and later in another and finally resulted in only the sickness of humans being left, was to a considerable extent brought about by structural changes in societies. Davies mentions the decline in the number of households keeping domestic cattle, the development of factory-produced butter and cheese, and also the increased possibilities of insurance against risks. This meant that fewer people were vulnerable to misfortune in these fields. A similar reduction in vulnerability in the realm of sickness – particularly with regard to children – took considerably longer. In connection with the sandy areas and peat lands in Drenthe, de Blécourt (1990: 256) speaks in this fashion of 'the conditions' – namely the economic, and especially the accompanying demographic developments – in which witchcraft accusations could exist, flourish and decline.

If someone was affected by a kind of misfortune which could in principle be attributed to bewitchment, then the formulation of a suspicion or accusation of witchcraft depended partly on the existence of motives and opportunities for manoeuvring someone else into the role of witch. The chance of this happening was greater when people were thrown back on one another in a local community, when they knew a great deal about each other, and when there was therefore plenty of occasion for conflicts and envy (Walz, 1993). This is also a theme which Davies explores when he advances the instability of local communities and urbanization as circumstances which contributed to the decrease in witchcraft accusations. In other words, what is at issue here is the structure of the situation, which to a greater or lesser extent 'invites' the attribution of misfortune to the evil intentions of another person. The less the local inhabitants depended on, and interfered with one another, the fewer the motives and opportunities for attributing their own misfortunes to bewitchments by other people. It may be added here that impediments to taking counter-measures, such as the official prohibition of the water ordeal in England as reported by Davies, indirectly contributed to the decrease in witchcraft accusations. From then on people had to manage without such a spectacu-lar demonstration and confirmation of the danger of witches.

Jonathan Barry (1996: 25–7) has recently rightly pointed out that the cultural context and transmission of witchcraft beliefs should receive more attention. In the event of misfortune people could draw on a variety of available cultural repertoires: witchcraft was one of them, alongside a whole range of religious and non-religious forms of knowledge and behaviour, even reaching as far as 'science', including medicine. Generally speaking, people could explain misfortune either in personal or impersonal terms. Following Alan Macfarlane's classification a 'personal' explanation could take three directions; the misfortune could be attributed to God (as punishment for ones own sins or the sins of the community), to another person (the witch or another scapegoat) or to oneself (ones own sins or otherwise). An 'impersonal' explanation, on the other hand, was based, in the terminology of Macfarlane (1970: 203), on impersonal forces which were set in motion at random (by chance) or according to certain, scientific, mechanistic laws. A certain relationship existed between the personal explanations in so far as people sought the (ultimate) cause of misfortunes in themselves. The stronger the sense of sin, the smaller the step to witchcraft. This partly explains why thinking in terms of bewitch-ment continued to possess relatively great appeal in orthodox Protestant circles, such the Württemberg Pietists, the English Methodists and the Dutch bible belt.

Cultures of misfortune provided not only explanations of, but also prescriptions for, adversity. In short, where prayers were of no help and the doctor was powerless, the unwitching specialist could bring relief. The effectiveness of the prescription ultimately tipped the scales. As long as doctors were unable to accomplish very much, there was a flourishing demand for unwitching specialists, and they could in turn generate fresh demand (de Blécourt, 1988). A similar argument applies to the Catholic and sometimes the Protestant clergy; in so far as the clergy were prepared to offer help in unwitching, they contributed to the continuity of witchcraft. This is at the same time one of the ways in which the cultural transmission took place – through the active help of church officials and unwitching specialists. The practice of bewitching and unwitching, and the attendant gossip and propaganda, were the best guarantees of the continuity of witchcraft. Seeing is believing.

In a more indirect way oral tradition also contributed to the cultural transmission of witchcraft. As bewitchment affairs became less common, and the chances decreased of ever coming into contact with witchcraft oneself, this form of tradition became even more important than in the past. However, where the narrative culture lost ground, at least as far as stories of concrete incidents were concerned, the younger generation remained deprived of this source of information. But even so, hearing is not seeing. A story about witchcraft from grandmother's or grandfather's time lacked the persuasiveness of an actual confrontation with a bewitchment. Our world may not yet be disenchanted, but it does not have far to go. The fact that nowadays some people label themselves as (good) witches shows that the risk of being branded as a maleficent witch has become negligible.

The process of 'disenchantment' has largely kept pace with that of secularization. Loss of ground by religion has in general been accompanied by loss of ground by witchcraft. As long as the Church cooperated in unwitching, whether intentionally or otherwise, and whether directly or indirectly, then not only was the link with the Church strengthened, but the reality of witchcraft was confirmed. And where the Bible was literally interpreted, witchcraft always found a favourable breeding ground.

Notes

Chapter 1

1. My thanks are due to Willem de Blécourt and Owen Davies for making manuscripts and literature available and for their comments on an earlier version of this essay, to Florike Egmond for providing archival material on a Dutch witchcraft case, to Hans de Waardt for his comments on an earlier version of the introduction and the chapter on The Netherlands, to Rachel M.J. van der Wilden-Fall for the translation of this essay into English, and the Royal Dutch Academy of Sciences for funding the translation. I should also like to thank Stuart Clark, Brian Levack, Roy Porter and, last but not least, August Gijswijt for their help and patience.

PART 3

Witchcraft and Magic in Enlightenment, Romantic and Liberal Thought

Roy Porter

CHAPTER 1

Controversy c. 1680–1800

INTRODUCTION

This volume has explored the ending of the judicial prosecution of witchcraft but the prolongation of such beliefs and practices at the grassroots. This final section now changes perspective, moving to 'history from above'. Panning from the late seventeenth century to the dawn of the twentieth, it addresses the questioning and rejection by the elite of the worldview that had sanctioned belief in witchcraft and magic, indeed the wider repudiation of the supernatural and the superstitious in the names of reason, science, civilization and progress.

What follows will examine the movement for ideological modernization launched by the Enlightenment and its offspring, especially what has variously been termed the secularization, naturalization, or at least dechristianization of the Western mind.[1] The broad-brush approach employed will inevitably blur many complexities, but it is vital to avoid treating the discrediting of witchcraft in isolation. Doubtless witch prosecutions shuddered to a halt partly because courtroom proceedings became too troublesome, contentious or embarrassing. But the repeal of witchcraft legislation was an expression of deeper shifts in elite outlooks, often represented as a joyous emancipation from dated dogmas repugnant to modernizers anxious to bury the past and to build a better future. The Enlightenment proclaimed '*sapere aude*' and one of the truths it dared to know was that witchcraft, magic and all their supernatural trappings were false or foolish phantasms (Gay, 1966–9).

What follows will examine the repudiation of outmoded beliefs and the promotion of outlooks distancing self-styled 'Moderns' from 'Ancients', and 'healthy' from 'pathological' attitudes – though it is crucial to note that the rejection of archaic creeds was never as cut-and-dried as its champions claimed. The ending of the persecution of witches was attended by new witch-hunts – and in any case wasn't the vaunted victory of science over faith a faith of its own? What was happening was not the victory of light over darkness but a cultural revamping. Indeed, the paeans to progress once raised by *philosophes* and positivists, liberals and Whig historians now seem highly problematic. With the benefit of cultural anthropology and the sociology of knowledge, today's historians have abandoned the appealing but question-begging evolutionism that once celebrated the ascent of man from magic to science, from religion to reason; celebrating the triumph of truth has given way to analysing structures of belief.[2]

The chapter opens by examining the challenge to witch-beliefs mounted in England. Thereafter, rather than repeating this story for other parts of Europe (there are many similarities, albeit with local variants of timing and circumstances), my emphasis will be upon what was distinctive in campaigns against 'error' mounted elsewhere – for example, encounters with vampires in Hungary and with shamans in Siberia. This leads to the next chapter which will turn to the ideological weaponry mobilized by the *philosophes* to fight 'superstition' and the supernatural.[3] Sorcery and magic did not just wither away; indeed, as Marijke Gijswijt-Hofstra has stressed, they continued to seed and shoot within the community, providing villagers with explanations of their lot in life and with the means to protect themselves or pursue their feuds. Such convictions had become alien to dominant elites and the state, however – at best objects of curiosity and at worst repugnant to reason and good sense. The last two chapters will conclude by exploring the strange fate of the supernatural in an era when its theological and metaphysical foundations being undermined.

THE DECLINE OF WITCH PRACTICES AND BELIEFS IN ENGLAND

Witch panics were by no means over. As related by Brian Levack earlier in this volume, Styria and the Tyrol exploded in the 1680s and 1690s, Poland became an epicentre between 1675 and 1725, and Hungary in the 1720s – while, across the Atlantic, Salem in Massachusetts provided one of the most shocking outbreaks of all in 1692, with 30 witches convicted. Witch trials continued in Bavaria through to the 1760s (Behringer, 1995), while, as late as 1782 a witch was tried and executed in Switzerland. Nevertheless, what makes the period distinctive is the spate of official prohibitions against witch-hunting, from Louis XIV's in 1682 to Maria Theresa's in 1768, and the repeal of witchcraft legislation, for example in England in 1736 and Sweden in 1779. Enlightened Europe took pride in abolishing yet another relic of barbarism.

By 1700 legal proceedings against witches were petering out in England.[4] The generation after 1570 had brought nearly two-thirds of all executions, and some of the key persecution manifestos, notably James I's *Daemonologie* (1597). Panics in Essex and Kent fanned by the Civil War sparked further executions, and the final sentence known to have been carried out occurred in Devon in 1682, when Temperance Lloyd, Susanna Edwards and Mary Trembles were sentenced for bewitching four women. The last assize court conviction was that of Jane Wenham in Hertfordshire in 1712, but after a highly politicized case, she was pardoned, a sign of official scepticism. The disdainful trial judge, Sir John Powell, 'expressed surprise when Thorne [an accuser] went into fits in court', and he 'rejected the usefulness as proof of witchcraft of a number of bent pins said to have been vomited'.[5] When Jane Clerk was indicted for witchcraft in 1717, the case against her was dismissed.

Nineteen years later Parliament actually repealed the statutes of Mary of Scotland (1563), Elizabeth I (1563), and James I and VI (1604), declaring that 'no prosecution, suit or proceedings shall be carried out against any person or persons for witchcraft, sorcery, inchantment, or conjuration'. While the 1736 Statute permitted the prosecution of those *pretending* to perform magic, it denied the reality of those powers. Witchcraft had been reduced to false pretences, an offence particularly troublesome to a commercial society.[6]

Thereafter, though witch practices and accusations continued, they were essentially confined to low culture, only occasionally erupting into the public sphere, as with the hideous case in 1751 in Tring, some 30 miles north of London, that culminated in the hanging of Thomas Colley, a butcher. Colley had headed a mob that hounded John and Ruth Osborne, claiming they were witches. The lynch-mob attack on the 70-year old couple was proclaimed in advance; anticipating trouble, the overseer of the poor sheltered them in the workhouse; when the mob besieged it they were moved to the church, but they were then dragged out to a pond, where Ruth Osborne was ducked by Colley, and, as a trial witness testified, 'that was the last time he perceived any life in her'. Her husband was then kicked and beaten to death (Carnochan, 1971; Sharpe, 1996: 3f.).

Reports appeared in polite organs like the *Gentleman's Magazine*, expressing outrage at the barbarity of the rabble. One moral they pointed was the fact that, while Colley was awaiting execution, a 'gentleman' visited him, 'to reason with him, and to convince him of his erroneous opinion, in believing that there was any such thing as witchcraft'. That envoy of enlightenment generously informed him that 'witches had no manner of existence but in the minds of poor infatuated people, in which they had been confirm'd by the tradition of their ancestors, as foolish and crazy as themselves'. The vulgar for their part ('so great was the infatuation of the people') nevertheless reckoned 'it was a very hard case, that a man should be hang'd for destroying an old wicked woman, who had done so much mischief by her abominable charms and witchcraft'. Two aspects of the Colley case thus stand out: by 1750 it was not the witch but the witch-hunter who suffered the law's penalty; and witchcraft had come to be represented as a conflict not between God and Satan but between civilized gentlemen, flanked by Church and State, and brutal rustics. Some forty years after the event, the parson-naturalist Gilbert White echoed the moral: noting 'it is the hardest thing in the world to shake off superstitious prejudices', he invited readers to remember the 'practices too gross for this enlightened age' perpetrated at Tring (*The Trial*, 1751; *The Remarkable Confession*, 1751; White, 1989: 265–6).

There was of course nothing new about scepticism: witchcraft was inherently implausible, critics had long argued; it depended on cozening and credulity, and had no cast-iron Biblical warrant. But early opponents of witch-trials, like the physician Johan Wier, whose *De praestigiis daemonum* appeared in 1563, had been arguing from within the same doctrinal framework as the witch-hunters, accepting the reality of Satan and spirits, if challenging them on *maleficium*, sabbats and the like. So long as Reformation and Tridentine doctrines remained authoritative, witches would be seen not as victims but as villains, heretical conspirators pledged, through confederacy with the Devil, to the confusion of God's Kingdom.[7]

It was only once an alternative or at least a modified world-view gained ground that witchcraft could be widely discredited or dismissed. That is broadly speaking what transpired after 1650. Liberal natural theology of the kind soon to be broadcast from the pulpit by the Boyle Lectures sidelined the God-versus-Satan psychomachy as versified in Milton's epic and instead enshrined a rational Deity presiding over a designer Universe (Jacob, 1976). The temper of the age of reason dismissed events like apparitions or convulsions as spurious, or explained them away through down-to-earth causes. The black arts could thus be mocked as silly superstitions, and demonology and *maleficium* lost their purchase.

Meanwhile new official arrangements were ministering over domains that had traditionally been the seedbeds of witch accusations. If, as some historians have argued, want of charity to a neighbour had often sparked witch charges, the Poor Law made relief the legal duty of the parish, and so perhaps deflected irritation away from the individual hag to the 'pauper problem' at large. In due course, the Devil became a character popular at the masquerade and witches would mainly figure in fairy stories. In the 1760s the 'Medmenham monks' of the Hellfire Club revelled in their notoriety as demoniacs, but none was a worshipper of any idol but Eros (McCormick, 1958; Summers, 1964: ch. vi; Castle, 1986: 50, 65).

CHANGING MIND-SETS: RELIGION, PHILOSOPHY AND SCIENCE

The eighteenth century inherited old disputes over witchcraft. Promoting their distinctive doctrines of matter and spirit, the sacred and the profane, Protestants and Catholics, Platonists and Aristotelians engaged in crossfire in an ideological minefield with respect to sorcery, magic and the 'invisible world'. Protestants took delight in exposing *false* miracles as Popish impostures, pagan leftovers or vulgar errors; but they affirmed *true* supernatural manifestations, thus corroborating the Gospel. In a tradition stemming from Johan Wier and from Reginald Scot's *Discoverie of Witchcraft* (1584), radical sceptics could even present themselves as the *echt* Christians even though denying the actuality of witchcraft: while the Devil existed, he had no power over material bodies. This view, however, cut little ice with theologians.[8]

The one shameless sadducee was Thomas Hobbes who, albeit paying lip-service to Christianity, formulated a philosophical materialism which ruled out the real presence of witches. 'The opinion that rude people have of fairies, ghosts and goblins and the power of witches' was attributed in his *Leviathan* (1651) to ignorance of how to distinguish 'dreams' from 'sense'. 'As for witches', he continued, 'I think not that their witchcraft is any reall power', though he approved of the punishment of such imposters for the 'false beliefe they have, that they can do such mischiefe'. Hobbesian materialism proved acceptable to none, and he was demonized, confirming the old dictum that denial of witchcraft was the Devil's work (Hobbes, 1968: 92).

Hobbes aside, authors in Restoration England affirmed belief in the supernatural, on the authority of reason and testimony, the Book of God's Word and the Book of God's Works. Yet the result was not consensus but confusion. Valentine Greatrakes, the 'Irish Stroker', claimed a divine gift of healing. Delighted to find signs of the operation of spirits, the Platonist Henry More accepted that Greatrakes' thaumaturgical powers 'may be the special gift of God in nature . . . wonderful at least, if not properly called miracles'. Others demurred: the Stroker's cures were impious and rabble-rousing, countered the royalist high-flyer David Lloyd in his *Wonders no Miracles* (1666); by touching for the King's Evil, Greatrakes was usurping theocratic powers (Duffy, 1981: 272; Bloch, 1973).

The physician and writer Sir Thomas Browne seemed to face two ways. His *Pseudodoxia Epidemica* (1672) trashed idle beliefs. But as a staunch Anglican and author of *Religio Medici*, he was ardently committed to traditional teachings about spirits. At the trial of Rose Cullender and Amy Duny at Bury St Edmunds in 1664–5, his testimony to witchcraft helped convict them (Stock, 1982: 63). A younger contemporary who likewise amphibiously pursued science (as an early Fellow of the Royal Society) while upholding witchcraft and magic was the antiquarian and astrologer John Aubrey. The supernatural and the natural were, for him, two faces of a single coin – 'Why should one think the Intellectual World less Peopled, than the Material?'. His papers teem with magical formulae, many being endorsed 'This hath bin oftin proved'. 'To make a man Gunne-proofe', he recorded, 'write these characters + Zada + Zadash + Zadathan + Abira + in virgin paper [I beleeve parchment] carry it always with you, and no gun-shott can hurt you'. 'If you will not beleive', he continued, 'hang the ring in a string about a Cocks neck, and shoot at him with a bowe or gun loaded with a bullet, and you will find the experiment true'. In his *Remaines of Gentilisme* he explained how to exorcise spirits and work charms. Nevertheless, as befitted an FRS, he regarded himself as a good Baconian, on one occasion getting a 'matter of fact' vouched for by 'a very understanding Gentleman, and not Super-stitious' (Hunter, 1975: 106f).

In these spiritual world controversies, Meric Casaubon's *Of Credulity and Incredulity* (1668) defined for many years to come the Anglican *via media*. Rejection of belief in witches opened the door to atheism, he warned; whatever the reservations about the individual case, the accumu-lated weight of reliable testimony tipped the balance in support of witchcraft (Casaubon, 1668; Hunter, 1985; Kors, 1990; Hunter and Wootton, 1992). A similar line was taken by the Cambridge scholar, Henry More. His *Antidote against Atheisme* (1653) presented information on 'the supernaturall effects observ'd in them that are bewitch'd and possess'd', so as to silence scoffing sceptics.[9] His arguments against saddu-ceeism were echoed by the younger Cambridge Platonist Ralph Cud-worth, who rebutted Hobbes's jibe that magic was fabricated by priests and princes to cow the people (Cudworth, 1743: ii, 654f.).

It would thus be misleading to represent the late seventeenth-century witchcraft debate as science dissolving superstition, because the 'new philosophy' was itself deployed to bolster supernaturalist beliefs. This is shown by the career of Joseph Glanvill, Anglican divine and Fellow of the Royal Society. Espousing More's Neoplatonism, his *Sadducismus triumpha-tus* (1668) attacked the sceptical conceit that witches were but 'creatures of melancholy and superstition'. Insisting that the reality of witches was 'not a matter of vain speculation' but matter of fact, he sought to prove witchcraft from Scripture and from 'a choice collection of modern relations' against the 'fool' who 'swaggers and huffs, and swears there are no WITCHES', but calls all such things 'ridiculous, incredible, foppish, impossible' (Glanvill, 1726: 3; 1668: 6; Burns, 1981: 49; Sharpe, 1996: 244–5). Denial of witches, Glanvill warned, leads to the 'Denial of Spirits, a Life to come, and all the other Principles of Religion': no witches, no salvation. Religion was to be rescued by the science of the supernatural. All this drew More and Glanvill into what became a further cockpit of controversy, the status of miracles, for witches were credited by demonologists with the capacity to perform if not actual miracles (*miracula*) at least wonders (*mira*).[10]

Glanvill's scientific validation of supernatural interventions met opposition, notably from John Webster, a Nonconformist medical practitioner. Writing from a Paracelsian-Helmontian position and convinced of occult natural powers, Webster's objective, in *The Displaying of Supposed Witchcraft* (1677), was to deny not wonders as such but the Devil's role in them. His experiences as a medical practitioner, which included treating the 'possessed', reinforced his scepticism. He had had patients whose families were 'perswaded' that they were 'possest', but what he diagnosed was disease (Webster, 1677: 124–5).

The Glanvill-Webster debate reveals how science was everyone's weapon in the witchcraft wars. Webster drew on the new natural philosophy to query the Devil's agency in the physical world, Glanvill for his part used it to demonstrate the existence of spirits. But was it not a rum do, scoffed the wits, if atheism could be confuted only by parading the powers of Satan? Did this not flatter the Prince of Darkness? Not at all, since it was manifestly true, as Robert Burton and many grave thinkers after him believed, that in this corrupt and contemptible *mundus senescens* 'the Devil reigns' (Burton, 1948: 214; Delumeau, 1978; Sharpe, 1996, 227f).

Respecting the unseen world, the Anglican middle way was a fine line: to believe too little was atheism, too much was superstition. Debates thundered on; and though the empirical and experimental style of scientific investigation continued to gain authority, feelings were more ambivalent about the mechanical philosophy accompanying it. The notion that Nature was governed by natural laws even then being discovered by the likes of Boyle, Hooke and Newton was of course appealing. But many shied away from the Cartesian mechanical universe, not least because it appeared to banish God and the soul (Schaffer, 1980; Hutchison, 1983).

EIGHTEENTH-CENTURY WITCHCRAFT DEBATES

The age of miracles was past: they had played their part in the founding of the faith, but salvation was now to be sought in Scripture. This conviction, basic to mainstream English Protestantism, had bearings upon the issue of witches' powers, that perennial problem for demonologists who attributed certain phenomena squarely to sorcery whilst holding others to be phantasms. For sceptics, since the age of miracles was past and God alone could perform miracles, the idea that witches could injure at a distance or fly off to a sabbat was not just preposterous but impious too (Sharpe, 1996: 241).

At the close of the century a work appeared congenial to such sceptical yet godly lines of thought. Between 1691 and 1693 Balthasar Bekker, a Dutch divine and admirer of Descartes, published the four-volume *De Betoverde Weereld*, translated into German in 1693 and into French the next year. It caused great offence, and Bekker was expelled from the ministry (Stock, 1982: 80; Attfield, 1985; Stronks, 1991).

The first volume, englished in 1695 as *The World Bewitch'd*, traced doctrines about demons back to pagans and papists. Demonic possession in the Bible was in reality but disease – though since what were involved were truly fatal conditions, *Christ's* cures were truly miraculous. Bekker was promoting a quiet Cartesianism. Spirits and demons might exist, but Scripture presented no proof that mortals could traffic with them: the Mosaic laws penalized cozeners and idolaters, and the witch of Endor was just an evil being. Supposed dealings with demons were not supported by cast-iron facts: all such matters could be accounted for by natural causes or chicanery. Uniting Calvinism and Cartesianism, *De Betoverde Weereld* maintained that the regularity of Nature ruled out witchcraft.[11]

It was false theology that had inflated the role of the Devil. 'If we consider the Scriptures with a perfectly open and unbiased mind', insisted Bekker, 'we shall certainly not attribute to the Devil those powers and activities which preconceived ideas led the commentators and translators to ascribe to him' (Hazard, 1953: 175). Seen through Cartesian eyes, Satan was a spirit; no spirit – not even the Devil – could act on 'extension' without a body as its medium; hence, the physical changes attributed to the Devil would have to be performed through matter and motion, and must submit to the regular laws of Nature. So, unless the Devil were embodied – which he wasn't – his alleged temptings and possessions were untenable (Bekker, 1695: Attfield, 1985: 390; Stronks, 1991: Preface to Book II). In any case, the Gospel, when correctly philologically inter-preted, taught that Christ's tempter was either a wicked man or a vision; witchcraft phenomena were subject to doubt and deception; and the Calvinist God being all-powerful, there was no logical possibility of the independent activities of a Devil (such would imply not monotheism but 'ditheism'); so, all things considered, 'the Empire of the Devil is a Chimaera'. Witchcraft delusions were, in short, the malady of weak minds. Those believing themselves bewitched or possessed were victims of their own naiveté; those practising divination were swindlers, guilty not of sorcery but chicanery.[12]

Doctrinal cleansing along lines similar to Bekker's, expunging superstition and enthusiasm, was influential in English religious thinking around 1700. Certain teachings, traditionally considered semi-heretical, gained ground. Both mortalism and Socinianism encouraged scepticism respecting notions of wandering spirits, paralleling Hobbes' boast that his doctrines laid such papist ghosts as purgatory, indulgences, and the invocation of saints (Stromberg, 1954; Almond, 1994: 67). Amongst rational Dissenters, passionate abhorrence of popish idolatry fed an icono-clastic mentality eternally suspicious of all manner of pretended spirits, paving the way for the fiercely monotheistic Christian materialism of Joseph Priestley in the late eighteenth century (Lincoln, 1938; Thomas, 1971: ch. iii).

The same decades also brought the comparable rise of Deism, associated with such figures as Toland, Collins, Chubb, Morgan, Wollaston and Woolston, who could operate under cover of John Locke's *The Reasona-bleness of Christianity* (1695). Ranging from irreverent and disingenuous wits like Charles Blount to sober believers, Deists insisted that any theological tenet which traduced reason would be an affront to the Supreme Being and the human mind. Some, rather as with Locke, believed Christianity passed the rationality test once purged of its popish relics; for more radical spirits, Christianity, at least as standardly under-stood, was irreparably superstitious, on account of such irrational elements as miracles and demons. Witchcraft was the machination of priestcraft, to frighten the people (Gay, 1968; Champion, 1992; Sharpe, 1996: 246).

Throughout the eighteenth century, many rationalizing impulses struggled to make the supernatural presentable, and the key problem for Christian apologists became the validity of miracles. The Church of England's position had been expounded by Edward Stillingfleet's *Origines Sacrae* (1662): miracles had been performed in Biblical times, and the Old and New Testament accounts were true. But, while affirming God's all-seeing Providence, 'we see no reason in the world for miracles to be continued where the doctrine of faith is settled'. To deny Scripture miracles was atheistic, but to expect new wonders was 'enthusiasm' (Stillingfleet, 1662: 142; Sharpe, 1996: 247).

On miracles, and hence more generally the supernatural, the key British sceptics were Thomas Woolston, Conyers Middleton and David Hume. An eccentric Deist, in *On the Miracles of Our Saviour* (1728–9) Woolston denied the New Testament healing miracles on various grounds. 'Faith and Imagination' might explain some; in others, such as Jesus curing blindness, there was clearly no miracle, for 'our Surgeons, with their Ointments and Washings', could achieve as much. The truly sensational miracles Woolston denied out of hand as 'monstrously romantick' – raising Lazarus from the dead was but 'Fable and Forgery'. Woolston boldly con-fronted Christ's own resurrection, relying on the old rabbinical argument that fanatics had absconded with the body. Woolston was convicted of blasphemy, but his tracts on miracles, published in 1727 and 1728, sold (said Voltaire) 30,000 copies in England and prompted over sixty replies (Burns, 1981: 10f.; Trapnel, 1994: 109). Amongst those, Bishop Thomas Sherlock's *Tryal of Witnesses of the Resurrection of Jesus* (1729) defended the credibility of human testimony: many had seen the risen Christ; while in his *Vindication of the Miracles of our Blessed Saviour* (1729–31), Bishop Richard Smalbroke charged Woolston with reducing the Devil and Hell 'to merely Mystical and Cabalistical Notions . . . to deprive them of all literal and real Existence' (Sherlock, 1729; Smalbroke, 1729–31).

The classicist Conyers Middleton's *A Free Enquiry into the Miraculous Powers* (1749) was widely read as a disguised denial of the reality of the New Testament miracles, since he confuted not only the Roman Catholic belief in continuing miracles (mere superstition) but also the respectable Anglican position that miracles continued in the primitive church, seeking, he claimed, to dissolve 'a chain of pretended Miracles' which deserved to be discredited because they debased Scripture. Middleton's scepticism was bolstered by reference to witchcraft. 'There is not in all history', he wryly insisted, 'any one miraculous fact, so authentically attested as the existence of witches. All Christian countries whatsoever have consented in the belief of them and provided capital laws against them: in consequence of which, many hundreds of both sexes have suffered a cruel death'. For all that, however, he crowed, writing after 1736, 'the belief of witches is now utterly extinct, and quietly buried' ([Middleton], 1749; 1751; Stock, 1982: 103; Sharpe, 1996: 250).

David Hume shifted the grounds for scepticism on miracles to the philosophy of knowledge and the psychology of belief. His 'Of Miracles' maintained that, in view of the seeming uniformity of the workings of Nature, any startling breach of them would inevitably be less believable than the suspicion of human error or deceit. Apparent miracles might stem from ignorance of natural causes; nor was human testimony of the miraculous persuasive, for too many psychological factors were involved (Burns, 1981: 142; Siebert, 1990; Tweyman, 1996).

Citadels of the supernatural thus came under fire in the boisterous polemics of the Augustan age. But, in gauging shifts in climates of thought, undue importance should not be attached to set-piece debates on miracles and the like. It was not pamphlet pyrotechnics that decided the fate of belief in witchcraft and the dominion of the Devil. Far more influential were deep-seated transformations of religious faith and sensibility amongst the educated elite in the post-Restoration generations. These may loosely be termed the victory of Latitudinarianism – roughly what Locke meant when he commended the 'reasonableness' of Christianity. What became professed amongst the polite and the propertied was a creed compatible with the new Lockean philosophy of mind and with Newtonian science.[13] Latitudinarianism represented the universe as well-designed, orderly and good, presided over by a benevolent and omnipotent Creator. The Earth was contrived for human use; in the light of an understanding of God's will and ways, it was man's right and duty to lead a virtuous and happy life, as prescribed by the laws of God and Nature. Views of this kind, advanced by prominent Anglican theologians from Archbishop Tillotson around 1690 to William Paley, author of the influential *Natural Theology* (1802), became the religion of moderate rational Protestants. Typical of the Latitudinarian vision of Creation was Joseph Addison, whose essays in the *Spectator*, played such a crucial role in promoting moderate Enlightenment views:

> The Spacious Firmament on high
> With all the blue Etherial sky
> And spangled Heav'ns, a Shining Frame
> Their great Original proclaim. (Willey: 1962: 51)

Whereas writers like Glanvill had looked to demons popping up as the confutation of atheism, Addison regarded cosmic order, illuminated by Newtonian laws, as the true proof of God. Needless to say, such ideas squared with the Whig oligarchy's notion of a well-governed polity – God's Universe was Walpole's England writ large.

This religious vision had no need for, or patience with, the fine print of Reformation scripturalism: the gallivantings of Old Testament Jews, semantic squabbles over predestination or transubstantiation, and doctrines like hellfire were all made to seem irrelevant, curious, or even inimical to basic morality to men of good will and freehold property. Why should Satan be granted such power if God were truly good and omnipotent? How could the Devil possibly have free rein if Creation operated through universal divine laws? Didn't the implication that evil enjoyed such sway sacrilegiously challenge Divine Beneficence? Rational religion was monotheistic and optimistic; the personification of Evil was a bugbear of benighted old believers, and of modern enthusiasts. In the greatest popularization of this new worldview, the *Essay on Man*, Alexander Pope instructed the reader against seeing Evil anywhere: 'Cease then, nor ORDER Imperfection name':

> All Nature is but Art unknown to thee;
> All Chance, Direction, which thou can'st not see;
> All Discord, Harmony, not understood,
> All partial Evil, universal Good:
> And, spite of Pride, in erring Reason's Spite,
> One truth is clear, 'Whatever is, is Right.' (Pope: 1965: 515)

The poetic antitheses of Pope's declaration of faith resembled the teaching of the influential theologian, Bishop Joseph Butler, that apparent imperfections in Creation were marks not of real evils but the limits of human understanding. And if, as Pope proclaimed, 'God said, *Let Newton be!* and all was light', what room could there be for the prince of darkness? (Cunliffe, 1992).

The new Latitudinarian ethos – Pelagian on sin, optimistic on the theodicy problem, and utilitarian in temper – called into question and, no less importantly, created a distaste for the paraphernalia of demonology that had haunted earlier generations. Gentlemanly Christians abandoned the Puritan fascination with doctrines of the millennium and hellfire. Such beliefs, along with the presence of a personal Devil, were now said, in coffee-house quips, to be the prattle of Dissenters and enthusiasts, notably (as will be explored below) the new menace of the Methodists. Moderates distanced themselves from those zealots whose preoccupation with portents and prophesyings served as salutary reminders of the crazed fanatics and fundamentalists of the Interregnum (Walker, 1964; Camporesi, 1991; Link, 1995; Stanford, 1996: 151f.).

Changing religious mentalities and sensibilities, and the embracing of an orderly, Newtonian universe, were reinforced at a more mundane level by new perceptions of the here-and-now befitting an age of reason. Interlocking advances in knowledge, science, technology and industry were boosting public confidence in the human capacity to know the natural and social order and hence to control it. And since to those with some power and prosperity, the workings of things seemed increasingly assured, old fears abated somewhat (Glacken, 1967; Spadafora, 1990). The Baconian gospel that knowledge is power was paying dividends in many fields of inquiry – chemical experimentation, mechanical advances, astronomy, navigation and so forth. And hopes were high of reducing to order the hidden springs of human action and social intercourse, as epitomized by David Hume's call for a Newton of the moral sciences. Data were being gathered about births and deaths, wealth and population; vital statistics were being tabulated by political arithmeticians; probability theory was promising to reveal the laws of life behind the chaotic surface; in the study of law and government, sensationalist psychology and the utilitarian felicific calculus were endeavouring to provide philosophical foundations for disciplines of pleasure, pain and punishment. Not least, the laws of the market were proclaimed, purportedly proving the self-regulating nature of the capitalist economy.

Behaviours traditionally explained in supernatural terms were now being subsumed within secular and impersonal explanations; suicide for instance, long held by theologians as diabolically triggered and a deliberate mutiny against God, was accepted in the eighteenth century as the act of those whose mental balance was upset; infanticide, likewise, came to be seen not as bewitchment but in the civil context of child-murder; while the Hanoverians abandoned the old thaumaturgical practice of 'touching for the King's Evil'. In due course Thomas Malthus, despite – or perhaps because of – being an Anglican clergyman, could claim to demonstrate in his *Essay on the Principle of Population* (1798) that catastrophes like war and famine had nothing to do with the Four Horsemen of the Apocalypse but followed inexorably from simple equations governing the balance of hunger and sex. In many domains there was taking place what, from a twentieth-century viewpoint, has been called a 'taming of chance', though less anachronistically it might be deemed the denial of the transcendental.[14]

This making of the mind-set of the human sciences – the basic expectation that social action is to be understood by impersonal, universal, natural and social law – went with a multitude of day-to-day indications that polite and propertied society, when confronting adversity, was less disposed than before to look to the Hand of God, and certainly not to the meddlings of Satan. It remained a hazardous world, but chance could now be limited through better information, regularly purveyed by the newspapers, and through practical resourses like smallpox inoculation, life and fire insurance, and banks. Faced with a household rat problem, the seventeenth-century astrologer Elias Ashmole used talismans to exorcise them; by the eighteenth century professional rat-catchers were advertising their services in the newspapers. The staging of public lotteries in Walpolean England symbolizes the new secular world-view.[15]

With confidence rising amongst opinion-makers as to the orderliness and controllability of nature and society, it is no surprise that the wits and *literati* of post-Restoration England should disparage those mired in 'superstition'. There was a sustained chorus of criticism targeted at vulgar folly (Malcolmson, 1973; P. Burke, 1978; Golby and Purdue, 1984). Presiding over the Alice Molland witch-trial in 1685, the judge Roger North slighted those who would subject witches to the swimming test, and took exception to the 'popular rage' and 'tattle' amongst the Exeter mob. The views of 'the common sort' were for him 'mere matter of fancy, as pigs dying, and the like' (North, 1890: iii, 131).

The classic expression of these new enlightened outlooks came as a rebuttal of the last full English defence of witchhunting. In 1715, Richard Boulton's *A Compleat History of Magick, Sorcery and Witchcraft* restated traditional orthodoxy: the Devil was dangerous and would worm his way into those sunk in despair. Convinced that 'the Devil comes to delude Men', Boulton affirmed the swimming test and the witch's mark to establish proof, though, to show how up-to-date he was, he also cited Boyle and Locke in support of the reality of spirits (Boulton, 1715–16: 3). Boulton was counterblasted in the Revd Francis Hutchinson's *An Historical*

Essay Concerning Witchcraft (1718). A Whiggish Anglican, Hutchinson was careful to uphold the possibility of the spirit world, declaring that 'sober belief' in spirits was 'part of every good Christian's faith'; but he insisted that such convictions were altogether different from 'the fantastick doctrines that support the vulgar opinion of witchcraft' (Hutchinson, 1718: vi; Bostridge, 1997: 193f.). 'The credulous multitude', Boulton was informed, 'will ever be ready to try their tricks, and swim the old women, and wonder at and magnify every unaccountable symptom and odd accident' (Hutchinson, 1718: viii). Most 'witchcraft' was explicable by natural causes; the scriptural references to it had been mistranslated; and popular ghost-lore was fiddle-faddle (Stock, 1982: 81; Sharpe, 1996: 284–5). The confessions of 'old Women' were 'not to be regarded' and the notion of compacts with the Devil was 'meer Imagination' (Hutchinson, 1718: 229–30).

Hutchinson rehearsed the old sceptical arguments of Wier, Scot, Webster and Bekker; but he also addressed the psychology of witch-belief as social panic. While never denying the hypothetical possibility of witchcraft, and carefully appending two sermons against Sadducceeism – one affirming Christ's miracles, the other the reality of angels – he shrewdly noted that witchcraft festered most in superstitious Catholic countries, and ventured that the powder-kegs of witch panics were inflammatory books and vainglorious witch-finders.

Hutchinson was the epitome of the moderate, progressive humanitarian Whig outlooks that wielded such influence in Georgian England. While Hobbes and Voltaire reduced everything to fraud, he judiciously made allowance for self-deception, hysteria, social pressure and labelling: people could easily be talked into believing they were witches ('Old women are apt to take such fancies of themselves': Hutchinson, 1718: 69). 'Imagine a poor old creature', he invited readers, appealing to their sympathies:

> under all the weakness and infirmities of old age, set like a fool in the middle of a room, with a rabble of the town round about her house: then her legs tied cross, that all the weight of her body might rest upon her seat. Then she must continue her pain four and twenty hours, without any sleep or meat . . . what wonder was it, if when they were weary of their lives, they confessed any tales that would please [their judges].[16]

A case like Jane Wenham's, living in a 'barbarous parish', showed 'how impossible it is for the most innocent Persons to defend themselves'. She was a meek innocent; in Hutchinson's reading it was thus the witch who was the victim of malice and deserving compassion (Hutchinson, 1718: 129, 131).

If Hutchinson set out the 'modern' view of witchcraft that was destined to prevail in Georgian enlightened society which equally extended sympathies towards other 'unfortunates' like prostitutes, orphans, dumb animals and slaves, by no means all publicists were of his mind. Boulton himself penned a rejoinder (Boulton, 1722), and, as Sharpe has shown, many clergymen continued to uphold witch beliefs, as for example Humphrey Michel, vicar of the Leicestershire parish of Horninghold. A staunch Tory, closet Jacobite, hammer of Dissenters and presenter of miscreants before the Church courts, Michel had no qualms about witchcraft. In June 1709 he recorded the swimming of two witches, one of whom, Mary Palmer, a cripple, 'though bound hand and feet, did not sink but swim'. A certain Goody Ridgway had 'in all probability' been bewitched, he believed, and he rebuked the behaviour of 'a supposed witch', who 'went out of the church when I had named and read my text, Deut Ch. 18, where is the word witch'.[17]

As these instances suggest, witchcraft, like everything else, became highly politicized in a 'divided society' rent by the 'rage of party' (Speck, 1967). High-flying Anglicans, Non-Jurors, crypto-Jacobites and Tories tended to support prosecution of witches – and Dissenters, swearers and sabbath-breakers too – as part of the duty of a confessional state to uphold orthodoxy; Whigs and Latitudinarians, by contrast, leant towards toleration and saw witchcraft as a by-product of priestcraft. To deny witchcraft could thus be a way of pulling the rug out from under the feet of High Anglicans and Tories.

Such factionalization is evident in the controversy surrounding the Wenham trial, a case provoking a flurry of controversial publications (Guskin, 1981–2). Supporters of proceedings against her included clergymen and her more respectable relatives, who approved of the guilty verdict (Sharpe, 1996: 288). But she was pardoned, and thereafter she lived out her life in a cottage provided, in a philanthropic gesture, by a Whig magnate. After making a point of visiting her, Hutchinson stated, in an evidently tendentious remark, that 'the whole county is now fully convinced that she was innocent'.[18] Whigs like Hutchinson liked to pretend they were expressing the sentiments of the nation, indeed of enlightened mankind. The wish may somewhat have been father to the reality, for it is remarkable that the repeal of the English and Scottish witchcraft laws in 1736 provoked virtually no parliamentary debate or opposition. The lengthy Whig dominion made the erasure of witchcraft from the political agenda a *fait accompli*.[19]

The press played a continuing role in educating the reading public in what became the new orthodoxies. As late as 1711 in *The Review*, Daniel Defoe was still making a clear declaration of the reality of witchcraft, as part of his Harleyan cross-party programme in favour of an all-embracing, godly, eirenic Christian commonwealth. But with shifting political allegiances, Defoe grew far more evasive, expressing scepticism in *The Political History of the Devil* (1726) about demonic pacts, and tending to turn the Devil into a caustic political metaphor: who needed Satan when the nation had Robert Walpole? Defoe turned from the power of the Devil to the diabolism of power. His later writings about witchcraft and the supernatural read less as apologetics than as Grub Street journalism as he became the leading popularizer of stories of the supernatural, for instance the celebrated *Apparition of Mrs Veal* (1706) ([Defoe], 1706; 1726; 1727; Stock, 1982: 91–3; Schaffer, 1989).

In contrast to Defoe, the Whiggish *Tatler* and *Spectator* systematically if discreetly taught tea-table society the party line on witchcraft as on every aspect of polite living. 'I believe in general that there is, and has been such a thing as witchcraft', stated Addison, parading his orthodoxy before continuing that he could 'give no credit to any particular instance of it'. That adroit face-saving formula established, he went on to explain how those old women mistaken for witches were poor and pitiable people victimized by the 'ignorant and credulous Parts of the World'. There were great dangers once some crone – call her Moll White – had got the 'Reputation of a Witch': 'If she made any Mistake at Church, and cryed *Amen* in a wrong place, they never failed to conclude that she was saying her Prayers backwards. . . . If the Dairy Maid does not make her Butter come so soon as she would have it, *Moll White* is at the bottom of the Churn. If a Horse sweats in the Stable, *Moll White* has been upon his Back'.

Every village had one:

> When an old Woman begins to doat, and grow chargeable to a Parish, she is generally turned into a Witch, and fills the whole Country with extravagant Fancies, imaginary Distempers, and terrifying Dreams. In the mean time, the poor Wretch that is the innocent Occasion of so many Evils begins to be frighted at her self, and sometimes confesses secret Commerce and Familiarities that her Imagination forms in a delirious old Age. This frequently cuts off Charity from the greatest Objects of Compassion, and inspires People with a Malevolence towards those poor decrepid Parts of our Species, in whom Human Nature is defaced by Infirmity and Dotage'.[20]

Addison and Hutchinson were of a mind: gentlemen no longer believed in witches. And many other contemporaries agreed that witch beliefs were superstitions disgraceful to a progressive age, along with the bugbears of popery and priestcraft. Thomas Gordon's 'Of Witchcraft' accused clerics of whipping up scares over witchcraft because they enjoyed a monopoly in countering it. In this they had been helped by mob credulity, but mankind was nevertheless progressing: 'an old Woman may be miserable now, and not be hanged for it'. Gordon prided himself upon his advanced religious posture, flattering himself that he was 'so much a heretick as to believe, that God Almighty, and not the Devil, governs the World'; like all enlightened people, he was pleased to believe he no longer dwelt in a devil-infested world (Gordon, 1724: 74–7; Stock, 1982: 82).

The Addisonian line, oozing humanitarianism and more than a whiff of condescension, resonated down the century from press and pulpit alike as the idiom of the *bien pensants*. In a sermon preached in 1736 after a suspected witch was 'swum', a Leicestershire parson Joseph Juxon called witchcraft into question. Suspects were typically 'such as are destitute of friends, bow'd down with years, laden with infirmities; so far from annoying others, as not to have it in their power to take care of themselves'. Yet so prevalent were phobias and superstition that 'there is always a party formed . . . against these poor, ignorant and helpless creatures'. Such accusations had to be nipped in the bud, not least because, though 'persons of ill fame be accused first . . . yet the suspicion may fall at last upon those of unblemished character and reputation', precipitating 'havock'. The phrases were becoming clichés (Juxon, 1736; Sharpe, 1996: 273–4).

Works addressing witchcraft, magic and the supernatural continued to appear in England throughout the century. They fall into various categories. Many were in the Addisonian mould, occupying the moral high ground, sniping at easy reactionary targets – 'The world has perhaps been imposed upon' by none more than pretenders to magic, declared *A System of Magick* (1727: i) – the anonymous author recommended laughing at all pretenders. *A Discourse on Witchcraft*, brought out to coincide with repeal, congratulated Englishmen upon living in an enlightened land at a happy time when the 'impostures' of priests and the folly of the 'superstitious and ignorant vulgar' were finally in retreat (*A Discourse*, 1736: iii, 6).

Newspapers in particular took pleasure in reporting sensational manifestations of witchcraft practices or bizarre superstitions, while entering a collusive superiority with their enlightened readers. 'The ridiculous notion of witches and witchcraft still prevails amongst the lower sort of people, as the following account will sufficiently evince', declared one such organ in 1773, before going on to narrate a cruel ducking meted out in Wiltshire to an alleged witch – she was then 'luckily' saved by a benign magistrate (*Reading Mercury and Oxford Gazette*, 15 March 1773). Also in a Wiltshire village, 'one Sarah Jellicoat escaped undergoing the whole discipline usually inflicted by the unmerciful and unthinking vulgar on witches', thanks, predictably, to the timely intervention of 'some humane gentlemen and the vigilance of a discreet magistrate' (*Lloyd's Evening Post*, 2 January 1761).

In the era of conspicuous humanity and sensibility, the witch could even become the heroine of such narratives, cast as a poor, lonely woman persecuted by bigots. Such sentimental strains were already present in Hutchinson – when Jane Wenham 'was denied a few Turnips' by the vicious parishioners, he tells us, 'she laid them down very submissively' (Hutchinson, 1718: 130–1). Christopher Smart's *The Genuine History of the Good Devil of Woodstock* (1802) invited imaginative and moral identification with a witch. All the villagers were nasty to destitute Jane Gilbert, called her a witch, and did her harm; but she bore it like a good Christian, sustained in part by compassionate superiors; finally she came into a legacy and behaved with Christian charity to her erstwhile persecutors.

A counter discourse aimed to defend the reality of witchcraft and its penumbra of beliefs, on the grounds that denial of the supernatural was the slippery slope to atheism – and indeed the very design of clandestine infidels. This genre warned readers against the scoffers skulking in coffeehouses and taverns. Published in the repeal year, *Pisteuo-Daimon*, for example, lamented that, amongst lovers of wit and buffoonery, it had become 'fashionable' to laugh 'at the Stories of Witches and Apparitions', but this reflected badly on modern irreverence and impiety, and led to treating 'the sacred Page itself, too often, in a ludicrous manner' ([Anon.], *Pisteuo-Daimon*, 1736: xlix; Redwood, 1976). *The History of Witches* (1775: Preface) likewise read scepticism towards witchcraft as all too symptomatic of an 'age of general debauchery, extravagence and dissipation'. This genre of writing rarely defended witch-hunting in so many words, but was suspicious of the motives of doubters and warned of the repercussions of disbelief.

Many books, however, simply rehashed tales of the supernatural for their entertainment value; *The Compleat Wizzard*, for instance, advertised itself as a 'collection of authentic and entertaining narratives of the real existence and appearance of ghosts, demons, and spectres: together with several wonderful instances of the effects of witchcraft'. Ghosts and witches became established in pulp literature. Through collecting ballads, Sir Walter Scott above all helped put such tales on the map as part of a fashionable genre of 'folk literature', while offering psychological explanations of their supernatural elements and denying the reality of ghosts (*The Compleat Wizzard*, 1770; Scott, 1802; 1830; Castle, 1995; Purkiss, 1996).

Finally there was a body of writings, small but persistent, which purveyed knowledge of alchemy, astrology and other occult arts, often cast in historical form. In 1783, for example, a translation was brought out of Agrippa's *Fourth Book of Occult Philosophy and Geomancy*. This work was careful to dissociate itself from false friends and unsavoury associations – 'Magic itself, which the ancients did so divinely contemplate, is scandalized with bearing the badge of all diabolical sorceries'. Accusations of such links were unjust since 'Magic and Witchcraft are far different sciences'. 'Agrippa' then proceeded to vindicate the arts of the magus, notably astrology (Agrippa, 1783). Francis Barrett's *The Magus, or Celestial Intelligencer* (1801) likewise offered itself as a 'complete system of occult philosophy' for the 'laborious and diligent student' (Barrett, 1801: i; Summers, 1964: ch. vi). Such works in their turn provoked a counter-literature, expressly intended to help readers see through the tricks of conjurors. The most distinguished of such attempts to expose 'magic' through revealing the real science behind the skulduggery was David Brewster's *Letters on Natural Magic, Addressed to Sir Walter Scott, Bart* (1834). Natural wonders, the distinguished Scottish scientist insisted, were more marvellous than all the tricks of art.[21]

CHALLENGES TO WITCH BELIEFS AND PRACTICES ON THE CONTINENT

Developments somewhat paralleling those in England also occurred in France, where Louis XIV's edict of 1682, an eloquent testament to centralizing absolutism, had virtually ended witchcraft prosecutions in the secular courts (Mandrou, 1968). Just as with the 1736 repeal in England, the old crime of witchcraft turned into 'so-called magic', and the decree was framed as a measure for punishing cunning folk, magicians, witches and poisoners. Nowhere did it explicitly deem 'witchcraft' an offence; those using charms and conjurations could still be prosecuted, but they would be accused of such offences as deception, profanity and sacrilege, poisoning or unlawful healing. Those falsely levelling witchcraft accusations might, however, now be charged with calumny. The edict reflected a world-view in which the Devil, if not abolished, was at least banished from the official record, and 'witches' were turned into deceivers of the gulled (Mandrou, 1968).

The year 1730 brought one of the most widely publicized witch cases in French history, the Cadière–Girard affair. The young Marie-Catherine Cadière accused her former Jesuit confessor, Jean-Baptiste Girard, of sorcery, bewitchment, 'spiritual incest' and procuring an abortion. This, the last notorious witchcraft case in France, significantly came before the ecclesiastical courts, confirming that French jurisprudence no longer recognized witchcraft as a criminal offence. Despite the authorities' efforts, practices and accusations continued as before in peasant circles, however; counter-witches and magical healers swarmed, many claiming a heavenly gift (Ramsey, 1988: 229f.)

Despite the containment of witchcraft as such, French religious politics, far more than in England, continued to be the stage of spectacular supernatural scandals, the most serious being those arising out of the convulsionaries in the wake of controversies raging between throne and alter and the Jansenists over the Papal bull Unigenitus (1713), which had condemned those dissident Augustinians. On 1 May 1727, François de Paris, a revered Jansenist deacon, died in Paris and was buried in the parish cemetery of Saint-Médard. Mourners began to flock to his grave; and 'miraculous' healings of apparently incurable diseases – tumours, paralysis, blindness, deafness, rheumatism – were posthumously wrought there by this holy man. A religious cult grew up; the crowds became unmanageable, and the affair spilled over into the charged arena of ecclesiastical politics.[22]

Anticonstitutionnaires (or appellants, that is opponents of the bull Unigenitus) latched onto the nascent Paris cult, hinting that the deacon's posthumous cures were an indication of Divine favour for their cause. They transformed the Saint-Médard events into a *cause célèbre* that challenged the Church authorities. What was increasingly recognized to be at stake was not merely a Papal bull but the very character of religious authority itself. The cult became disorderly and threatening, but if the cemetery cures were indeed authentic, how could the Church authorities take action against it without seeming to discredit all miracles? It was all summed up in the spoof couplet which ran through Paris:

> De par le roi défense à Dieu
> De faire miracle en ce lieu.

The civil and ecclesiastical establishment had good cause to look upon the cult of François de Paris with mounting apprehension. In July 1731 'convulsive agitations' broke out at the tomb. Outraged at the increasingly tumultuous displays, *Constitutionnaire* detractors denounced such paroxysms as an outrage. In the throes of their convulsions, attractive women were allowing themselves to become indecently exposed in full public view. Condemned as either the tools of the Devil or the products of deception or derangement, the convulsionaries became the targets of measures taken to halt them, including a decree published on 22 August 1731, in which the Roman Inquisition declared invalid all the miracles attributed to the deacon's intercession, and a royal ordinance promulgated on 27 January 1732, shut down the parish cemetery – moves that left the *anticonstitutionnaires* more convinced than ever of the corruption infecting both Church and State (Kreiser, 1978: 194).

'Convulsionary' became a term of opprobrium synonymous with fanaticism in the eyes of Church authorities and (curious allies!) the *philosophes* alike (Besterman, 1971: 155). The Jansenist leadership too was in a rare pickle over the disciples of François de Paris. Expectations of miracles and similar supernatural signs had traditionally loomed large in the Jansenist mind, since they were thought to provide marks of Divine favour and consolation. Yet in the end many Jansenist theologians denied the portents and questioned the cures. Such a position received its strongest backing from Pierre Nicole, whose scepticism was symptomatic of the agonizing ambiguities towards the supernatural expressed within post-Tridentine Catholicism. The magistrates of the Parlement of Paris and a majority of appellant clergy and theologians also ultimately joined with the *constitution-naire* bishops and the throne in repudiating the convulsionary movement (Kreiser, 1978: 72). By mid-1732 the anti-convulsionary Jansenists had themselves launched a campaign to discredit the miracles and their supporters, while on 17 February 1733, the royal council issued a decree prohibiting convulsionary activities, in public and private alike.

Things quietened down, but by then the damage had been done, further splitting the Church and giving perfect ammunition to the *philo-sophes*. Not only could they mock the ludicrous and grotesque events at Saint-Médard, but they had the pious over a barrel respecting the healing miracles which had allegedly occurred there: if for reasons of its own, the Catholic Church saw fit to discredit 'miracles' which happened in the here-and-now, on its own doorstep and before people's very eyes, how could any other 'miracle' in the Christian canon be sustained?

David Hume broached the subject in his discussion of the difficulties of evaluating testimony. Adopting a position sceptical of all miracles, he wrote implying that the 'miraculous' cures at Saint-Médard were better attested than those of Jesus Christ. In undermining the former, Jesuit theologians were cutting off their nose to spite their face (Besterman, 1971: 311; Kreiser, 1978: 398f.). Indeed, many believers felt deeply disconcerted by the weighty evidence supporting the miraculous character of many of the disavowed Paris cures – since they were forced to rescue the Gospel events by denying all similarity between the 'miracles' per-formed by Christ and the 'prodigies' attributed to François de Paris. The more the theologians wrangled, the more hazy grew the status of miracles. The Saint-Médard episode was thus a free gift to Enlightenment critics in their challenge to the supernatural.

In some parts of Europe ecclesiastical authorities continued energetically to hunt down those allied to the Devil or engaging in the occult arts. In Portugal for instance,[23] throughout the eighteenth century the Inquisition brought to light widespread folk magico-medical practices involving charms, prayers and blessings, potions and unguents. Many so-called *saludadores* (blessing men) were arraigned – often farmers or shepherds who confessed to blessing animals' drinking water, to protect them from diseases like rabies; some considered themselves illuminated; others were accused of being a *curandeiro* (witch-doctor). Under examination, the Inquisitors tried to induce victims to confess to having called upon the Devil. They would challenge the accused's ability to act by his own will, suggesting that 'in this foul way, maybe the Devil acted, putting into his mind the usual Devilish tricks, and he will save himself by saying he knew it by divine inspiration'.

Despite such trials, the magical healers survived, practising cures, rites and blessings. This was inevitable, given the paucity of regular doctors, especially in the countryside. The Inquisition conducted no more *autos da fe* after 1770; the last torturing of a witch was in 1764, and the last whipping of a witch was carried out in 1785. Initially the punishment of banishment was widely used, but such sentences gradually decreased; the last to be convicted was sent to the galleys in 1802.

In certain enlightened absolutist states, by contrast, action against the diabolical was orchestrated not by the Church but by the civil authorities; the result was a difference in emphasis, less punishing the guilty than eradicating ignorance and error. This was the case in the Habsburg Empire, where in the 1720s and 1730s witch persecutions in the Hungarian territories rose to a pitch comparable to the panics elsewhere – a 'delay' also characteristic of other countries on the 'periphery' of Europe, including Scandinavia (Klaniczay, 1990a: 168; Ankarloo, 1993).

Maria Theresa followed the example of Louis XIV (1682) and Frederick William I of Prussia (1728), in bringing witch-hunting to an end. What roused her to action was a particular kind of monster, the vampire, sightings of which in Moravia aroused great anxiety in Vienna. Vampirism attracted considerable attention – more than routine witch-burnings in the same period in Hungary, Poland, Austria and Germany – since for churchmen, the notion was acutely threatening, involving as it did a blasphemous reversal of key Christian dogmas, including resurrection and the Eucharist (Barber, 1988). If in France, witch persecutions were brought to an end partly as a result of public scandals inspired by notorious cases of diabolical possession – e.g., the Ursuline nuns of Loudun (1633) – in the Habsburg Empire, it was the vampire scandals that precipitated abolition.

In 1755 in Hermersdorf, a village near the Silesian-Moravian border, the corpse of Rosina Polakin was exhumed, in response to the community's conviction that she was a vampire who attacked them at night. Her body was found to be undecomposed, with blood still running in the veins. According to custom, the deceased's family was made to drag the corpse through a gap the graveyard wall, before being beheaded and burnt.[24]

On the advice of her chief physician, Gerard van Swieten, Maria Theresa sent in two of her court doctors, Johannes Gasser and Christian Vabst. When they urged her to use the law to stamp out such repulsive 'superstitions', she issued a 'Rescriptum' forbidding 'magia postuma' and condemning other 'superstitions', including soothsaying, digging for treasure, divination and witch-persecution. In 1756 a commission was set up in Vienna which drew up a new statute forbidding witch-hunting. Designed to 'uproot superstition and to promote the rational judgement of crimes involving magic and sorcery', the law, part of the new Constitutio Criminalis Theresiana, bears all the hallmarks of enlightened absolutism:

> It is well known to what intolerable extremes the craze concerning sorcery and witchcraft has lately extended. Its foundations were laid by the inclination of the stupid and vulgar crowd toward superstition. Silliness and ignorance, which gave rise to simple-minded amazement and superstitious practices, have finally led to a situation in which gullibility had gained ground everywhere among the people, who have become incapable of distinguishing reality from illusion. (Klaniczay, 1990a: 170)

The new witchcraft law distinguished four categories of cases: those originating from fantasy, imagination or fraud; those deriving from mental illness; those when a person had performed the rituals of a diabolic pact; and those where there was infallible proof of real sorcery. Judges were to consult doctors. They were required to refrain from torturing the accused, from inspecting for witch-marks or using the archaic ducking-ordeal. As for punishments, fraud was of course condemned, mental instability was to be treated, blasphemy to be punished by banishment, and, as for 'real' devilish sorcery, the Empress covered herself by declaring that 'if such an extraordinary event should happen, We reserve to Ourselves the right to decide about its due punishment'. Henceforth in the Habsburg Empire it became virtually impossible for anybody to be sent to the stake as a result of a witchcraft accusation. In 1768 functionaries were commanded to desist from initiating legal proceedings 'unless they have very clear proofs' (Klaniczay, 1990a: 171).

The brain behind the abolition campaign was Gerard van Swieten, Maria Theresa's court-physician. 'This imaginary illness, due to perverted fantasy, was last analysed marvellously by the immortal van Swieten in his treatise on Vampires', wrote Istvan Weszpremi, a contemporary doctor:

> By dint of wise advice he managed to convince the queen to chase the illness from the mind of the uneducated and superstitious people, so since that time such absurdities cannot be heard about within the territories of our country. (Klaniczay, 1990a: 171)

Leiden-born, Van Swieten had studied under Herman Boerhaave, before being invited in 1743 to become *protomedicus* at the court of Maria Theresa. His *Remarques sur le Vampyrisme de Sylesie de l'an 1755* judiciously acknowledged the reality of miracles, divine omnipotence and even Satan's power. Yet, he added, 'since the natural sciences have made such progress, many things formerly regarded as marvels have turned out to have natural causes', proceeding to advance medical arguments for the continuing presence of blood-like bodily fluids in corpses weeks after death.[25]

The public discrediting of superstition culminated in 1767 in a massive synthesis published in Vienna by Konstantin Franz von Cauz. *De cultibus magicis* praised the Queen for 'chasing this barbaric superstitious ignorance from the brains of the people', honouring Van Swieten for initiating the package of abolition measures (Klaniczay, 1990a: 177–8). Finally, in 1781, the Emperor Joseph II issued the Edict of Toleration: throughout his realm, witchcraft and magic were nonentities and so no longer punishable.

If vampirism was discounted and curbed, however, the image lived on in metaphor. The *philosophes* shifted public concern from real vampires to symbolic 'bloodsuckers': 'One does not hear about vampires in London nowadays', bantered Voltaire:

> I can however see merchants, speculators, tax-collectors, who have sucked the blood of the people in broad daylight, but who were definitely not dead, although they have been corrupted quite enough. These real bloodsuckers do not live in cemeteries but in very pleasant palaces. (Klaniczay, 1990a: 185)

It was no longer the blood of the exhumed corpses, but that of the 'social bloodsuckers' that was to flow, as was proclaimed in the Hungarian translation of the Marseillaise:

> The bloodsucking tyrant race
> Points his arms against your breasts
> And dips his ugly hands into your blood
> If he cannot make you his serf
> Take up arms, champions. (Klaniczay, 1990a: 188)

Vampire scandals carried a weighty message for the Habsburg rulers: the pressing need to civilize the East European savage – an Enlightenment mission that could come only from 'above' and from the 'west'. Such thinking dictated Maria Theresa's royal decrees and also the reports of her physicians and officials who enjoyed scolding the ignorance of Slavic peasants and the poisonous effects of Orthodox 'superstition'.

Comparable to the vampire under the Habsburgs was the shaman in Russia. Eighteenth-century travellers were fascinated by the shamans and witches (shamankas) they found in those regions (Flaherty, 1992: 7). In 1763 the Scot John Bell described the 'charming sessions' he witnessed among the Buryat-Mongols in southern Siberia and, as befitted a Calvinist surgeon, took pleasure in anatomizing the fraudulence of the shaman's cures and the credulity of the people. The seance was flagrant vaudeville:

> He was desired to exhibit some specimen of his art . . . he turned and distorted his body into many different postures, till, at last, he wrought himself up to such a degree of fury that he foamed at the mouth, and his eyes looked red and staring. He now started up on his legs, and fell a dancing, like one distracted, till he trod out the fire with his bare feet.
>
> These unnatural motions were, by the vulgar, attributed to the operations of a divinity . . . He now performed several legerdemain tricks; such as stabbing himself with a knife, and bringing it up at his mouth, running himself through with a sword and many others too trifling to mention.

Whatever Bell's personal views about Biblical miracles and the like may have been, one thing was clear: he was not going to be taken in by the cavortings of Russian savages: 'In short, nothing is more evident than that these shamans are a parcel of jugglers, who impose on the ignorant and credulous vulgar' (Bell, 1763: 253–5).

Another medical man, Daniel Gottlieb Messerschmidt, who witnessed how a shaman 'leaped about like a crazy person, and grabbed with one hand into the hot ashes lying in the fireplace', likewise exposed the performance as trickery (Flaherty, 1992: 46–8). Stephan Krascheninnikow, a botanist on the Bering expeditions, also took it upon himself to debunk the frauds of 'the most famous Shaman Carimlacha . . . particularly that of stabbing his belly with a knife, and letting a great quantity of blood run out, which he drank'. He was not impressed by what he saw: 'this he performed in such an awkward manner, that any one, who was not blinded by superstition, might easily discover the trick' (Flaherty, 1992: 54–5).

Shamans became a key exhibit in the European inquest on the supernatural. The Swiss-born Johann Georg Zimmermann (1728–95) explained that such superstitious practices took root when simple folk were mystified as to the causes of their afflictions and so were vulnerable to imposture:

> Philosophy alone heals superstition. Wherever there is no philosophy, it is haunted. There are the witches; there are the spirits; there are the goblins; there the evil prevails all over.[26]

The Austrian physician Johann Peter Frank likewise surveyed the shamans' prognostications and activities – from rain-making to hexing – and branded them as hoaxes: 'The raptures, the soothsaying, and that sort of goings-on are always based on similar causes, deception or illnesses' (Zimmermann, 1763–4: iv, 626).

To Catherine the Great, shamanism was less a philosophical problem than a national scandal, representing all the dark, obscurantist forces resisting her policies of Enlightenment. Determined to change her Empire's image from Asiatic backwardness to European rationality, she likened the shamans and their followers to convulsionaries, enthusiasts and assassins (Flaherty, 1992: 118). Seeking to dissociate her empire from shamanism, she countered the Abbé Jean Chappe d'Auteroche's *Voyage en Siberie* (1761), which painted Russia as a nation of shamans, with a refutation of her own, a 300-page *Antidote*. She even criticized the *encyclopédistes* for including articles on shamanism and other paranormal subjects, which she considered as a reprehensible sop to depraved fashion. The *Encyclopédie* (1765) indeed made various references to shamans which reflected badly on Russia, including a description of Yakut customs in the entry on Russia:

> They have no other priests but shamans – types of sorcerers in whom they have much faith, and who deceive them through a multitude of tricks and hoaxes, by which there is but one nation rude enough to be seduced.[27]

Entries like this even provoked her to try her pen at writing a comedy, *Der sibirische Schaman, ein Lustspiel* (1786) (Flaherty, 1992: 119).

Amidst diverse contexts and in different ways educated opinion and government authorities in various European nations thus turned away from the acceptance of witchcraft, magic and the supernatural: such phenomena were no longer compatible with the self-image as modernizers that enlightened elites and rulers embraced. As in the Habsburg campaign against vampires, it was sometimes necessary to take legal steps. It was generally preferable, however, to define the phenomena as figments of the imagination, as throwbacks or as objects of ridicule, and thereby define or laugh them out of existence.

CHAPTER 2

The Enlightenment Crusade

INTRODUCTION

The debunking of witchcraft, possession and all such frauds and follies was central to the *écrasez l'infâme* crusade of the radical Enlightenment, spearheading emancipation on a broad front – of science from superstition, progress from prejudice. If God had said 'Let Newton be and all was light', how could there by any powers of darkness? How shocking that people were still bedevilled by such bugbears and old crones were still being burned![1]

For Voltaire and his allies the propaganda war on witchcraft and magic had a quite specific enemy, Roman Catholicism, for the Church was the mother of superstition (Raymond, 1967; Mason, 1981). Every *exposé* they made of any folly – be it animal cults in ancient Egypt or the oracles of Greece – could and would be read, by those in the know, as a veiled attack upon the Church. From Bayle and the English Deists onwards, Enlightenment freethinkers set religion on the slab, anatomizing the sacred with secular steel. Paganism was dissected, for instance, in Fontenelle's *The History of Oracles*, to show how its superstitions were a perversion of true religion; Christian heresies were also exposed, to cut out corruptions and purify doctrine; and in time Christianity itself became the pathological specimen, in attempts such as David Hume's to lay bare the natural history of religion. Hence by happenstance or design, analysis of witchcraft and magic became exemplary of the general demystification at large: bringing the enchanted world down to earth, setting truth on its feet (Manuel, 1957).

VOLTAIRE AND THE *PHILOSOPHES*

'What is magic'? asked Voltaire, answering briskly: 'It is the secret of doing what nature cannot do. It is an impossible thing'.[2] Twenty-five of the 600 articles in his *Philosophical Dictionary* dealt with it, while many others touched upon it and his *Essai des Moeurs* and other writings turn over the question (Voltaire, 1756). Voltaire was, or affected to be, outraged about the evils resulting from such mumbo-jumbo, observing that 'superstition is, immediately after the plague, the most horrible flail which can inflict mankind. There are still sorcerers within six leagues of me, on the frontiers of Franche-Comte, at Saint-Claude' (Libby, 1935: 208). Men come in two sorts, he bantered, knaves and fools; and the former had always cheated the latter – hardly surprisingly, since so endemic were credulity, fear and the spell-binding mystique of the marvellous that the crudest hoaxes worked.

How had it arisen? Voltaire often alluded to the Asiatic origin of all absurdity; the Jews then passed it on ('they were especially given to magic, because it . . . is the height of human extravagance') (Libby, 1935: 211; Stanford, 1996: 33); and finally the Church fathers promoted it – Origen, Tertullian, Lactantius and Augustine. Through them all manner of pretended prodigies got attributed to the Devil (Link, 1995: 81). 'The Church has always condemned magic but she has always believed in it', he reflected: 'she did not excommunicate sorcerers as deluded madmen but as men who really held commerce with Devils' (Libby, 1935: 215). Thus magic, like devotion, rose in the East and then became enshrined in Christian teachings.

Voltaire said little of magic in the Middle Ages, though he noted of Friar Bacon:

> This Roger . . . tells us that you can prolong life with spermaceti, and aloes, and dragon's flesh, but that you can render yourself immortal with the philosopher's stone. . . . However, despite all these terrifying absurdities and chimeras, we must admit that this Bacon was an admirable man for his century. What a century! (Libby, 1935: 216)

He traced the Renaissance flowering of the occult in the writings of Pico della Mirandola and others, and in the Reformation too, for the Protestants acknowledged demonic possession, thaumaturgy and sorcery – as did Bodin and other intellectuals who should have known better. Hence witch- and heretic-burnings spread. 'The worst of the matter', he contended, was that

> all the people, seeing that magistrates and the church were believers in magic, were all the more invincibly persuaded of its existence; as a result, the more sorcerers were persecuted, the more appeared. From whence came so general and so unhappy an error? From ignorance. (Libby, 1935: 217)

The upshot of this entrenchment of superstition was that 'there has never been a more universal empire than that of the Devil'. How then could he be dethroned? By 'Reason':

A number of learned men in Europe . . . began to believe . . . that all oracles, all miracles which antiquity had boasted were merely the work of imposters; . . . The Devil thus lost a great deal of his credit until at last the honest Bekker . . . wrote his boring book against the Devil and proved by a hundred arguments that he did not exist.[3]

So had the Devil finally been driven out of contemporary France? No! '*The Critical History of Superstitious Practices* by Le Brun of the Oratory is very strange', Voltaire noted: 'he wishes to ridicule sorcery and is himself ridiculous enough to believe in its power'. Despite Locke, Shaftesbury and the English Deists, 'vampires have actually been believed in and the Reverend Dom. Augustin Calmet . . . has printed and reprinted the history of vampires with the permission of the Sorbonne'. As late as 1777 he wailed:

> are we in the century of Montesquieu and of Beccaria? . . . Yet magic is still spoken of . . . It is still more strange that in our century when reason seems to have made some progress there can have been printed in 1749 an *Examination of the Devils of Loudon by M. Menardie, priest*. (Libby, 1935: 223)

Voltaire did not confine his attacks to demonology and hocus pocus. Astrology too was 'a most ridiculous imposture', because 'we ought to admit in physics no action without contact, until we have found some power which acts at a distance as gravitation does'. How credulous of Grotius to conduct horoscopes of Louis XIII's eldest son! Almanacs spread gibberish, alchemy was folly (Libby, 1935: 224) and popular medicine required scepticism:

> that crabs are good for the blood because they become red like blood when they are cooked; that eels cure paralysis because they wriggle . . . these ideas and a thousand others were errors of ancient charlatans who judged without reasoning, and who being deceived deceived others. (Libby, 1935: 226)

Exasperation and anger explode like fire-crackers throughout the *Philosophical Dictionary*. 'What can you reply to a man who rolls his eyes, twists his mouth and says he has a Devil in his body? Each person feels what he feels'. Yet it was mortifying that 'in our century there are still sick people who believe themselves possessed of a Devil' (Libby, 1935: 229).

Such obsession with witches was a blot on the human race. For Voltaire, witch trials were high on the list of those 'judicial murders which tyranny, fanaticism, or even error or weakness, have committed with the sword of justice'. Credulity encouraged 'belief in fascination and witchcraft'; this was even made a part of the Christian creed; and thereafter 'nothing was to be seen but priests drawing out devils from those who were said to be possessed'. Magistrates ('who should have been more understanding than the vulgar') went around trying, condemning and sentencing in an age when 'it was a sacred duty to put girls to the torture in order to make them confess that they had lain with Satan, and that they had fallen in love with him in the form of a goat . . . They were burned at last, whether they confessed or denied; and France was one vast theatre of judicial carnage'.[4]

Magic should be confronted as a mortal enemy because it meant the suspension of the critical and reasoning faculties. Its basis was phantasmagoric:

> Manes, umbrae, simulacra are the expressions of Cicero and of Vergil. The Germans say 'Geist', the Spanish 'duende, trasgo', the Italians seem to have no word for it. The French alone use 'esprit'. The correct word for all the nations should be phantom, imagination, reverie, idiocy, deceit. (Libby, 1935: 232)

The irreverent paradox-monger, Pierre Bayle, had led the attack on fictions and fraud in his *Pensées diverses sur la comète* (1683) and *Dictionnaire historique et critique* (1696); (Labrousse, 1983; Schaffer, 1987; Whelan, 1989: 11). Voltaire was his true disciple.

Voltairian raillery at the supernatural as a chimera and cheat was broadly reflected in the *Encyclopédie*, though the entries in that work are not always easy to interpret, often being deadpan in tone but tongue-in-cheek (Shorr, 1932; Lough, 1968; 1971; Wilkins, 1975; Darnton, 1979). According to the article of that name, the most menacing enemy of all was 'superstition', worse even than atheism: 'la superstition est un tyran despotique qui fait tout céder à ses chimères'.[5] The contributors thanked their lucky stars for living in a 'siècle éclairé', when the 'chimères' and 'folies' of the past were in some measure losing their grip. No longer, it was stated, presumably prescriptively, did anyone really believe in 'des loups-garou, des esprits, des lamies, des larves, des liliths, des lémures, des spectres, des génies, des démons, des fées, des revenans, des lutins' (*Encyclopédie*: Loup-garou, ix, 703; Goulemot, 1980). But if they wore a hopeful face, or whistled in the dark, the contributors also emphasized the enduring outworks of superstition and folly: Parisian duchesses still dashed off to consult old clairvoyants about their love-life. The *encyclopédistes* took superstitions and the occult seriously enough to devote great space to the subject and hammer home their condemnations (*Encyclopédie*:Pythagorisme, xiii, 630).

On the occult arts verdicts varied. Alchemy got considerable coverage and a crumb of sympathy. Yet, while not condemned out of hand, it leant too much towards the hermetic, and failed the test of modern empiricism, and in 'Adeptes' and 'Théosophes' Diderot spoke slightingly of alchemists (*Encyclopédie*: *Adeptes*, i, 131; *Théosophes*, xvi, 254; Copenhaver, 1990). Fortune-telling was utterly scorned. Astrology – 'cette ridicule prévention' – was still in favour in almanacs, groaned the *abbé* Mallet in 'Astrologie', but d'Alembert was presumably bantering when he said that it was so senseless 'qu'à peine le plus bas peuple ajoûte-t-il quelque foi aux prédictions de nos almanachs' (*Encyclopédie*: *Astrologue*, i, 783; *cf.* Bailly, 1785). Diderot too trashed astrology, yet in 'Influence des astres', the doctor and occasional contributor, Ménuret, took a more moderate line, citing the importance Hippocrates and Galen had assigned to phases of the moon in illness, respectfully mentioning Richard Mead's *Of the Power and Influence of the Sun and the Moon on Humane Bodies*, and noting the planetary effects upon madmen (*Encyclopédie*: *Astrologue*, i, 783; *cf.* Mead, 1712). Overall, however, the occult and the esoteric arts received short shrift in the *Encyclopédie*: the more civilised a people, the less magic there was. 'Magie' came in three types – divine magic, by which God made known his plans to the elect (and which, perhaps, no longer existed); natural magic, by which man might discover the secrets of nature through use of scientific instruments such as the microscope; and, finally, accursed supernatural magic. In general it was the offspring of fear and superstition, and women were extraordinarily susceptible (*Encyclopédie*: *Magie*, ix, 854; Lough, 1969: 147).

What then of specifically religious manifestations of the praeternatural? Older *philosophes* would have witnessed the St Médard affair on their very doorstep. Who were these *convulsionnaires*? They were a 'secte de fana-tiques', disavowed by level-headed Jansenists. Neither possessed by the Devil nor divinely inspired, they were evidently suffering from hysterical frenzy (*Encyclopédie*: *Possession du démon*, xiii, 168–9; *Pythagorisme*, xiii, 630).

'Divination' presented Diderot's historical assessment of the subject. He rejected the demonological view that prediction of the unknown resulted from a pact with the Devil. The itch to predict the future had taken root amongst the Egyptians, Greeks, the Romans and the Jews. Using Noël Antoine Pluche's *Histoire du ciel* and Condillac's *Traité des systèmes*, Diderot explained how, in ancient Egypt, certain objects that were originally of merely symbolic significance became fetishes and began to be worshipped for their own sake, and the sun, moon and stars became deified. *Philosophes* must expose and oppose all such superstition (Wilkins, 1975: 1761–2; Rossman, 1974; Pluche, 1739; Condillac, 1749).

Witchcraft came under fierce attack. It was all a kind of charlatanry, a pathological spectacle. Witch trials had often been pursued for personal gain or out of lust for power. 'Démonomanie' might also be an illness; its prime symptom was belief that one was possessed by the Devil or the

Holy Spirit (*Encyclopédie: Démonomanie*, iv, 821). The article on 'Sabbat' cited Malebranche, who had deemed witchcraft the result of a wild imagination, fuelled by fear. In 'Incube' the contributor, following Wier and Bekker, discounted the materiality of the Devil and his terrestrial presence and power (*Encyclopédie: Sabbat*, xv, 456; *Sorciers*, xvi, 370; *Incube*, viii, 660). On this issue, 'Possession du démon' was explicit: it restated Bekker's position that the Devil, being a spirit, would need God's aid to harm a victim physically. 'Possession' was a mental malady curable by medicine; exorcism was regarded by the *Encyclopédie* as a relic of the past. Impotence caused by magic was discussed in 'Nouement d'aiguillette', where Jaucourt claimed that the ailment was essentially psychological, the product of a fearful imagination (*Encyclopédie: Possession du démon*, xiii, 167–9; *Exorcisme magique*, vi, 272; Minerva, 1983).

The *Encyclopédie* took certain battles against superstition as won, as in the case of oracles. Jaucourt summarised Fontenelle's view that oracles were entirely phoney, gross priestly impositions upon the herd (*Encyclopédie: Oracle*, xi, 531–7). Other superstitions were plain silly: cabalistic and number magic, chimeras, geomancy, chiromancy and so forth. In an enlightened age such nonsense was dying out. And, with the advance of humanity, better understanding was emerging of quirks like somnambulism or hysteria. Such behaviour was not of supernatural origin: where it was not fraudulent, it must be the product of pathology, physical or mental.[6]

If Voltaire and the *Encyclopédie* led the charge, all *philosophes* did their bit for the war effort against the supernatural and all such leger-demain that had so long served to exploit and oppress the people, but which might now afford insights into the pathology or perversions of human nature. In his *Traité des systèmes*, Condillac argued that fear was the root of superstition. At the time of some catastrophic event, men had divined the position of the sun, moon and stars and concluded that the heavens were to blame. This led to the wearing of talismans and charms in hopes of currying the favour of the gods or winning their protection. Dreams came to be regarded as unique revelations from Above. It had been natural for the savage mind to adopt such beliefs. Condillac's message was clear: weakness, fear and ignorance were the springs and supports of superstition, and all such thinking was vain and infantile (Condillac, 1749; Knight, 1968).

In 1765 Jean Castilhon (1718–1799), a *philosophe* who wrote many articles for the *Encyclopédie* supplement, published his *Essai sur les erreurs et les superstitions*. Superstition was 'un culte de religion minutieux, mal dirigé, mal ordonné, rempli d'une infinité de préjugés'. The spirit of reason had, however, helped to erode belief in astrology, at least in England and France. 'Un art peu malfaisant, qui ... emprunte ... le secours et le ministère du diable', witchcraft was not to be feared; magicians should be punished but not burnt. Imagination was the mother of superstition; credulity had barbaric consequences; but reason's day was dawning (Castilhon, 1765: 59–60; Mercier, 1781: iv, 301; Rosen, 1972: 258). A later critic, J. B. Salgues, argued in his *Des erreurs et des préjugés répandus dans la société* (1810–11) that contemporary interest in the extra-ordinary was the product of ignorance amongst the poor and idle imaginations amongst the rich. He dismissed popular superstitions out of hand: imposters abused credulity, usually to obtain money (Wilkins, 1975: 125–8).

THE STATUS OF SUPERSTITION

It was by no means only *philosophes* and *encyclopédistes*, however, who criticized superstition. That was also the mission of a cadre of religious *érudits* dedicated, rather like certain English Deists, to weeding Catholicism clean of the accumulated undergrowth of time, aiming by such means to strengthen well-rooted trees.[7] Whereas the *philosophe* wished to liberate man from mental chains, encouraging him to use reason to take his destiny into his own hands, his theologian counterpart wished to purify religion and wean believers off practices which were the relics of paganism or the work of Satan. David Gentilcore has remarked how, amongst late-seventeenth century Italian Jesuits, superstition was defined as 'any of a wide range of popular rituals to heal, cause injury, predict the future or bind someone in love, the efficacy of which – the Roman Catholic Church believed – was due to an expressed or tacit pact with the Devil' (Gentilcore, 1993: 134).

Jean Baptiste Thiers' *Traité des superstitions* (1679) was an early attempt to counter the infiltration of the Roman Catholic Church by superstitious and sacrilegious practices. Thiers denounced diabolic prophecy, astrology, belief in lucky and ominous days, and recourse to talismans and charms, all of which involved supping with Satan. Affirming the reality of the Devil, he denounced any activity which might presuppose a diabolic pact. Some superstitions, however, were merely the result of vulgar errors, perhaps being rooted not in the Devil but in the frailties of human nature (Wilkins, 1975: 108–10; Thiers, 1679/1741: i, 208–9; Goulemot, 1980).

Also in this mould was the Oratorian Pierre Le Brun's *Histoire critique des practiques superstitieuses* (1702), a work dedicated to sifting genuine natural phenomena from chicanery (and, as we have seen, ridiculed for its pains, yet also plundered by Voltaire). Le Brun attacked astrology, talis-mans, etc., on the grounds that such activities contravened natural law and were therefore baseless. But other out-of-the-way phenomena were harder to evaluate. Was the divining rod authentic? Since it sometimes worked, Le Brun tentatively concluded that it quivered because of the action of spirits, whose existence was, of course, attested by the Bible and the Church Fathers.

Le Brun's claim to attention lay, rather as with Browne and Glanvill, in advocacy of strict scientific criteria and rules of evidence to authenticate so-called miraculous effects. Some did not pass the test, as with the case of the holy navel, a venerated relic. This, according to medical opinion, could never have been part of the umbilical cord as it was 'une matière très dure, semblable à de petites pierres, avec quelque poussière graveleuse' (Le Brun, 1702). Another cleric, Alphonse Costadau, anatomized the abnormal in a monumental eight-volume *Traité historique et critique des principaux signes dont nous nous servons pour manifester nos pensées* (1717). 'Signes' were either natural, divine or diabolic. Diabolical signs included oracles, talismans, elixirs and divination, all condemned as 'absolument superstitieuses' since they supposed 'un pacte avec le Démon'. Like Le Brun and Thiers, Costadau judged those who meddled with the forbidden guilty of heresy (Costadau, 1717).

The most eminent product of this clerical stable-cleaning endeavour was Dom Calmet. Aiming to strengthen religion by refining it, his *Dissertations sur les apparitions* (1746) investigated spirit manifestations in the *Bible*, comparing them with similar indications in other cultures. The majority of apparitions were illusions, and great care must be taken in handling them, to avoid being humbugged. Calmet also examined claims for resurrection from the dead, dealing in particular with the Transylvanian epidemic of vampirism (discussed in the previous chapter). Ever cautious, he pointed out that no credible witness had seen, touched or questioned the imagined vampires: there must be a natural solution. Searching for rational explanations, however, was a high-risk strategy for defenders of the faith.[8]

THE ROLE OF MEDICINE

In the witchcraft and magic controversies, medicine too increasingly made its voice heard: after all, if possession manifestations weren't cozenage or truly the work of supernatural spirits, then what else could trances and convulsions be but sickness (be it of the mind or body) and therefore the domain of the doctors? Medical involvement in the abnormal proceeded on two fronts.

For one thing professional doctors in every nation were engaged in a war of attrition against wonder-working healers and mountebanks, many of whom had assumed for themselves a priestly or magus-like aura, selling

'Cordials Angelical, Royal, Golden, Imperial', as one critic complained (Ramsey, 1988: 230f.; Porter, 1989). As avowed enemies of such *maiges* and charlatans, enlightened doctors campaigned for practical reform – e.g., regulation of the secret remedies trade. Dubbing all counter-witchcraft and magical healing a form of quackery that traded on rustic gullibility was a common discrediting ploy. Thus in his treatise on vulgar medical errors Jean d'Iharce described how, while *devins* avoided saying

> that they have, like the witches, a pact with the Devil . . . they make every effort to suggest it and never fail . . . They put into play all sorts of superstitions to entice those who are idiotic enough to consult them. (d'Iharce, 1783: 421)

Enlightened physicians characterized non-orthodox healers as barefaced shams who exploited peasant ingenuousness. Unsympathetic towards popular culture, their goals were simple: they wanted to annihilate error.

Thus doctors dismissed their rivals; but they also claimed possession over the possessed. The effects of supposed *maleficium* or demonic possession were plain for all to see. The smitten would fall into contortions, vomiting pins, screaming in weird tongues, displaying abnormal strength. In the Reformation era, such had widely been supposed to be the Devil's work – but was it not more likely that the cause was disease? 'Possession' and 'obsession' thus presented challenges to medical expertise. The witchcraft question became a struggle about jurisdiction over the body (Walker, 1981; Harley, 1996; Sharpe, 1996: 197).

Christian doctrines positing the reality of possession were rarely denied by outright regular physicians. But they strongly asserted that apparent manifestations of demonic possession and *maleficium* might be disease symptoms, due perhaps to morbid humours, above all melancholy (black bile). The individual case could be decided only by the experienced physician, on the basis of reliable diagnostic tests and expert clinical judgment (MacDonald, 1981; 1991).

As time went on physicians grew more insistent that such manifestations were routinely signs of sickness, and they found receptive ears among the educated classes. This was in part a mark of the rising clout and confidence of the medical profession in an age of scientific breakthroughs that had produced such luminaries as William Harvey. But it was in large measure a product of anguished reactions to religious and political crises. The Thirty Years War on the Continent (1618–48), and, in Britain, the Civil Wars (1642–51), triggered a violent reaction against all manner of religio-political dogmatism and extremism, condemned as ruinous to the Christian commonwealth and to individual security alike. Calvinist 'saints', Machiavellian Jesuits, plebeian Anabaptists, Ranters, regicidal fanatics, and other sectaries with antinomian leanings were accused of self-righteous zeal, of the blind presumption that the divine Word dwelt in themselves, that to the pure all things were pure, and that the Lord had granted an avenging sword to the godly.

From the mid-seventeenth century and then ritualistically all through the eighteenth, a barrage of abuse was hurled against all such self-styled saints and prophets, on grounds historical, scriptural, theological, demon-ological, philosophical and personal. A further style of discrediting – indeed one gaining in ideological appeal – lay in charges of psychopathol-ogy; the claim that such religious extremism and all its associated manifes-tations were symptomatic of mental disorder: *soi-disant* saints and puffed-up prophets were literally brain-sick (Knox, 1950; Heyd, 1995).

It was not difficult, of course, for medical men and polemicists drawing upon medico-psychological reasoning to point to crystal-clear affinities between the manifestations of the religious lunatic fringe and lunatics proper: glossolalia, convulsions, paroxysms, seizures, visions and halluci-nations, monstrous violence (as with regicides), weepings and wailings – were not these all symptoms of derangement? Hence charismatic individ-uals or entire religious sects might be demonized on medical authority: enthusiasm, zeal and other forms of transcendental experience could be medicalized into psychopathology, either by foes seeking to defame them or by doctors truly trying to treat converts and convulsionaries. That was a trump card repeatedly played in Britain to counter the threats posed in the seventeenth century by the significantly named Quakers, Shakers and Ranters and then, on a massive scale after the 1730s, against Methodists – 'Methodistically mad' became the smart insult.[9]

In broad terms, the symptoms were easily medicalized: all modes of odd speech or outlandish behaviour causing public disorder was readily labelled 'disordered'. There was less agreement, however, as to precise diagnosis. Some followed Henry More in likening the dreaded 'enthusiasm' to epilepsy; black bile was still commonly invoked by those deploying humoral aetiologies deriving from the Greeks, and the new mechanical philosophy (iatrophysics and iatrochemistry) proved extremely serviceable from the 1660s in suggesting that organic defects (inflamed fibres, vascular obstructions, or smoky vapours ascending into the head from obstructed guts) would produce purely secondary 'religious' manifestations such as convulsions or coma. The diagnostic label, hysteria – due perhaps to a wandering womb or to weak nerves – explained the bizarre emotional lability of female proselytes and fasting nuns (MacDonald, 1981; S. Jackson, 1986; Porter, 1987).

It was not only physicians who were attracted to the strategy of medicalizing possession and *maleficium*. Naturalistic explanations were congenial to the mind-set of Latitudinarian clergy in post-Restoration England, for example, and they often recommended medical means to cure troubled spirits (though belief in conscience-searching and Providence often led them also to divine the finger of God in such afflictions).[10] The Nonconformist minister Richard Baxter was widely consulted in cases of apparent demonic possession. Although he made therapeutic use of prayer and Bible readings, he held that melancholy was primarily a physical disorder: to think otherwise would encourage displays of enthusiasm and so encourage the Devil's wiles. Melancholy was not itself satanic but could provide opportunities for the Tempter to worm his way into the faithful (Baxter, 1691: 171–85; 1696: pt 3, 85–6; 1713: 81).

Anglicans tended to adopt a naturalistic stance supported by medical authority. While initially believing in exorcism, Thomas Willis, Anglican, royalist, founder of neurology and a figure of notable medical stature, increasingly excluded the Devil from physical interference with the brain. Though conceding the possibility of demonic activity, he defined most supposed cases as merely natural. His work was recognized by the elite as offering plausible explanations of diseases which 'have usually by ignorant People been ascribed to Witchcraft and possessions of the Devil' (Willis, 1667: 70, 90–1; Martensen, 1993). Encountering cases of alleged possession, the Dissenting physician John Webster was equally short with such claims, denying demonic possession in modern times, and sneering at the 'strange lustrations, suffumigations and other vain superstitious Rites and Ceremonies' the vulgar used to cure diseases or drive away evil spirits (Webster, 1677: 273, 335; Harley, 1989: 120–1).

In some parts of Europe, debate on matters demonological long raged amongst academic physicians,[11] partly because Johan Wier's *De praestigiis daemonum* (1563) had provided a sceptical text that sparked lasting controversy. Around 1700, the great Halle medical professor, Friedrich Hoffmann, was at the centre of attempts to clarify the issue. In a doctoral dissertation, his student Gottfried Büching reaffirmed the Devil's influence over both the mind and the human body, via the elements, especially the air. The Devil could commandeer the natural spirits in the body, inducing violent contortions, praeternatural strength, fits, spasms, pain, uterine suffocation, St Vitus Dance and epilepsy. Doctors must, however, learn to distinguish diabolical invasions from mundane maladies. A cause could be accepted as supernatural, maintained Büching, in the presence of the following signs: convulsions with no prior symptoms, blaspheming, knowledge of future or hidden things, speaking in languages of which the patient had no knowledge, unnatural strength, vomiting of objects like pins, keys, splinters of wood or stones, or discharging objects from the ear, vagina or penis.

Other German medics, however, rejected demonological doctrines. In Jena in 1693 a Dr Ernst Heinrich Wedel devoted his dissertation to upholding the claim that 'spectres are fictitious representations, against the law of nature'. Visions were errors of fantasy conjured up under the influence of fear, or produced by damage to the sensory organs or by cerebral illness (Diethelm, 1970; King, 1974a; 1974b).

In 1725 Hoffmann returned to the fray, once again lending his illustrious name to the support of demonology, and stating that the Devil acted upon witches through the animal spirits. Another of his students contended that it was possible for the Devil, by divine permission, to appropriate natural forces to produce visions, by invading an eye which had been damaged by an illness or by precipitating diseases of the brain. Demonology thus continued to exert a certain hold over German academic medicine, and though that waned, as late as 1776, Boerhaave's student, Anton de Haen, whom van Swieten had brought to Vienna, seemingly contradicted his teachers by publishing *De magia*, a defence of demonology from an orthodox religious point of view.

Beyond the halls of German universities, however, medicine broke earlier with demonological ideas. In Britain, all prominent physicians dealing with depression of the spirits from the late seventeenth century onwards – Richard Blackmore, Richard Mead, George Cheyne, Nicholas Robinson and their circles – viewed religious melancholy wholly naturalistically, indeed somatically. Referring to the visions of early Quakers and other sectaries, Robinson, an avid follower of Newton, claimed they were 'nothing but the effects of mere madness, and arose from the stronger impulses of a warm brain' (Robinson, 1729: 247; Porter, 1983; Suzuki, 1992).

Richard Mead's *Medica Sacra* (1755), a commentary on diseases described in the Bible, provided rational explanations for cases of possession and other scriptural diseases traditionally cited as proofs of possession. In Mead's judgment, such beliefs were 'vulgar errors . . . the bugbears of children and women'. He was one of the trend-setting Whig elite eager to join the chorus of condemnation against the benighted witchcraze:

> my soul is seized with horror on recollecting, how many millions of innocent persons have been condemned to the flames in various nations since the birth of Christ, upon the bare implication of witchcraft: while the very judges were perhaps blinded by vain prejudices, or dreaded the incensed populace, if they acquitted those, whom the mob had previously adjudged guilty. (Mead, 1755: xi)

The fashionable court physician rejoiced that as a modern Englishman 'I have lived to see all laws relating to witchcraft entirely abolished', ascribing the persistence of such laws in other nations to 'ignorance of natural causes' (Mead, 1755: xiii).

In practice, faced with the clinical realities of suffering and treatment, physicians everywhere were extricating themselves from demonology by the turn of the eighteenth century. In 1723 the medical faculty at Halle was asked for an opinion on a matter of diabolical possession. Though long on record as acknowledging the reality of the Devil's powers, Hoffman claimed in his discussion – the subject was a 21-year-old farm-hand alleged to have made a diabolic pact – to be guided solely by medical criteria. The Faculty's judgment, which he formulated, was that Satan's power to seduce a person must naturally be accepted, but in this particular case other factors had to be taken into account: lack of intelligence and education, a severe head injury, and heavy brandy drinking for several years. The diagnosis was that the case was delusional (King, 1974a; Geyer-Kordesch, 1994).

Highly revealing of the trend towards medicalization is Hoffmann's *Medicina consultatoria* (1725–39), a multi-volumed account of his cases as an official consultant to the Halle medical faculty. One from 1718 concerns a young male aristocrat. The notes presented him as a weak and over-sensitive man given to smoking and drinking drams. At 13 he had had a relationship with a 'disreputable woman', pledging marriage in an oath written in blood. His mother thought him bewitched; she and his Lutheran confessor confronted him; he disavowed his actions, beating his fiancée until she returned the document. The brief also mentioned loud praying, ostentatious sighing, and paroxysms leading to catatonia; he would not eat out of fear of choking to death.

In his judgement on the case, Hoffmann drew extensively on the professional language of medicine:

> This morbus is called *pro affectu melancholico*, originating in feebleness, especially of the brain and nerves, when the whole *systema nervorum* is weak by nature, perhaps also *ex dispositione haereditaria*, compounded by a rotten diet of tobacco and spirits, that was afterwards aggravated through an over-scrupulous conscience and lengthy depression; all this contributed to disorderly *motibus spasticis*. (Geyer-Kordesch, 1994)

He ended the *consilium* by emphasizing that 'because this disease has fully natural causes, there can be no indication of supernatural causes or witchcraft'. The recommended therapy involved a strict daily regimen of nourishing food, riding and exercise, the taking of prescribed medicines, and a ban on tobacco and alcohol. Clearly the aim was to quash 'speculation' involving invisible powers in nature.

Hoffmann's clinical experiences were mirrored elsewhere. On the job, doctors tended to be professionally dismissive of the supposed interventions of the Devil. Practising in Northern England (where 'ignorance, popery and superstition doth much abound'), John Webster found that the common people, when suffering from 'epilepsy, palsie, convulsions and the like', were prone to 'perswade themselves that they are bewitched, forespoken, blasted, fairy-taken, or haunted with some evil spirit'. Trying to convince the vulgar that they were not suffering from diabolical interference was, however, a thankless task:

> say what you can they shall not believe you, but account you a physician of small or no value, and whatsoever you do to them, it shall hardly do them any good at all, because of the fixedness of their depraved and prepossessed imagination. But if you indulge their fancy, and hang any insignificant thing about their necks, assuring them that it is a most efficacious and powerful charm, you may settle their imaginations, and then give them that which is proper to eradicate the cause of their disease, and so you may cure them, as we have done in great numbers. (Webster, 1677: 323)

A century later Dr Erasmus Darwin, practising in the Midlands, was equally frustrated by popular credence in the workings of Satan. In his *Zoonomia; or, The Laws of Organic Life* (1794), he treated certain aspects of Christian doctrine as pathological, and stabbed a finger of blame at the Wesleyans:

> *Orci timor.* The fear of Hell. Many theatric preachers among the Methodists successfully inspire this terror, and live comfortably upon the folly of their hearers. In this kind of madness the poor patients frequently commit suicide; although they believe they run headlong into the Hell which they dread! Such is the power of oratory, and such the debility of the human understanding! (Porter, 1987: 73; McNeil, 1987)

Common folk, Darwin held, were especially susceptible, and 'the maniacal hallucination at length becomes so painful that the poor insane flies from life to become free of it'. He adduced numerous case-histories of desperate sufferers whose 'scruples' had plunged them into religious madness, and often thence to despair and death, as for example:

> Mr—, a clergyman, formerly of this neighbourhood, began to bruise and wound himself for the sake of religious mortification . . . As he had a wife and family of small children, I believed the case to be incurable; as otherwise the affection and employment in his family connections would have opposed the beginning of this insanity. He was taken to a madhouse without effect, and after he returned home, continued to beat and bruise himself, and by this kind of mortification, and by sometimes long fasting, he at length became emaciated and died . . . what cruelties, murders, massacres, has not this insanity introduced into the world. (Porter, 1987: 74)

Throughout the Enlightenment, witchcraft sceptics gratefully seized upon the medico-psychiatric argument: the enthusiasm of persecuting zealots and the despair of their victims were equally manifestations of maladies. If the courts threw out witchcraft accusations, opined one author in the Wenham debate, 'hereafter we may not have that waste of human blood in every village, upon the wild testimonies of a parcel of brain-sick people'.[12]

As abnormal behaviour was appropriated by the medical gaze, females in particular became pathologized – hardly surprisingly, as it was women whom the witch panic had primarily demonized in the first place.[13] As historians recently have emphasized, the new science had profound gender implications. It proclaimed man's right to probe and penetrate mother earth, and linked discreditable beliefs – *maleficium*, superstition – with the fickle female imagination. Attention became focused on *maladies des femmes*, disorders supposedly deriving from the labile female reproductive economy. The complications attending menarche, menstruation, pregnancy, birth and menopause were commonly stressed, as was the influence of the female imagination on the formation of the foetus, on convulsions and hysteria. Not least, as both practitioners and clients of charlatanry, women were thought to present particular obstacles to medical progress (Gilman *et al.*, 1993: 91f.; L. Wilson, 1993).

The controversies over the convulsionaries of St Médard in the 1730s, discussed from the religious viewpoint in the previous chapter, posed terrible dilemmas: why would God have chosen as his prophets foolish women in a trance and incapable of the use of reason? 'How can it be', pondered baffled Jansenists, 'that God is supposed to communicate to girls who have themselves shaken, pulled about by men, suspended upside down in the air, and placed in shocking postures, and that he works through them in a miraculous manner in order to have them announce to the church some very great wonders?' (L. Wilson, 1993: 18).

Medicine was called in to solve such mysteries and to sit in judgment on the convulsions. Fearful of the potential for public disorder in these gatherings and responding to the Church's dread of religious scandal, the Crown launched medical inquiries, and in 1732 the lieutenant-general of police, René Hérault, summoned two dozen doctors and surgeons to the Bastille to examine seven convulsionary prisoners. Attempting to determine if the jerks and twitchings were involuntary or could be provoked at will, they found that the convulsionaries could actually induce contractions and hence concluded that the spasms were neither genuine nor supernatural (L. Wilson, 1993: 22).

Another commission investigated Anne Lefranc's 'miraculous cure'. This ageing spinster, who for some thirty years had suffered from partial blindness and paralysis, had experienced a miraculous cure at the cemetery.

Was it authentic? (Kreiser, 1978: 120f.). The most damaging testimony came from her own family. Her brother accused her of perpetrating a hoax, and asserted that her afflictions were far from being cured. Medical experts gave their opinions: her principal infirmity was, they decided, an *affection hystérique* stemming from menstrual irregularity. Since all her 'ailments' had arisen from this problem, no miracle could be involved in her cure. The authorities claimed the Jansenists were using a fake miracle to dupe the pious:

> A cure may be regarded as miraculous only when the malady was incurable or when the afflicted person has recovered his health in a manner so perfect and so sudden that it is clear that such a change could not possibly be attributed to a natural cause; without one of these two circumstances no cure, however surprising it may appear, can be regarded as a true miracle, because nature keeps hidden within its bosom the principles of such an effect. (Kreiser, 1978: 125)

Anne Lefranc's alleged cure, by contrast, was but 'a succession of suppositions, deceptions, and lies'. There was nothing odd in this official scepticism. A principal aim of the Post-Tridentine Papacy, after all, had been to quash popular 'ignorance' and 'credulity', and to cultivate a purified and more elevated sense of the sacred (Kreiser, 1978: 126).

In 1735 Archbishop Vintimille directed his inspector general, Nigon de Berty, to conduct yet another inquiry. Its findings were that the convulsionaries had blown up natural recoveries into miracles thanks to 'an overactive imagination, or the malice of the Devil'. Some of them were, admittedly, in need of medical assistance; the majority, however, were to be censured as frauds who had conspired with the Devil to deceive the public, undermining the moral order and subverting the authority of church and state (L. Wilson, 1993: 23).

If doctors tended to argue for the naturalization of convulsions, this did not, however, entail absolution from blame. Although a physiological basis was posited, this was in turn said to be rooted in a flagrant eroticism which doctors typically held could and should have been controlled by the will. Those failing to master their impulses were suffering from a pathological condition and were to be denounced or pitied.

Amongst the physicians involved with the *convulsionnaires* the most eminent was the Jansenist Philippe Hecquet. He interpreted the convulsions as symptoms of the vapours or hysterical affections, sexually-based disorders unique to women. (Males subject to convulsions were considered effeminate and melancholic, their malady being diagnosed as hypochondria.) Hecquet ascribed these phenomena to various natural causes – 'hysteria', 'erotic vapours', 'melancholia', 'derangement', 'imagination', and the like – which fell within the remit of medicine. Yet he also suspected most of them of a self-seeking duplicity in a long tradition of hysterical connivers who included the Ursulines of Loudun:

> how many astonishing scenes have been presented to the public throughout all time by hysterical or vaporous girls or women, whose enthusiastic operations have appeared so extraordinary that some have been attributed to God, others to the Devil. (L. Wilson, 1993: 28)

Terming these vapours 'shameful' and 'criminal', Hecquet reflected that they were generally experienced by adolescent girls, ageing spinsters and widows. The cure was obvious: marriage. Failing that, recourse could be had to an arsenal of traditional methods, including blood-letting (L. Wilson, 1993: 29). Hecquet's preferred medical therapy for these convulsionaries, however, was to remove them from the limelight and place them under the supervision and discipline of physicians like himself. The women were to be isolated, intimidated, flogged, and dunked in cold water: that would soon put an end to the vapours and might even restore their virtue.[14]

Constitutionnaire theologians were more likely to attribute the convulsionaries' actions to 'diabolic intervention'. Fits, blaspheming, glossolalia, sacrilegious acts of profanation and other bodily contortions proved that satanic forces were at work.[15] For physicians, on the other hand, supernatural phenomena became diagnosed as hysteria. But in both cases the judgmentalism was much the same, however: the medical contention that the sex was hysterically disposed mirrored the Christian doctrine that it was in women's nature to sin and deceive. 'The supremacy of malice which is in woman when she lets herself go', pontificated Hecquet, 'along with the natural penchant of her sex toward seduction is proven, for Scripture says that there is no malice comparable to that of a woman who wants to be evil' (L. Wilson, 1993: 29).

CONCLUSION

This and the previous chapters have been examining critiques of witchcraft beliefs and practices, polemical, philosophical, theological and medical. It is now generally accepted that the witch-hunts and trials which peaked in the seventeenth century resulted from the superimposition upon traditional supernatural outlooks and practices of a new demonology, associated with Reformation and Counter-Reformation theologies, Renaissance magic, and renewed crusades against heresy and heathenism – movements reinforced by the advent of printing and the spread of literacy, the centralizing juridical and administrative ambitions of the new monarchies, and much else. The intensified desire of the godly to evangelize and police the people made conditions ripe for a witchcraze (Moore, 1987). If so – if witches were thus the victims of the demonological obsessions of Western élites – it is hardly surprising that panics about witches waned in the eighteenth century, since those in the saddle, or at least some of the most influential opinion-makers, were ceasing to subscribe to such theologies, indeed in many cases were energetically repudiating them in the name of civilization and progress. Christian transcendentalism no longer seemed to provide the blueprint for an orderly, smooth-running commercial society. Witches ceased to be prosecuted and began to be patronized; rustics were now ridiculed for believing what the Establishment had taught before.

The emphasis so far has been on the learned conception of the witch and the intellectual confutations of witch-beliefs and magic mounted in the long eighteenth century. They clearly carried weight in elite circles. But there was more to the transformation than that. It also had much to do with a shifting balance of social elites, a move from the supremacy of the clergy and the church as the dominant agency of beliefs to the emergence of the Habermasian public sphere and the fourth estate: if once the sermon had been mightier than the sword, soon it would be the pen. With such a shift in societies increasingly swayed by commercial interests, there were to be new witches for old; the modern scapegoats included the poor at large, criminals, vagrants, the disabled and all those other folks whom Foucault has regarded as the targets of that street-sweeping which was the 'great confinement' (Foucault, 1961; Spierenburg, 1991). The next two chapters will turn their attention to witchcraft and magic after their official demise, and probe a posthumous life – indeed a resurrection in new guises.

CHAPTER 3

Culture and the Supernatural c.1680–1800

INTRODUCTION

The Enlightenment views just surveyed – philosophical, social, scientific, medical – set about replacing biblical supernaturalism with a modern ideology of Nature and reason. But there was more to change than the simple triumph of science over superstition which the *philosophes* proclaimed.

For one thing, as already implied, at the grassroots 'superstitions' did not dissolve like mist in the sunshine but proved highly tenacious – driving reformers to despair! And the educated themselves continued to uphold a mixed bag of beliefs. Take the Anglican minister, James Woodforde, a graduate of Oxford University and a Norfolk clergyman from 1773 to his death in 1803. Faithfully kept for almost 45 years, Woodforde's diary reveals a Janus-faced figure, with one foot in the old world and the other in the new – probably quite typical of the times.

The medical remedies Woodforde used are a patchwork of modern medicine and folk cures, derived from a variety of sources, including books of popular medicine like William Buchan's *Domestic Medicine* (1769) (Lawrence, 1975; Porter, 1992). Though he could be condescending towards villagers and their benighted beliefs, some of the parson's remedies clearly had their origin in magic. He developed a stye on his eye:

> As it is commonly said that the Eye-lid being rubbed by the tail of a black cat would do it much good if not entirely cure it, and having a black cat, a little before dinner I made a trial of it, and very soon after dinner I found my Eye-lid much abated of the swelling and almost free from Pain. I cannot therefore but conclude it to be of the greatest service to a Stiony on the Eye-lid. (Beresford, 1924–31: iii, 253; Hultin, 1974; 1975)

Woodforde can hardly have failed to make the association between black cats and witchcraft. Indeed he deliberately used black objects therapeutically on other occasions. On 6 May 1790 he bought an astonishing 18 yards of black ribbon, 'to put around our Necks to prevent sore throats'; another time he spent a morning 'spreading family Plaister on black silk' (Beresford, 1924–31: v, 274).

That old favourite the moon formed part of Woodforde's health map. Feeling 'poorly, weak and faint' on 18 September 1800, he blamed it on the new moon. The symptoms returned on 29 May 1801, and again the new moon was accountable (believing himself a touch epileptic, he considered that lunar phases induced that condition).[1] Thus old beliefs lingered in the wrinkles of the eighteenth-century educated mind.

Enlightened elites might moreover find occasion to take up for their own purposes what otherwise they might have poohpoohed as foolish, as in the 'French Prophets' episode. In 1706 three Camisard refugees arrived in London from Languedoc. Though regarded with suspicion by the mainstream Huguenot churches, they developed a hold over those disposed to interpret their faith-healing and miracle-working as proofs of Providence. The Prophets announced the Apocalypse, calling upon Londoners to repent; and in the summer 1707, one of their English adherents, John Lacy, began speaking in tongues, levitating, and exhibiting healing gifts, restoring sight to a 16-year-old blind girl. Controversy followed, resulting, in the next four years, in some 60 pamphlets. While support largely came from religious sectaries, some leading intellectuals, Whigs and Low Churchmen, including Isaac Newton's successor as Lucasian professor in Cambridge, William Whiston, were glad to affiliate with the Prophets to further their anti-Catholic, anti-Sun King lobbying; and the Newtonian mathematician, Fatio de Duillier, became an energetic spokesman for their millennial prophesyings (Jacob, 1976; 1978; Schwartz, 1978; 1980; Heyd, 1995). Other prominent advocates of Newtonian physics and mechanical medicine, particularly the fashionable society physician, Dr George Cheyne, had no difficulty in embracing mystical religious beliefs (Shuttleton, 1994). And towards the close of the century sectarian supernaturalism joined forces with incipient Romanticism. William Blake, whose religious faith was rooted in various Protestant sects including Swedenborgianism, delighted in the prophetic:

> Now I a fourfold vision see,
> And a fourfold vision is given to me;
> 'Tis fourfold in my supreme delight
> And threefold in soft Beulah's night
> And twofold always. May God us keep
> From Single vision & Newton's sleep!'[2]

In any case, supernaturalism surged back in repeated revivals, ambiguously in the Pietist movement in Protestant Germany and amongst certain individuals like Emmanuel Swedenborg, but more directly in English Methodism, whose founder, John Wesley, was adamant as to the authenticity of witchcraft, reasserting Joseph Glanvill's baseline position –

'the giving up of witchcraft is, in effect, giving up the Bible' – and regretting that 'the English in general . . . have given up all account of witches and apparitions as mere old wives' fables'. 'Pope John' reproved the bigotry of the modern infidel who bellowed 'so dogmatically against what not only the whole world, heathen and Christian, believed in past ages, but thousands, learned as well as unlearned, firmly believe at this day' (Wesley, *Journal*, 1906: iii, 330; Rack, 1989: 387f.; Abelove, 1991; Plasha, 1993; Davies, 1997b: 255).

Wesley had no doubt he had witnessed the Devil's work with his own eyes. In 1746 he encountered a woman 'whom Satan had bound in uncommon manner for several years'; in 1770 he saw a case of convulsive fits that had persisted ten years, which led him to infer witchcraft. Personal experience was but one proof amongst many: 'I cannot give up to all the deists in Great Britain the existence of witchcraft', he reflected in 1776, 'till I give up the credit of all history, sacred and profane' – 'I have not only as strong, but stronger proofs of this, from eye and ear witnesses, than I have of murder, so I cannot rationally doubt of one any more than the other' (Curnock, 1909–16: vi, 109; Telford, 1931: vii, 300; Sharpe, 1996: 253). On this issue Wesley never wavered: as late as 1785, when he was in his eighties, he insisted: 'while I live I will bear the most public testimony I can to the reality of witchcraft'. Yet reading Richard Baxter's *Certainty of the World of Spirits* gave him pause for thought: 'How hard it is to keep the middle way; not to believe too little or too much' (Curnock, 1909–16: v, 265; vi, 109; v, 374–5; iii, 250–1; v, 32–5; iii, 537; v, 311; v, 103; Stock, 1982: 94–5.

Wesley was concerned not just with precepts but with practical thaumaturgy. In 1739 he recorded a case of possession near Bristol. Sally Jones, a 19-year-old, was a 'terrible sight. . . . The thousand distortions of her whole body showed the dogs of hell were gnawing at her heart'. Convinced Satan possessed her, she told him 'Six days ago you might have helped me. But it is past. I am the devil's now. I have given myself to him. His I am. Him I must serve. With him I must go to hell' (Wesley, 1747; Curnock, 1909–16: ii, 298, 301–2; A. Hill, 1958; Sharpe, 1996: 253–4).

In 1762 at Halifax, Wesley recorded a most instructive case, involving a 22-year-old woman undergoing paroxysms. What is the disorder? he asked the physicians. 'Old Dr Alexander' said it was 'what formerly they would have called being bewitched'. 'And why should they not call it so now?', retorted Wesley, answering his own rhetorical question: 'because the infidels have hooted witchcraft out of the world; and the complaisant Christians, in large numbers, have joined with them in the cry' (Curnock, 1909–16: v, 374–5). As well as the wiles of Satan, he also believed in the mysterious ways of God, instancing the Catholic girl who went blind when she read the Catholic mass book, but regained her sight upon opening the Scriptures.

The Methodists' fixation upon the demonic became notorious. Of her childhood nurse the patrician Lady Mary Wortley Montagu wrote that 'she took so much pains from my infancy, to fill my head with super-stitious tales and false notions, it was none of her fault that I am not at this day afraid of witches and hobgoblins or turn'd Methodist'.[3] Indeed, as with other expressions of evangelical and revivalist faith, Methodism provoked holy wars, at least of words, being seen as a return of the 'enthusiasm' the Anglican hierarchy associated with the seventeenth-century Puritan sectaries and plebeian 'mechanic preachers' whose zeal had threatened to turn the world upside down (Oliver, 1978; Harrison, 1979; Garrett, 1975).

All such complexities and *caveats* notwithstanding, the eighteenth cen-tury clearly brought, at least amongst educated elites, a waning of belief in Hell and the Devil, in witchcraft and magic. This should not, however, be accepted at face value as the much-trumpeted triumph of Truth: ideological change was driven by social tensions and conflicts. The following pages will sketch these social dimensions, examining culture wars and suggesting that what was at stake was not just the progress of science but the politics of politeness, as competing elites jockeyed for control of potent intellectual resources and symbols, to affirm their identities, consolidate their legitimacy and belittle rivals. It will further be argued that it would be misleading to suppose that witchcraft and magic were simply purged from elite culture. There occurred a return of the repressed; expelled through the door, the supernatural was let back in masquerade through the window, in art and literature, in aesthetic and imaginative incarnations and in a frisson for spectacle – private pleasures that could threaten no real harm.

THE REFORMATION OF POPULAR CULTURE

The eighteenth-century Quality decried and dissociated themselves from much of the time-honoured common culture to which their grandparents had subscribed. In their quest for decorum and distinction, grandees detached themselves from parochial and calendar customs like wassailing or harvest-home, and set about cleaning up or closing down traditional popular outlets – cruel sports like bear-baiting – which were increasingly declared to be offensive to reason, morality, sobriety, and law and order. This *Kulturkampf* involved beliefs too, though what was occurred was mostly local and sporadic skirmishing. Magic and the occult arts became targets of cultural contestation as the Establishment distanced itself from an all-encompassing inherited culture and sought to police the boundaries between the polite and the plebeian (Malcolmson, 1973; P. Burke, 1978; Elias, 1978–83; Golby and Purdue, 1984; Stallybrass and White, 1986).

Throughout the Renaissance astrology had formed part of this common culture, acceptable to courtiers, clergy and countryfolk alike. In England the practice peaked around the mid-seventeenth century with William Lilly and his great rival, the royalist John Gadbury, both of whom enjoyed a national following (Geneva, 1995). After the Restoration, however, educated circles decisively shrugged it off. The new science – Newtonianism in particular – naturally had something to do with this rejection. Traditional geocentric cosmology had stressed the intimate correspondences between the macro- and the microcosm, the heavens and mankind. But if, as the new astronomy revealed, the heavens were neither perfect nor unchanging, and the Earth was but a paltry planet in an infinite Universe, the doctrines of astrology had questions to answer.

The repudiation of astrology was principally, however, a response to Restoration politics. During the Civil War and Interregnum the art had indelibly tainted itself with plebeian radicalism, republicanism and reckless political prophecy; and by consequence astrology became ritually dismissed as vulgar and hazardous. By 1700 those Fellows of the Royal Society who had been sympathetic to astrology – for instance, John Aubrey – were dead, and no eminent metropolitan astrologers stepped into their shoes. But though its appeal to sophisticated circles was waning, it retained its hold. A network of provincial and lesser astrologers continued practising, albeit, as Patrick Curry has shown, on the margins. Like other facets of the occult, astrology did not become 'refuted' and give up the ghost; rather it adapted, coming to occupy a modified niche in a more polarized cultural environment (Bollème, 1969; Capp, 1979; Curry, 1989; 1992; Sharpe, 1996: 270–1).

Almanacs sales held up, but their nature changed, as the art underwent internal reform. One kind of almanac fed the reader with 'A Discourse on the Invalidity of Astrology'; many early eighteenth-century productions shed all prophecies whatsoever; and some compilers made a show of repudiating judicial astrology. Openly hostile, Richard Saunders' almanac derided astrology's want of scientific foundation, mocking Lilly, Gadbury, and the 'frightful stuff' put out by the leading early eighteenth-century adept, John Partridge (Capp, 1979: 239).

As ever with culture wars, ridicule and satire proved favourite weapons. In his *Dictionnaire*, Pierre Bayle mocked astrology as the creed of the ignorant and infantile, unbefitting modern man, bantering to his readers that he would not even trouble them with formal disproofs. Such dismissiveness was infectious. In 'Predictions for the year 1708', Jonathan Swift, writing under the pseudonym of Isaac Bickerstaff, lampooned the political predictions of the old almanac-makers, his chief target being the staunch Whig, John Partridge. 'Bickerstaff' solemnly foretold that Partridge would die of a fever at 11 p.m. on 29 March 1708 – followed by Louis XIV on 29 July, and the Pope on 11 September. The jest was a huge hit. A solemn account duly appeared of Partridge's predicted demise. The hapless astrologer tried to prove his continued existence, but his plight was hopeless – his incredible protestations were rebutted by the wits. Astrology had been reduced to a joke (David, 1966; Redwood, 1976; Capp, 1979: 243–5).

Earnest popular educators were confident that it was not ridicule but the march of mind that would finally see astrology off. For that reason, in 1828 the appearance was hailed of *The British Almanac*, published by the Society for the Diffusion of Useful Knowledge, for it provided a wealth of factual information but was quite astrology-free. 'From that hour', it was piously declared, 'the empire of astrology was at an end'. As with Partridge's, the obituary proved wildly premature (Capp, 1979: 167–81).

Other bodies of knowledge underwent similar revampings. From the late seventeenth century, fortune-telling, palmistry, physiognomy and similar Renaissance occult arts lost credit amongst intellectual trend-setters, though continuing to be practised up and down the country by an assortment of adepts and amateurs. In medical matters, top people likewise distanced themselves from ancient magical and herbal lore, including the theory of emblems or correspondences, trusting more to trained professional physicians and surgeons; after Queen Anne British monarchs significantly stopped touching for the King's Evil (in France the Bourbons continued till the nineteenth century). Mothers *à la mode* conspicuously abandoned the old village midwife in favour of the fashionable – but not necessarily safer – new male *accoucheur* (Chamberlain, 1981; Porter, 1985; 1995b; Riddle, 1992; A. Wilson, 1995).

The politics of such cultural contests have been the subject of animated debate. Some historians, notably Robert Muchembled in his reading of 'acculturation' in early modern France, believe that church and state consciously and systematically set about trying to curb and cleanse popular knowledges, habits, festivals and sexual customs, so as to impose their central authority upon the localities. In his eyes, attacks 'from above' on witchcraft and popular magic stemmed in large measure from the post-Tridentine drive to eliminate vestigial paganism and emplace a disciplined Christian order. Fears that witchcraft was an expression of popular power were real enough, but they were also deliberately fanned by the elite. Muchembled's interpretations have been criticized for exaggerating both the conspiratorial nature of elite activities and their efficacy; in the French countryside at least, folkways proved hardy perennials; as with horticultural pruning, attacks on them might only strengthen resistance.[4]

Rather like Muchembled, other historians have stressed how the new shibboleths of reason, nature and science fulfilled not only 'liberating' but also socially controlling functions, serving the interests of the dominant classes through the forging of cultural hegemony. Margaret Jacob and Larry Stewart have particularly drawn attention to the socio-political messages of the Newtonian worldview being propagated in England by the beneficiaries of the Glorious Revolution of 1688 and the Hanoverian Succession. Cosmic law and order were invoked to bolster the Whig oligarchy; natural theology taught that Nature was designed for human use and enjoyment, thereby providing rationales for capitalism; and the old mutual 'moral economy' was assailed by a new individualistic, competitive political economy, which claimed to be modelled on Newtonian atomism and to reflect the laws of God and Nature (Jacob, 1976; 1988: 116f.; Thompson, 1991; Stewart, 1992).

In both such readings – the coercive and the hegemonic – the process envisaged is one of the stifling and subduing by the powers-that-be of an entrenched popular supernaturalism through policing or propaganda agencies. But other models of cultural change might be applied, ones stressing not suppression but exchange and seduction. In England at least the triumph of modernizing outlooks arguably occurred less through imposition than infiltration, indeed in large degree through supply-and-demand market mechanisms operating in a blossoming commercial society in which consumerism was becoming a key force for change (McKendrick *et al.*, 1982; Brewer and Porter, 1993; Brewer and Staves, 1995; Bermingham and Brewer, 1995). Better communications, the mushrooming of the newspaper press, of journals, magazines and other kinds of light-reading as well as educational and instructional books; the refurbishment of cities as leisure centres, decked out with coffee-houses, taverns, assembly rooms, comfortable churches, theatres and other sites of public resort; and the rise of writers, journalists, educators, lecturers and similar cultural entrepreneurs and service occupations – all such developments made it easier for provincials and country folks to grow quite *au fait* with smart metropolitan culture and for a growing segment of the nation to tune in to its fashionable channels. The growing prominence of information media and commercial culture within a flourishing exchange economy may have done far more for the marginalization of witchcraft and its kin in the more advanced regions of Europe than any direct political, legal or ecclesiastical action, dictated by throne or altar. 'The sale of books in general has increased prodigiously within the last twenty years', reflected the English bookseller James Lackington in 1792:

> The poorer sort of farmers, and even the poor country people in
> general, who before the period spent their winter evenings in relating

stories of witches, ghosts, hobgoblins &c, now shorten the winter nights by hearing their sons and daughters read tales, romances, &c, and on entering their houses, you may see Tom Jones, Roderic Random, and other entertaining books stuck up on their bacon racks.[5]

As a bookseller Lackington had an axe to grind, and his cameo of novel-reading cottagers is not wholly credible; but even the no-nonsense Samuel Johnson confirmed the role of the free trade in knowledge in spreading and reproducing a new rationality when he declared that 'the mass of every people must be barbarous where there is no printing and consequently knowledge is not generally diffused. Knowledge is diffused among our people by the newspapers' (Boswell, 1946: i, 424; Porter, 1997b). Surveying the seemingly insatiable demand for contraband literature in France – saucy novels, scandal sheets, society satires, and lashings of erotica – Robert Darnton has implied that the new commercial culture was so dazzling that it almost irresistibly, and notwithstanding government censorship, won over provincial elites and disarmed traditional religious piety and devotion. Those who could shop, chat in coffee houses poring over the papers, attend popular scientific lectures and go to the theatre, had other interests, hopes and fears, than witches.[6] Religion had for centuries been not just a faith but a way of life, revolving around the liturgy and rituals of the church. At least in the burgeoning urban and commercial societies of North-West Europe, however, that church-centred culture was being outshone by the emergence of what Habermas has dubbed the 'public sphere'. Dominated by an urban institutions, and by the press and print culture these sustained, that public sphere, be it in Birmingham, Bruges or Bordeaux, was primarily secular (Money, 1977; Habermas, 1989; Spierenburg, 1991; Calhoun, 1992; Eley, 1992; Sommerville, 1992; K. Wilson, 1995; Brewer, 1997).

A generation ago Keith Thomas asked whether the technological advances of an industrializing society furthered such trends by obviating or diminishing the need to look to magic for power. Did new inventions come to work 'like magic'? Probably not, but the eighteenth century certainly brought practical innovations that promised greater stability and security, including banks, insurance, hospitals and better fire-fighting services. These perhaps had some impact. Equally important surely was the growing and reassuring sense of orderly routine in townsdwellers' lives: pocket-watches, newspapers appearing twice or thrice weekly like clockwork, scheduled coach and freight services, more effective marketing arrangements that largely put an end to famine – and not least the safety-net provided by poor laws that stopped people from starving to death (Thomas, 1971; Barry, 1996).

This background of material consolidation helped to slot a final and crucial piece of the modernizing cultural jigsaw into place: a sense of progress, or at least a more upbeat mood. Across Europe, cultural boosters were trumpeting expectations of self-betterment and social advance. Eyes trained on improved worldly prospects were less likely to be obsessed with Otherworldly destinies, eschatological cataclysms or even Heaven and Hell. Amongst people heartened by this growing sense of self-reliance, fears of injury from demonic enemies surely subsided: there were quite enough threats to well-being that were more mundane and tangible: unpaid bills, bad debts, trade slumps, idle apprentices – all the inevitable daily dilemmas of the bourgeoisie, for which one blamed not Satan but one's servants or the state (Lowe, 1982; Spadafora, 1990).

As the Lackington and Johnson quotations suggest, contemporaries were in no doubt as to how material life impacted upon attitudes and beliefs. They certainly pondered mental change. 'The searching into Natural knowledge', remarked John Aubrey, 'began but since or about the death of King Charles the first'; previously

twas held a strange presumption for [any] man to attempt improvement of any knowledge whatsoever, even of Husbandry it selfe; they thought it not fitt to be wiser than their fathers & not good manners to be wiser than their neighbours; and a sin to search into the wayes of nature. (Hunter, 1975: 103–4)

Aubrey had sensitive antennae.

SURVIVAL: ART AND LITERATURE

However scorned and spurned during the age of reason, the demonic and the magical did not so much disappear from polite culture as change their face and place. Once disclaimed and tamed, they became available for cultural repackaging, notably in the domains of literature and the arts which were themselves enjoying phenomenal growth (Purkiss, 1996; Brewer, 1997).

There was, of course, nothing new in such artistic representation. The supernatural had always been a staple of literature; it suffuses Shakespeare, as in the ghost in *Hamlet*, the witches in *Macbeth*, Prospero in the *Tempest*, the fairy world of *A Midsummer Night's Dream*, and the portrayal of Joan of Arc as a witch in *Henry VI* (Briggs, 1962). Yet later witches on the English stage attest shifting outlooks. If somewhat laughable, Shakespeare's witches had mainly been powerful, sinister and magical, but those in Thomas Shadwell's *The Lancashire-Witches* (1681) and *Tegue o Divelly the Irish Priest* (1682) were pure comic relief in a pot-boiling pro-Whig satire produced to wring anti–Papist propaganda out of the disclosure of the

Popish Plot; Mother Demdike, Mother Chattox and the rest were made to fly across the boards with the aid of stage machinery, an apt dramatic exposure of the artifice of it all. The popularity of Shadwell's play – it enjoyed some 50 performances between 1703 and 1729 – suggests how the crude witch image had become a political football, exploited by jubilant Whigs to conjure up a hideous but hilarious burlesque of the fiendish Tories and wild Irish. In *Dido and Aeneas* (1689), Henry Purcell used a trio of witches, as in *Macbeth*; but Purcell's cackling hags were essentially grotesque low-life figures, like bawds or barmaids. Witchcraft was moving from the tragic to the comic muse. A few years later, Allan Ramsay's pastoral drama, *The Gentle Shepherd* (1715) introduced a new figure: a harmless domesticated 'witch' who, however, was feared and invested with supernatural powers by the boorish rustics (Stock, 1982: 83–4; Keates, 1995; Sharpe, 1996: 291).

Fantasy devils loom large in the supernatural paraphernalia of Augustan satire, notably Pope's *The Rape of the Lock*. In *The Dunciad*, Pope playfully evoked a daemonic universe in which infernal goddesses – 'Cloacina' and 'Dulness' – possessed mortals and required propitiation in a mock-classical extravaganza involving sorcerers, dragons, gorgons, fiends and wizards. The Augustans could still present the supernatural, but mainly by camping it up. 'A poet who should now make the whole action of his tragedy depend upon enchantment and produce the chief events by the assistance of supernatural agents', Samuel Johnson perceived, 'would be censured as transgressing the bounds of probability, be banished from the theatre to the nursery, and condemned to write fairy tales instead of tragedies' (Butt, 1963: iv, 527–8; Wimsatt, 1969: 128).

A similar demonizing of targets for satirical ends appears in William Hogarth's 1762 engraving, 'Credulity, Superstition and Fanaticism'. Originally called 'Enthusiasm Delineated', this conjured up the (by then) ludicrous confederation of Satan, witches and spirits, to mock the Methodists. In this depiction of a ranting sermon, a grotesque congregation of men and women appears in the throes of hysterical frenzy, while a thermometer, resting on Joseph Glanvill's *Sadducismus Triumphatus* and John Wesley's *Sermons*, takes the temperature of the Methodists' brains on a scale running from despair and suicide up to raving madness. The creator of all this mental mania is the enthusiastic preacher in the pulpit, clutching in one hand a puppet of the devil, and in the other a witch doll, wearing a steeple black hat and astride a broomstick (Rudwin, 1959; Paulson, 1974: 404f.; Castle, 1995; Sharpe, 1996: 257–8, 291–2).

Witch personae could thus blossom as comic grotesques at the very time when real witches were disappearing from the daily fears of the educated. In due course the connotations of witchiness would also change: the stereotypical village hag would be superseded by the *femme fatale* and the vamp, while the old devil figure perhaps evolved into the new bogeyman/antihero of the negro, provocatively blending blackness with virility (Easlea, 1980: 249–50; Dabydeen, 1985; Dijkstra, 1986; Honour, 1989; Link, 1995). Meanwhile the shawl-clad crone, with her conical black hat, living in a cottage with her cat, and stirring a cauldron, lived on in Romantic fairy-tales, children's fiction and, in the twentieth century, in Disney (Bettelheim, 1977; Pickering, 1981; Goldstein, 1984; Bottigheimer, 1996).

In such migrations, witches assumed a new symbolic reality; the *psychological* truth, so to speak, of witch beliefs and the supernatural came out into the open. Charles Lamb, friend of the Romantic poets and children's writer, explored in his essays the ambivalent experiences of having been a child receptive to ghosts and goblins. In 'Witches, and Other Night Fears', he assumed the persona of a little girl and imagined being terrified by the picture of the raising of Samuel in Stackhouse's *History of the Bible*. She could not go to her aunt for comfort, as she had convinced herself that the old woman was a witch: 'I shrunk back terrified and bewildered to my bed, where I lay in broken sleeps and miserable fancies, till the morning'. It is a narrative which echoes one of Lamb's earliest poems:

> As when a child on some long winter's night
> Affrighted clinging to its Grandma's knees
> With eager wond'ring and perturbed delight
> Listens strange tales of fearful dark decrees
> Muttered to wretch by necromantic spell;
> Or of those hags, who at the witching time
> Of murky midnight ride the air sublime,
> And mingle foul embrace with fiends of Hell;
> Cold Horror drinks its blood.

Here Lamb thematically internalizes, psychologizes and sexualizes the witch figure in a manner that proved endlessly fascinating to Romantic, Bohemian and Decadent authors throughout the nineteenth century, particularly in Britain and Germany, ensuring that fairy stories, notably those of the brothers Grimm, were as much for adults as for children.[7]

Supernatural characters were also being recruited to fulfil various roles in French fictions. Laurent Bordelon's satirical *Les souffleurs, ou la pierre philosophale d'Arlequin* (1695) includes a magician, Polichinel, who hurls down fire upon the scornful but is finally exposed, like Tartuffe, as a fraud. Bordelon enjoyed ridiculing demonic activity and superstitions, listing in horror in his *Diversités curieuses pour servir de récréation à l'esprit* (1699) 85 diverse types of divination then being practised. His *Histoire es imaginations extravagantes de Monsieur Oufle* (1710) – Oufle being an anagram of Le Fou – was translated into English in 1711 as *A History of the Ridiculous Extravagances of Monsieur Oufle; Occasion'd by his reading Books treating of Magick, the Black-Arts, Daemoniacks, Conjurers, Witches, Hobgoblins, Incubus's, Succubus's, and the Diabolical-Sabbath; of Elves, Fairies, Wanton Spirits, Genius's, Spectres and Ghosts; of Dreams, the Philosopher's Stone, Judicial Astrology, Horoscopes, Talismans, Lucky and Unlucky Days, Eclipses, Charms, and All Sorts of Apparitions, Divinations, Charms, Enchantments, and Other Superstitious Practices, With Notes containing a Multitude of Quotations out of those Books, which have either Caused such Extravagant Imaginations, or may Serve to Cure Them.* The title tells all. A foolish, crazed adept of the esoteric arts, Oufle has a magic library stuffed with works by Agrippa, Pico della Mirandola, Johannes Trithemius, Paracelsus, Robert Fludd and all those other antiquated scholar-magus figures the Enlightenment loved to mock (Shumaker, 1972; Wilkins, 1975).

Further lampooning of magic and those foolish enough to believe in it forms the theme of the *Lettres cabalistiques* (1741) of the Marquis d'Argens. This fictitious philosophical correspondence between two cabbalists, assorted spirits, and Astaroth, the authorial *persona*, exposes the inanity of conjurations. The insinuation is that religion originated from superstition and an itch to know the unknowable; in eighteenth-century France it was only the educated élite who had transcended superstition (Wilkins, 1975). For Sébastien Mercier, likewise, the supernatural was a figment of the imagination. His *Songes d'un hermite* show him distressed by those who take it seriously, leading him to comment on the 'folies des nations depuis les magiciens de Pharaon jusqu'au saint du cimetière Saint-Médard' (Mercier, 1770: xxxii, 296; Wilkins, 1975).

Alongside this reworking of the supernatural into a vehicle or butt of satire, fundamental developments were taking place in literary and artistic criticism. The dark and irrational elements then being banished from enlightened religion and natural philosophy were being granted a privileged place in new artistic values and genres: the cult of Longinus and the later popularity of Edmund Burke's *On the Sublime and Beautiful* (1757) generated the aesthetics and poetics of the supernatural. Burke provided the psychological explanation of the allure of the sublime: it was terror enjoyed in security. In the gothic sublime, dread of ghosts, witches and demons could be savoured from the comfort and safety of one's theatre-box or drawing-room sofa (E. Burke, 1757; Hipple, 1957; Monk, 1960; Eagleton, 1990; Furniss, 1993).

The new aesthetics had far-reaching implications, far transcending admiration for mountains and spectralization (Nicolson, 1959). For some it could even provide a resurrection of the kinds of religion exposed to the withering Enlightenment critique of irrationalism, thereby revising and reinvesting the very notion of the holy. In a discussion of the New

Testament demons and miracles mounted by Anthony Blackwall, reliance on the evidences of Christianity was eclipsed by the psychology of faith. The man possessed with Legion, Blackwall suggested, was described in a strikingly animated way:

> Who is not shocked with horror and trembling at the first appearance of the raging Demoniac. . . . Then with what religious awe, reverence and tenderness of devotion do we view the mild Saviour of the human race commanding the infernal Legion to quit their possession to the miserable sufferer! (Blackwall, 1725: 250–4, quoted in Stock, 1982: 107)

Here Scripture was being sold almost as a theatrical spectacle commanding suspension of disbelief and so achieving spiritual credit.

Examining the raising of Lazarus, Blackwall likewise underscored the theatrical qualities of suspense, amazement and disbelief in the miracle; similarly with Christ's healing of the leper and calming the waves. St Paul had often been accused of obscurity, Blackwall conceded, but therein lay his strength and unique spiritual attraction. It was almost as though Blackwell was implying that the truth of Bible miracles lay primarily in their appeal to refined, quivering sensibilities (Blackwall, 1725: 277–8).

Nor was Blackwall alone in almost turning the Bible into what Poe would style a work of mystery and imagination. In 1769 James Usher, a Catholic convert, published *Clio or, Discourse on Taste*, in which he praised enthusiasm and the religious sublime for their power of terror, curiosity and exultation: 'In the sublime we feel ourselves alarmed, our motions are suspended, and we remain for some time until the emotion wears off, wrapped in silence and inquisitive horror'. Following Burke, Usher observed that obscurity, irregularity, terror and awe constituted the sublime, and all of those were primarily associated with the 'idea of invisible and immense power' – in other words, God. Moderns might deride such emotions as superstitious, but terror and awe were integral to true religious experience (Usher, 1769: 101, 107–9, 116, 237–40; Stock, 1982, 107–8).

The achievement of the sublime in psychologizing, and thereby updating and revalidating, the supernatural shows most clearly in the cult of the Gothic, a genre ushered in by Horace Walpole's *The Castle of Otranto* (1765); and later in Romanticism, in the novels of Mrs Radcliffe, Matthew Monk Lewis and, in a more complex fashion, Mary Shelley's *Frankenstein* (1818) (Punter, 1980; Andriano, 1993; Bann, 1994; Clery, 1995: 172f.). Such works trade in stock elements: the mist-shrouded castle, the villain sworn to the Devil, ghosts, spectres, sorcerers and witches, a flirting with the weird, the uncanny, the bizarre, with sado-masochistic sexuality – and, underpinning all, the Burkeian obsession with dread and the infinite unknown. Supernatural elements like spectralization triggered new sexual frissons; the old demoniacal themes of possession, incubi and succubi were eroticized, for instance, by Fuseli (Castle, 1995). Eerily juxtaposing the satiric and the Romantic, the down-to-earth and the imaginary, the hideous images of Goya's *Caprichos* similarly present the dialectic in revolutionary Spain between the Enlightenment and the call of traditional culture. If the sleep of reason produces monsters, what are Goya's monsters meant to be? satires on the disorders of the times, or ogres of his own imagining? (Powell, 1956; Park and Daston, 1981; Levitine, 1983; Held, 1987; Tomlinson, 1992; Ilie, 1995).

Romanticism represents the point at which supernaturalism left the church and entered the studio and the garret: throughout the nineteenth century it would principally be writers and artists who would explore the issues of innocence and evil, the worldly and the eternal, so long the territory of the theologians. Eventually these would become the domain of psychoanalysis (Rudwin, 1922; 1926; 1959; Abrams, 1971).

REBIRTH: THE OCCULT IN THE SECULAR WORLD

Witchcraft, magic and the supernatural were thus both theatricalized and psychologically internalized by new literary and artistic movements. The passionate poet or painter had the devil in his brain — he was, in fact, possessed by the demon of art. Yet Mozart's Queen of the Night was only stagily scary, and the only spooks in *Northanger Abbey* (1818) were the ones that fevered Catherine Morland's adolescent imagination. Cut down to size in this way, and further satirized in Peacock's *Nightmare Abbey* (1818) whose Coleridgean Mr Flosky declares that modern literature is 'hag-ridden', the irrational and abnormal could safely enjoy a public comeback, not just in writing but in new or curious scientific guises, in variations upon a dominant Newtonianism. The fringe sciences springing up in the eighteenth and nineteenth centuries were, to some degree, survivals from former ages that had retained some of their old symbolic trappings; but they were also trying to assume a glory borrowed from the prestigious new sciences. As it closed ranks, the scientific community began to dub such activities as pseudo-sciences or non-sciences: like so many other ascribed identities, this was half-resented and half-welcomed.[8]

Such disciplines as alchemy, astrology and animal magnetism, and the fringes of physiognomy and phrenology evidently enjoyed a certain vogue before tending to settle down in a new niche in the nineteenth century as the 'occult'. In this process, non-regular sciences helped reinstate the terrain of the supernatural discredited by the mechanical philosophy and

Enlightenment, thereby paving the way for facets of modern psychology and the paranormal (Ellenberger, 1970; Inglis, 1977).

In the launching of new sciences, great importance was attached to the restoration of the old Renaissance magi. In the *Encyclopédie*, and in works such as Bordelon's *History of . . . Monsieur Oufle*, magic had been laughed out of court. Indeed, even practitioners lamented the parlous fate of the esoteric in the modern world: in his *A Complete Illustration of the Celestial Science of Astrology; Or, The Art of Foretelling Future Events and Contingencies*, Ebenezer Sibly rounded on 'the stupid prejudices of the times against the real and venerable science of astrology' (Debus, 1982). But once the occult had been purged of the demoniacal, the future looked brighter in an era craving spectacle, excitement, and insight.

The esoteric sciences needed new magi, and that is why Franz Anton Mesmer was a man ripe for his times (Darnton, 1968; Gauld, 1992; Crabtree, 1993). After studying medicine at Vienna, he was granted the doctorate in 1766 with a *Physical-Medical Treatise on the Influence of the Planets*, which maintained that celestial bodies exercised a terrestrial influence. Citing Newton's theory of tides, he held that 'a tide also occurs in the human body, thanks to the same forces which cause the expansion of the sea and also the atmosphere'. Tides acted on nerves to excite magnetism. The property sensitizing the body to universal gravitation was termed 'animal magnetism'. Through harnessing this Mesmer claimed to be able to relieve internal obstructions, restore menstrual periods, cure haemorrhoids and stimulate the inner flow that was essential to health (Flaherty, 1995: 276).

His fame spreading, Mesmer was called in by the Elector of Bavaria in the case of Father Johann Joseph Gassner, who was causing embarrassment through his fame as a popular exorcist. It was a decisive moment. Seizing the opportunity to counterpose himself as a man of science and enlightenment, Mesmer managed to replicate all of Gassner's wonders, but to give empirical explanations for them on the basis of his own theory. Whereas Gassner produced convulsions in sinful subjects whose demon he claimed to be exorcising, Mesmer provoked crises caused by 'tidal disharmony', which he cured through touching and stroking with magnets. Despite this apparent victory of science over superstition, the medical faculty of Vienna grew intensely suspicious; having him declared a public menace, they forced his departure (Flaherty, 1995: 277).

Mesmer relocated in Paris, and sought once more to achieve professional stature through publicizing his scientific claims. In his *Dissertation on the Discovery of Animal Magnetism* (1779), he set out the 27 propositions underlying his theory: animal magnetism was 'the property of the animal body which brings it under the influence of heavenly bodies, and the reciprocal action occurring among those who are surrounded by it' (Flaherty, 1995: 278). His *Catechism on Animal Magnetism* (1784) offered adepts instruction in the secrets of his methods. The power of magnetism could be augmented by establishing direct interconnections among several people. One way was to form a chain by holding hands; another was the *baquet*.

As Mesmer's fame spread, he found his *métier* in showmanship. 'M. Mesmer's house', observed a contemporary,

> is like a divine temple upon which all the social orders converge: abbés, marquises, grisettes, soldiers, doctors, young girls, accoucheurs, the dying, as well as the strong and vigorous – all drawn by an unknown power. There are magnetizing bars, closed tubs, wands, ropes, flowering shrubs, and musical instruments including the harmonica, whose piping excites laughter, tears, and transports of joy. (Flaherty, 1995: 278)

The mystical atmosphere of his Parisian clinics served to put patients in the right frame of mind before the charismatic doctor made his grand entrance carrying a magic (i.e., magnetized) iron wand. The seances became ritualized in ways paralleling shamanistic curing sessions, and Mesmer was often taunted by critics as a juggler or shaman (Flaherty, 1992).

Rather as with the Saint-Médard convulsionaries, the government intervened in 1784 and set up a royal commission to investigate. This concluded there was no scientific validity to Mesmer's theories: imagination, delusion and suggestibility explained all the phenomena he produced. It also supplied a confidential report on the moral implications of Mesmer's procedures, condemning the excessive physical intimacy between healers and patients, through which animal magnetism posed threats to female virtue.

Like the medical consultants appointed to investigate the Saint-Médard convulsionaries, the Commissioners focused on female sexuality. Women were attracted to the movement and their hysterical susceptibility to convulsions made them vulnerable. Being more imaginative, emotional and sensual, they were by nature more inclined to convulsions. The relationship between the male magnetizer and his female patient, characterized by touching, was perilously erotic. Women were stimulated by the emotions the magnetizers aroused and were eager to participate in more advanced experiments in private – all, of course, in the name of healing. The findings of the Commission drove Mesmer out of Paris, despite his protestations of scientific respectability.[9]

The fascinating point is that, looking back in old age, Mesmer acknowledged that such mysterious phenomena as the sicknesses he healed and the events he orchestrated were as old as human infirmities, and they always misled the human psyche, which tended to assign them to supernatural causes or to (evil) spirits. Such phenomena included 'the oracles, inspirations, the sibyls, prophesies, divinations, witchcraft, magic, the demonology of the ancients; and in our day, the opinions on convulsives and being possessed' (Flaherty, 1995: 280). The reason why the Establishment distrusted his work, he suggested, was simple:

> It is because my assertions regarding the processes and the visible effects of animal magnetism seem to remind people of ancient beliefs, of ancient practices justly regarded for a long time as being errors of trickery. (Flaherty, 1995: 280)

The *philosophes* had tried to exorcise the ghosts of the past, but to no avail; Mesmer was raising those spirits once again. And for that reason, animal magnetism became sufficiently acceptable to serve as a legitimate explanation for a host of matters heretofore considered magical. Mesmer's contemporary, Joseph Ennemoser, for example, explained in his history of magic:

> magnetism gives us information about the existence and action of the life of dreams, and the power of creation, and in general about the sports and whims of fancy . . . In fine, Magnetism is able to give the meaning of the symbolic enigmas of ancient mysteries, which were considered quite insoluble, or which appeared matter for the most varied explanation. In the same manner, the manifold declarations of ecstatic seers and mystic philosophers, which are treasured up by persons initiated into the mysteries, will now become more intelligible by means of magnetism. (Flaherty, 1995: 282)

Another figure, Franz Joseph Gall (1758–1828), was responsible for inventing a further discipline that occupied the indeterminate middle ground between approved science, quackery and the occult: phrenology. Having received his medical degree from Vienna in 1785, Gall pursued his investigations of the human brain, maintaining 'the brain is exclusively the organ of the soul'. His phrenology or organology became a cultish science and social philosophy; practical phrenologists were soon giving individual character readings, sometimes performing blindfolded in public, yet, rather as with Mesmer, claiming to possess the secrets which would unlock the soul and resolve social ills. Phrenology developed as both a popular social philosophy and as an end-of-the-pier marvel (Cooter, 1984; Young, 1990).

Another charismatic figure whose teachings were to have equally wide-ranging repercussions was the Swiss pastor Johann Caspar Lavater. His physiognomical writings revived an art which had been derided throughout the Enlightenment, largely on account of its decidedly occultist associations. Lavater's aim was to validate physiognomy as a discipline above suspicion of charlatanry. In the course of four large folio volumes, he reminded readers of its illustrious history deriving from the ancient Egyptians through the Renaissance up to modern times. So closely was physiognomy associated with the Renaissance magi, Lavater confessed, echoing some of Mesmer's preoccupations, that he feared being accused of sorcery (Lavater, 1775–8; Tytler, 1982).

The momentous legacy of mesmerism, physiognomy and the other fringe sciences just mentioned lay in the fact that, by reconfiguring old arts, they carved out new conceptual spaces, thereby making a contribution to the occult and to later nineteenth-century spiritualism. They also facilitated the invention of the human sciences, by disclaiming the mechanization of nature and stressing the importance of delving into the inner workings of the soul (Oppenheim, 1985; Barrow, 1986; Owen, 1989; Flaherty, 1995: 283).

Finally it is worth glancing at the rise of freemasonry as an exemplification of the reincarnation of occult mysteries within an institution, a comprehensive anti-church. The masonic movement took root in England and Dutch Republic and spread through much of Europe. Its initial impulse lay in an anti-absolutist, anti-Catholic idealism, concerned to bond an inner spiritual brotherhood (Robison, 1798; Knoop and Jones, 1947; Dumas, 1967; Jacob, 1981; 1992; McIntosh, 1992; Weisberger, 1993; Flaherty, 1995: 283; Roberts, 1995; Piatigorsky, 1997). It attracted to itself a string of exceedingly exotic and rather shamanistic figures, including Martinès de Pasqually, Jean Baptiste Willermoz and Cagliostro. In key respects freemasonry created a body of values and practices that repudiated supernaturalistic Christianity in the name of Enlightenment, while simultaneously reproducing, in miniature, the rituals and mysteries of a church – this explains the vitriolic hatred towards it expressed by defenders of Christian orthodoxy, who viewed it as a heretical anti-church, the Devil's work.

Therein, of course, lay one of the ironies of the movements which have just been described. Repudiation of traditional Christian supernaturalism often led to its replacement with new cults which, at least superficially, bore them a suspicious resemblance. Likewise the desire to demystify the universe resulted only in a further mystifying of the mind. Not least, as the growing policing of the poor and other marginalized groups, and then the French Revolutionary Terror, were to show only too clearly, the ending of traditional witch-hunts hardly made Europe a more humane place.

CHAPTER 4

The Disenchantment of the World in the Nineteenth Century

> Notable enough too, here as elsewhere, wilt thou find the potency of Names; which indeed are but one kind of such Custom-woven, wonder-hinding Garments. Witchcraft, and all manner of Specterwork, and Demonology, we have now renamed Madness, and Diseases of the Nerves. Seldom reflecting that still the new question comes upon us: What is Madness, What are Nerves? (Carlyle, 1987: 196–7)

The striking new hospital medicine pioneered in revolutionary Paris operated by means of what Michel Foucault termed the 'gaze'. Inspecting the bodies of countless poor patients on the wards and then in the morgue, and mapping signs and symptoms onto lesions, pathological anatomy logged the empire of disease and death (Foucault, 1963).

In a similar way, when nineteenth-century scholars and gentlemen gazed out beyond the parsonage or the club, what they were struck by was the pathology of the popular mind; everywhere the masses were credulous and prejudiced – and all the more annoyingly so, for was this not meant to be the age of improvement? Like naturalists hunting butterflies and beetles, folklorists went out and netted the strange superstitions of goatherds and gardeners, along with their dialects, ballads, costumes, dances, calendar customs and proverbs. While their more footloose friends sailed off to study the savage mind in Brazil or Borneo, Sunday ethnographers preserved fables in the Dordogne or darkest Devon (Dorson, 1968a, 1968b; Allen, 1976; P. Burke, 1978; Stocking, 1987). Though prophets of progress might proclaim that archaic beliefs were withering away, more often what was actually found testified to the appalling resilience of ancient ways and wisdom. 'An old woman bitterly complained to me', the Cornish Quaker Barclay Fox jotted in his diary on 2 December 1842:

> that she had been bewitched by another old woman, Philly Hicks, whom she attacked yesterday for the innocent purpose of drawing blood which it seems would break the spell. She says ever since she set

her eye on her she has felt a strange crawling all over her body. (Brett, 1979: 296)

As a spontaneous journal entry, this sounds trustworthy. But much of the material published in learned journals or the newspapers should not be taken at face value, telling us more about the minds of the observers than the mentalities of the observed. Often it was voyeuristic, presenting the lower orders as benighted and bizarre, as with this newspaper item:

Burial superstition

Great excitement has been caused by the mysterious disappearance from Kilmally burial-ground, near Ennis, of the coffins containing the remains of Mr. Marcus Deane, J.P., and Miss Barnes, an English governess in Mr. Deane's family. The general opinion is that the remains have been carried away and buried in some other spot to prevent their removal out of the parish to the new cemetery, which, according to a superstition, would entail famine and pestilence on the parishioners. (*Shrewsbury Chronicle*, 3 October 1884; Foster, 1993)

It can surely have been no accident that this hair-raising tale was being told about the bog Irish at a time of mounting Anglo-Irish political tensions. And what should we make of this 'singular case of superstition', about a girl who had drowned in a canal?

The child's mother said she had kept her little girl at home because she had 'a dread' upon her in consequence of having three nights in succession dreamed of baking bread. She had lost other children, and on each occasion had similar dreams before the child died. Owing to her dream she had kept the girl away from school, and had refused to allow her to leave the house. (*Shrewsbury Chronicle*, 6 September 1884)

From the outset, 'singular' and 'superstition' establish the judgmental framework. A mother who kept her child away from school was likely to be the sort of womam sunk in superstitions.Folklorists had fish of their own to fry, leading them to sensationalize, sentimentalize or censor the data they dredged up. And as with anthropologists and missionaries overseas, their responses were mixed. A collector might deplore the brutish customs of the yokels, while in the same breath rueing the 'olden days' of an imagined 'merrie England'. The fact that, in England at least, folklore hunters and gatherers clearly felt in a cleft stick — should one pillory, pity or praise the world then being lost? — signals the rapidity of rural change in the workshop of the world, that nation of capital-intensive farming, enclosure, railways, state education and mass literacy — all of which were corroding the castle of custom. Scoured by such tides of change, village ways and wisdom were patronized by modernizers as 'popular superstitions' – or cherished by romantics as hallowed traditions, the precious life-blood of the Anglo-Saxon or Celtic heritage.[1]

Innovation threw 'survivals' into relief. The Reverend John Christopher Atkinson's *Forty Years in a Moorland Parish* (1892) recorded how, on his arrival there as vicar in 1847, the villagers of Danby in North Yorkshire had been believers in witchcraft. 'I have no doubt at all', he assured readers, 'of this very real and very deep-seated existence of a belief in the actuality and the power of the witch' (Atkinson, 1891: 72–3; Sharpe, 1996: 276), listing the persistence of practices familiar centuries earlier: shape-changing, *maleficium* targeted against livestock, recourse to cunning folk for counter-magic and practical healing. The main local 'conjuror' had been the Stokesley 'wise man'. 'To this fellow', Atkinson recounted,

> people whose education, it might have been expected, would have raised them above such weaknesses, flocked; many came to ascertain the thief, when they had lost property; others for him to cure themselves or their cattle of some indescribable complaint. Another class visited him to know their future fortunes; and some to get him to save them from being balloted into the militia – all of which he professed himself able to accomplish. (Atkinson, 1891: 111; de Blécourt, 1994)

At the dawn of the twentieth century, villagers in remote rural Essex still believed in magic; witches brought on illness and even paralysis and visited victims with plagues of lice. Witchcraft worked within a wider cosmology helping people to make sense of existence and handle adversity (Maple, 1965, 1971; Thompson, 1991). Some commentators rejoiced in those gnarled roots. There 'lingers still among the uneducated classes', wrote the leading folklorist Edwin Hartland about Gloucestershire,

> a number of traditions – songs, tales, proverbs, riddles, games, customs, institutions, leechcraft, superstitions – distinct from and only partially sanctioned by the religion, the literature, the science and arts, which together sum up what we understand by civilisation. These traditions constitute our Folklore.[2]

But while Hartland hoped this heritage could survive alongside 'civilization', others lamented the imminent extinction of country ways, a consequence (thought the gloomy Darwinist novelist Thomas Hardy) of the new 'political economy' that was driving capital-intensive farming:

> the recent supplanting of the class of stationary cottagers, who carried on the local traditions and humours, by a population of more or less migratory labourers, which has led to a break of continuity in local history, more fatal than any other thing to the preservation of legend, folk-lore, close inter-social relations and eccentric individualities. For

these the indispensable conditions of existence are attachment to the soil of one particular spot by generation after generation. (Hardy, 1874: 38–9; Bushaway, 1995: 192)

Many in England echoed Hardy's lamentation over a vanishing culture. The hectoring Enlightenment language of 'vulgar errors' softened into sentimentality: in 1831 a writer referred with some affection to the 'popular superstitions of the present day, at which the rising generation may smile when the credulous are dead and only remembered for their fond belief'.[3]

But while antiquarians might treasure folk-beliefs, others, especially Evangelical clergymen, remained committed to combatting them as dangerous relics of paganism or popery. In 1830 the Somerset clergyman John Skinner sought to convince a parishioner that the source of his sickness did not lie in witchcraft: 'I endeavoured as much as possible to do away with those unfortunate fancies he labours under about being bewitched, but I fear I shall not succeed' (Coombs and Coombs, 1971: 401). In a Lincolnshire village at the same time the minister was campaigning against 'popular superstition': 'I have never waived an opportunity of . . . endeavouring to eradicate a superstition which tended to weaken the influence of Christianity in an uninstructed mind'; yet amongst the locals 'these hateful corroders of happiness are far from being extirpated. Credulity and superstition still reign with tyrannic sway in many hearts' (*Gentleman's Magazine*, cii [1832], 591; Obelkevitch, 1976). With their iconoclastic hatred of idolatry, Protestant Dissenters too were as distrustful of vestiges of popish magic as Reginald Scot had been three centuries earlier. Growing up in the 1860s, George Sturt pointed to a stubborn family religiosity as the reason why his own upbringing had been untainted by the supernatural. 'We had no country "charms"', he recalled,

no rural lore at all, though my mother had been born and brought up in a farm-house . . . and the reason was almost certainly that my mother's own mother had a strong religious disapproval of such ideas. I never heard of fairies as if they were anything real; or of ghosts, or spirits, or omens. (Sturt, 1977: 136–7)

In France the battle-lines were rather differently drawn up. Agrarian change was glacially slow; a permanent peasantry dominated village life, and what commentators recorded was not the threats to folkways as in England but their tenacity.[4] Broadly speaking this folk culture was despised by the educated, not least the clergy. It is no accident that it was French philosophical anthropologists like Lévy-Bruhl who were to champion the condescending ethnocentric notion of a 'primitive mentality', putting pre-logical, magical primitive beliefs firmly in their place.[5]

Nineteenth-century France presents a peasant culture highly, and some-times violently, resistant to élite weeding or eradication. There had long flourished near Biesnau in Burgundy a miraculous fountain, whose patron was the apochryphal Saint Bon. It was reputedly capable of curing every disease, and a certain old 'voyageuse', Petrouille, was among those who consulted it. In 1827, however, the authorities, anxious to put a stop to this silly nonsense, prosecuted her. Local opinion denounced the proceed-ings and many testified to her good faith, one elderly peasant affirming that: 'Petrouille . . . is a good Christian, and I know nothing about her which doesn't accord with the faith'. The efforts of the Church and the *curé* to enlighten the people proved unavailing (Devlin, 1987: 46).

And episodes like that were endlessly repeated throughout the French countryside. 'Mindless' *paysan* rituals drew reproof from their betters. 'People go to confession and communion', it was commented, with evident disgust,

> give alms, observe some superstitious customs, buy crucifixes, rosary-beads with which they touch the demi-god's statue; they rub their foreheads, knees, paralysed arms on miraculous stones; throw pins and farthings into fountains, dip their shirts into them to be cured, and their belts to give birth painlessly. (Devlin, 1987: 52)

The anti-clerical radical, A. S. Miron, expressed similar disdain for the popular pilgrimage to Pierrefixte, near Nogent-le-Rotrou, where the fountain of Saint John the Baptist was said to cure all annually on 23 June (significantly, midsummer as well as the saint's day). The ritual went like this: the sick had to soak a linen rag in the holy waters, and then massage the afflicted part. Miron attacked the habit of plunging young children into the waters and was especially offended by the sight of young women stripping down at the fountain: 'At last, in 1848 when I was in charge of the administration of the district, I issued a prefectorial edict making this prohibition definitive' – only to find the locals retaliated, claiming their ancient liberties were being usurped (Devlin, 1987: 53). By and large anti-clerical intellectuals attacked such practices as Catholic superstition, while the clergy would denounce them as relics of pagan nature-worship (Devlin, 1987: 59).

Like Voltaire a century earlier, critics were shocked at the bizarreness of the practices they found. One popular 'miracle' was the temporary resuscitation of dead babies. Infants who had expired before baptism might be brought on pilgrimage to the chapel of Notre-Dame-des-Faisses at Ribiers in the Hautes-Alpes, where mass was celebrated for their resurrec-tion: they were supposed to come momentarily to life and then be baptised, thereby ensuring that they would escape limbo and ascend without detour to heaven. These 'miracles' commanded great interest till the custom was stamped out by two priests (Devlin, 1987: 64–5).

The year 1857 – just before Bernadette Soubirous witnessed the Immaculate Conception at Lourdes – brought the greatest scandal in the French countryside: an 'epidemic possession' broke out in Morzine in the Haute-Savoie, at the peak of which, in 1861, over a hundred villagers were affected. The possessed hurled insults, swore and blasphemed; they displayed uncommon strength or an astounding command of foreign tongues; some seemed to receive supernatural messages and fell to prophesying (Maire, 1981). On one occasion, the deputy-mayor, Jean Berger, was chased for three hours by dozens of men, women and children armed with pitchforks, accusing him of visiting the community with a malady. Finally, after 15 years of chaos, a stop was put to the epidemic: a posse of police and soldiers were sent in, and some of the possessed were marched off to hospital – a much-feared fate; fits in church and on the streets ceased, and the outbreak died away (Devlin, 1987: 138).

Morzine was a reminder of how folk customs had always given voice to local grievances and protests, and certain visionary leaders emerged from below, capitalizing on such traditions. Eugène Vintras from Tilly-sur-Seulles acquired a large following. In August 1839 he had his first vision – a threadbare old man, who revealed that he had been sent by God to establish his prophetic mission. Assuming the prophet's mantle, Vintras began to take down and proclaim the divinely-sent words. Initially such prognostications were confined to 'misfortunes which will befall man, punishments that are near at hand, divine wrath' and so forth, but soon he was predicting 'the arrival of a great King on the throne of France' (Devlin, 1987: 143). It was time for the Establishment to strike back. Bishops denounced Vintras from the pulpit and forbade him to receive communion; Popes Gregory XVI and Pius XI followed suit; Louis Philippe also turned his attention to Vintras when in 1841 he persisted in announcing the accession to the throne of a new monarch; arrest and trial followed, and he was condemned to five years in prison (Devlin, 1987: 151).

Another such prophet was one Thomas-Ignace Martin, a labourer from the Chartres area, who claimed to hold conversations with the Archangel Gabriel. As Martin's apocalyptic visions grew increasingly political, he attracted the attention of the bishop, the prefect and the Minister of Police. Finally he was locked up in Charenton, the Paris lunatic asylum where he came under the supervision of the eminent alienist, Philippe Pinel. Supernatural happenings were acceptable only if, as with Bernadette Soubirous, they could be wholly stage-managed by the Church: the scandalous anarchy of earlier convulsionary episodes had not been forgotten (Goldstein, 1984, 1987; Devlin, 1987: 163).

Popular culture characteristically caused trouble by challenging and reversing official hierarchies and value-systems (Stallybrass and White, 1986). Priests might be ascribed second identities by the peasantry quite aside from their ecclesiastical office, being made to double as folk heroes or demons. Ancient tradition commonly held *curés* responsible for storms, and peasants swore that priests directed the winds. The Abbé Meschinet was an early devotee of photography. A bunch of country-folk watched him with suspicion when he set up his apparatus and dived under the black cape. Just then a hailstorm broke out. Armed with pitchforks and sticks, the peasants fell upon him, yelling that he was a sorcerer who had just whipped up a tempest (Devlin, 1987: 207–8; Ramsey, 1988: 270; *cf.*, for England, Obelkevitch, 1976).

Just like the priests, physicians might equally be cast in an unwelcome role, viewed not as healers but as sorcerers or as ministers of death. The ancestral persona of the *semeur de peste* ('sower of plague'), akin to a magician or sorcerer, could be projected onto the doctor suspected of being the agent appointed to enact the rancour of the rich towards the poor (Devlin, 1987: 210). In the Hautes-Alpes, sorcerers were believed to murder by means of poison, and this was also the technique employed, according to popular myth, by the *semeur de peste*. Thus doctors caused epidemics.

Priests too were sometimes identified as responsible for outbreaks: in 1854, when cholera broke out in the Gatinais, clerics reported that 'almost everywhere, priests have been accused of giving the cholera'. Accusations against doctors were in part expressions of popular distrust of institutional medicine. Rabies sufferers (rumour had it) were smothered to death in hospitals, while Breton peasants were unwilling to be admitted into such institutions, being convinced that patients were subjected to experimentation. The poor suspected the authorities of trying to kill them: during cholera epidemics, it was repeatedly reported that the doctors, in cahoots with officialdom, were poisoning the poor (Delaporte, 1986; Devlin, 1987: 212).

Doctors were not actually trying to do that, but elite observers certainly held some rather venomous attitudes. Enlightenment rationalists, as shown in earlier, had diagnosed popular superstition as the ally of tyranny and oppression. Following in their footsteps, later French radicals targeted superstition because they saw the idiocy of rural life as a drag on progress. Few expressed affection for folkways: they wanted to eliminate them. And while the *philosophes* had experienced a certain faith in the populace, or at least a belief in the virtue of 'natural' man and the power of education (Payne, 1976), this tended to evaporate when the new nine-teenth-century science of psychology (individual and crowd) presented man as an irrational being driven by passion and prejudice – themes that will be further explored below (Le Bon, 1920; Nye, 1975; Moscovici, 1981).

A few intellectuals, however, countered the trend and idealized *les paysans* and their mysterious ways, even, for the first time, elevating witches into folk-heroes. The suggestion that witches formed a popular underground resistance came from the Romantic historian Jules Michelet. His *La sorcière* (1862) presented witchcraft as a protest movement of medieval serfs, and the sabbat as a clandestine nocturnal conclave where villagers convened to feast, enacting pagan rites and folk dramas parodying lord and priest. All centred on the witch, who was, Michelet maintained, a priestess presiding over an ancient fertility cult, the people's champion against the feudal tyrant. The sabbat culminated with her copulating with a giant fertility figure, equipped with a massive phallus, representing Satan. All this was a product of the populist Michelet's mythopoeic imagination, ever feverish when women were involved. Yet his fantasy that witchcraft was a subversive movement had a future ahead of it, later being modified by Margaret Murray and finally revived by some modern feminists.[6]

However tenacious the old ways, even in peasant-dominated France their grip was eventually relaxed. But few attributed this 'breaking of the spell' to the force of reason as earlier envisaged by the Enlightenment (Spierenburg, 1991). Contemporaries rather believed that plebeian habits were imperceptibly being eroded by impersonal agencies: the penetration of urban culture, newspapers and the power of print, formal schooling, military conscription – all crumbled the cake of custom. That pioneering collector of popular antiquities, John Aubrey, had long before divined how much the waning of popular superstition owed to the corrosive impact of social disruption: 'When the wars came and with them liberty of conscience and liberty of inquisition, the phantoms vanished' (Dick, 1972: 29). The noted English folklorist William Howitt also thought that superstition was withering thanks to 'modern ambition, modern wealth, modern notions of social proprieties, modern education', all of which were 'hewing at the root of the poetical and picturesque, the simple and the candid in rural life' (Howitt, 1838: 483); while the encroachment of capitalist relations, especially the privatization of the common fields, was widely seen as undermining shared culture: 'enclosure acts have played havoc with the past', observed J. Harvey Bloom, who collected materials in the Cotswolds (Bloom, 1930: iii–iv). Reminiscing about her 1880s Oxfordshire childhood, Flora Thompson recalled asking if witches still existed. 'No, they seem to have all died out', mother replied: 'There haven't been any in my time: but when I was your age there were plenty of old people who had known or even been ill-wished by one' (Thomson, 1973: 266–7). Thompson then went on to spin a familiar tale of how material innovation changed mentalities:

the world was at the beginning of a new era, the era of machinery and scientific discovery. Values and conditions were changing everywhere. Even to simple country people the change was apparent. The railways had brought distant parts of the country nearer, newspapers were coming into every house; machinery was superseding hard labour, even on the farm to some extent; food bought at shops, much of it from distant countries, was replacing the home-made and the home-grown. Horizons were widening. (Thompson, 1973: 68–9)

The parallels with other arcadian myths – the bucolic golden age or the stable nuclear family – are plain: things had always been as they should be not so very long before. Such explanations for the decline of folklore are, of course, themselves formulaic and folkloric. The point about accounts like Flora Thompson's is not their truth but their ritual quality – in other words, their own tenacity as myths of modernization.

THE GRAND THEORY OF SECULARIZATION

Bolstering Enlightenment ideas with eye-witness experiences, pundits continued to inveigh against the follies of witchcraft and magic. What was novel in the nineteenth century was the attempt to replace polemic and condemnation with a grand panorama of mental and social change. An age of revolution looked to philosophies of history for the meaning of things; and anyway the times had a penchant for stupendous syntheses, from Dr Casaubon's key to all mythologies to the Spenglerian *Decline of the West*.[7]

What Hegel undertook for the Idea of freedom and Marx for class, others attempted for the natural history of consciousness, sketching out a dynamics of transformation from religion to reason. Supplanting the old Biblical eschatology of the Four Kingdoms, theories now swept from savagery to civilization. They traced the rise of Reason in individual and society, or pursued an anthropology of the ascent of man through successive stages of mental development. In other words, they studied 'secularization' – though that term is largely anachronistic, loaded and imperfect. '"Secularization" began as an emotive word, not far in its origins from the word "anticlericalism"', Owen Chadwick has reflected:

Sometimes it meant a freeing of the sciences, of learning, of the arts, from their theological origins or theological bias. Sometimes it meant the declining influence of churches, or of religion, in modern society. Then the sociologists, heirs of Comte, aided by certain historians and anthropologists, did a service by showing how deep-seated religion is in humanity and in the consensus which makes up society. They therefore made the word unemotional; a word used to describe a process, whatever that process was, in the changing relationship between religion and modern society, a process arising in part out of the industrial revolution and the new conditions of urban and mechanical life, in part out of the vast growth in new knowledge of various kinds. (Martin, 1978; Chadwick, 1990: 264; Sommerville, 1992)

As Chadwick hints, an early and highly influential arrival at the meta-historical ball was Positivism. Building upon Condorcet's Enlightenment rationalism and its St Simonian successors, Auguste Comte charted in his multi-volume *Cours de philosophie positive* the maturation of mind understood in terms of an ascent ('the law of intellectual progress') from the theological, through the metaphysical, up to the positivistic or scientific plane. The evolution of rationality matched and mirrored improvements in material civilization that brought nebulous transcendental speculations down to earth. 'The truth is', commented Thomas Carlyle, 'men have lost their belief in the Invisible, and believe and hope, and work only in the Visible' (Carlyle, 1829).

The key to science lay in the capacity to formulate the laws governing the phenomena of Nature and society, thanks to which authentic mastery of nature would supersede the fruitless rites of otherworldly cults and magic. In Comte's non-Christian but not anti-religious sociology, the superannuated clergy would be superseded by a priesthood of science administering the rites of a religion of humanity. Understood broadly as the endorsement of the universal empire of natural law to human development, Comtian positivism proved hugely influential amongst nineteenth-century *savants*, especially when integrated into a fully evolutionary framework, as by Herbert Spencer. The empire of natural law put paid to marvels; the law of progress explained why magic had once been believed in (Manuel, 1962; Peel, 1971; Evans–Pritchard, 1981: 43; Aron, 1989; Olson, 1993).

Key elements in the Positivist agenda were taken to their logical conclusion by Emile Durkheim, not least his confidence that it was science's mission progressively to reveal the laws governing seemingly free or random human actions like suicide. Durkheim programmatically made society the subject of science, to be understood in terms of social laws and functions. With society itself becoming, so to speak, consecrated or fetishized, all the old sacred players (God, Satan, the eucharist) were temporalized and problematized, and pre-scientific notions of the sacrosanct were decoded as the confusions of more primitive styles and stages of thinking. Within Durkheimian sociology it was no longer asked whether magic and the supernatural were true. The question was what role they had traditionally served in sanctifying society, and how their erstwhile functions had been discredited.[8]

Roughly comparable but rather distinct developments were in train in the Germanic tradition. Stimulated by *Sturm und Drang* and Romantic stirrings, Herder's writings reversed traditionally negative attitudes towards the populace and turned the *Volk* (its legends, spirit and above all its tongue) into objects of esteem. Whereas the *philosophes* had condemned the peasantry as a cesspit of error, in post-Herderian German thinking the nation became the fount of wisdom. German Biblical scholarship was meanwhile attempting, in a somewhat parallel way, to recapture the inner spirit of Judaism and early Christianity, using techniques of intuitive rationalization that were the seeds of *Geistesgeschichte* and of Weberian *Verstehen*. Such concerns in turn stimulated the 'anthropology' of the Young Hegelians and their materialist critics alike, including Feuerbach and the young Karl Marx. And all such approaches were more or less suffused with Hegel's conviction that the history of Mind evinced a rationality maturing by its own inner unfolding: rationality was the evolution of spirit in the world (Marcuse, 1955; Hughes, 1958; Passmore, 1968; P. Burke, 1978: 268f.; Leaf, 1979: 81f.).

This historical sociology of consciousness was, however, given a more pessimistic twist by Max Weber. Though far from disputing the world-historical march of rationalisation, Weber denied its purposeful personification as a self-directing and self-realizing force in its own right. On the contrary, the supreme irony as Weber saw it was that rationalization, while real, was an unintended by-product of Protestant faith. Nor could the much-vaunted rise of rationality even be reckoned as an unambiguous gain, for the 'disenchantment of the world' it had effected had divorced fact from value, reason from feelings, man from nature, individual from society. And, at bottom, what was the rationality of the modern capitalist state but an 'iron cage'? Weber's disillusioned sociology in some respects mirrors Nietzsche's pathological poetics: rationality might have been achieved, but had that been good for man's health? (Weber, 1930; Weber, 1946: 138–9; Hawthorn, 1976). Small surprise that in Germany in particular moves to revitalize the folk inheritance gained ground.

Dominated by evolutionary models forumulated by Darwin and Spencer, England too produced its crop of anthropological theorists. Fundamentally rationalist in temper and training, most were fascinated by ubiquitous animistic and supernatural beliefs which they interpreted through a developmental lens as what Edward Tylor termed 'survivals' and 'vestiges' – 'living fossils' so to speak. He wrote of the evolutionary development from 'savage through barbaric to civilized life'. In an influential model, William Robertson Smith traced an evolutionary passage from ritual to myth (and thence to religion and finally to literature), while evolutionism provided Sir James Frazer in *The Golden Bough* with the key to his interpretation of magic and religion as precocious but premature attempts at scientific reasoning (Tylor, 1871; Frazer, 1890–1915; Hodgen, 1936; Burrow, 1966; Kuper, 1988; Shamdasani, 1996: 436f.).

Such anthropological theories, and many others besides, threaded in and out of each other like dancers at a ball. Their collective significance, however, lay in transforming the critique of the supernatural from a tactical war waged by Enlightenment free-thinkers into academic ortho-doxy. *Philosophes* had seen superstition as something to be fought; later theorists historicized and naturalized it into a passing stage in the historical evolution of mind. By laying the foundations for anthropology and sociology, they conferred upon human science, the naturalistic study of mankind, an authority comparable to that so long possessed by the Christian theology it supplanted. The superstitious, the supernatural, and even the varieties of religious experience themselves were henceforth to be conceptualized in no other way but as enigmas or anomalies to be resolved by the higher and all-encompassing explanatory categories of natural and social science.

Nothing, of course, was graven in stone. Nineteenth-century anthro-pology itself rapidly came to seem like one of the survivals it studied. And the present century has brought wave upon wave of challenges to the dominant secular, mechanical, reductionist scientific paradigms (Berman, 1981; Capra, 1983; Harrington, 1996). The paradox has been often asserted that science itself is the modern superstition; and new oracles have sought to resurrect old myths or create novel ones, more holistic, more respectful to Nature than Christianity and its heir, science. Calls have been made for the recovery of the sacred (Lovelock, 1979; Midgley, 1992). 'For more than 99 per cent of human history', reflects Morris Berman,

> the world was enchanted and man saw himself as an integral part of it. The complete reversal of this perception in a mere 400 years or so has destroyed the continuity of the human experience and the integrity of the human psyche. It has very nearly wrecked the planet as well. The only hope it seems to me, lies in the reenchantment of the world. (Berman, 1981: 22)

Nevertheless the official Western mind remains disenchanted, and it would now take a miracle to supplant dominant scientific materialism with an alternative metaphysics that was truly transcendental.

THE PSYCHOPATHOLOGY OF WITCHCRAFT AND MAGIC

Paralleling this anthropology of the primitive mind, past and present, the nineteenth century brought a medicalizing or psychologizing drive, an offshoot of the anatomo–pathological method mentioned at the outset of this chapter. With the witch-craze safely consigned to the past, no longer were specialists in psychopathology condemned to serve as the Inquisitors' adjutants, performing tests on anaesthetized skin and wandering wombs. At last, flexing their professional muscles, doctors could declare independence and produce their own grand psychopathological doctrines, based upon historical evidence, clinical expertise and theoretical models. Looking backwards, nineteenth-century psychiatrists began to sit in lofty judgment on the psychological temper of earlier epochs, diagnosing as deeply disturbed those murky late medieval times of eschatological fears, heretic-hunting and witch-burning. They would anatomatize the delusions of all who in previous centuries had made pacts with the Devil and his minions. At last the bizarre physical symptomatologies and weird flights of fancy of witches and their victims, or of those displaying convulsions or the dancing mania, could finally be revealed as the products of individual or mass psychopathology. Psychiatry could now dedicate its own hall of fame to those physicians who, from Wier onwards, precociously announced these fundamental medico-psychological truths to a deaf or disbelieving world. Through such means psychiatry claimed to serve science and humanity, by exposing the fallacies of the witch-hunters and their latter-day successors and apologists. Especially in Third Republic France but also in the Reich during Bismarck's *Kulturkampf*, the bitter battles between the Church and the *avant garde* intelligentsia politicized psychiatry. Anti-clerical clinicians touted psychiatric models as rebuttals of theological mystification (Goldstein, 1987; Ellis, 1990).

In thus laying bare the hidden history of the psyche and reasoning about the abnormal, psychological medicine staked its claim to be heard in the present, capable of diagnosing the disorders of modern society and exercising jurisdiction over disputed clinical cases (as at Morzine). The mental balance of new mass society became highly controversial, of course, as revolution remained in the air but Enlightenment faith in the perfectibility or at least improvability of human nature was challenged, after the Terror, by gloomier theories of human psychology allegedly based upon the science of difference and deterioration. Concepts of 'moral insanity' called the reign of rationality into question, and from around 1850 Morel, Moreau de Tours and other French psychiatrists began to draw attention to the presence of degenerates, impaired by psychiatric disorders that were congenital and inheritable. Thereafter degenerationist theory gained ground, leading to the notion of recidivism developed by Cesare Lombroso, and providing fuel for eugenics. Degenerationist pathography would both explain the Devil and also obviate him (Pick, 1989; Dowbiggin, 1991).

Asylum superintendants believed they had ample evidence in their wards for their retrospective diagnoses of witches and the possessed back in the age of faith. Day-in, day-out, routine clinical experience revealed no shortage of patients who still, in the nineteenth century, believed they were in the clutch of diabolical powers or experiencing angelic revelations. Before the very eyes of the doctors and their students, patients would shriek, be struck dumb, or speak in tongues; would suffer seizures, fall into a stupor, or would become paralysed or anaesthetized – all like former saints or demoniacs. Especially under the controlled stimulus of hypnosis, first revealed by Mesmer and refined by later clinicians, notably Jean-Martin Charcot at the Salpêtrière, Paris's huge female madhouse, patients would disassociate, presenting themselves in dissonant personalities and guises precisely like those in earlier centuries by ventriloquised demons. What could such patients be but vestiges or living history, recapitulating the behaviour of those bewitched and bedevilled in the sixteenth century? No wonder psychiatrists believed that they had in their hand the key that would finally unlock some of the mysteries of human history (Charcot, 1987; 1991; Harris, 1989: 155f.; Gauld, 1992: 272f.).

That key was the hysteria diagnosis (Gilman *et al.*, 1993; Micale, 1995). Influential nineteenth century physicians believed that hysteria – it was largely, though not exclusively, a female malady – provided the solution to the bizarre episodes of witchcraft and convulsionary phenomena in the past. Hysteria became the subject of scores of medical texts, and made the fame and fortunes of Charcot, Breuer, Janet, Freud and other towering medical figures, as it became regarded as the open sesame to the impenetrable enigmas of mind/body interaction – religious rapture, sexual deviation, suicidal despair, and, above all, that mystery of mysteries, woman. Ontogeny recapitulated phylogeny, and psychiatrists believed that they could see the history of the human psyche unfolding in the clinic or on the couch (Schaps, 1982; Dijkstra, 1986; Masson, 1986; Showalter, 1986; Steinbrügge, 1995).

To clinch their credentials for pronouncing on religion and history, some schools of psychiatry, *par excellence* those associated with Charcot's aggressively naturalizing circle, proposed a bold metahistory drawing on Comte's scheme of the evolution of thinking from the theological up to the scientific plane. Such a progressive schema implied that sickness had, at the dawn of civilization, been misattributed to Otherworldly agencies (spirit-possession, necromancy, etc.), subsequently being mystified into formulaic verbiage (so-called humours, animal spirits, complexions, temperaments) dissembling as explanations. Growing out of such mumbo-jumbo, physicians had finally learned to ground their art upon the realities of anatomy, physiology and neurology. By abandoning myths for measurement, words for things, metaphysics for metabolism, medicine was finally grasping the laws of organic life. According to Charcot, hysteria would be solved by pursuing the science of the body, to be precise, neurophysiology (Goldstein, 1982).

Such views were congenial to nineteenth century psychological doctors. 'Only when bodily functions are deranged', warned the mid-Victorian British physician, Bevan Lewis, do 'we become . . . conscious of the existence of our organs' (Lewis, 1889: 143). Imbalances of body and mind held the secret of hysterical behaviour. In his cautions about consciousness, Lewis was of a mind with field leaders like Charles Mercier, David Skae, Henry Maudsley and Thomas Clouston, who saw hysteria as an expression of excessive introspection, self-preoccupation and narcissistic eroticism (Clark, 1988). Allowed to dwell upon herself, feared Maudsley, the hysteric would most likely sink into insanity (Maudsley, 1873: 79); for, as the patient progressively abandoned her 'power of will' – 'a characteristic symptom of hysteria in all its Protean forms' – she would fall into 'moral perversion', losing:

> more and more of her energy and self-control, becoming capriciously fanciful about her health, imagining or feigning strange diseases, and keeping up the delusion or the imposture with a pertinacity that might seem incredible, getting more and more impatient of the advice and interference of others, and indifferent to the interests and duties of her position. (Maudsley, 1873: 80)

Such descriptions perfectly accounted for a long line of female visionaries, witches and deviants.

Though briefly Charcot's student, Freud somewhat cuts across this explanatory strategy. Freud had been trained into the Germanic school of neurophysiology, whose creed (paralleling the positivist) espoused the triple alliance of scientific method, medical materialism and intellectual progress: explanations of the living had to be somatically-grounded. Though initially endorsing this programme, during the 1890s Freud shifted to a psychodynamic stance, formulating a battery of mentalist neologisms – the unconscious, the *ego*, *id*, and *super ego*, the death wish, etc. – which organicists derided as throwbacks to Comte's 'metaphysical' stage. (Freud regarded himself as victimized for his pains, energetically cultivating a self-image as a persecuted heretic.)[9] Through such analyses, hysteria became a catch-all diagnosis for all that was odd.

As earlier shown, certain sixteenth and seventeenth century doctors like Edward Jorden had claimed that *some* cases of alleged possession and *maleficium* were manifestations of disease. It was therefore not a huge leap to the nineteenth-century psychiatric conviction that *every* such instance necessarily was. Anti-clerical psychiatrists might then venture one stage further; having shown that demonism was psychopathological, might religion itself, with its saintly behaviour, mortification of the flesh, fasting, visions, ecstasies and holy trances be neither more nor less? After all, as a good Comtian, Charcot took it as axiomatic that, being a real disease, hysteria must be biologically universal: '*L'Hystérie a toujours existé, en tous lieux et en tous temps*'. With his colleague, Anselm Richer, he set about demonstrating that a reliable pictorial record existed of hysterics in history. On the basis of an examination of religious paintings deriving from Medieval and Counter-Reformation times – an exercise in what came to be called 'retrospective medicine' – their *Les démoniques dans l'art* (1887) contended that the mystics and saints, the St Catherine's and St Theresa's, as well as the demoniacs of Christian history had typically been hysterics akin to those cavorting in their clinics (Charcot and Richer, 1887; Didi-Huberman, 1982; Gilman, 1982).

This daring attempt by militant psychiatry to snatch all non-normal behaviour away from the altar and the confessional was specific to the emergent politics of French anti-clericalism. Philippe Pinel, the leading Paris psychiatrist around 1800, had by no means been hostile to religion (Weiner, 1994). The turning point had came with the 1830 Revolution, which stimulated a revitalized Catholicism and the retaliatory rediscovery of demonology by liberal psychiatrists (Vandermeersch, 1991, 1994). At first, the witch-hunts were referred to rather loosely. In the 1830s, Esquirol and Brierre de Boismont alluded to earlier times when witchcraft, diabolical possession, vampirism and the *convulsionnaires* were common, but assumed that these weird events were things of the past. 'This illness became very rare', assured Esquirol, speaking about demonology, 'due to the fact that religious education, the better rearing of children and widespread schooling have equally enlightened all social classes' (Esquirol, 1838: i, 254). Religion posed no difficulties for him as long as it remained within rational bounds.

Things changed, however. 'Esquirol pretended', stated Macario in 1843:

> and other authors have repeated what he said – that demonomania is extremely rare in the nineteenth century and that this kind of lunacy is only to be found in uneducated, superstitious and pusillanimous people. It is said that the demons were replaced by a groundless fear of the police, of magnetism, of electricity . . . Esquirol as well as the authors writing after him were wrong. (Macario, 1843)

And the reason for that, he thought, was that the leading psychiatrists 'observed lunatics only in Paris'; peasants in the provinces – it became such a familiar tale – were a different kettle of fish.

Macario viewed possession or demonomania as a form of melancholia or lypemania, its characteristic description being an almost 'demonic' vitality. He additionally pointed to the witch-craze so as to highlight the bloody effects of religion, praising Wier for his courage in repudiating demonomania. Martin Luther should have been diagnosed as ill in view of his beliefs about the Devil (Macario, 1843).

At the same time, French psychiatry was concentrating its attention on the question of hallucinations. Brierre de Boismont explored the history of visions, ecstasies and other religious phenomena (Brierre de Boismont, 1845), while Louis Calmeil's *De la folie* (1845) was a study of hallucinations, combative in tone, which was destined to become popular, thanks to its contentious accounts of such topics as 'The Demonopathy of the Nuns at Cambray', 'A Case of Hystero-Demonopathy at the Monastery of St. Brigit', and so forth (Calmeil, 1845). Meanwhile in Germany the physician Karl Marx published a work in praise of the doctors who had resisted the witchcraft mania (Marx, 1859; Vandermeersch, 1991: 360–1).

At that moment the Morzine epidemic (discussed above) providentially broke out, proving, contrary to Esquirol, that possession phenomena had not disappeared at all. For more than eighteen years, a 'hystero-demono-pathy' epidemic flourished, afflicting dozens of villagers convinced they were possessed by the Devil and sparking unbelievable scenes of hysteria (Constans, 1862; Maire, 1981). This replay of history was the Devil's gift to psychiatry, and the doctors took full advantage of their good fortune.

In 1865, a special lecture on Wier was delivered by Auguste Axenfeld at the Paris Faculté de Médecine; and he was also honoured by the famous Salpêtrière neurologist, Desirée Magloire Bourneville. Charcot's *protégé* was absorbed by religious pathologies: why did hysteria manifest itself in prolonged fasting, ecstasies and prostration? Why did hysterics hallucinate the Devil? It was arranged for Wier's *De praestigiis daemonum* to be translated into French, and Bourneville contributed the foreword, presenting the author as the patron saint of psychiatry. Wier was praised for striving to

> demonstrate that the crimes the witches were accused of were fictitious; that those women were not criminals but patients suffering from mental illness; that they should not be sentenced by priests, monks nor judges; that they consequently should not be put in prison, tortured and burned but that they should be entrusted to the care of physicians. (Bourneville, 1885: iv; Vandermeersch, 1991; Brais, 1993).

In his own way and slightly later Freud – ever dogmatically anti-religious, as witness his *Die Zukunft einer Illusion* (1927) – drew upon Wier to help resolve the identity of historical witches and the bewitched on the one hand, and modern hysterical patients on the other. Probably on the basis of a reading of the *Malleus maleficarum*, Freud also, if fleetingly and privately, perceived how, if hysterics were the witches of modern times, it must follow that modern psychiatrists had stepped into the shoes of the old witchfinders. Faced with the hysterics' deviousness, he confided to his buddy Wilhelm Fliess his sympathy for the 'harsh therapy of the witches' judges', behaving a little like one of the old witch-finders towards patients such as 'Dora'.[10] On a similar note, the English hysteria doctor, Robert Carter, had earlier remarked that the hysteric who faked disease thereby 'betrays the cloven foot' (Carter, 1853: 122; Carlson and Kane, 1982; Porter, 1993: 233f.). Perhaps the panicky reactions of these rationalist psychiatrists equally betray a cloudy awareness that the distinction which they would have liked to be able to make between science and superstition was not at all secure. There was a devil within the unconscious.

From the late nineteenth century it became psychiatric orthodoxy that witches and their victims had been suffering from 'mass-neuroses'. The *Malleus maleficarum* constituted a splendid psychiatric textbook, proclaimed the Russian-born American psychiatrist, Gregory Zilboorg, if only the word 'patient' were substitued for 'witch'. Such candour from the psychiatrists lends plausibility to Thomas Szasz's view that the mental patient in the clutches of compulsory psychiatry was the historical successor to the persecuted witch, and the psychiatrist the heir of the inquisitor: society always requires scapegoats and the ending of the witch-hunt unleashed a new 'witch-hunt' conducted by the doctors.[11]

THE RETURN OF THE REPRESSED

Late nineteenth-century anti-clerical psychiatrists felt the need to be so truculent precisely because religion, perplexingly enough, was hardly waning away in a century that brought the manifestations of Lourdes and Marpingen ('the German Lourdes'), Fatima and Knock (Donat, 1988; Blackbourn, 1993). Under pressure from science, rationalism and liberalism, the Christian churches revitalized their faith. In tandem there arose a new movement, spiritualism, animated by a consuming concern with the paranormal that uncannily mirrors the preoccupations of Casaubon, More, Glanvill and others back in the seventeenth century. The aspiration was to confirm the existence of an Unseen World not on the say-so of prelates but on the proofs of science and the senses (Inglis, 1977, 1986, Brandon, 1983; Oppenheim, 1985; Owen, 1989).

In hopes of establishing a forum of inquiry and rational debate, the Society for Psychical Research was founded in London in 1882, with the aim of subjecting to scientific study spiritual manifestations fancied by sceptics to be mere products of emotionalism or trickery. Alleged cases of telepathy and thought-transference were experimentally tested. Spiritualism enjoyed its golden age, with a hard core of several thousand firm believers, including eminences like Alfred Russel Wallace, and a wider public interest including dabblers in high places like Mr Gladstone (Williams, 1985).

Nevertheless the reality of spirits remained elusive. While many spiritualists considered their activities utterly compatible with Christianity – in the Netherlands and to a degree in England, spiritualists included amongst their ranks well-known Protestant ministers – many pillars of orthodoxy demurred; the Rev. John Bryant Clifford in 1873 published his *Modern Witchcraft, or Spiritualism, a Sign of the Times* which equated the spiritualism of his day with 'modern witchcraft' (Clifford, 1873; Sharpe, 1996: 294). Honest Christians might be deeply distrustful of the spiritualists, casting them as the new enthusiasts, tricksters or sorcerers, meddling in matters better left alone and exploiting the gullible and vulnerable.

Though some scientists were Glanvills, most treated spiritualism rather as the *philosophes* had reacted to demonism. Darwin's bulldog Thomas Huxley dismissed it as the fag-end of a primitive superstition:

> The only case of 'Spiritualism' I have ever had the opportunity of examining into for myself was as gross an imposture as ever came under my notice. But supposing the phenomena to be genuine – they do not interest me. If anyone would endow me with the faculty of listening to the chatter of old women and curates in the nearest provincial town, I should decline the privilege, having better things to do. And if the folk in the spiritual world do not talk more wisely and sensibly than their friends report them to do, I put them in the same category. The only good that I can see in the demonstration of the 'Truth of Spiritualism' is to furnish an additional argument against suicide. Better live a crossing-sweeper, than die and be made to talk twaddle by a 'medium' hired at a guinea a seance. (Brandon, 1983: 250; Basham, 1992)

Vocal medical voices, including that of the editor of the *British Medical Journal*, Ernest Hart, came out against spiritualism (Hart, 1898). And the psychiatrists – once more! – concluded that spiritual manifestations were, after all, expressions of hysteria or suggestibility, when they were not downright humbug (Brown, 1983; Shortt, 1984; Gauld, 1992). The nineteenth century closed with both the Christian churches and the scientific establishment suspicious of spiritualism's attempt to recoup the unseen world. In the twentieth century it would be psychoanalysis and other forms of psychology which continued to provide the basis for belief in modes of reality (interior space) beyond the material and the mundane (Rose, 1985, 1990; Inglis, 1986; Rose and Miller, 1986).

Conclusion: Secularization

Secularization, the last four chapters have been suggesting, was more than the campaign of reason against religion or the march of science. It was, to cast the explanatory net far more broadly, in part an unintended consequence of the spiritualization of religion and the utter division between the sacred and the profane upon which Protestantism insisted; it also came about because of the enormous transformation of material life itself within the public sphere under urban market capitalism. Religion had once been the fabric of existence; it was transformed into one storey of living within a temporal mansion (Chadwick, 1975; Sommerville, 1992).

But to say this is not to deny a major role to beliefs in the decay of witchcraft and magic. The campaigns of the freethinkers and *philosophes* of the eighteenth century played their part; so did the founders of anthropology and the human sciences in the nineteenth, in making nature and reason the platform for conceptualizing man and society. There was a deep shift in worldview, away from an earlier scriptural eschatology; liberal thinkers were no longer willing to credit that in a benign and well-designed Creation, Satan, devils and witches could enjoy the lead roles demonology had prescribed. Individualism and progress became the official watchwords; and when the question of the discontents of civilization was raised, it was to inner demons that they were ascribed (Cohn, 1975). Rationalists liked to represent this as progress − the banishment of bugaboos; a sceptical voice might counter that after two centuries of warfare, the phantom enemies were more entrenched than ever, while science and the state had become the new persecutors.

Notes

Chapter 1

1. For discussion see Chadwick (1990). I wish to thank the following for their invaluable research assistance and stimulating discussions: Emily Garner, Mark Gosbee, Nathan Powell, Sally Scovell and Rajeev Vinaik. Jonathan Barry and Rhodri Hayward have offered particularly helpful criticisms, as have my co-authors and the genreal editor of this enterprise. Sheila Lawler, Jan Pinkerton and Mary Shaw have done wonders with typing and the spell-check.

2. 'There are no pages of human history more filled with horror than those which record the witch-madness of three centuries', wrote H. C. Lea (1939: xxx–xxxi). The publication date offers a silent commentary on liberal assumptions. For historiographical revisionism on the Enlightenment, see Outram (1995) and Hulme and Jordanova (1990). For anthropology and sociology, see Gellner (1973); Barnes *et al.* (1995); Geertz (1973).

3. 'Superstition' is, of course, totally tendentious; generally it means someone else's religion: see Wilkins (1972).

4. Sharpe (1996), 226–7. My debts to this major book will be obvious.

5. *A Full and Impartial Account* (1712), 21–8. Largely reportage, this is hostile to Wenham, as is Bragge (1712); see Sharpe (1996), 230; Bostridge (1997), 132f. This is a key book, to which I am greatly endebted.

6. *An Act to Repeal the Statute* (1736); Russell (1980), 123. The 1736 Act remained in force until 1951, when it was replaced by the Fraudulent Mediums Act. Ending the persecution of witches was an achievement, but any humanitarian reading must be set against the spiralling of capital statutes in the Walpole era, particularly those protecting property.

7. Sharpe (1996), 32. For Scripture as master narrative, see C. Hill (1993; 1971).

8. Walker (1981); Barry (1996) is historiographically incisive.

9. More (1653), 110–29; Brann (1980); Clark (1997), 305. Another bulky work using Glanvill to shore up witchcraft was Bovet (1684), who recommended that both black and white witches should be executed in obedience to *Exodus* xxii, 18; see Sharpe (1996), 241. Bovet's chief agenda was anti-popery.

10. Glanvill (1726), 3, 223, 224; those denying witches were 'Anti-Scripturists' (p. 228). See Hall (1990); Hutchison (1983).
11. Attfield (1985), 389. The Dutch controversy over Bekker (Stronks, 1991) was repeated in Germany, where at Halle Bekker's arguments were taken up by Christian Thomasius, P. J. Spener and others whose Pietistic leanings countered 'superstitious' Christianity.
12. Attfield (1985), 390; Easlea (1980), 218. Bekker was confuted by Beaumont (1705), who used the standard Glanvillian argument that 'the whole visible World has proceeded from the invisible World' (p. 397).
13. Locke (1695); Spellman (1993); Byrne (1996); Cragg (1950; 1964); Rupp (1986); Brooke (1991). Newton's own views about Providence and miracles were complex, but popular Newtonianism sold the image of a world of order: Buchdahl (1961); Dijksterhuis (1961).
14. Such changes cannot be adequately documented here. But see Mac-Donald (1986); Jackson (1996), 46f.; Glass (1973); Hirschman (1977); S. Letwin (1965); W. Letwin (1963); for quantification and probability, see Gigerenzer *et al.* (1989); Bernstein (1996); Hacking (1975; 1990); Daston (1987; 1988); Frängsmyr *et al.* (1990). For naturalizing society see Fox *et al.* (1995); Gusdorf (1960); Olson (1991; 1993). See also Lowe (1982); Cohen (1982); Hundert (1986).
15. Giedion (1948); Black (1986); Miller (1957). By a nice irony, the pioneering historian of English witchcraft, C. L'Estrange Ewen, later turned his attention to the national lotteries which, perhaps more than anything else, symbolically contradicted the metaphysics of witchcraft: (1929; 1932).
16. Hutchinson (1718), 63. Hutchinson was backed, and Boulton attacked, by Daillon (1723).
17. Pruett (1978); Sharpe (1996), 287. Deuteronomy 18: 10 reads: 'There shall not be found among you any one that . . . useth divination, or an observer of times, or an enchanter, or a witch'.
18. Hutchinson (1718), 130–1: Wenham was 'a pious sober woman'. Hutchinson invited accusers to put themselves into her shoes: 'I verily believe . . . that such a Storm as she met with, might have fallen upon them if it had been their Misfortune to have been poor, and to have met with such Accidents as she did, in such a barbarous Parish as she liv'd in' (p. 131).
19. Bostridge (1996); Sharpe (1996), 290–1. The Act stated that 'no prosecution, suit, or proceeding' could be launched in a court in Great Britain 'against any person or persons for witchcraft, sorcery, inchantment, or conjuration, or for charging another with any such offence'. It did, however, claim to protect 'ignorant persons' from

being defrauded by cheats pretending to tell fortunes, or to be able to find stolen goods: An Act (1736).

20. Bond (1965): 117 (14 July 1711), vol. i, pp. 480–2. Addison's play, *The Drummer* (1716), inspired by Glanvill's tale of the 'Drummer of Tedworth', naturalized and ridiculed poltergeist phenomena. But Addison, ever moderate, attacked Sadduceeism too, through the unprincipled freethinker Tinsel.

21. Brewster (1834); Brewster dealt with optical illusions, eye-diseases and the like which explained ghosts and spectra, and he revealed conjurors' tricks.

22. The following discussion relies on Kreiser (1978); for the French background see Briggs (1989; 1996a).

23. The following material on Portugal comes from Corrêa De Melo (1992).

24. Klaniczay (1990a), 170. At the beginning of the eighteenth century the French botanist Pitton de Tournefort gave a horrifying account of the dissection of a Greek revenant on the island of Mykonos:

> We saw a rather different and quite tragic scene on the same island occasioned by one of those corpses that are believed to return after their burial. The one of whom I shall give an account was a peasant of Mykonos, naturally sullen and quarrelsome – a circumstance to be noted concerning such matters. He had been killed in the fields, no one knew by whom nor how. Two days after he had been buried in a chapel in the town, it was bruited about that he had been seen walking during the night, taking long strides; that he came into houses and turned over furniture, extinguished lamps, embraced people from behind, and played a thousand little roguish tricks. At first people only laughed, but the matter became serious when the most respectable people began to complain. Even the popes acknowledged the fact, and doubtless they had their reasons. People did not fail to have masses said, but the peasant continued his little escapades without mending his ways. After a number of meetings of town leaders and of the priests and monks, they concluded that it would be necessary – in accord with I don't know what ancient ceremony – to wait 9 days after the burial.
>
> On the 10th day they said a mass in the chapel where the body lay, in order to drive out the demon that they believed to be concealed in it. The body was disinterred after the mass, and they set about the task of tearing out its heart. The butcher of the town, quite old and very maladroit, began by opening the belly rather than the chest. He rummaged about for a long time in the entrails,

without finding what he sought, and finally someone informed him that it was necessary to cut into the diaphragm. The heart was torn out to the admiration of all the bystanders. But the body stank so terribly that incense had to be burned . . .

In so general a prepossession, we chose not to say anything. They would have treated us not just as fools but as infidels. How is one to bring an entire population back to its senses?

Quoted in Barber (1988), 21–3.

25. Klaniczay (1990a), 173. Van Swieten's liberal attitudes presumably derived from his Dutch roots, for the Netherlands had been in the vanguard of scepticism. It was there that witch-hunting claimed the fewest victims – about 30 executions in total – and was earliest ended: the last known execution took place in 1603.

26. Zimmermann likened the mental hysteria to the dangers of convents and similar institutions: Zimmermann (1763–4), ii, 105–6, quoted in Flaherty (1992), 101.

27. The *Encyclopédie* entry on shamans runs:

SHAMANS . . . is the name that the inhabitants of Siberia give to impostors who perform the functions of priests, jugglers, sorcerers, and medicine men. These shamans purport to have influence over the Devil, whom they consult to predict the future, to heal illnesses, and to do tricks that seem supernatural to an ignorant and superstitious people. . . . And the whole comedy ends with the audience giving money to the shaman, who at this point prides himself on his show of indifference comparable to other imposters of the same kind.[118]

Quoted in Flaherty (1992), 123.

Chapter 2

1. For readings of the radical Enlightenment, sympathetic and hostile, see Jacob (1981), and Crocker (1959) respectively. For the Enlightenment creation of 'modern paganism', see Gay (1966–9); for superstition see Besterman (1971), 382. Voltaire termed superstition 'a despotic tyrant'.

2. See Libby (1935), 205, a valuable digest. Certain defenders of orthodoxy later turned the tables and cited Voltaire and the *philosophes* as proof of the continued agency of the Devil; see Fiard (1803).

3. Libby (1935), 219. In 'Oracles' Voltaire jauntily described how the Church Fathers raised the Devil: 'Ce pauvre diable, qu'on disait rôti dans un trou sous la terre, fut tout étonné de se trouver le maître du monde': Voltaire (1879), vol. iv, 136–46 (p. 141); see also Wilkins (1973; 1975).

4. Morley (1927), vii, 191; see also xii, 34; iii, 236–7; cited in Sharpe (1996), 6.
5. *Superstition*, xv, 670. The *Encyclopédie* was published in 17 volumes (Paris: chez Briasson, 1751–80); it ·has been reprinted (Geneva: Slatkine reprints, 1989); it is that edition which is cited in the following references.
6. The article on Cabbala reeks of anti-semitism. Inspired by Basnage (1710), *Juifs* mocked the obscurity of the Talmud and its gross contradictions. See also *Nombres*, xi, 205–6; Wilkins (1975), 1768–9.
7. Such works provided the *philosophes* with materials for their anti-Christian critiques, rather as Edward Gibbon plundered the researches of pious historian-philologists for his anti-Christian history.
8. Calmet (1746). Calmet denied promoting superstition. Most ghost tales, he maintained, were impositions; lycanthropy was a delusion; vampires could be accounted for by trances. Naturally he did not embrace materialism, but neither did he feel defensive about his scepticism towards witchcraft: Stock (1982), 93–4; Porset (1989).
9. Lytes (1960); see the entry on 'Enthusiasm' by Voltaire in Besterman (1971), 187, which opens 'The Greek word means *disturbance of the entrails*'.
10. See for example [Rogers] (1691); Moore (1692). The following pages draw heavily upon Harley (1989).
11. Diethelm (1970), from whom the following discussion is derived.
12. *A Full Confutation* (1712), 5; Wenham's persecution was the result of 'priestcraft' (p. 6).
13. Some feminist historians have interpreted the witch-hunt as first and foremost a woman-hunt – 'a ruling-class campaign of terror directed against the female peasant population' according to Ehrenreich and English (1974), 6. For a fuller appraisal see Roper (1994); Sharpe (1996), 182.
14. There is a striking parallel between Hecquet's preferred treatment of convulsionaries and the plan for curing hysterical women devised in the mid-nineteenth century by the British physician Robert Carter. Both involve a medical exorcism ritual: Carlson and Kane (1982); Porter (1993), 262f.
15. L. Wilson (1993), 29. How closely medical 'treatments' mirror the punishments meted out to witches!

Chapter 3
1. Beresford (1924–31), v, 316. On the moon and medical folklore see Porter (1995). A parallel to Woodforde's amphibianism is William Dyer of Bristol: Barry (1985).

2. Thompson (1993); Mee (1992); Keynes (1966), letter 24, 22 November 1802, p. 818. Blake's 'The Marriage of Heaven and Hell' remarked that Milton was 'of the Devil's party without knowing it'. Blake quipped that in England – the England of the gin craze – 'Spirits are Lawful, but not Ghosts' (787).

3. Quoted in Sharpe (1996), 254; for perverting infant imaginations, see the discussion of Charles Lamb below.

4. Muchembled (1985) – a view later toned down (1988). Muchembled's strong 'acculturation model' has been energetically criticized by Briggs (1989), 382f. In some respects his reading corresponds with David Gentilcore's view of the attitude of the Church in Italy: 'There is fear on the Church's part that these uncanonized, but locally acknowledged, holy wonder-workers might be duped by the devil into serving his own ends': (1993), 135. The resilience of traditional folkways comes out in Loux (1978; 1979). For a recent reading of witchcraft as popular protest see Ginzburg (1990).

5. Lackington (1810), 257. See also Feather (1985); Black (1986); Wiles (1965). For France, see Darnton (1982). As Keith Thomas observed, 'eighteenth-century England was not a traditional society in the sense that fifteenth-century England had been': (1971), 606.

6. Darnton (1996); Chartier (1992). Note that my argument is not that the new information culture put an end to bugbears. But someone whose grandfather had been worried about witches might now, thanks to the new cultural channels and media, be more worried about the Whigs or about the French.

7. In Lamb's pseudo-Jacobean drama, *John Woodvil*, one passage, later cancelled, runs:

> I can remember when a child the maids
> Would place me on their lap, as they undrest me,
> As silly women use, and tell me stories
> Of Witches – Make me read 'Glanvil on Witchcraft',
> And in conclusion show me in the Bible,
> The old family-Bible with the picture in it,
> The 'graving of the Witch raising up Samuel,
> Which so possest my fancy, being a child,
> That nightly in my dreams, an old Hag came
> And sat upon my pillow. . . . Spite of my manhood,
> The Witch is strong upon me every night.

On the above, see Summerfield (1984), 254–62, and Lamb, 'Witches, and Other Night Fears', *London Magazine* (October 1821), 384. The religious work referred to is Stackhouse (1733). Lamb's assumption that the child absorbs witch beliefs from her nurse echoes John Locke, who had written:

> The *Ideas* of *Goblines* and *Sprights* have really no more to do with Darkness than Light, yet let but a foolish Maid inculcate these often on the Mind of a Child, and . . . he shall never be able to separate them again so long as he lives, but Darkness shall ever afterwards bring with it those frightful Ideas.

Locke (1690), 43. Several of Wordsworth's poems feature witchcraft, including 'Goody Blake and Harry Gill'; see Bewell (1989), 154.

8. Peacock (1969), 68. The following depends heavily on Flaherty (1995), 271–91.

9. Darnton (1968), 62f. The controversies over Mesmerism, as with the Convulsionaries, reveal the role of sexual symbolism. Parisian doctors used the image of the convulsive woman (the pseudo-witch) to attack the warped values of an aristocratic culture they were intent on reforming; their provincial colleagues regarded the convulsive woman as a symptom of the erroneous beliefs of a popular culture they were bent on uprooting: L. Wilson (1993), 149.

Chapter 4

1. Bushaway (1982; 1995). For nostalgia, see Boyes (1995), and Chase (1989). Historians have learned to be wary of 'ancient traditions': Hobsbawm and Ranger (1983). Recent historians have stressed that 'magic' and 'superstition' were found not only in the countryside: Davies (1997c).

2. Hartland (1892), 4–5. For Hartland, folklore involved an epistemological divide: it was the 'beliefs and practices of the uneducated' collected by 'clergymen, medical men, elementary schoolmasters, and ladies in various stations of life', and others full of 'human sympathy with their lowlier neighbours': *ibid.*, 6–7. See Dorson (1968a), 230.

3. Hone (1864 [1831–2]), 125. As a publisher of radical-populist sympathies, Hone was positive towards folk wisdom. Brand (1777) had been an important pioneering work, presenting folk materials relatively non-judgmentally, rather as Bishop Percy's *Reliques* popularized ballads. Considering witchcraft as 'a striking article of Popular Mythology', he noted that it 'bids fair soon to be entirely forgotten' ('Sorcery or Witchcraft').

4. The following summarizes Devlin (1987), and Kuselman (1983), drawing also on Weber (1979) and Ramsey (1988), 264f.

5. See Lévy-Bruhl (1923); Levi-Strauss (1962). English writers tended to turn Blacks and the Irish, but not the natives of Hampshire, into deviant 'Others'.

6. Michelet (1862); Orr (1976). Darnton (1984) is insightful upon peasant folk heroes. On witchcraft as popular protest see Ginzburg (1990); for feminists see Bovenschen (1978).

7. Bann (1984, 1990); Burrow (1981); for grand Victorian theories explaining religion, see White (1896); Draper (1874). It is amusing that George Eliot chose to recycle Casaubon's name. It provides an echo to the first chapter.

8. Lukes (1973); Durkheim (1961, 1989); Durkheim and Mauss (1970); Harris (1968), 71; Evans-Pritchard (1981), 153f. Twentieth-century historians of witchcraft and magic in their turn have been influenced by mainstream anthropology, with ambiguous consequences: Thomas (1975); Salmon (1989).

9. Freud cannot adequately be explored here but insights and references are offered in Young-Bruehl (1994) and Forrester (1994). The transition from Romanticism to Freud is well analyzed in Castle (1995).

10. Masson (1986), 225. Freud admitted how his views were homologous to those of the demonologists: 'all of my brand-new prehistory of hysteria is already known and was published a hundred times over, though several centuries ago ... why are their [the witches'] confessions under torture so like the communications made by my patients in psychic treatment[?]'. Freud to Fliess, 17 Jan 1897, in Masson (1986), 224. Freud of course gave an erotic reading to the symbolism of witchcraft: the witch's broomstick was the 'great lord Penis': see Swales (1982). It is also easy to hear echoes of witch beliefs in Melanie Klein's notions of 'bad breast'.

11. Zilboorg (1935), 181, 205; Mora (1994). Zilboorg's belief that Wier was the 'founder of clinical psychiatry (p. 207) long exercised a hold over psychiatrists: for a critique see Schoeneman (1977, 1982), 1028–32. See Szasz (1970), who writes: 'psychiatry is an institution of social and political control serving inquisitorial functions, since heresy could be destroyed only by destroying heretics' (p. 20).

Bibliography

Abelove, H. (1991) *The Evangelist of Desire: John Wesley and the Methodists* (Palo Alto).

Abrams, M. H. (1971) *Natural Supernaturalism: Tradition and Revolution in Romantic Literature* (London).

An Act to Repeal the Statute . . . Intituled, an Act Against Conjuration, Witchcraft, and Dealing with Evil and Wicked Spirits (1736) (London).

Addison, J. (1716) *The Drummer* (London).

Agrippa, H. C. (1783) *Henry Cornelius Agrippa's Fourth Book of Occult Philosophy and Geomancy. Magical Elements of Peter de Abano. Astronomical Geomancy: The Nature of Spirits; and Arbatel of Magic* (London).

Allen, D. E. (1976) *The Naturalist in Britain: A Social History* (London).

Almond, P. (1994) *Heaven and Hell in Enlightenment England* (Cambridge).

Alver, B. G. and Selberg, T. (1987) 'Folk medicine as part of a larger concept complex', *ARV. Scandinavian Yearbook of Folklore*, 43: 21–44.

Andriano, J. (1993) *Our Ladies of Darkness: Feminine Demonology in Male Gothic Fiction* (University Park).

Ankarloo, B. (1990) 'Sweden: The mass burnings (1668–76)', in B. Ankarloo and G. Henningsen, eds (1990): 285–317.

— (1994) 'Magies scandinaves et sorciers du nord' in R. Muchembled, ed. *Magie et sorcellerie en Europe du Moyen Age à nos jours* (Paris): 195–213.

— and Henningsen, G. eds (1990) *Early Modern European Witchcraft: Centres and Peripheries* (Oxford).

[Anon.] (1676) *The Doctrine of Devils* (London).

[Anon.] (1682) *A Tryal of Witches at the Assizes Held at Bury St. Edmonds for the County of Suffolk* (London).

[Anon.] (1695) *Solon Secundus, or Some Defects in the English Laws* (London).

[Anon.] (1704) *A True and Full Relation of the Witches at Pittenweem* (Edinburgh).

[Anon.] (1727) *A System of Magick; Or, a History of the Black Art. Being an Historical Account of Mankind's Most Early Dealing with the Devil; and How the Acquaintance on Both Sides First Began . . .* (London).

[Anon.] (1736) *Pisteuo-Daimon, The Witch of Endor: Or, a Plea for the Divine Administration by the Agency of Good and Evil Spirits, Written Some Years Ago . . .* (London).

[Anon.] (1895) 'The "witch-burning" at Clonmel', *Folk-lore*, 6: 373–84.

Argyrou, V. (1993) 'Under a spell: the strategic use of magic in Greek Cypriot society', *American Ethnologist*, 20: 256–71.

Aron, R. (1989) *Main Currents in Sociological Thought*, vol. 1, translated by R. Howard and H. Weaver (New York).

Atkinson, J. C. (1891) *Forty Years in a Moorland Parish: Reminiscences and Researches in Danby in Cleveland* (London): 72–3; cited in James Sharpe (1996) *Instruments of Darkness: Witchcraft in England, 1550–1750* (London): 276.

Attfield, R. (1985) 'Balthasar Bekker and the decline of the witch-craze: the old demonology and the new philosophy', *Annals of Science*, 42: 383–95.

Bader, G. (1945) *Die Hexenprozesse in der Schweiz* (Affolteren).

Bailly, J. S. (1785) *Histoire de l'astronomie moderne* (new edn., Paris).

Baldick, C. (1990) *In Frankenstein's Shadow: Myth, Monstrosity, and Nineteenth-Century Writing* (Cambridge).

Bann, S. (1984) *The Clothing of Clio: A Study of Representations of History in Nineteenth-Century Britain and France* (Cambridge).

— (1990) *The Inventions of History: Essays on the Representation of the Past* (Manchester).

— ed. (1994) *Frankenstein, Creation and Monstrosity* (London).

Baranowski, B. (1952) *Procesy czarownic w Polsce w XVII i XVIII wieku* (Lodz).

Barber, P. (1988) *Vampires, Burial and Death: Folklore and Reality* (New Haven).

Barnes, B., Bloor D. and Henry, J. (1995) *Scientific Knowledge: A Sociological Analysis* (London).

Barrett, F. (1801) *The Magus, or Celestial Intelligencer; Being a Complete System of Occult Philosophy. In Three Books: Containing the Antient and Modern Practice of the Cabalistic Art, Natural and Celestial Magic, &c. . . .: Exhibiting the Sciences of Natural Magic; Alchymy, or Hermetic Philosophy . . . the Constellatory Practice, or Talismanic Magic . . .: Magnetism, and Cabalistical or Ceremonial Magic . . . and Conjuration of Spirits. To which is added Biographia Antiqua, or the Lives of the Most Eminent Philosophers, Magi, &c. The Whole Illustrated with a Great Variety of Curious Engravings* (London).

Barrow, L. (1986) *Independent Spirits: Spiritualism and English Plebeians, 1850–1910* (London).

Barry, J. (1985) 'Piety and the patient: Medicine and religion in eighteenth-century Bristol', in R. Porter, ed. *Patients and Practitioners: Lay Perceptions of Medicine in Pre-Industrial Society* (Cambridge): 145–75.

— (1994) 'Public infidelity and private belief? The discourse of spirits in

Enlightenment Bristol', unpublished paper at the conference on 'Healing, magic and belief in Europe, 15th-20th centuries' (Woudschoten, The Netherlands).

— (1996) 'Introduction: Keith Thomas and the problem of witchcraft', in J. Barry, M. Hester and G. Roberts, eds (1996): 1–45.

—, Hester, M. and Roberts, G. eds (1996) *Witchcraft in Early Modern Europe: Studies in Culture and Belief* (Cambridge).

Baschwitz, K. (1963) *Hexen und Hexenprozesse* (Munich).

Basham, D. (1992) *The Trial of a Woman: Feminism and the Occult Sciences in Victorian Literature and Society* (Basingstoke).

Basnage, J. (1710) *Histoire des juifs* (Paris).

Baumgarten, A. R., (1987) *Hexenwahn und Hexenverfolgung im Naheraum. Ein Beitrag zur Sozial- und Kulturgeschichte* (Frankfurt am Main etc.).

Baumhauer, J. F. (1984) *Johann Kruse und der 'neuzeitlich Hexenwahn'. Zur Situation eines norddeutschen Aufklärers und einer Glaubensvorstellung im 20. Jahrhundert untersucht anhand von Vorgängen in Ditmarschen* (Neumünster).

Baxter, R. (1691) *The Certainty of the World of Spirits* (London).

— (1696) *Reliquiae Baxterianae* (London).

— (1713) *Preservatives against Melancholy and Overmuch Sorrow* (London).

Beaumont, J. (1705) *An Historical, Physiological and Theological Treatise of Spirits, Apparitions, Witchcrafts, and Other Magical Practices . . . With a Refutation of Dr. Bekker's 'World Bewitch'd', and Other Authors that have Opposed the Belief of Them* (London).

Becker, A. (1700) *Disputatio Juridica de Jure Spectrorum* (Halle).

Behar, R. (1989) 'Sexual witchcraft, colonialism, and women's powers: Views from the Mexican Inquisition', in A. Lavrin, ed. *Sexuality and Marriage in Colonial Latin America* (Lincoln and London): 178–206.

Behringer, W. (1987) *Hexenverfolgung in Bayern: Volksmagie, Glaubenseifer und Staatsräson in der Frühen Neuzeit* (München).

— (1995) 'Der "Bayerische Hexenkrieg". Die Debatte am Ende der Hexenprozesse in Deutschland', in S. Lorenz and D. R. Bauer, eds (1995b): 287–313.

Bekker, B. (1695) *The World Bewitched* (London).

Bell, J. (1763) *Travels from St. Petersburg in Russia, to Diverse Parts of Asia* (Glasgow).

Beresford, J., ed. (1924–31) *The Diary of a Country Parson: The Revd James Woodforde*, 5 vols (Oxford).

Berman, M. (1981) *The Re-enchantment of the World* (Ithaca).

Bermingham, A. and Brewer, J., eds (1995) *The Consumption of Culture, 1600–1800: Image, Object, Text* (London).

Bernard, R. (1630) *A Guide to Grand Jury Men . . . in Cases of Witchcraft* (London).

Bernstein, P. L. (1996) *Against the Gods: The Remarkable Story of Risk* (New York).

Besterman, T., ed. (1971) *Voltaire: Philosophical Dictionary* (Harmondsworth).

Bethencourt, F. (1990) 'Portugal, A scrupulous inquisition', in B. Ankarloo and G. Henningsen, eds (1990): 403–22.

— (1994) 'Un univers saturé de magie: l'Europe méridionale', in R. Muchembled, ed. *Magie et sorcellerie en Europe du Moyen Age à nos jours* (Paris): 159–94.

Bettelheim, B. (1977) *The Uses of Enchantment: The Meaning and Importance of Fairy Tales* (New York).

Bever, E. (1983) 'Witchcraft in early modern Wuerttemberg', Ph.D. thesis (University of Princeton).

Bewell, A. (1989) *Wordsworth and the Enlightenment: Nature, Man and Society in the Experimental Poetry* (New Haven).

Black, G. F. (1937–8) 'A calendar of cases of witchcraft in Scotland, 1510–1727', *Bulletin of the New York Public Library*, 41: 811–47, 917–36; 42: 34–74.

Black, J. (1986) *The English Press in the Eighteenth Century* (London).

Blackbourn, D. (1993) *Marpingen: Apparitions of the Virgin Mary in Bismarckian Germany* (Oxford).

Blackstone, W. (1769) *Commentaries on the Laws of England* (Oxford).

Blackwall, A. (1725) *The Sacred Classics Defended and Illustrated* (London).

Blécourt, W. de (1983) *Atroce injurien. Een scriptie over toverij in Nederland en haar bestudering met bijzondere aandacht voor Drenthe*, unpublished thesis (University of Amsterdam).

— (1986a) 'Van heksenprocessen naar toverij', in W. de Blécourt and M. Gijswijt-Hofstra, eds (1986): 2–30.

— (1986b) 'Meppelse toverij aan het eind van de achttiende eeuw', in de Blécourt and Gijswijt-Hofstra, eds (1986): 203–40.

— (1988) 'Duivelbanners in de noordelijke Friese Wouden, 1860–1930', *Volkskundig bulletin*, 14: 159–87.

— de (1989a) 'Heksengeloof: toverij en religie in Nederland tussen 1890 en 1940', in P. Geschiere and W. van Wetering, eds *De geldigheid van magie. Heksen, demonen en economische verandering*. Special issue *Sociologische gids*, 36: 245–66.

— (1989b) 'Specialistes in geluk. Waarzegsters in Groningen, Friesland, Drenthe en Overijssel in de 19e en het begin van de 20e eeuw', *Etnofoor*, 2: 71–90.

— (1990) *Termen van toverij. De veranderende betekenis van toverij in Noordoost-Nederland ussen de 16de en 20ste eeuw* (Nijmegen).

— (1991) 'Four centuries of Frisian witch doctors', in M. Gijswijt-Hofstra and W. Frijhoff, eds (1991): 157–66.

— (1992) 'Op zoek naar genezeressen. Waarzegsters in Noordoost-Nederland', *Medische antropologie*, 4: 56–69.

— (1993) 'Spuren einer Volkskultur oder Dämonisierung? Kritische Bemerkungen zu Ginzburgs "Die Benandanti"', *Kea. Zeitschrift für Kulturwissenschaften*, 5: 17–29.

— (1994) 'Witch doctors, soothsayers and priests. On cunning folk in European historiography and tradition', *Social history*, 19: 285–303.

— (1996) 'On the continuation of witchcraft', in J. Barry, M. Hester and G. Roberts, eds (1996): 335–52.

— (1999) 'The witch, her victim, the unwitcher and the researcher. The continued existence of traditional witchcraft', in B. Ankarloo and S. Clark, eds. *Witchcraft and Magic in Europe: The Twentieth Century* (London).

— and Gijswijt-Hofstra, M. eds (1986) *Kwade mensen. Toverij in Nederland.* Special issue of *Volkskundig bulletin*, 12 (Amsterdam).

— and Pereboom, F. (1991) 'Insult and admonition: Witchcraft in the Land of Vollenhove, seventeenth century', in M. Gijswijt-Hofstra and W. Frijhoff, eds (1991): 119–31.

Bloch, M. (1973) *The Royal Touch: Sacred Monarchy and Scrofula in England and France*, trans. by J. E. Anderson (London).

Bloch-Raymond, A. and Frayssenge, J. (1987) *Les êtres de la brume et de la nuit. Peurs, revenants et sorcières des Grands Causses hier et aujourd'hui* (Montpellier).

Bloom, J. H. (1930) *Folklore, Old Customs and Superstitions in Shakespeare Land* (London).

Bodin, J. (1580) *De la démonomanie des sorciers* (Paris).

Bodó, M. (1751) *Jurisprudentia criminalis secundum praxim et constitutiones Hungaricas* (Pozsony)

Bollème, G. (1969) *Les almanaches populaires aux 17e et 18e siècles* (Paris).

Bond, D., ed. (1965) *The Spectator*, 5 vols (Oxford).

Boškovic-Stulli, M. (1991–2) 'Hexensagen und Hexenprozesse in Kroatien', *Acta Ethnographica Hungarica*, 37: 143–71.

Bostridge, I. (1991) 'Debates about witchcraft in England 1650–1736', D.Phil thesis (University of Oxford).

— (1996) 'Witchcraft Repealed', in J. Barry, M. Hester, and G. Roberts, eds (1996): 309–34.

— (1997) *Witchcraft and its Transformations c.1650-c.1750* (Oxford).

Boswell, J. (1946) *The Life of Samuel Johnson*, 2 vols (London).

Bottigheimer, R. B. (1996) 'Fairy Tales and Folk-tales', in Hunt, P., ed. *International Companion Encyclopaedia of Children's Literature* (London): 152–65.

Boulton, R. (1715–16) *A Compleat History of Magick, Sorcery and Witchcraft*, 2 vols (London).

— (1722) *The Possibility and Reality of Magick, Sorcery and Witchcraft*

Demonstrated. Or, a Vindication of a Compleat History of Magick, Sorcery and Witchcraft (London).

Bourneville, D. M. (1885) *Histoires, disputes et discours des illusions et impostures des diables . . .* (Paris).

Bovenschen, S. (1978) 'The contemporary witch, the historical witch, and the witch myth: The witch, subject of the appropriation of nature and the object of the domination of nature', *New German Critique*, 15: 83–119.

Bovet, R. (1684) *Pandaemonium, or the Devil's Cloyster. Being a Further Blow to Modern Sadduceism, Proving the Existence of Witches and Spirits* (London).

Boyer, P. and Nissenbaum, S. (1974) *Salem Possessed* (Cambridge, Mass.).

Boyes, G. (1995) *The Imagined Village: Culture, Ideology and the English Folk Revival* (Manchester).

Bragge, F. (1712) *Witchcraft Farther Display'd Containing I. An Account of the Witchcraft Practis'd by Jane Wenham of Walkerne, in Hertfordshire, Since her Condemnation . . . II. An Answer to the Most General Objections Against the Being and Power of Witches . . .* (London).

Brähm, F. (1709) *Disputatio Inaug. de Fallacibus Indiciis* (Halle).

Brais, B. (1993) 'Desiré Magloire Bourneville and French anticlericalism during the Third Republic', in D. Porter and R. Porter, eds *Doctors, Politics and Society* (Amsterdam): 107–39.

Brand, J. (1777) *Observations on Popular Antiquities* (London).

Brandon, R. (1983) *The Spiritualists: The Passion for the Occult in the Nineteenth and Twentieth Centuries* (London).

Brann, N. L. (1980) 'The conflict between reason and magic in seventeenth-century England: A case study of the Vaughan-More Debate', *Huntingdon Library Quarterly*, 43: 103–26.

Brett, R. L., ed. (1979) *Barclay Fox's Journal* (London).

Brewer, J. (1997) *The Pleasures of the Imagination: English Culture in the Eighteenth Century* (London).

— and Porter, R., eds (1993) *Consumption and the World of Goods in the 17th and 18th Centuries* (London).

— and Staves, S., eds (1995) *Early Modern Conceptions of Property* (London).

Brewster, D. (1834) *Letters on Natural Magic, Addressed to Sir Walter Scott, Bart* (London).

Brierre de Boismont, A. (1845) *Des hallucinations, ou histoire raisonnée des apparitions* (Paris; 2nd edn 1852; 3rd edn 1862).

Briggs, K. M. (1962) *Pale Hecate's Team* (New York).

Briggs, R. (1989) *Communities of Belief: Cultural and Social Tensions in Early Modern France* (Oxford).

— (1996a) *Witches and Neighbours: The Social and Cultural Context of European Witchcraft* (London).

— (1996b) '"Many reasons why": witchcraft and the problem of multiple explanation', in J. Barry, M. Hester and G. Roberts, eds (1996): 49–63.

Bronne, C. (1957) 'Une affaire de sorcellerie en Flandre, en 1815', *Synthèses, Revue Internationale*, 12, number 131: 228–40.

Brooke, H. (1991) *Science and Religion: Some·Historical Perspectives* (Cambridge).

Brown, E. M. (1983) 'Neurology and Spiritualism in the 1870s', *Bulletin of the History of Medicine*, 57: 563–77.

Brown, P. H., ed. (1900) *Register of the Privy Council of Scotland, 1627–1628*, 2nd ser., 2 (Edinburgh).

Broye, C. (1990) *Sorcellerie et superstitions à Genève XVIe–XVIIIe siècles* (Genève).

Brunnemann, J. (1727) *Discours von dem betrüglichen Kennzeichen der Zauberei*, 2nd ed. (Halle).

Buchdahl, G. (1961) *The Image of Newton and Locke in the Age of Reason* (London).

Burke, E. (1757) *On the Sublime and Beautiful* (London).

Burke, P. (1978) *Popular Culture in Early Modern Europe* (London).

Burns, R. M. (1981) *The Great Debate on Miracles: From Joseph Glanvill to David Hume* (Lewisburg).

Burr, G. L., ed. (1903) 'The witch persecutions', *Translations and Reprints from the Original Sources of European History*, 3: no. 1 (Philadelphia).

— ed. (1914) *Narratives of the Witchcraft Cases* (New York).

Burrow, J. W. (1966) *Evolution and Society: A Study in Victorian Social Theory* (Cambridge).

— (1981) *A Liberal Descent: Victorian Historians and the English Past* (Cambridge).

Burton, R. (1948) *The Anatomy of Melancholy*, edited by D. Floyd, and P. Jordan-Smith (New York; 1st edn 1621, London).

Bushaway, B. (1982) *By Rite: Custom, Ceremony and Community in England, 1700–1880* (London).

— (1995) '"Tacit, unsuspected, but still implicit faith": Alternative belief in nineteenth-century rural England', in T. Harris, ed. (1995): 189–215.

Butt, J., ed. (1963) *The Poems of Alexander Pope* (London).

Byloff, F. (1934) *Hexenglaube und Hexenverfolgung in den österreichischen Alpenländern* (Berlin and Leipzig).

Byrne, J. (1996) *Glory, Jest and Riddle: Religious Thought in the Enlightenment* (London).

Byrne, P. F. (1967) *Witchcraft in Ireland* (Cork).

Calef, R. (1700) *More Wonders of the Invisible World* (London).

Calhoun, C. (1992) 'Introduction: Habermas and the public sphere', in C. Calhoun, ed. *Habermas and the Public Sphere* (Cambridge): 1–50.

Calmeil, L. F. (1845) *De la folie* (Paris).

Calmet, A. (1746) *Dissertations sur les apparitions* (Paris); translated as (1759) *Dissertations upon the Apparitions of Angels, Daemons, and Ghosts, And Concerning the Vampires of Hungary, Bohemia, Moravia, and Silesia* (London).

Camporesi, P. (1991) *The Fear of Hell: Images of Damnation and Salvation in Early Modern Europe*, trans. L. Byatt (Cambridge).

Camus, D. (and Thomas, L.-V.) (1988) *Pouvoirs sorciers. Enquête sur les pratiques actuelles de sorcellerie* (Paris).

Capp, B. (1979) *English Almanacs, 1500–1800: Astrology and the Popular Press* (Ithaca).

Capra, F. (1983) *The Turning Point: Science, Society and the Rising Culture* (London).

Carlson, E. T. and Kane, A. (1982) 'A different drummer: Robert B. Carter on nineteenth-century hysteria', *Bulletin of the New York Academy of Medicine*, 58: 519–34.

[Carlyle, T.] (1829) 'Signs of the Times', *Edinburgh Review*, 59: 439–59 (453).

Carlyle, T. (1987) *Sartor Resartus* (Oxford).

Carnochan, W. B. (1971) 'Witch-hunting and belief in 1751: The case of Thomas Colley and Ruth Osborne', *Journal of Social History*, 4: 389–403.

Carpzov, B. (1670) *Practicae novae imperialis Saxonicae rerum criminalium* (Leipzig).

Carter, R. B. (1853) *On the Pathology and Treatment of Hysteria* (London).

Casaubon, M. (1668) *Of Credulity and Incredulity in Things Natural, Civil and Divine* (London).

Castilhon, J. (1765) *Essai sur les erreurs et les superstitions* (Amsterdam).

Castle, T. (1986) *Masquerade and Civilization: The Carnivalesque in Eighteenth Century English Culture and Fiction* (London).

— (1995) *The Female Thermometer: Eighteenth-Century Culture and the Invention of the Uncanny* (New York).

Cervantes, F. (1991) 'The devils of Querétaro: Scepticism and credulity in late seventeenth-century Mexico', *Past & Present*, 130: 51–69.

Chadwick, O. (1975) *The Secularization of the European Mind in the Nineteenth Century* (Cambridge).

Chamberlain, M. (1981) *Old Wives' Tales: Their History, Remedies and Spells* (London).

Chambers, R. (1861) *Domestic Annals of Scotland* (Edinburgh).

Champion, J. A. I. (1992) *The Pillars of Priestcraft Shaken: The Church of England and its Enemies, 1660–1730* (Cambridge).

Chapelle, Abbé de la (1772) *Le Ventriloque ou l'engastrimythe* (London).

Charcot, J.-M. (1987) *Charcot the Clinician: The Tuesday Lessons – Excerpts from Nine Case Presentations on General Neurology Delivered at the Salpêtrière Hospital in 1887–88*, translated and with commentary by C. G. Goetz (New York).

— (1991) *Clinical Lectures on Diseases of the Nervous System*, ed. by R. Harris (London).

— and Richer, P. (1887) *Les démoniaques dans l'art* (Paris).

Chartier, R. (1992) *L'Ordre de livres: Lecteurs, auteurs, bibliothèques en Europe entre XIVe et XVIIIe siècles* (Aix-en-Provence); translated by L. Cochrane as *The Order of Books: Readers, Authors and Libraries in Europe between the 14th and 18th Centuries* (Cambridge, 1994).

Chase, M. (1989) *The Imagined Past: History and Nostalgia* (Manchester).

Clark, M. (1988) '"Morbid introspection", unsoundness of mind, and British psychological medicine, c.1830–1900', in W. F. Bynum, R. Porter, and M. Shepherd, eds *Anatomy of Madness* (London): 3: 71–101.

Clark, S. (1984) 'The scientific status of demonology', in B. Vickers, ed. *Occult and Scientific Mentalities in the Renaissance* (Cambridge): 351–74.

— (1990) 'Protestant demonology: Sin, superstition and society (c.1520–c.1630), in B. Ankarloo and G. Henningsen, eds (1990): 45–81.

— (1997) *Thinking with Demons: The Idea of Witchcraft in Early Modern Europe* (Oxford).

Clery, E. J. (1995) *The Rise of Supernatural Fiction* (Cambridge).

Clifford, Rev. J. B. (1873) *Modern Witchcraft, or Spiritualism, a Sign of the Times* (London).

Cockburn, J. S. (1972) *A History of English Assizes 1558–1714* (Cambridge).

Cohen, P. C. (1982) *A Calculating People: The Spread of Numeracy in Early America* (Chicago).

Cohn, N. (1975) *Europe's Inner Demons: An Enquiry Inspired by the Great Witch-Hunt* (New York).

Colson, O. (1898) 'La sorcellerie au pays wallon. Etat actuel de la croyance', *Wallonia*, 6: 55–64.

Commenda, H. (1960) 'Gesellschaft der Schatzgräber, Teufelsbeschwörer und Geisterbänner, Linz 1792', *Historisches Jahrbuch der Stadt Linz, 1960*: 171–95.

The Compleat Wizzard; Being a Collection of Authentic and Entertaining Narratives of the Real Existence and Appearance of Ghosts, Demons, and Spectres: Together with Several Wonderful Instances of the Effects of Witchcraft, etc. To which is Prefixed, an Account of Haunted Houses (1770) (London).

Condillac, E. B. de (1749) *Traité des systèmes* (La Haye).

Conrad, J. L. (1983) 'Magic charms and healing rituals in contemporary Yugoslavia', *Southeastern Europe*, 10: 99–120.

— (1987) 'Bulgarian magic charms: ritual, form, and content', *Slavic and East European Journal*, 31: 548–62.

Constans, A. (1862) *Relation sur une epidemie d'hystéro-demonopathie en 1861* (Paris).

Contreras, J. and Henningsen, G. (1986) 'Forty-four thousand cases of the

Spanish Inquisition (1540–1700): Analysis of a historical data bank', in G. Henningsen and J. Tedeschi, eds (1986): 100–29.

Coombs, H., and Coombs, P., eds (1971) *Journal of a Somerset Rector 1803–1834* (Bath).

Cooter, R. (1984) *The Cultural Meaning of Popular Science: Phrenology and the Organization of Consent in Nineteenth-Century Britain* (Cambridge).

Copenhaver, B. P. (1990) 'Natural magic, Hermetism, and occultism in early modern science', in D. C. Lindberg and R. S. Westman, eds *Reappraisals of the Scientific Revolution* (Cambridge): 261–302.

Corrêa De Melo, M. C. (1992) 'Witchcraft in Portugal during the eighteenth century, analysed through the accusations of the Tribunal do Santo Oficio de Evora', in *Transactions of the Eighth International Congress on the Enlightenment, Bristol 21–27 July 1991: Studies on Voltaire and the Eighteenth Century*, 303: 573–8.

Costadau, A. (1717) *Traité historique et critique des principaux signes dont nous nous servons pour manifester nos pensées* (Lyon).

Cotta, J. (1616) *The Trial of Witch-Craft* (London).

Crabtree, A. (1993) *From Mesmer to Freud: Magnetic Sleep and the Roots of Psychological Healing* (New Haven).

Cragg, C. R. (1950) *From Puritanism to the Age of Reason* (Cambridge).

— (1964) *Reason and Authority in the Eighteenth Century* (Cambridge).

Crocker, L. G. (1959) *An Age of Crisis: Man and World in Eighteenth Century French Thought* (Baltimore).

Cromartie, A. (1995) *Sir Matthew Hale, 1609–76* (Cambridge).

Cudworth, R. (1743) *The True Intellectual System of the Universe*, 2 vols (London; 1st edn 1693).

Cunliffe, C., ed. (1992) *Joseph Butler's Moral and Religious Thought* (Oxford).

Curnock, N., ed. (1909–16) *The Journal of the Rev. John Wesley, A.M.*, 8 vols (London).

Curry P. (1989) *Prophecy and Power: Astrology in Early Modern England* (Cambridge).

Curry, P. (1992) *A Confusion of Prophets: Victorian and Edwardian Astrology* (London).

Dabydeen, D. (1985) *Hogarth's Blacks: Images of Blacks in Eighteenth Century English Art* (Kingston).

Daillon, J. de (1723) *Daimonologia: or, a Treatise of Spirits. Wherein Several Places of Scripture are Expounded, Against the Vulgar Errors Concerning Witchcraft, Apparitions, etc. To which is added, An Appendix, Containing Some Reflections on Mr. Boulton's Answer to Dr. Hutchinson's Historical Essay* (London).

Dalton, M. (1630) *The Country Justice* (London).

Damaska, M. (1978) 'The death of legal torture', *Yale Law Journal*, 86: 860–84.

Darnton, R. (1968) *Mesmerism and the End of the Enlightenment in France* (Cambridge).

— (1979) *The Business of Enlightenment: A Publishing History of the Encyclopédie, 1775–1800* (Cambridge).

— (1982) *The Literary Underground of the Old Regime* (Cambridge).

— (1984) *The Great Cat Massacre and Other Episodes in French Cultural History* (New York).

— (1996) *The Forbidden Best-Sellers of Pre-Revolutionary France* (London).

Daston, L. (1987) 'The domestication of risk: Mathematical probability and insurance 1650–1830', in L. Krüger, L. Daston, and M. Heidelberger, eds *The Probabilistic Revolution* (Ann Arbor): 237–60.

— (1988) *Classical Probability in the Enlightenment* (Princeton).

David, H., ed. (1966) *Jonathan Swift: Bickerstaff Papers and Pamphlets on the Church* (Oxford).

Davies, O. (1995) 'The Decline of Popular Belief in Witchcraft and Magic', Ph.D. thesis (University of Lancaster).

— (1996) 'Healing charms in use in England and Wales 1700–1950, *Folklore*, 107: 19–32.

— (1996–7) 'Hag-riding in nineteenth-century West Country England and Modern Newfoundland: an examination of an experience-centred witchcraft tradition', *Folk Life*, 35: 36–53.

— (1997a) 'Cunning-folk in England and Wales during the eighteenth and nineteenth centuries', *Rural History*, 8: 91–107.

— (1997b) 'Methodism, the clergy, and the popular belief in witchcraft and magic', *History*, 82: 252–65.

— (1997c) 'Urbanization and the decline of witchcraft: an examination of London', *Journal of Social History*, 30: 597–617.

Davies, R. Trevor (1947) *Four Centuries of Witch-Beliefs. With Special Reference to the Great Rebellion* (London).

Deacon, R. (1976) *Matthew Hopkins: Witch-Finder General* (London).

Debus, A. G. (1982) 'Scientific truth and occult tradition: The medical world of Ebenezer Sibly (1751–1799)', *Medical History*, 26: 259–78.

Decker, R. (1981–2) 'Die Hexenverfolgungen im Herzogtum Westfalen', *Westfälische Zeitschrift*, 131/132: 339–86.

— (1995) 'Die Haltung der römischen Inquisition gegenüber Hexenglauben und Exorzismus am Beispiel der Teufelsaustreibungen in Paderborn 1657', in S. Lorenz and D. R. Bauer, eds (1995b): 97–115.

DeDieu, J.-P. (1986) 'The archives of the Holy Office of Toledo as a source for historical anthropology', in G. Henningsen and J. Tedeschi, eds (1986): 158–89.

— (1987) 'The Inquisition and popular culture in New Castile', in S.

Haliczer, ed. *Inquisition and Society in Early Modern Europe* (London and Sydney); 129–46.

— (1989) *L'administration de la foi. L'Inquisition de Tolède (XVIe–XVIIIe siècle)* (Madrid).

[Defoe, D.] (1704–13) *The Review* (London).

— (1706) *A True Relation of the Apparition of Mrs Veal* (London).

— (1726) *The Political History of the Devil* (London).

— (1727) *Essay on the History and Reality of Apparitions* (London).

Delaporte, F. (1986) *Disease and Civilization: The Cholera in Paris, 1832* (Cambridge).

Delumeau, J. (1978) *La peur en Occident XIVe–XVIIIe siècles* (Paris).

Demos, J. (1982) *Entertaining Satan: Witchcraft and the Culture of Early New England* (New York).

Denier, M.-C. (1990) 'Sorciers, présages et croyances magiques en Mayenne aux XVIIIe et XIXe siècles', *Annales de Bretagne et des Pays de L'Ouest (Anjou, Maine, Touraine)*, 97: 115–32.

Desplat, C. (1988) *Sorcières et diables en Béarn (fin XIVe – début XIXe siècle)* (Pau).

Devlin, J. (1987) *The Superstitious Mind: French Peasants and the Supernatural in the Nineteenth Century* (New Haven).

Dick, O. L., ed. (1972) *Aubrey's Brief Lives* (London).

Diderot, D., and d'Alembert, J. (1751–80) *l'Encyclopédie* (Paris) (reprinted: Geneva, 1989).

Didi–Huberman, G. (1982) *Invention de l'hystérie: Charcot et l'iconographie photographique* (Paris).

Dienst, H. (1987) 'Hexenprozesse auf dem Gebiet der heutigen Bundesländer Voralberg, Tirol (mit Südtirol), Salzburg, Nieder- und Oberösterreich sowie des Burgenlandes', in H. Valentinitsch, ed. *Hexen und Zauberer* (Graz): 265–90.

— (1992) 'Von Sinn und Nutzen multidisziplinärer Auswertung von Zaubereiprozessakten. Zur Entstehung einer diesbezüglichen Datenbank in Österreich', *Mitteilungen des Instituts für österreichische Geschichtsforschung*, 100: 354–75.

Diethelm, O. (1970) 'The medical teaching of demonology in the 17th and 18th Centuries', *Journal of the History of the Behavioral Sciences*, 6: 3–15.

Dijksterhuis, E. J. (1961) *The Mechanisation of the World Picture* (Oxford).

Dijkstra, B. (1986) *Idols of Perversity: Fantasies of Feminine Evil in Fin de Siècle Culture* (Oxford).

A Discourse on Witchcraft. Occasioned by a Bill Now Depending in Parliament, to Repeal the Statute Made in the First Year of the Reign of King James I, Intituled An Act against Conjuration, Witchcraft, and Dealing with Evil and Wicked Spirits . . . (1736) (London).

Donat, J. (1988) 'Medicine and religion: On the physical and mental disorders that accompanied the Ulster Revival of 1859', in W. F. Bynum, R. Porter, and M. Shepherd, eds *Anatomy of Madness*, vol. 3 (London): 125–50.

Dorson, R. M. (1968a) *The British Folklorists: A History* (London).

— (1968b) *Peasant Customs and Savage Myths: Selections from the British Folklorists*, 2 vols (London).

Douglas, M. (1973) *Natural Symbols: Explorations in Cosmology* (Harmondsworth).

Douxchamps-Lefevre, C. (1987) 'A propos de la sorcellerie dans le Namurois au 18e siècle. Le procès à charge de Joseph Saucin, manant de Spy (1762–1763)', in [M.-]S. Dupont-Bouchat, ed. *La sorcellerie dans les Pays-Bas. De hekserij in de Nederlanden* (Kortrijk-Heule): 71–7.

Dowbiggin, I. (1991) *Inheriting Madness: Professionalization and Psychiatric Knowledge in Nineteenth-Century France* (Berkeley).

Drake, S., ed. (1866) *The Witchcraft Delusion in New England* (Roxbury).

Draper, J. W. (1874) *History of the Conflict between Religion and Science* (New York).

Duffy, E. (1981) 'Valentine Greatrakes, the Irish stroker: Miracles, science and orthodoxy in Restoration England', *Studies in Church History*, 17: 251–74.

Dumas, F. R. (1967) *Cagliostro* (London).

Dupont-Bouchat, M.-S. (1978) 'La Répression de la sorcellerie dans le duché de Luxembourg aux XVIe et XVIIe siècles', in M.-S. Dupont-Bouchat *et al.*, *Prophètes et sorciers dans les Pays-Bas XVIe-XVIIIe siècles* (Paris): 41–154.

— (1984) 'Sorcellerie et superstition: l'attitude de l'Eglise dans les Pays-Bas, XVIe-XVIIIe siècle,' in H. Hasquin, ed. *Magie, sorcellerie, parapsychologie* (Brussels): 61–83.

— (1987) 'La répression des croyances et des comportements populaires dans les Pays-Bas: l'Eglise face aux superstitions (XVIe-XVIIIe s.)', in [M.-]S. Dupont-Bouchat, ed. *La sorcellerie dans les Pays-Bas. De hekserij in de Nederlanden* (Kortrijk-Heule): 117–43.

— (1994) 'Le diable apprivoisée. La sorcellerie revisitée: magie et sorcellerie au XIXe siècle', in R. Muchembled, ed. *Magie et sorcellerie en Europe du Moyen âge à nos jours* (Paris): 235–66.

Durkheim, E. (1961) *The Elementary Forms of the Religious Life* (New York; first French edn 1912).

— (1989) *Suicide: A Study in Sociology* (London; first edn 1897).

— and Mauss, M. (1970) *Primitive Classification*, translated by R. Needham, 2nd edn (London).

Eagleton, T. (1990) *The Ideology of the Aesthetic* (Oxford).

Easlea, B. (1980) *Witch-hunting, Magic and the New Philosophy: An Introduction to Debates of the Scientific Revolution 1450–1750* (Hassocks).

Eerden, P. C. van der (1992) 'Cornelius Loos und die *magia falsa*', in H. Lehmann and O. Ulbricht, eds. *Vom Unfug des Hexen-Processes. Gegner der Hexenverfolgungen von Johann Weyer bis Friedrich Spee* (Wiesbaden): 136–160.

Ehrenreich, B., and English, D. (1974) *Witches, Midwives and Healers: A History of Women Healers* (London).

Eley, G. (1992) 'Nations, publics and political cultures: Placing Habermas in the nineteenth century', in C. Calhoun, ed. *Habermas and the Public Sphere* (Cambridge and London): 289–339.

Elias, N. (1978) *The Civilizing Process*, vol. 1, *The History of Manners* (New York); (1982) vol. 2, *Power and Civility* (New York); (1983) vol. 3, *The Court Society* (New York).

Ellenberger, H. F. (1970) *The Discovery of the Unconscious: The History and Evolution of Dynamic Psychiatry* (New York).

Ellis, J. D. (1990) *The Physician-Legislators of France: Medicine and Politics in the Early Third Republic 1870–1914* (Cambridge).

Ellison, R. C. (1993) 'The Kirkjuból affair: a seventeenth-century Icelandic witchcraft case analysed', *The seventeenth century*, 8: 217–43.

Esquirol, E. (1838) *Des maladies mentales* (Paris).

Evans-Pritchard, Sir E. (1981) *A History of Anthropological Thought* (London).

Ewen, C. L'E. (1929) *Witch Hunting and Witch Trials: The Indictments for Witchcraft from the Records of 1373 Assizes held for the Home Circuit A.D. 1559–1736* (London).

— (1932) *Lotteries and Sweepstakes: An Historical, Legal and Ethical Survey of Their Introduction, Suppression and Re-Establishment in the British Isles* (London).

— (1933) *Witchcraft and Demonianism* (London).

Favret-Saada, J. (1977) *Les mots, la mort, les sorts* (Paris).

Feather, J. (1985) *The Provincial Book Trade in Eighteenth Century England* (Cambridge).

Fiard, Abbé (1803) *La France trompée par les magiciens et démonolâtres du dix-huitième siècle* (Paris).

[Filmer, Sir R.] (1653) *An Advertisement to the Jury-Men of England Touching Witches* (London).

Fiume, G. (1994) 'The old vinegar lady, or the judicial modernization of the crime of witchcraft', in E. Muir and G. Ruggiero, eds *History from Crime: Selections from Quaderni storici* (Baltimore and London): 65–87.

Flaherty, G. (1992) *Shamanism and the Eighteenth Century* (Princeton).

— (1995) 'The non-normal sciences: Survivals of Renaissance thought in the eighteenth century', in C. Fox, R. Porter, and R. Wokler, eds (1995): 271–91.

Forrester, J. (1994) '"A whole climate of opinion": Rewriting the history of psychoanalysis', in M. S. Micale, and R. Porter, eds *Discovering the History of Psychiatry* (New York): 174–90.

Foster, R. (1993) *Paddy and Mr. Punch: Connections in Irish and English History* (London).

Foucault, M. (1961) *La folie et la déraison: Histoire de la folie à l'âge classique* (Paris); translated by R. Howard and abridged as *Madness and Civilization: A History of Insanity in the Age of Reason* (New York, 1965).

— (1963) *Naissance de la clinique: Une archéologie du regard médical* (Paris); translated by A. M. Sheridan Smith as *The Birth of the Clinic* (London, 1973).

Fox, C., Porter, R. and Wokler, R., eds (1995) *Inventing Human Science: Eighteenth-Century Domains* (Berkeley).

Fox, S. J. (1968) *Science and Justice: The Massachusetts Witchcraft Trials* (Baltimore).

Frängsmyr, T., Heilbron, J. L. and Rider, R. E., eds (1990) *The Quantifying Spirit in the 18th Century* (Berkeley).

Frank, J. P. (1804–1819) *System einer vollständigen medicinischen Polizey*, 6 vols (Mannheim).

Frank, S. P. (1987) 'Popular justice, community and culture among the Russian peasantry, 1870–1900', *Russian Review*, 46: 239–65.

Frazer, Sir J. (1890–1915) *The Golden Bough: A Study in Magic and Religion*, 9 vols (London).

Freud, S. (1930) 'Civilization and its Discontents', in *The Standard Edition of the Complete Psychological Works of Sigmund Freud*, translated and edited by J. Strachey *et al.* (London, 1953–74), 21: 64–145.

Frijhoff, W. (1984) 'Satan en het magisch universum. Raakvlakken, wisselwerking, reminiscenties in Oost-Gelderland sedert de zestiende eeuw', *Tijdschrift voor geschiedenis*, 97: 382–406.

— (1991) 'Witchcraft and its changing representation in Eastern Gelderland, from the sixteenth to twentieth centuries', in M. Gijswijt-Hofstra and W. Frijhoff, eds (1991): 167–80.

A Full and Impartial Account of the Discovery of Sorcery and Witchcraft Practis'd by Jane Wenham of Walkerne in Hertfordshire (1712) (London).

A Full Confutation of Witchcraft: More Particularly of the Depositions Against Jane Wenham, Lately Condemned for a Witch; at Hertford. In which Modern Notions of Witches are Overthrown, and the Ill Consequences of Such Doctrines are Exposed by Arguments; Proving that Witchcraft is Priestcraft, In a Letter from a Physician in Hertfordshire to his Friend in London (1712) (London).

Furniss, T. (1993) *Edmund Burke's Aesthetic Ideology: Language, Gender and Political Economy in Revolution* (Cambridge).

Gaboriau, P. (1987) *La pensée ensorcelée: la sorcellerie actuelle en Anjou et en Vendée* (s.l. Le cerde d'or, Jean Huguet).

Gari Lacruz, A. (1980) 'Variedad de Competencias en el delito de brujeria 1600–1650 en Aragon', in *La Inquisición Española: nueva visión, nuevos horizontes* (Madrid): 319–27.

Garrett, C. (1975) *Respectable Folly: Millenarians and the French Revolution in France and Britain* (Baltimore).

Gaskill, M. (1994a) 'Witchcraft and power in early modern England: the case of Margaret Moore', in J. Kermode and G. Walker, eds *Women, Crime and the Courts in Early Modern England* (London): 125–9.

— (1994b) 'Attitudes to crime in Early Modern England with special reference to witchcraft, coining and murder', Ph.D thesis (University of Cambridge).

— (1996) 'Witchcraft in early modern Kent: stereotypes and the background to accusations', in J. Barry, M. Hester and G. Roberts, eds (1996): 257–87.

Gauld, A. (1992) *A History of Hypnotism* (Cambridge and New York).

Gay, P. (1966–9) *The Enlightenment: An Interpretation*, 2 vols (New York).

— (1968) *Deism: An Anthology* (Princeton).

Geertz, C. (1973) *The Interpretation of Cultures* (New York).

Geis, G. and Bunn, I. (1981) 'Sir Thomas Browne and witchcraft', *International Journal of Law and Psychiatry*, 4: 1–11.

Gellner, E. (1973) 'The savage and the modern mind', in R. Horton and R. Finnegan, eds *Modes of Thought: Essays on Thinking In Western and Non-Western Societies* (London): 162–81.

Geneva, A. (1995) *Astrology and the Seventeenth-Century Mind: William Lilly and the Language of the Stars* (Manchester).

Gentilcore, D. (1992) *From Bishop to Witch. The System of the Sacred in Early Modern Terra d'Otranto* (Manchester and New York).

— (1993) 'The church, the Devil and the healing activities of living saints in the kingdom of Naples after the Council of Trent', in O. Grell, and A. Cunningham, eds *Medicine and the Reformation* (London): 134–55.

Gentleman's Magazine (1832) Part 2, edition 102.

Gestrich, A. (1995) 'Pietismus und Aberglaube. Zum Zusammenhang von popularem Pietismus und dem Ende der Hexenverfolgung im 18. Jahrhundert' in S. Lorenz and D. R. Bauer, eds (1995b): 269–86.

Geyer-Kordesch, J. (1985) 'The cultural habits of illness: The enlightened and the pious in eighteenth-century Germany', in R. Porter, ed. *Patients and Practitioners* (Cambridge): 177–204.

— (1994) 'Whose Enlightenment?: Medicine, witchcraft, melancholia and pathology', in R. Porter, ed. *Medicine in the Enlightenment* (Amsterdam): 113–27.

Giedion, S. (1948) *Mechanization Takes Command: A Contribution to Anonymous History* (New York).

Gigerenzer, G., Swijtink, Z., Porter, T., Daston, L., Beatty, J. and Kruger, L. (1989) *The Empire of Chance* (Cambridge).

Gijswijt-Hofstra, M. (1986) 'Toverij in Zeeland, een status quaestionis', in W. de Blécourt and M. Gijswijt-Hofstra, eds (1986): 107–51.

— (1989) 'Witchcraft in the Northern Netherlands', in A. Angerman *et al.*, eds *Current Issues in Women's History* (London): 75–92.

— (1990) 'The European witchcraft debate and the Dutch variant', *Social History*, 15: 181–94.

— (1991a) 'Six centuries of witchcraft in the Netherlands: themes, outlines, and interpretations', in M. Gijswijt-Hofstra and W. Frijhoff, eds (1991): 1–36.

— (1991b) 'Witchcraft before Zeeland magistrates and church councils, sixteenth to twentieth centuries', in M. Gijswijt-Hofstra and W. Frijhoff, eds (1991): 103–18.

— (1991–2) 'Witchcraft and tolerance: the Dutch Case', *Acta Ethnographica Hungarica*, 37: 401–12.

— (1992) 'Recent witchcraft research in the Low Countries', in N. C. F. van Sas and E. Witte, eds *Historical research in the Low Countries* (Den Haag): 23–34.

— (1997) 'Een onttoverde wereld? Tegenslag en toverij in West-Europa na de "heksenprocessen"', in M. Gijswijt-Hofstra and F. Egmond, eds *Of bidden helpt? Tegenslag en cultuur in West-Europa, ca 1500–2000* (Amsterdam): 119–34.

— and Frijhoff, W., eds (1987) *Nederland betoverd. Toverij en hekserij van de veertiende tot in de twintigste eeuw* (Amsterdam).

— and Frijhoff, W., eds (1991) *Witchcraft in the Netherlands from the fourteenth to the twentieth century* (Rotterdam).

Gilman, S. (1982) *Seeing the Insane: A Cultural History of Madness and Art in the Western World* (New York).

— and King, H., Porter, R., Rousseau, G. S. and Showalter, E. (1993) *Hysteria Beyond Freud* (Berkeley).

Ginzburg, C. (1983) *The Night Battles: Witchcraft and Agrarian Cults in the Sixteenth and Seventeenth Centuries*, trans. J. and A. Tedeschi (London).

— (1990) *Ecstasies: Deciphering the Witches' Sabbath*, trans. R. Rosenthal (London).

Glacken, C. J. (1967) *Traces on the Rhodian Shore: Nature and Culture in Western Thought from Ancient Times to the End of the Eighteenth Century* (Berkeley).

Glanvill, J. (1668) *Plus Ultra: Or, the Progress and Advancement of Knowledge Since the Days of Aristotle: In an Account of Some of the Most Remarkable Late Improvements of Practical, Useful, Learning* (London).

— (1726) *Saduccismus Triumphatus*, 4th edn (London).

Glass, D. V. (1973) *Numbering the People: The Eighteenth-Century Population Controversy and the Development of Census and Vital Statistics in Britain* (Farnborough).

Godbeer, R. (1992) *The Devil's Dominion: Magic and Religion in Early New England* (Cambridge).

Goedelmann, J. G. (1592) *De Magis, Veneficis et Lamiis* (Frankfurt).

Golby, J. M. and Purdue, A. W. (1984) *The Civilization of the Crowd: Popular Culture in England, 1750–1900* (London).

Goldschmidt, P. (1705) *Verworffener Hexen- und Zauberer-Advocat* (Hamburg).

Goldstein, B. P. (1984) *Lessons to be Learned: A Study of Eighteenth-Century English Didactic Children's Literature* (New York).

Goldstein, J. (1982) 'The hysteria diagnosis and the politics of anticlericalism in late nineteenth-century France', *Journal of Modern History*, 54: 209–39.

— (1984) '"Moral contagion": A professional ideology of medicine and psychiatry in eighteenth- and nineteenth-century France', in G. L. Geison, ed. *Professions and the French State 1700–1900* (Philadelphia): 181–222.

— (1987) *Console and Classify: The French Psychiatric Profession in the Nineteenth Century* (Cambridge).

Gordon, T. (1724) *The Humourist*, 3rd ed. (London).

Göttsch, S. (1991) 'Hexenglauben und Schadenzauber. Zur disziplinierung leibeigener Untertanen', *Kieler Blätter zur Volkskunde*, 23: 55–65.

Goulemot, J. M. (1980) 'Démons, merveilles et philosophie à l'âge classique', *Transactions of the Fifth International Congress of the Enlightenment* (Oxford), 2: 1009–22.

Gregory, A. (1991) 'Witchcraft, politics and "good neighbourhood" in early seventeenth-century Rye', *Past and Present*, 133: 31–66.

Grevius, J. (1624) *Doma Tribunal Reformatum* (Hamburg).

Gusdorf, G. (1960) *Introduction aux sciences humaines: Essai critique sur leurs origines* (Paris).

Guskin, P. J. (1981) 'The context of English witchcraft: The case of Jane Wenham (1712)', *Eighteenth Century Studies*, 15: 48–71.

Habermas, J. (1989) *The Structural Transformation of the Public Sphere: An Inquiry into a Category of Bourgeois Society*, translated by T. Burger (Cambridge).

Hacking, I. (1975) *The Emergence of Probability* (Cambridge).

— (1990) *The Taming of Chance* (Cambridge).

Hale, J. (1702) *A Modest Inquiry into the Nature of Witchcraft* (Boston).

Hale, Sir M. (1972) *Pleas of the Crown: A Methodical Summary 1678*, ed. P. R. Glazebrook (London).

Haliczer, S. (1990) *Inquisition and Society in the Kingdom of Valencia, 1478–1834* (Berkeley, Los Angeles and Oxford).

Hall, A. R. (1990) *Henry More: Magic, Religion and Experiment* (Oxford).

Hardy, T. (1874) *Far From the Madding Crowd* (reprinted London, 1974): 38–9.

Harley, D. (1989) 'Mental illness, magical medicine and the Devil in northern England, 1650–1700', in R. French, and A. Wear, eds *The Medical Revolution of the Seventeenth Century* (Cambridge): 114–44.

(1996) 'Explaining Salem: Calvinist psychology and the diagnosis of possession', *American Historical Review*, 101: 307–30.

Harrington, A. (1996) *Re-enchanted Science* (Princeton).

Harris, M. (1968) *The Rise of Anthropological Theory* (New York).

Harris, R. (1989) *Murders and Madness: Medicine, Law and Society in the Fin de Siècle* (Oxford).

Harris, T., ed. (1995) *Popular Culture in England, c. 1500–1850* (Houndmills, Basingstoke and London).

Harrison, J. F. C. (1979) *The Second Coming: Popular Millenarianism, 1780–1850* (London).

Harsnett, S. (1603) *A Declaration of Egregious Popish Impostures* (London), reprinted in F. W. Brownlow, *Shakespeare, Harsnett and the Devils of Denham* (Newark, 1993).

Hart, E. (1898) *Hypnotism, Mesmerism and the New Witchcraft* (London).

Hartland, E. S., ed. (1892) *Country Folk-Lore: Printed Extracts: Gloucestershire* (London).

Hastrup, K. (1990a) 'Iceland: sorcerers and paganism', in B. Ankarloo and G. Henningsen, eds (1990): 383–401.

— (1990b) *Island of Anthropology: Studies in Past and Present Iceland* (Odense).

Hauber, E. D., ed. (1738) *Biblioteca sive acta et scripta magica* (Lemgo).

Haustein, J. (1995) 'Bibelauslegung und Bibelkritik: Ansätze zur Überwindung der Hexenverfolgung', in S. Lorenz and D. R. Bauer, eds (1995b): 249–67.

Hawthorn, G. (1976) *Enlightenment and Despair: A History of Sociology* (Cambridge).

Hay, D., *et al.*, eds (1975) *Albion's Fatal Tree: Crime and Society in Eighteenth-Century England* (London).

Hazard, P. (1953) *The European Mind (1680–1715)* (London).

Heikkinen, A. and Kervinen, T. (1990) 'Finland, the male domination', in B. Ankarloo and G. Henningsen, eds (1990): 319–38.

Held, J. (1987) 'Between the bourgeois Enlightenment and popular culture: Goya's festivals, old women, monsters and blind men', *History Workshop Journal*, 23: 39–58.

Henningsen, G. (1975) 'Hekseforfølgelse efter "hekseprocessernes tid"', *Folk og kultur*, 4: 98–151.

— (1980) *The Witches' Advocate: Basque Witchcraft and the Spanish Inquisition (1609–1614)* (Reno, Nevada).

— (1982) 'Witchcraft in Denmark', *Folklore*, 93: 131–7.

— (1984) 'Sort magi, spådomskunst og heksemishandling 1855', *Folk og kultur*, 13: 75–84.

— (1988) 'Witch persecution after the era of the witch trials', *ARV. Scandinavian Yearbook of Folklore*, 44: 103–53.

— (1990) '"The ladies from outside": An archaic pattern of the witches' sabbath', in B. Ankarloo and G. Henningsen, eds (1990): 191–215.

— (1991–2) 'The white sabbath and other archaic patterns of witchcraft', *Acta Ethnographica Hungarica*, 37: 293–304.

— and Tedeschi, J., eds (1986) *The Inquisition in Early Modern Europe* (Dekalb, Ill.).

Herzfeld, M. (1981) 'Meaning and morality: a semiotic approach to evil eye accusations in a Greek village', *American Ethnologist*, 8: 560–74.

Heyd, M. (1995) *"Be Sober and Reasonable": The Critique of Enthusiasm in the Seventeenth and Early Eighteenth Centuries* (Leiden).

Hill, A. W. (1958) *John Wesley Among the Physicians* (London).

Hill, C. (1971) *Antichrist in Seventeenth Century England* (London).

— (1993) *The English Bible and the 17th-Century Revolution* (London).

Hipple, W. J. (1957) *The Beautiful, the Sublime, and the Picturesque in Eighteenth-Century Aesthetic Theory* (Carbondale).

Hirschman, A. O. (1977) *The Passions and the Interests: Political Arguments for Capitalism before its Triumph* (Princeton).

The History of Witches, Ghosts, and Highland Seers: Containing Many Wonderful Well-attested Relations of Supernatural Appearances. Not Published Before in any Similar Collection. Designed for the Conviction of the Unbeliever, and the Amusement of the Curious (1775) (Berwick).

HMC (1894) *The Manuscripts of the Duke of Roxburghe*. Historical Manuscripts Commission Fourteenth Report, Appendix III (London).

Hobbes, T. (1968) *Leviathan: or, the Matter, Forme and Power of a Commonwealth Ecclesiasticall and Civil*, ed. C. B. Macpherson (Harmondsworth).

Hobsbawm. E. and Ranger, T., eds (1983) *The Invention of Tradition* (Cambridge).

Hodgen, M. (1936) *The Doctrine of Survivals: A Chapter in the History of Scientific Method in the Study of Man* (London).

Hoffer, P. C. (1996) *The Devil's Disciples: Makers of the Salem Witchcraft Trials* (Baltimore).

— and Hull, N. E. (1984) *Murdering Mothers: Infanticide in England and New England* (New York).

Holmes, C. (1993) 'Women: Witnesses and witches', *Past and Present*, 140: 45–78.

Hone, W., ed. (1831–2) *The Year Book* (London: reprinted 1864).

Honour, H. (1989) *The Image of the Black in Western Art*, vol. 4, *From the American Revolution to World War I* (Cambridge).

Howell, T. B. (1816) *A Complete Collection of State Trials* (London)

Howitt, W. (1838) *Rural Life of England* (London).

Hughes, H. S. (1958) *Consciousness and Society: The Reorientation of European Social Thought 1890–1930* (New York).

Hulme, P. and Jordanova, L., eds (1990) *Enlightenment and its Shadows* (London).

Hultin, N. C. (1974) 'Some aspects of eighteenth-century folk-medicine', *Southern Folklore Quarterly*, 38: 199–209.

— (1975) 'Medicine and magic in the eighteenth century: The diaries of James Woodforde', *Journal of the History of Medicine*, 30: 359–66.

Hundert, E. J. (1986) 'A cognitive idea and its myth: Knowledge as power in the lexicon of the Enlightenment', *Social Research*, 53: 133–57.

Hunter, M. (1975) *John Aubrey and the Realm of Learning* (London).

— (1985) 'The problem of "atheism" in early modern England', *Transactions of the Royal Historical Society*, 5th ser., 35: 135–57.

— and Wootton, D., eds (1992) *Atheism from the Reformation to the Enlightenment* (Oxford).

Hutchinson, F. (1718) *An Historical Essay Concerning Witchcraft. With Observations Upon Matters of Fact; Tending to Clear the Texts of the Sacred Scriptures, and Confute the Vulgar Errors about that Point, and also Two Sermons. One in Proof of the Christian Religion; the Other Concerning the Good and Evil Angels* (London).

Hutchison, K. (1983) 'Supernaturalism and the mechanical philosophy', *History of Science*, 21: 297–333.

d'Iharce, J.-L. (1783) *Erreurs populaires sur la médicine* (Paris).

Ilie, P. (1995) *The Age of Minerva*, vol. i. *Counter-rational Reason in the Eighteenth Century. Goya and the Paradigm of Unreason in Western Europe* (Philadelphia).

Inglis, B. (1977) *Natural and Supernatural: A History of the Paranormal* (London).

— (1986) *The Hidden Power* (London).

Jackson, M. (1996) *New-Born Child Murder: Women, Illegitimacy and the Courts in Eighteenth-century England* (Manchester and New York).

Jackson, S. W. (1986) *Melancholia and Depression from Hippocratic Times to Modern Times* (New Haven).

Jacob, M. C. (1976) *The Newtonians and the English Revolution, 1689–1720* (Ithaca).

— (1978) 'Newton and the French prophets: New evidence', *History of Science*, 16: 134–42.

— (1981) *The Radical Enlightenment: Pantheists, Freemasons and Republicans* (London).

— (1988) *The Cultural Meaning of the Scientific Revolution* (New York).

— (1992) *Living the Enlightenment: Freemasonry and Politics in 18th Century Europe* (New York).

James VI (1597) *Daemonologie* (Edinburgh), ed. G. B. Harrison (London, 1924).

Jenkins, R. P. (1977) 'Witches and fairies: supernatural aggression and deviance among the Irish peasantry', *Ulster Folklife*, 23: 33–56.

Jobe, T. H. (1981) 'The Devil in Restoration science: The Glanvill-Webster witchcraft debate', *Isis*, 72: 343–56.

Johansen, J. Chr. V. (1990) 'Denmark: The sociology of accusations', in B. Ankarloo and G. Henningsen, eds (1990): 339–65.

— (1991), *Da Djaevelen var ude . . . Trolddom i det 17. århundredes Danmark* (Odense).

— (1991–2) 'Witchcraft, sin and repentance: the decline of Danish witchcraft trials', *Acta Ethnographica Hungarica*, 37: 413–23.

Jones, G. P. (1947) *The Genesis of Freemasonry: An Account of the Rise and Development of Freemasonry in its Operative, Accepted and Early Speculative Phases* (Manchester).

Jorden, E. (1603) *A Briefe Discourse of a Disease Called Suffocation of the Mother* (London)

Juxon, J. (1736) *A Sermon upon Witchcraft: Occasion'd by a Late Illegal Attempt to Discover Witches by Swimming. Preached at Twyford in the County of Leicester, July 11, 1736* (London).

Kalberg, S. (1993) *Max Weber's Historical Sociology* (Cambridge).

Karlsen, C. (1987) *The Devil in the Shape of a Woman: Witchcraft in Colonial New England* (New York).

Keates, J. (1995) *Purcell: A Biography* (London).

Keynes, G., ed. (1966) *Blake's Complete Writings* (London).

King, L. S. (1974a) 'Friedrich Hoffmann and some medical aspects of witchcraft', *Clio Medica*, 9: 299–309.

(1974b) 'Witchcraft and medicine: Conflicts in the early eighteenth century', in G. A. Lindeboom, *Circa Tiliam* (Leiden): 122–39.

Kittredge, G. L. (1929) *Witchcraft in Old and New England*, (Cambridge, Mass.).

Kivelson, V. A. (1991) 'Through the prism of witchcraft: gender and social change in seventeenth-century Muscovy', in B. Evans Clements, B. Alpern Engel and C. D. Worobec, eds *Russia's Women: Accommodation, Resistance, Transformation* (Berkeley, Los Angeles and Oxford): 74–94.

Klaits, J. (1982) 'Witchcraft trials and absolute monarchy in France', in R. Golden, ed. *Church, State and Society under the Bourbon Kings of France* (Lawrence, Kans.): 148–72.

Klaniczay, G. (1987) 'Decline of witches and rise of vampires in the 18th century Habsburg monarchy', *Ethnologia Europaea*, 17: 165–80.

— (1990a) *The Uses of Supernatural Power: The Transformation of Popular Religion in Medieval and Early Modern Europe* (Cambridge).

— (1990b) 'Hungary: The accusations and the universe of popular magic', in B. Ankarloo and G. Henningsen, eds (1990): 219–55.

— (1991–2) 'Witch-hunting in Hungary: Social or cultural tensions?', *Acta Ethnographica Hungarica*, 37: 67–91.

— (1994) 'Bûchers tardifs en Europe centrale et orientale', in R. Muchembled, ed. *Magie et sorcellerie en Europe du Moyen Age à nos jours* (Paris): 215–31.

— Kristóf, I. and Pócs, É., eds (1989) *Magyarországi Boszorkányperek* I and II (Budapest).

— and Pócs, É., eds (1991–2) *Witch Beliefs and Witch Hunting in Central and Eastern Europe*, Special Issue *Acta Ethnographica Hungarica*, 37.

Kneubühler, H.-P. (1977) *Die Überwindung von Hexenwahn und Hexenprozess* (Diessenhofen).

Knight, I. (1968) *The Geometric Spirit: The Abbé de Condillac and the French Enlightenment* (New Haven).

Knoop, D. and Jones, G. P. (1947) *The Genesis of Freemasonry: An Account of the Rise and Development of Freemasonry in its Operative, Accepted and Early Speculative Phases* (Manchester).

Knoop, D. and Weisberger, R. W. (1993) *Speculative Freemasonry and the Enlightenment: A Study of the Craft in London, Paris, Prague and Vienna* (Boulder).

Knox, R. A. (1950) *Enthusiasm* (London).

Kors, A. C. (1990) *Atheism in France, 1650–1729*, vol. I, *The Orthodox Sources of Disbelief* (Princeton).

— and Peters, E., eds (1972) *Witchcraft in Europe: 1100–1700: A Documentary History* (Philadelphia).

Kovács, Z. (1973) 'Die Hexen in Russland', *Acta Ethnographica Hungarica*, 22: 51–87.

Kramer, H. and Sprenger, J. (1928) *The Malleus Maleficarum*, ed. M. Summers (London).

Kramer, K.-S. (1983) 'Schaden- und Gegenzauber im Alltagsleben des

16.–18. Jahrhunderts nach archivalischen Quellen aus Holstein', in C. Degn, H. Lehmann and D. Unverhau, eds *Hexenprozesse. Deutsche und skandinavische Beiträge* (Neumünster): 222–39.

Kreiser, B. R. (1978) *Miracles, Convulsions and Ecclesiastical Politics in Early 18th Century Paris* (Princeton).

Kristóf, I. (1991–2) ' "Wise women", sinners and the poor: The social background of witch-hunting in a 16th-18th century Calvinist city of Eastern Hungary', *Acta Ethnographica Hungarica*, 37: 93–119.

Kunstmann, H. H. (1970) *Zauberwahn und Hexenprozess in der Reichstadt Nürnberg* (Nuremberg).

Kuper, A. (1988) *The Making of Primitive Society* (London).

Kuselman, T. A. (1983) *Miracles and Prophecies in Nineteenth-Century France* (New Brunswick, NJ).

Labouvie, E. (1987) 'Hexenspuk und Hexenabwehr. Volksmagie und volkstümlicher Hexenglaube', in R. van Dülmen, ed. *Hexenwelten. Magie und Imagination vom 16.-20. Jahrhundert* (Frankfurt am Main): 49–93.

— (1990) 'Wider Wahrsagerei, Segnerei und Zauberei. Kirchliche Versuche zur Ausgrenzung von Aberglaube und Volksmagie seit dem 16. Jahrhundert', in R. von Dülmen, ed. *Verbrechen, Strafen und soziale Kontrolle*, Studien zur historischen Kulturforschung (Frankfurt am Main): 15–55.

— (1991) *Zauberei und Hexenwerk. Ländlicher Hexenglaube in der frühen Neuzeit* (Frankfurt am Main).

— (1992) *Verbotene Künste. Volksmagie und ländlicher Aberglaube in den Dorfgemeinschaften des Saarraumes (16.-19.Jahrhundert)* (St Ingbert).

— (1993) 'Verwünschen und Verfluchen: Formen der verbalen Konfliktregelung in der ländlichen Gesellschaft der Frühen Neuzeit', in P. Blickle, ed. *Der Fluch und der Eid* (Berlin): 121–45.

— (1995) 'Absage an den Teufel. Zum Ende dörflicher Hexeninquisition im Saarraum', in S. Lorenz and D. R. Bauer, eds (1995b): 55–76.

Labrousse, E. (1983) *Bayle*, trans. by D. Potts (Oxford).

Lackington, J. (1810) *Memoirs of the Forty Five First Years of the Life of James Lackington*, 13th edn (London).

Lamoine, G., ed. (1992) *Charges to the Grand Jury 1689–1803* (Camden Society, 4th ser. 43).

Langbein, J. H. (1974) *Prosecuting Crime in the Renaissance: England, Germany, France* (Cambridge, Mass.).

— (1976) *Torture and the Law of Proof* (Chicago).

Lapoint, E. C. (1992) 'Irish immunity to witch-hunting, 1534–1711', *Éire-Ireland*, 27: 76–92.

Larner, C. (1977) 'Two late Scottish witchcraft tracts: *Witchcraft Proven* and

The Tryal of Witchcraft', in S. Anglo, ed. *The Damned Art* (London): 227–45.

— (1981) *Enemies of God: The Witch Hunt in Scotland* (Baltimore).

— (1984) *Witchcraft and Religion* (Oxford).

—Lee, C. H. and McLachlan, H. V. (1977) *Source-Book of Scottish Witchcraft* (Glasgow).

Lavater, J. C. (1775–8) *Physiognomische Fragmente* (Leipzig).

Lawrence, C. (1975) 'William Buchan: Medicine laid open', *Medical History*, 19: 20–35.

Laymann, P. (1629) *Processus iuridicus contra sagas et veneficos* (Cologne).

Le Bon, G. (1920) *The Crowd: A Study of the Popular Mind* (London) (original French edition, 1895).

Le Brun, P. (1702) *Histoire critique des practiques superstitieuses* (Paris).

Lea, H. C. (1939) *Materials Towards a History of Witchcraft*, arr. and ed. by A. C. Howland, 3 vols (Philadelphia).

Leaf, M. J. (1979) *Man, Mind and Science: A History of Anthropology* (New York).

Lecky, W. E. H. (1910) *History of the Rise and Influence of the Spirit of Rationalism in Europe* (London).

Lecouteux, C. (1985) 'Hagazussa – Striga – Hexe', *Hessische Blätter für Volks- und Kulturforschung*, NF 18: 57–70.

— (1995) 'Hexe und Hexerei als Sammelbegriff', in S. Lorenz and D. R. Bauer, eds (1995a): 31–44.

Leerssen, J. (1996) *Remembrance and Imagination: Patterns in the Historical and Literary Representation of Ireland in the Nineteenth Century* (Cork).

Letwin, S. (1965) *The Pursuit of Certainty* (Cambridge).

Letwin, W. (1963) *The Origins of Scientific Economics* (London).

Levack, B. P. (1980) 'The great Scottish witch hunt of 1661–1662', *Journal of British Studies*, 20: 90–108.

— (1995a) *The Witch-Hunt in Early Modern Europe*, 2nd ed. (London).

— (1995b) 'Possession, witchcraft and the law in Jacobean England', *Washington and Lee University Law Review*, 52: 1613–40.

— (1996) 'State-building and witch-hunting in early modern Europe'', in J. Barry, M. Hester and G. Roberts, eds (1996): 96–115.

Levi-Strauss, C. (1962) *La pensée sauvage* (Paris).

Levitine, G. (1983) 'Goya and l'abbé Bordelon', in H. Mason, ed. *Transactions of the Sixth International Congress on the Enlightenment* (Oxford).

Lévy-Bruhl, L. (1923) *Primitive Mentality* (London).

Lewis, B. (1889) *A Textbook of Mental Diseases* (London).

Libby, M. S. (1935) *The Attitude of Voltaire to Magic and the Sciences* (New York).

Lincoln, A. H. (1938) *Some Political and Social Ideas of English Dissent, 1763–1800* (Cambridge).

Linebaugh, P. (1991) *The London Hanged: Crime and Civil Society in the Eighteenth Century* (London).

Link, L. (1995) *The Devil: A Mask Without a Face* (London).

Liu, T. P. (1994) 'Le Patrimoine Magique: reassessing the power of women in peasant households in nineteenth-century France', *Gender and History*, 6: 13–36.

Lloyd's Evening Post, 2 January 1761.

Locke, J. (1690) *An Essay Concerning Humane Understanding* (London).

— (1695) *The Reasonableness of Christianity* (London).

Löher, H. (1676) *Hochnötige unterhanige wemütige Klage der frommen Unschültigen* (Amsterdam).

Loos, C. (1592) *De vera et de falsa magia* (Cologne).

Lorenz, S. (1981) 'Johann Georg Goedelmann—Ein Gegner des Hexenwahns?', in R. Schmidt, ed. *Beiträge zur pommerschen und mecklenberischen Geschichte* (Marburg): 61–105.

— (1982) *Aktenversendung und Hexenprozess* (Frankfurt am Main)

— (1995) 'Die letzten Hexenprozesse in den Spruchakten der Juristfakultäten: Versuch einer Beschreibung', in S. Lorenz and D. R. Bauer, eds (1995b): 227–47.

— and Bauer, D. R., eds (1995a) *Hexenverfolgung. Beiträge zur Forschung* (Würzburg).

— and Bauer, D. R., eds (1995b) *Das Ende der Hexenverfolgung* (Stuttgart).

Loriga, S. (1994) 'A secret to kill the king: magic and protection in Piedmont in the eighteenth century', in E. Muir and G. Ruggiero, eds *History from Crime. Selections from Quaderni storici* (Baltimore and London): 88–109.

Lough, J. (1968) *Essays on the Encyclopédie of Diderot and d'Alembert* (London).

— (1969) *The Encyclopédie of Diderot and d'Alembert: Selected Articles* (Cambridge).

— (1971) *The Encyclopédie* (London).

Loux, F. (1978) *Sagesse du corps: Santé et maladie dans les proverbs réginaux françaises* (Paris).

— (1979) *Practiques et savoirs populaires: Le corps dans la société traditionnelle* (Paris).

Lovelock, J. (1979) *Gaia: A New Look at Life on Earth* (Oxford).

Lowe, D. (1982) *History of Bourgeois Perception* (Brighton).

Lukes, S. (1973) *Emile Durkheim. His Life and Work: A Historical and Critical Study* (Harmondsworth).

Lytes, A. (1960) *Methodism Mocked* (London).

Macario, M. (1843) 'Etudes cliniques sur la démonomanie', *Annales médico-psychologiques*, 1: 440–85.

McCormick, G. D. K. (1958) *The Hell-fire Club: The Story of the Amorous Knights of Wycombe* (London).

MacDonald, M. (1981) *Mystical Bedlam: Madness, Anxiety and Healing in Seventeenth Century England* (Cambridge).

— (1986) 'The secularization of suicide in England, 1600–1800', *Past and Present*, 3: 50–100.

— (1990) *Witchcraft and Hysteria in Elizabethan London: Edward Jorden and the Mary Glover Case* (London).

Macfarlane, A. (1970) *Witchcraft in Tudor and Stuart England* (London).

McIntosh, C. (1992) *The Rose Cross and the Age of Reason: Eighteenth-Century Rosicrucianism in Central Europe and its Relationship to the Enlightenment* (Leiden).

McKendrick, N., Brewer, J. and Plumb, J. H. (1982) *The Birth of a Consumer Society: The Commercialization of Eighteenth-Century England* (London).

Mackenzie, Sir G. (1672) *Pleadings in Some Remarkable Cases* (Edinburgh).

— (1678) *The Laws and Customs of Scotland in Matters Criminal* (Edinburgh).

— (1691a) *A Vindication of the Government of Scotland during the Reign of Charles II* (Edinburgh).

— (1691b) 'A Discourse on the Four First Books of the Digest', British Library, Sloane MS. 3828.

McNeil, M. (1987) *Under the Banner of Science: Erasmus Darwin and his Age* (Manchester).

Madar, M. (1990) 'Estonia I: Werewolves and poisoners', in B. Ankarloo and G. Henningsen, eds (1990): 257–72.

Maesschalck, I. (1995) '"Wacht u, o mensch, van bygheloof". Toverij en superstitie in de Zuidnederlandse prediking van de 17de en de 18de eeuw', unpublished thesis (Catholic University, Leuven).

Maffei, S. (1750) *Arte Magica Dileguata* (Verona).

Maire, C.-L. (1981) *Les posedées de Morzine 1857–1873* (Lyons).

Malcolmson, R. (1973) *Popular Recreations in English Society 1700–1850* (Cambridge).

Mandrou, R. (1968) *Magistrats et sorciers en France au XVIIe siècle: une analyse de psychologie historique* (Paris).

Mantzel, E. (1738) *Ob wohl noch Hexenprozesse entstehen möchten* (Rostock).

Manuel, F. E. (1957) *The Eighteenth Century Confronts the Gods* (Cambridge).

— (1962) *The Prophets of Paris: Turgot, Condorcet, Saint-Simon, Fourier and Comte* (Cambridge).

Maple, E. (1960) 'Cunning Murrell: A study of a nineteenth-century cunning man in Hadleigh, Essex', *Folklore*, 71: 37–43.

— (1965) 'Witchcraft and magic in the Rochford Hundred', *Folklore*, 76: 72–115.

— (1971) *Superstition and the Superstitious* (New York).

Marcuse, H. (1955) *Reason and Revolution* (London).

Martensen, R. L. (1993) 'The circles of Willis: Physiology, culture, and the formation of the "neurocentric" body in England, 1640–1690', D. Phil. thesis (University of California, San Francisco).

Martin, D. (1978) *A General Theory of Secularization* (Oxford).

Martin, R. (1989) *Witchcraft and the Inquisition in Venice, 1550–1650* (Oxford).

Marx, K. F. H. (1859) *Ueber die Verdienste des Aertze um das Verschwinden der daemonische Krankheiten* (Göttingen).

Mason, H. (1981) *Voltaire: A Biography* (Baltimore).

Masson, J. M. (1986) *A Dark Science: Women, Sexuality and Psychiatry in the Nineteenth Century* (New York).

— ed. (1986) *The Complete Letters of Sigmund Freud to Wilhelm Fliess, 1887–1904* (Cambridge, Mass.).

Mather, C. (1692) *Wonders of the Invisible World* (Boston).

Mather, I. (1693) *Cases of Conscience Concerning Evil Spirits Personating Men* (Boston).

Mathisen, T. R. (1988) 'Continuity and change in the tradition of folk medicine', *ARV. Scandinavian Yearbook of Folklore*, 44: 169–98.

Matter, F., Blécourt, W. de, Dekker, T., Frijhoff, W. and Gijswijt-Hofstra, M., eds (1990) *Toverij in Nederland, 1795–1985. Bibliografie* (Amsterdam).

Maudsley, H. (1873) *Body and Mind* (London).

Mead, R. (1712) *Of the Power and Influence of the Sun and the Moon on Humane Bodies* (London).

— (1755) *Medica Sacra: Or, a Commentary on the Most Remarkable Diseases Mentioned in the Holy Scriptures* (London).

Mee, J. (1992) *Dangerous Enthusiasm: William Blake and the Culture of Radicalism in the 1790s* (Oxford).

Meili, D. (1980) *Hexen in Wasterkingen. Magie und Lebensform in einem Dorf des frühen 18. Jahrhunderts* (Basel).

Meinders, H. A. (1716) *Unvorgreifliche Gedancken* (Lemgo).

Mello, J. van (1984) 'Een geval van hekserij met moord te Geraardsbergen–Onkerzele in 1815', in W. P. Dezutter and R. van de Walle, eds *Volkskunde in Vlaanderen. Huldeboek Renaat van der Linden* (Brugge): 172–5.

Mercier, L.-S. (1770) *Songes d'un hermite* (Paris).

— (1781) *Tableau de Paris* (Hambourg).

Merzbacher, F. (1970) *Die Hexenprozesse in Franken* (Munich).

Meyfarth, J. (1635) *Christliche Erinnerung an gewaltige Regenten und gewissen-*

haffte Prädicanten wie das abscheuliche Laster der Hexerey mit Ernst auszurot-ten (Schleusingen).

Micale, M. (1995) *Approaching Hysteria: Disease and its Interpretations* (Princeton).

Michelet, J. (1862)) *La sorcière* (Paris).

[Middleton, C.] (1749) *A Free Inquiry into the Miraculous Powers Which are Supposed to Have Subsisted in the Christian Church* (London).

— (1751) *Vindication of the Free Inquiry* (London).

Midelfort, H. C. E. (1972) *Witch Hunting in Southwestern Germany, 1562–1684* (Stanford)

— (1979) 'Witch hunting and the domino theory', in J. Obelkevich, ed. *Religion and the People* (Chapel Hill, NC): 277–88.

Midgley, M. (1992) *Science as Salvation: A Modern Myth and its Meaning* (London).

Millar, J. ed. (1809) *History of the Witches of Renfrewshire* (Paisley).

Miller, G. (1957) *The Adoption of Inoculation for Smallpox in England and France* (London).

Minerva, N. (1983) 'Démonologie tératologiques et lumières: un aspect de l'imagination fantastique et de l'anti-philosophie au dix-huitième siècle', *Transactions of the Sixth International Congress on the Enlightenment* (Oxford): 22–3.

Money, J. (1977) *Experience and Identity: Birmingham and the West Midlands, 1760–1800* (Manchester).

Monk, S. H. (1960) *The Sublime: A Study of Critical Theories in Eighteenth Century England* (Ann Arbor).

Monter, E. W. (1976) *Witchcraft in France and Switzerland: The Borderlands during the Reformation* (Ithaca and London).

— (1990a) 'Scandinavian witchcraft in Anglo-American perspective', in B. Ankarloo and G. Henningsen, eds (1990): 425–34.

— (1990b) *Frontiers of Heresy: The Spanish Inquisition from the Basque Lands to Sicily* (Cambridge).

— (1994) 'Poursuites précoces. La sorcellerie en Suisse', in R. Muchem-bled, ed. *Magie et sorcellerie en Europe du Moyen Age à nos jours* (Paris): 47–58.

— and Tedeschi, J. (1986) 'Towards a statistical profile of the Italian Inquisitions, sixteenth to eighteenth centuries', in G. Henningsen and J. Tedeschi, eds (1986): 130–57.

Moore, J. (1692) *Religious Melancholy* (London).

Moore, R. I. (1987) *The Formation of a Persecuting Society: Power and Deviance in Western Europe, 950–1250* (Oxford).

Mora, G. (1994) 'Early American historians of psychiatry, 1910–1960', in M. Micale and R. Porter, eds *Discovering the History of Psychiatry* (New York): 53–80.

More, H. (1653) *An Antidote Against Atheisme: or an Appeal to the Natural Faculties of the Minde of Man, Whether There Be Not a God* (London).

Morley, J., ed. (1927) *The Works of Voltaire*, 22 vols (New York).

Moscovici, S. (1981) *L'Age des foules: Un traité historique de psychologie des masses* (Paris).

Muchembled, R. (1979) *La sorcière au village, XVe–XVIIIe siècles* (Paris).

— (1981) *Les derniers bûchers. Un village de Flandre et ses sorcières sous Louis XIV* (Paris).

— (1985) *Popular Culture and Elite Culture in France, 1400–1750*, trans. L. Cochrane (London).

— (1987) *Sorcières, justice et société aux 16e et 17e siècles* (Paris).

— (1988) *L'Invention de l'homme moderne: sensibilitiés, moeurs et comportements collectif sous l'ancien régime* (Paris).

— (1991–2) 'Variations sur le énigme: la fin des bûchers de sorcellerie', *Acta Ethnographica Hungarica*, 37: 373–8.

— (1994) 'Terres de contrastes: France, Pays–Bas, Provinces–Unies', in R. Muchembled, ed. *Magie et sorcellerie en Europe du Moyen Age à nos jours* (Paris): 99–132.

Naess, H. E. (1990) 'Norway, the criminological context', in B. Ankarloo and G. Henningsen, eds (1990): 367–82.

Nenonen, M. (1992) *Noituus, taikuus ja noitavainot* (Helsinki).

— (1993) '"Envious are all the people, Witches watch at every gate": Finnish witches and witch trials in the 17th Century', *Scandinavian Journal of History*, 18: 77–91.

Nicolas, A. (1682) *Si la Torture est un moyen seur à verifier les crimes secrets: dissertation morale et juridique* (Amsterdam).

Nicolson, M. J. (1959) *Mountain Gloom and Mountain Glory: The Development of the Aesthetics of the Infinite* (Ithaca).

North, R. (1890) *The Lives of the Right Hon. Francis North . . . Together with an Autobiography of the Author*, ed. A. Jessop, 3 vols (London).

Notestein, W. (1911) *A History of Witchcraft in England* (Washington).

Nye, R. (1975) *The Origins of Crowd Psychology: Gustave LeBon and the Crisis of Mass Democracy in the Third Republic* (London).

Obelkevitch, J. (1976) *Religion and Rural Society: South Lindsey 1826–1875* (Oxford).

Oliver, W. H. (1978) *Prophets and Millenialists: The Uses of Biblical Prophecy in England from the 1790s to the 1840s* (Auckland).

Olson, R. (1991) *Science Deified and Science Defied: The Historical Significance of Science in Western Culture*, vol. 2: *From the Early Modern Age through the Early Romantic Era, ca. 1640 to ca. 1820* (Berkeley).

— (1993) *The Emergence of the Social Sciences, 1642–1792* (New York).

O'Neil, M. R. (1984) 'Sacerdote ovvero strione: ecclesiastical and super-stitious remedies in 16th-century Italy', in S. L. Kaplan, ed. *Understanding Popular Culture: Europe from the Middle Ages to the Nineteenth Century* (Berlin etc.): 53–83.

— (1987) 'Magical healing, love magic and the Inquisition in late sixteenth-century Modena', in S. Haliczer, ed. *Inquisition and Society in Early Modern Europe* (London and Sydney): 88–114.

— (1991–2) 'Missing footprints: Maleficium in Modena', *Acta Ethnographica Hungarica*, 37: 123–42.

Oorschot, T. G. M. van (1995) 'Ihrer Zeit voraus: Das Ende der Hexenverfolgung in der *Cautio Criminalis*', in S. Lorenz and D. R. Bauer, eds (1995b): 1–17.

Oppenheim, J. (1985) *The Other World: Spiritualism and Psychical Research in England 1850–1914* (Cambridge).

Orr, L. (1976) *Jules Michelet: Nature, History and Language* (Ithaca).

Outram, D. (1995) *The Enlightenment* (Cambridge).

Owen, A. (1989) *The Darkened Room: Women, Power and Spiritualism in Late Nineteenth Century England* (London).

Paiva, J. P. (1992) *Práticas e crenças mágicas: o medo e a necessidade dos mágicos na Diocese de Coimbra (1650–1740)* (Coimbra).

Park K. and Daston, L. (1981) 'Unnatural conceptions: The study of monsters in sixteenth-century France and England', *Past and Present*, 92: 20–54.

Passmore, J. (1968) *The Perfectibility of Man* (London).

Paulson, R. (1974) *Hogarth: His Life, Art and Times* (New Haven).

Payne, H. D. (1976) *The Philosophes and the People* (New Haven).

Peacock, T. L. (1969) *Nightmare Abbey* (Harmondsworth).

Peel, J. D. Y. (1971) *Herbert Spencer: The Evolution of A Sociologist* (London).

Peters, E. (1978) *The Magician, the Witch and the Law* (Philadelphia).

— (1985) *Torture* (Oxford).

Piatigorsky, A. (1997) *Who's Afraid of Freemasons? The Phenomenon of Freemasonry* (London).

Pick, D. (1989) *Faces of Degeneration: Aspects of a European Disorder c.1848–1918* (Cambridge).

Pickering, S. F. Jr. (1981) *John Locke and Children's Books in Eighteenth-Century England* (Knoxville).

Pinies, J.-P. (1983) *Figures de la sorcellerie languedocienne. Brèish, endevinaire, armièr* (Paris).

Plasha, W. (1993) 'The social construction of melancholia in the eighteenth century: Medical and religious approaches to the life and work of Samuel Johnson and John Wesley', M.Litt thesis (University of Oxford).

Pluche, N. A. (1739) *Histoire du ciel* (Paris).

Pope, A. (1965) 'Essay on Man', in J. Butt, ed. *The Poems of Alexander Pope* (London).

Porset, C. (1989) 'Vampires et lumières', *Studies on Voltaire and the Eighteenth Century*, 266: 125–50.

Porter, R. (1983) 'The rage of party: A glorious revolution in English psychiatry', *Medical History*, 27: 35–50.

— (1985) 'Making faces: Physiognomy and fashion in eighteenth-century England', *Etudes anglaises*, 28: 385–96.

— (1987) *Mind Forg'd Manacles: Madness and Psychiatry in England from Restoration to Regency* (London).

— (1989) *Health for Sale: Quackery in England 1650–1850* (Manchester).

— ed. (1992) *The Popularization of Medicine, 1650–1850* (London).

— (1993) 'The body and the mind: The doctor and the patient: Negotiating hysteria', in S. Gilman, H. King, R. Porter, G. Rousseau and E. Showalter, *Hysteria Beyond Freud* (Berkeley): 225–85.

— (1995a) 'From the sacred disease to epilepsy', in G. Berrios and R. Porter, eds *A History of Clinical Psychiatry: The Origin and History of Psychiatric Disorders* (London): 164–73.

— (1995b) 'The people's health in Georgian England', in T. Harris, ed. (1995): 124–42.

— (1997a) 'Accidents in the eighteenth century', in R. Cooter and B. Luckin, eds *Accidents in History: Injuries, Fatalities and Social Relations* (Amsterdam): 90–106.

— (1997b) 'English society in the 18th century revisited', in J. Black, ed. *The Eighteenth Century* (London): 29–50.

Pott, M. (1995) 'Aufklärung und Hexenglaube: Philosophische Ansätze zur Überwindung der Teufelspakttheorie in der deutschen Frühaufklärung', in S. Lorenz and D. R. Bauer, eds (1995b): 183–202.

Powell, N. (1956) *Fuseli's 'The Nightmare'* (London).

Proust, P. (1962) *Diderot et l'Encyclopédie* (Paris).

Pruett, J. H. (1978) 'A late Stuart Leicestershire parson: The Reverend Humphrey Michel', *Transactions of the Leicestershire Archaeological and Historical Society*, 54: 26–38.

Punter, D. (1980) *The Literature of Terror: A History of Gothic Fictions from 1785 to the Present Day* (London).

Purkiss, D. (1996) *The Witch in History: Early Modern and Twentieth Century Representations* (London).

Rack, H. D. (1989) *Reasonable Enthusiast: John Wesley and the Rise of Methodism* (Philadelphia).

Ramsey, M. (1988) *Professional and Popular Medicine in France, 1770–1830: The Social World of Medical Practice* (Cambridge).

Raymond, A. G. (1967) 'L'Infâme: superstition ou calomnie?', *Studies on Voltaire and the Eighteenth Century*, 57: 1291–1306.

Reading Mercury and Oxford Gazette, 15 March 1773.

Redwood, J. (1976) *Reason, Ridicule and Religion: The Age of Enlightenment in England, 1660–1750* (London).

The Remarkable Confession and the Last Dying Words of Thomas Colley . . . (1751) (London).

Riddle, J. M. (1992) *Contraception and Abortion from the Ancient World to the Renaissance* (Cambridge).

Robbins, R. H. (1959) *The Encyclopedia of Witchcraft and Demonology* (New York).

Roberts, M. M. (1995) 'Masonics, metaphor and misogyny: A discourse of marginality?', in P. Burke and R. Porter, eds *Languages and Jargons: Contributions to a Social History of Language* (Cambridge): 133–54.

Robinson, N. (1729) *A New System of the Spleen* (London).

Robison, J. (1798) *Proofs of a Conspiracy against all the Governments and Religions of Europe, Carried on in Secret Meetings of Free Masons, Illuminati, and Reading Societies* (Edinburgh).

Roeck, B. (1988) 'Christlicher Idealstaat und Hexenwahn zum Ende der Europaischen Verfolgungen', *Historisches Jahrbuch*, 108: 379–405.

[Rogers, T.], (1691) *A Discourse Concerning Trouble of Mind and the Disease of Melancholy* (London).

Roodenburg, H. (1990) *Onder censuur. De kerkelijke tucht in de gereformeerde gemeente van Amsterdam, 1578–1700* (Hilversum).

Rooijakkers, G., Dresen-Coenders, L. and Geerdes, M., eds (1994) *Duivelsbeelden. Een cultuurhistorische speurtocht door de Lage Landen* (Baarn).

Roper, L. (1994) *Oedipus and the Devil: Witchcraft, Sexuality and Religion in Early Modern Europe* (London).

Rose, N. (1985) *The Psychological Complex: Psychology, Politics and Society in England, 1869–1939* (London).

— (1990) *Governing the Soul: The Shaping of the Private Self* (London).

— and Miller, P. (1986) *The Power of Psychiatry* (Oxford).

Rosen, G. (1972) 'Forms of irrationality in the 18th Century', in H. E. Pagliaro, ed. *Studies in 18th Century Culture: Irrationalism in the 18th Century* (Cleveland): 255–88.

Rossman, V. R. (1974) 'L'Onomancie, exemple de satire dans l'*Encyclopédie*', *Studies on Voltaire and the Eighteenth Century*, 127: 223–30.

Rudwin, M. (1922) *Supernaturalism and Satanism in Chateaubriand* (Chicago).

— (1926) *Satan et le satanisme dans l'oeuvre de Victor Hugo* (Paris).

— (1959) *The Devil in Legend and Literature* (La Salle).

Rupp, E. G. (1986) *Religion in England, 1688–1791* (Oxford).

Russell, J. B. (1980) *A History of Witchcraft, Sorcerers, Heretics, and Pagans* (London).

Salmon, J. H. M. (1989) 'History without anthropology: A new witchcraft synthesis', *Journal of Interdisciplinary History*, 19: 481–6.

Sánchez Ortega, M. H. (1991) 'Sorcery and eroticism in love magic', in M. E. Perry and A. J. Cruz, eds *Cultural Encounters: The Impact of the Inquisition in Spain and the New World* (Berkeley, Los Angeles and Oxford): 58–92.

— (1992) 'Women as source of "Evil" in Counter-Reformation Spain', in A. J. Cruz and M. E. Perry, eds *Culture and Control in Counter-reformation Spain* (Minneapolis): 196–215.

Sander, K. (1991) *Aberglauben im Spiegel schleswig-holsteinischer Quellen des 16. bis 18. Jahrhunderts* (Neumünster).

Sassen, M. J. (1697) *Disputatio . . . de abusu et usu torturae* (Halle).

Schaffer, S. (1980) 'Natural philosophy', in G. S. Rousseau and R. Porter, eds *The Ferment of Knowledge: Studies in the Historigraphy of Eighteeenth-Century Science* (Cambridge): 55–91.

— (1987) 'Newton's comets and the transformation of astrology', in P. Curry, ed. *Astrology, Science and Society* (Woodbridge): 219–43.

— (1989) 'Defoe's natural philosophy and the worlds of credit', in J. Christie and S. Shuttleworth, eds *Nature Transfigured: Science and Literature, 1700–1989* (Manchester): 13–44.

Schaps, R. (1982) *Hysterie und Weiblichkeit: Wissenschaft über die Frau* (Frankfurt am Main).

Scheffler, J. (1994) 'Hexenglaube in der ländlichen Gesellschaft. Lippe im 19. und 20. Jahrhundert', in G. Wilbertz, G. Schwerhoff and J. Scheffler, eds *Hexenverfolgung und Regionalgeschichte. Die Grafschaft Lippe im Vergleich* (Bielefeld): 263–96.

Schiffmann, A. C. (1987) 'The witch and crime: the persecution of witches in twentieth-century Poland', *ARV. Scandinavian Yearbook of Folklore*, 43: 147–65.

Schlüter, D. (1991) *Betovering en vervolging. Over toverij in Oost-Nederland tussen de 16de en 20ste eeuw* (Enschede).

Schmidt, E. (1940) *Inquisitionsprozess und Rezeption* (Leipzig).

Schmitz, N. (1977) 'An Irish wise woman – fact and legend', *Journal of the Folklore Institute*, 14: 169–79.

Schöck, I. (1978) *Hexenglaube in der Gegenwart*. Tübinger Vereinigung für Volkskunde (Tübingen).

— (1987) 'Hexen heute. Traditioneller Hexenglaube und aktuelle Hexenwelle', in R. van Dülmen, ed. *Hexenwelten. Magie und Imagination vom 16.-20. Jahrhundert* (Frankfurt am Main): 282–305.

— (1995) 'Das Ende der Hexenprozesse – das Ende des Hexenglaubens?', in S. Lorenz and D. R.Bauer, eds (1995a): 375–89.

Schoeneman, T. J. (1977) 'The role of mental illness in the European witch hunts of the sixteenth and seventeenth centuries: An assessment', *Journal of the History of the Behavioral Sciences*, 13: 337–51.

— (1982) 'Criticisms of the psychopathological interpretation of witch-hunts: A review', *American Journal of Psychiatry*, 134: 1028–32.

Schormann, G. (1977) *Hexenprozesse in Nordwestdeutschland* (Hildesheim).

— (1981) *Hexenprozesse in Deutschland* (Göttingen).

Schwartz, H. (1978) *Knaves, Fools, Madmen, and 'That Subtile Effluvium': A Study of the Opposition to the French Prophets in England, 1706–1710* (Gainesville).

— (1980) *The French Prophets: The History of a Millenarian Group in Eighteenth-Century England* (Berkeley).

Scot, R. (1930) *The Discoverie of Witchcraft*, ed. M. Summers (London).

Scott, W. (1802) *Minstrelsy of the Scottish Border*, 2 vols (Kelso).

— (1830) *Letters on Demonology and Witchcraft* (London).

Scottish Record Office (1674) JC 2/14. Books of Adjournal of the High Court of Justiciary, 1673–8.

— (1680) JC 2/15. Books of Adjournal of the High Court of Justiciary, 1678–82.

Scott-Moncrieff, W. G., ed. (1905) *Proceedings of the Justiciary Court from 1661 to 1678* (Scottish History Society, 48).

Scully, S. (1995) 'Marriage or a career? Witchcraft as an alternative in seventeenth-century Venice', *Journal of Social History*, 28: 857–76.

Sebald, H. (1978) *Witchcraft: The Heritage of a Heresy* (New York and Oxford).

(1995) *Witch-Children* (Amherst, NY).

Shamdasani, S. (1996) 'C. G. Jung and the making of modern psychology', Ph.D. thesis (University of London).

Sharpe, J. A. (1991) 'Witchcraft and women in seventeenth-century England: some Northern evidence', *Continuity and Change*, 6: 179–99.

— (1992) *Witchcraft in Seventeenth-Century Yorkshire: Accusations and Counter Measures*, Borthwick Papers, no. 81 (York).

— (1996) *Instruments of Darkness: Witchcraft in England, 1550–1750* (London).

Sherlock, T. (1729) *The Tryal of Witnesses of the Resurrection of Jesus* (London).

Shorr, P. (1932) *Science and Superstition in the Eighteenth Century* (New York).

Shortt, D. (1984) 'Physicians and psychics: the Anglo-American medical response to spiritualism, 1870–1890', *Journal of the History of Medicine*, 39: 339–55.

Showalter, E. (1986) *The Female Malady: Women, Madness, and English Culture, 1830–1980* (New York).

Shrewsbury Chronicle, 6 September 1884.

— 3 October 1884.

Shumaker, W. (1972) *The Occult Sciences in the Renaissance* (Berkeley).

Shuttleton, S. (1994) 'Methodism and Dr George Cheyne's "More Enlightening Principles"', in R. Porter, ed. *Medicine and the Enlightenment* (Amsterdam): 317–35.

Siebert, D. T. (1990) 'Johnson and Hume on miracles', in J. W. Yolton, ed. *Philosophy, Religion and Science in the Seventeenth and Eighteenth Centuries* (Rochester): 122–6.

Smalbroke, R. (1729–31) *A Vindication of the Miracles of our Blessed Saviour*, 2 vols (London).

Smart, C. (1802) *The Genuine History of the Good Devil of Woodstock: The Story of Jane Gilbert, a Supposed Witch* (London).

Smith, K. C. (1977) 'The wise man and his community', *Folk Life*, 15: 24–35.

Soldan, W. G. and Heppe, H. (1912) *Geschichte der Hexenprozesse*, ed. M. Bauer, 2 vols (Munich; repr. Hanau, n.d.).

Soman, A. (1978) 'The Parlement of Paris and the Great Witch Hunt (1565–1640), *Sixteenth Century Journal*, 9: 31–44.

— (1985) 'La décriminilisation de la sorcellerie en France', *Histoire, économie et société*, 4: 179–203.

— (1986) 'Witch lynching at Juniville', *Natural History*, 95: 8–15.

— (1988) 'Le rôle des Ardennes dans la décriminilisation de la sorcellerie en France', *Revue historique ardennaise*, 23: 23–45.

— (1989) 'Decriminalizing witchcraft: Does the French experience furnish a European model?', *Criminal Justice History*, 10: 1–22.

— (1992) *Sorcellerie et justice criminelle (16e-18e siècles)* (Vermont).

Sommerville, C. J. (1992) *The Secularization of Early Modern England: From Religious Culture to Religious Faith* (New York).

Spadafora, D. (1990) *The Idea of Progress in Eighteenth Century Britain* (New Haven).

Speck, W. A. (1967) *The Divided Society: Parties and Politics in England, 1694–1716* (London).

[Spee, F.] (1631) *Cautio Criminalis* (Rinteln)

— (1660) *Advis aux criminalistes sur les abus qui se glissent dans les procès de sorcelleries* (Lyon)

Spellman, W. M. (1993) *The Latitudinarians and the Church of England* (Athens, Georgia).

Spierenburg, P. (1991) *The Broken Spell: A Cultural and Anthropological History of Preindustrial Europe* (London).

Stackhouse, T. (1733) *A Compleat History of the Holy Bible* (London).

Stallybrass, P. and White, A. (1986) *The Politics and Poetics of Transgression* (Ithaca).

Stanford, P. (1996) *The Devil: A Biography* (London).

Steinbrügge, L. (1995) *The Moral Sex: Woman's Nature in the French Enlightenment* (New York).

Stewart, L. (1992) *The Rise of Public Science: Rhetoric, Technology, and Natural Philosophy in Newtonian Britain, 1660–1750* (Cambridge).

Stillingfleet, E. (1662) *Origines Sacrae: Or, a Rational Account of the Grounds of the Christian Faith, as to the Truth and Divine Authority of the Scriptures and the Matters Therein Contained* (London).

Stock, R. D. (1982) *The Holy and the Daemonic from Sir Thomas Browne to William Blake* (Princeton).

Stocking, G. (1987) *Victorian Anthropology* (New York).

Stromberg, R. N. (1954) *Religious Liberalism in Eighteenth Century England* (London).

Stronks, G. J. (1991) 'The significance of Balthasar Bekker's *The Enchanted World*', in M. Gijswijt-Hofstra and W. Frijhoff, eds *Witchcraft in the Netherlands:* 149–56.

Sturt, G. (1977) *A Small Boy in the Sixties* (Brighton).

Summerfield, G. (1984) *Fantasy and Reason: Children's Literature in the Eighteenth Century* (London).

Summers, M. (1964) *Witchcraft and Black Magic* (London).

— (1965) *The History of Witchcraft and Demonology* (1st edition 1924; London).

Suzuki, A. (1992) 'Mind and its disease in Enlightenment British medicine', D.Phil. thesis (University of London).

Swales, P. (1982) 'A fascination with witches', *The Sciences*, 22: 21–5.

Szasz, T. S. (1970) *The Manufacture of Madness* (New York; London, 1972).

Tanner, A. (1626–7) *Theologia Scholastica* (Ingolstadt).

Taylor, J. M. (1908) *The Witchcraft Delusion in Colonial Connecticut, 1647–1697* (New York).

Tazbir, J. von (1980) 'Hexenprozesse in Polen', *Archiv für Reformationsgeschichte*, 71: 280–307.

Tedeschi, J. (1990) 'Inquisitorial law and the witch', in B. Ankarloo and G. Henningsen, eds (1990): 83–118.

— (1991) *The Prosecution of Heresy: Collected Studies on the Inquisition in Early Modern Italy* (Binghamton, NY)

Telford, J., ed. (1931) *The Letters of the Rev. John Wesley*, 8 vols (London).

Tenneur, R. le (1991) *Magie, sorcellerie et fantastique en Normandie* (Paris).

Terpstra, J. U. (1965) 'Petrus Goldschmidt aus Husum', *Euphorion*, 59: 361–83.

Thiers, J. B. (1679/1741) *Traité des superstitions*, 4 vols (Paris: vol 1 first pub in 1679).

Thomas, K. V. (1971) *Religion and the Decline of Magic: Studies in Popular Beliefs in Sixteenth- and Seventeenth-Century England* (London).

— (1975) 'An anthropology of religion and magic', *Journal of Interdisciplinary History*, 6: 91–110.

Thomasius, C. (1701) *De Crimine Magiae* (Halle).

— (1703) *Kurtze Lehr-Sätze von dem Laster der Zauberey* (Halle).

— (1705) *De Tortura ex foris Christianorum proscribenda* (Halle).

— (1712) *De origine ac progressu processus inquisitorii contra sagas* (Halle).

— (1986) *Über di Hexenprozesse*, ed. R. Lieberwirth (Weimar).

Thompson, E. P. (1975) *Whigs and Hunters: The Origin of the Black Act* (London).

— (1991) *Customs in Common* (London).

— (1993) *Witness Against the Beast: William Blake and the Moral Law* (Cambridge).

Thompson, F. (1973) *Lark Rise to Candleford* (Harmondsworth).

Tomlinson, J. A. (1992) *Goya in the Twilight of Enlightenment* (New Haven).

Traimond, B. (1988) *Le pouvoir de la maladie. Magie et politique dans les Landes de Gascogne, 1750–1826* (Bordeaux).

Trapnell, W. H. (1994) *Thomas Woolston: Madman and Deist?* (Bristol).

Trevor-Roper, H. R. (1969) *The European Witchcraze of the Sixteenth- and Seventeenth-Centuries and Other Essays* (New York).

— (1972) *Religion, the Reformation and Social Change*, 2nd edn (London).

Trusen, W. (1995) 'Rechtliche Grundlagen der hexenprozesse und ihrer Beendigung', in S. Lorenz and D. R. Bauer, eds (1995b): 203–26.

The Tryal of Thomas Colley . . . (1751) (London).

Tschaikner, M. (1991) ' "Also schlecht ist das Weib von natur . . .": Grundsätzliches zur Rolle der Frau in den Vorarlberger Hexenverfolgungen', in A. Niederstätter and W. Scheffknecht, eds *Hexe oder Hausfrau. Das Bild der Frau in der Geschichte Vorarlbergs* (Sigmaringendorf): 57–76.

Tweyman, S., ed. (1996) *Hume on Miracles* (Bristol).

Tylor, Sir E. B. (1871) *Primitive Culture: Researches into the Development of Mythology, Philosophy, Religion, Art, and Custom* (London).

Tytler, G. (1982) *Physiognomy in the European Novel* (Princeton).

Unsworth, C. R. (1989) 'Witchcraft beliefs and criminal procedure in early modern England', in T. G. Watkin, ed. *Legal Record and Historical Reality* (London): 71–98.

Unverhau, D. (1983) 'Akkusationsprozess-Inquisitionsprozess. Indikatoren für die Intensität der Hexenverfolgung in Schleswig-Holstein', in C.

Degn, H. Lehmann and D. Unverhau, eds *Hexenprozesse: Deutsche und Skandinavische Beiträge*, Studien zur Volkskunde und Kulturgeschichte Schleswig Holsteins 12 (Neumünster): 59–142.

Usher, J. (1769) *Clio: or, a Discourse on Taste*, 2nd ed. (London).

Vandermeersch, P. (1991) 'The victory of psychiatry over demonology: The origin of the nineteenth-century myth', *History of Psychiatry*, 2: 351–63.

— (1994) ' "*Les Mythes d'Origine*" in the history of psychiatry', in M. S. Micale and R. Porter, eds *Discovering the History of Psychiatry* (New York and Oxford): 219–31.

Várkonyi, A. (1991–2) 'Connections between the cessation of witch trials and the transformation of the social structure related to medicine', *Acta Ethnographica Hungarica*, 37: 426–77.

Voltaire, F. M. A. (1756) *Essai des moeurs*, 7 vols (Geneva).

— (1879) *Dictionnaire philosophique*, in *Oeuvres complètes de Voltaire* (Paris): vol. iv.

— (1971) 'Enthusiasm', in T. Besterman, ed. *Voltaire: Philosophical Dictionary* (1971): 187.

Vukanović, T. P. (1989) 'Witchcraft in the central Balkans I: Characteristics of witches', *Folklore*, 100: 9–24.

Waardt, H. de (1989) 'Met bloed ondertekend', in P. Geschiere and W. van Wetering, eds *De geldigheid van magie. Heksen, demonen en economische verandering*, Special issue *Sociologische gids*, 36: 224–44.

— (1991a) *Toverij en samenleving. Holland 1500–1800* (Den Haag).

— (1991b) 'Prosecution or defense: Procedural possibilities following a witchcraft accusation in the province of Holland before 1800', in M. Gijswijt-Hofstra and W. Frijhoff, eds (1991): 79–90.

— (1994) 'Oudewater. Eine Hexenwaage wird gewogen – oder: Die Zerstörung einer historischen Mythe', *Westfälische Zeitschrift*, 144: 249–63.

— (1995) 'Rechtssicherheit nach dem Zusammenbruch der zentralen Gewalt', in S. Lorenz and D. R. Bauer, eds (1995b): 129–52.

Walker, D. P. (1964) *The Decline of Hell: Seventeenth-Century Discussions of Eternal Torment* (London).

— (1981) *Unclean Spirits: Possession and Exorcism in France and England in the Late Sixteenth and Early Seventeenth Centuries* (London).

Walvaart, H. te (1995) 'Mit toverijen becladdet – Toverij in de Heerlijkheid Borculo 1610–1800', in M. Saatkamp and D. Schlüter, eds *Van Hexen un Düvelslüden. Über Hexen, Zauberei und Aberglauben im niederländisch-deutschen Grenzraum* (Vreden): 33–47.

Walz, R. (1993) *Hexenglaube und magische Kommunikation im Dorf der frühen Neuzeit. Die Verfolgungen in der Grafschaft Lippe* (Paderborn).

Wasser, M. and Yeoman, L., eds (1998) 'The trial of Geillis Johnstone for witchcraft 1614', in *Miscellany* (Scottish History Society) 4th ser, 1998, forthcoming.

Weber, E. (1979) *Peasants into Frenchmen: The Modernization of Rural France 1870–1914* (London).

Weber, M. (1930) *The Protestant Ethic and the Spirit of Capitalism* (London).

— (1946) 'Wissenschaft als Beruf', in English translation as 'Science as a vocation', in H. H. Gerth and C. W. Mills, eds *From Max Weber: Essays in Sociology* (New York): 129–56.

— (1965) *The Sociology of Religion*, translated by E. Fischoff (London).

Webster, J. (1677) *The Displaying of Supposed Witchcraft. Wherein is affirmed that there are many sorts of Deceivers and Imposters and Divers persons under a passive Delusion of Melancholy and Fancy* (London).

Weiner, D. B. (1994) ' "*Le Geste de Pinel*": The history of a psychiatric myth', in M. S. Micale and R. Porter, eds *Discovering the History of Psychiatry* (New York): 232–48.

Weisberger, R. W. (1993) *Speculative Freemasonry and the Enlightenment: A Study of the Craft in London, Paris, Prague and Vienna* (Boulder, Co.).

Weisman, R. (1984) *Witchcraft, Magic and Religion in 17th-Century Massachusetts* (Amherst).

Wesley, J. (1747) *Primitive Physick: Or, an Easy and Natural Method of Curing Most Diseases* (London).

— (1906) *The Journal of the Rev. John Wesley*, 4 vols (New York).

Weyer, J. (1991) *Witches, Devils, and Doctors in the Renaissance: Johann Weyer, 'De Praestigiis Daemonum'*, ed. G. Mora and B. Kohl, with E. Midelfort and H. Bacon, trans. J. Shea (Binghamton) (orig. 1568).

Whelan, R. (1989) *The Anatomy of Superstition: A Study of the Historical Theory and Practice of Pierre Bayle* (Oxford).

White, A. D. (1896) *A History of the Warfare of Science with Theology in Christendom*, 2 vols (London).

White, G. (1989) *The Natural History of Selborne* (Ware) (1st. ed. 1789).

Wiles, R. (1965) *Freshest Advices: Early Provincial Newspapers in England* (Columbus).

Wilkins, K. S. (1972) 'The treatment of the supernatural in the *Encyclopédie*', in *Studies on Voltaire and the Eighteenth Century*, 90: 1757–71.

— (1973) 'Attitudes to witchcraft and demonic possession in France during the eighteenth century', *Journal of European Studies*, 3: 348–62.

— (1975) 'Some aspects of the irrational in 18th-century France', *Studies on Voltaire and the Eighteenth Century*, 115: 107–200.

[Willard, S.] (1692) *Some Miscellany Observations on Our Present Debates respecting Witchcrafts* (Philadelphia).

Willey, B. (1962) *The Eighteenth Century Background: Studies on the Idea of Nature in the Thought of the Period* (London).

Williams, J. P. (1985) 'Psychical research and psychiatry in late Victorian Britain', in W. F. Bynum, R. Porter, and M. Shepherd, eds *The Anatomy of Madness* (London): vol. 1, 1233–54.

Willis, T. (1667) *Pathologiae Cerebri* (Oxford).

Wilson, A. (1995) *The Making of Man Midwifery* (London).

Wilson, K. (1995) *The Sense of the People: Politics, Culture and Imperialism in England, 1715–1785* (Cambridge).

Wilson, L. (1993) *Women and Medicine in the French Enlightenment: The Debate over Maladies des Femmes* (Baltimore).

Wimsatt, W. K. (1969) *Dr Johnson on Shakespeare* (Harmondsworth).

Wolf, H.-J. (1995) *Geschichte der Hexenprozesse* (Erlensee).

Worobec, C. D. (1995) 'Witchcraft beliefs and practices in pre-revolutionary Russia and Ukrainian villages, *Russian Review*, 54: 165–87.

Young, R. M. (1990) *Mind, Brain, and Adaptation in the Nineteenth Century* (New York).

Young-Bruehl, E. (1994) 'A history of Freud biographies', in M. S. Micale and R. Porter, eds *Discovering the History of Psychiatry* (New York): 157–73.

Zenz, E. (1981) 'Cornelius Loos--ein Vorläufer Friedrich von Spees im Kampf gegen den Hexenwahn', *Kurtrierisches Jahrbuch*, 21: 146–53.

Zguta, R. (1977a) 'The ordeal by water (swimming of witches) in the East Slavic world', *Slavic Review*, 36: 220–30.

— (1977b) 'Witchcraft Trials in 17th-century Russia', *American Historical Review*, 82: 1187–1207.

Zilboorg, G. (1935) *The Medical Man and the Witch During the Renaissance* (Baltimore).

Zimmermann, J. G. (1763–4) *Von der Erfahrung in der Arzneykunst*, 2 vols (Zurich).

Index

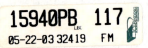